Arguments and Reason-Giving

Arguments and Reason-Giving

MATTHEW W. MCKEON

OXFORD
UNIVERSITY PRESS

OXFORD
UNIVERSITY PRESS

Oxford University Press is a department of the University of Oxford. It furthers
the University's objective of excellence in research, scholarship, and education
by publishing worldwide. Oxford is a registered trade mark of Oxford University
Press in the UK and certain other countries.

Published in the United States of America by Oxford University Press
198 Madison Avenue, New York, NY 10016, United States of America.

CIP data is on file at the Library of Congress
ISBN 978–0–19–775163–3

DOI: 10.1093/oso/9780197751633.001.0001

Printed by Integrated Books International, United States of America

MIX
Paper
FSC FSC® C183721

For Beth, Kelly, Matthew, Paige, and Shannon with gratitude
for the joy of arguing over the years

Contents

PART II: FORMAL VALIDITY, RATIONAL PERSUASION, ARGUMENTATIVE RATIONALITY, INTELLECTUAL HONESTY, AND INTELLECTUAL INTEGRITY

Preface

This book advances a model of arguing that involves using arguments to advance the premises as reasons for believing that the conclusion is true. I have been thinking about various dimensions of such arguing on and off since my "Statements of Inference and Begging the Question," *Synthese* 194 (2017), 1919–43. In this paper, I advance a pragmatic account of begging the question according to which a use of an argument begs the question just in case it is used as a statement of inference, and it fails to state an inference arguers or addressees can perform given what they explicitly believe. Accordingly, what begs questions are uses of arguments as statements of inference, and the root cause of begging the question is an argument's failure to state an inference performable by the reasoners the arguer targets.

I came to understand arguments used as statements of inference as reason-giving uses of arguments. My conception of a reason-giving use of argument seemed to me to be in the ballpark of first-step characterizations of argument in textbooks and the scholarly literature in informal logic and argumentation theory. As I highlight in Chapters 1 and 2, such characterizations of argument motivate the idea that in using an argument to advance reasons for the conclusion one claims that the premises are such reasons. Since I understand reason-giving by means of using an argument to be intentional, I thought it plausible to think that when you use an argument in a reason-giving way you believe what you claim, i.e., you believe that your premises are reasons for the conclusion in the sense that you intend. Of course, this is compatible with there being other uses of arguments that do not involve believing this.

This rudimentary picture of reason-giving uses of arguments portrays premises as reasons for belief. The epistemological notion of reasons for belief came to inform my understanding of various types of reason-giving uses of arguments. My subsequent review of the relevant epistemological literature on reasons for belief prompted me to see that different types of reason-giving uses of arguments can be distinguished depending on whether the premises are advanced as reasons to believe the conclusion, reasons someone has to believe it, reasons for someone to believe it, or reasons for which someone believes it.

Taking arguments used as statements of inference to be reason-giving uses of arguments so understood motivated my thinking about the nature of the inferences stated by arguments used in reason-giving ways. These inferences are distinctive in that they are accompanied by a linking belief to the effect that the inferential premises are reasons for believing the conclusion in the intended sense. I came to see that some norms guiding such inferences may be derived from norms for reason-giving uses of arguments.

My conception of reason-giving uses of arguments developed to the point that I thought it deserved a book-length treatment. I started writing during the summer of 2021 and finished a draft of the book in summer of 2023. As chair of my department, there were certainly plenty of distractions. Of course, this time overlaps with the pandemic years. Also, there was a mass shooting on campus at my university during Spring Semester 2023. Thankfully, supportive faculty colleagues and the dean of my college allowed me to be productive throughout these difficult academic years. I am grateful.

My primary motivation for writing the book is twofold. First, I desire to advance a model of arguing that is both descriptive (some of us some of the time so argue) and aspirational (more of us so arguing when we argue would improve the argument culture, certainly in the United States). I consider my work here as a means of promoting greater intentionality with respect to our arguing, whether in our personal or our professional lives. What exactly are you doing when you give reasons for believing something by means of using an argument? Second, my conception of reason-giving uses of arguments is multifaceted to the degree that its development calls on not only work in argumentation theory and informal logic, but also work in philosophy of language, philosophy of logic, epistemology, and intellectual virtue theory. I have written the book in the hope that readers will appreciate how argumentation theory and informal logic usefully informs work in these other sub-disciplines in philosophy. For example, I discuss reason-giving uses of arguments, a topic in argumentation theory and informal logic, in a way that provides a conceptual framework for shedding new light on topics of concern in other sub-disciplines in philosophy such as the rationality of belief, the normativity of logic for reasoning, and intellectual honesty and integrity.

My strategy for pronoun uses throughout the book is as follows. First, I use what I take to be the preferred pronouns of the people I mention. Second, I follow the pronouns used by authors when commenting on their examples. Finally, I use impersonal pronouns (they, them, their) when talking in the abstract about people, say in the many scenarios I use to illustrate key points (e.g., suppose person S uses their argument to . . .).

Most of the book is new material, but parts of some chapters draw on work that has been published elsewhere.

- Chapter 2, section 2.3.3, "Arguments in Formal Logic," draws from "What Does Formal Logic Have to Do with Arguments?," *Metaphilosophy* 53 (2022), 696–708.
- Chapter 3, section 3.4, "How, Exactly, Are Inference Claims Conveyed by One's Statement of an Argument?," is based on my "Inference Claims as Assertions," *Informal Logic* 41(3) (2021), 359–90.
- My discussion of Toulmin in Chapter 4, section 4.2.3, "Inference and Critical Thinking," overlaps in parts with "Arguments and Reason-Giving," *Argumentation* 36 (2022), 229–47.
- Chapter 6 is based on "Argument, Inference, and Persuasion," *Argumentation* 35 (2021), 339–56.
- Chapter 8's discussion (section 8.4) of why one's reason-giving use of argument lacks intellectual integrity unless the premises are one's reasons for which one believes the conclusion draws from "On the Rationale for Distinguishing Arguments from Explanations," *Argumentation* 27 (2013), 283–303.

I thank the publishers for permission to reuse and/or work from this material.

I also thank the reviewers for Oxford University Press. Their work improved the final version of the book. Finally, I thank Lucy Randall and Brent Matheny and my other editors at OUP, for their work in seeing the manuscript through to publication.

Using the names of my children and my wife in the scenarios and illustrations throughout the book somewhat mitigated the loneliness of the many hours spent working on it. Special thanks to my wife for her patience in giving me personal space to work on this project and for accommodating my periods of absence during the time it took to complete it.

1

Introduction

Arguments, understood initially as premise-conclusion complexes of propositions,[1] figure in our practices of giving reasons. Among other uses, we use arguments to advance reasons to explain why we believe or did something, to justify our beliefs or actions, to persuade others to do or to believe something, and (following Pinto 2001b) to advance reasons to worry or to fear that something is true. This book is about our uses of arguments to advance their premises as reasons for believing their conclusions, i.e., as reasons for believing that their conclusions are true. The focus here is reason-giving centered on such reason-to-believe uses of arguments. Accordingly, the book does not discuss uses of arguments to advance their premises as reasons for believing that the conclusion is plausible, compelling, reasonable, nontrivial, helpful, plausibly deniable, or possible in principle. For ease of reference, hereafter I'll refer to uses of arguments to advance their premises as reasons for believing that their conclusions are true simply as *reason-giving uses of argument*. The book focuses on reason-giving uses of arguments that have three features, put briefly as follows.

First, they are essentially intentional uses of arguments. One uses an argument in a reason-giving way only if one intends the premises to be reasons for believing the conclusion. I call the operative intention the *argumentative intention*. Second, when one uses an argument in a reason-giving way, one claims that the premises one advances are reasons for believing the conclusion. Borrowing from Hitchcock (2007a, 2011), I call this claim an *inference claim*. The content of one's inference claim reflects one's argumentative intention. Accordingly, one's inference claim says, in effect, that the premises are reasons for believing the conclusion (in the sense that one intends). Third, one's argumentative intention is rational insofar as it is associated with one's inference-claim belief. When one uses an argument in this reason-giving

---

[1] As I say below, the book adopts the formal logician's notion of an argument as an ordered pair of a set of premise propositions and a conclusion proposition. I won't have much to say about the nature of propositions.

Arguments and Reason-Giving. Matthew W. McKeon, Oxford University Press. © Oxford University Press 2024. DOI: 10.1093/oso/9780197751633.003.0001

way, one intends and thereby believes, perhaps incorrectly, that the premises are reasons for believing the conclusion in the sense that one intends. That is, one believes that one's inference claim is true.

To elaborate, I take argumentative intentions to be essential features of reason-giving uses of arguments. Intuitively, if you use an argument but don't intend the premises you advance to be reasons for believing the conclusion, then you are not using the argument in a reason-giving way. So, in order for one's case-making to be reason-giving one must intend the premises one advances to be reasons for believing the conclusion. Less obviously, I also take inference claims to be essentially associated with reason-giving uses of arguments. For example, if you advance an argument and assert that you are not claiming that the premises are reasons for believing the conclusion, then this signals an absence of an argumentative intention and that you are not using your argument in a reason-giving way. However, I don't believe that reason-giving uses of arguments are essentially associated with inference-claim beliefs, because the operative argumentative intentions may not be rational.

An argumentative intention without the associated inference-claim belief isn't rational. Suppose a person S uses an argument to make a case for the conclusion and insincerely claims that the premises are reasons for believing it. That is, suppose that S doesn't believe their inference claim. If S nevertheless intends the premises to be reasons for believing the conclusion, then S's argumentative intention isn't rational. Compare: it isn't rational to intend to take one's wife out to dinner when one doesn't believe that one has a wife. Likewise, it isn't rational to intend one's premises to be reasons for believing the conclusion when one doesn't believe that they are such reasons. I'll say that an argumentative intention with the associated inference-claim belief satisfies the *inference-claim belief requirement* for being rational. The reason-giving uses of arguments that are of interest in this book are associated with argumentative intentions that satisfy the *inference-claim belief requirement* for being rational.

Arguing occurs in a variety of contexts and serves a variety of aims. Arguments are given in bull sessions with friends, on Madison Avenue, around the kitchen table with family, in scholarly articles, during board meetings, in courtrooms, on news programs, and so on. Clearly, not all uses of arguments are genuinely reason-giving, because not all users of arguments intend the premises they advance to be reasons for believing their conclusion. For example, one may construct an argument just to look smarter than one's interlocuter (borrowed from Hoffman 2016, p. 378). In a bull session with friends about the best team or best movie, arguing may be merely playful. Here participants may use arguments that they believe are wildly fallacious and deliberately mispresent one another's views (borrowed from Blair 2011, p. 25). Also, case-making may be deceptive in contexts when one intends one's audience to take one to be genuinely engaged in reason-giving when one isn't, say a press secretary defending administration policy without intending what is advanced to be reasons for believing that the policy is correct.

In sum, according to the conception of reason-giving uses of argument developed in this book, the operative intention is what I call the argumentative intention. One intends one premises to be reasons for believing the conclusion. This argumentative intention is reflected in the associated inference claim, which says, in effect, that the premises are reasons for believing the conclusion (in the sense one intends). Furthermore, argumentative intentions associated with the reason-giving uses of argument of interest here satisfy the inference-claim belief requirement for being rational. This conception captures what I mean by a *reason-giving use of argument* or the *use of an argument in a reason-giving way*. Again, what distinguishes the reason-giving uses of arguments of interest in this book is that the associated argumentative intentions are rational insofar as they satisfy the inference-claim belief requirement.

I'll make the case that an essential element of the inferential reasoning expressed by an argument so used is belief of the associated inference claim. My direct support for this is twofold. First, when you use an argument in such a reason-giving way, you have inferred the conclusion from the premises because you believe that collectively they are reasons—in the sense you intend—for believing the conclusion. Second, this inference is expressed by the argument as you use it. Taken together, these two claims suggest that one's inference is not expressed by an argument a person S uses in a reason-giving way unless one has the linking belief that the premises are reasons for believing the conclusion in the sense S intends. Such a linking belief is an essential element of an inference expressed by an argument so used.

In short, essential to one's reason-giving use of an argument and the inference it expresses is believing that the premises one advances are reasons for believing the conclusion in the sense that one intends. Whether this involves believing that the premises are true depends on the type of *reason for belief* that one intends the premises to represent. That there are a variety of reasons for belief (e.g., see Audi 1993) reflects the richness of our practice of using arguments in reason-giving ways, which in turn accords with the multifarious uses of arguments.

For example, one may attempt to justify a belief by advancing premises as reasons one has to believe it. A reason one to has believe something is a proposition that, possibly in conjunction with other propositions, provides at least some evidence that it is true (Audi 1993, p. 235). Accordingly, if one intends the premises one advances to be reasons one has to believe the conclusion, then one thinks that the premises are true. However, one may argue for a conclusion from one's interlocuter's beliefs or commitments not all of which one believes are true. Also, one may argue for a conclusion from assumptions or claims that one regards as merely possible in order to decide what to do or believe. In such cases, one advances premises that are reasons for one's interlocuter to believe the conclusion and that are hypothetical or suppositional reasons to believe the conclusion, respectively. In neither case does using an argument in a reason-giving way require that one believes that the premises are true. What it does require is that one believes that the premises one advances are reasons for believing the conclusion in the intended sense.

Acknowledging a variety of reason-giving uses of arguments accords with the commonly accepted view in the informal logic literature that it is wrong to define arguments in terms of just one use of them, as there are many different legitimate uses of arguments (following Biro and Siegel 2006a; Blair 2011; Goldman 1994; et al.). The book's conception of a reason-giving use of an argument motivates understanding arguments in the abstract, e.g., as premise-conclusion complex of propositions, rather than primarily in terms of one use of such complexes such as to persuade addressees of the conclusion (as in Pinto 2001c) or to justify the conclusion (as in Lumer 2005). In Chapter 2, I motivate my understanding of arguments in terms of the formal logician's notion of an argument as an ordered pair of a set of premise propositions and a conclusion proposition. Accordingly, the existence of an argument is not contingent on its ever being used to advance reasons for believing its conclusion or even on it being humanly possible to so use it. However, in order to use an argument so construed in a reason-giving way one must believe that the premises are reasons of some sort for believing the conclusion. That is, one must believe what I call an *inference claim*.

Again, an inference claim associated with a reason-giving use of an argument roughly says, in effect, that the premises are reasons for believing the conclusion. According to Chapter 3's account of inference claims, they are associated with reason-giving uses of arguments and are not components of arguments (and so are not premises of arguments). Furthermore, since there is a variety of reason-giving uses of arguments, it is to be expected that the contents of the associated inference claims vary depending on the operative notion of *reasons for belief* that the premises are intended to be.

The inferential reasoning expressed by arguments used in a reason-giving way is at the forefront in Chapter 4. Again, an essential element of an inference expressed by an argument used in a reason-giving way is believing that the premises are reasons of some sort for believing the conclusion. Borrowing from Dewey (1933) and Mercier and Sperber (2017), I call such an inference a *reflective inference*. Reflective inferences are what cognitive psychologists call type-2 processes of reasoning (e.g., Evans 2020; Kahneman 2011; Stanovich 2009). Among the features of reflective inferences are that they are consciously performed, perhaps cognitively demanding, and criterial in the sense that the inferer is trying to fulfill appropriate standards of adequacy, which may in fact be unfulfilled. Reason-giving uses of arguments are at the core of reflective inferences so understood in that if you perform a reflective inference, you use an argument in a reason-giving way, and if you use an argument in a reason-giving way, you perform the reflective inference expressed by the argument so used. So, if you perform a reflective inference, you believe the inference claim associated with the argument that you use in a reason-giving way. Your inference-claim belief is the linking belief of your reflective inference.

In Chapter 5, I argue that if your reason-giving use of an argument is good, then the corresponding inference claim is true. That is, it is true that the premises are reasons for believing the conclusion in the intended sense. Given that reason-giving uses of arguments are at the core of reflective inferences, we should expect that your reason-giving use of an argument being good suffices to make your corresponding reflective inference warranted. Chapter 5 accounts for this in terms of the claim that if the linking belief of a reflective inference is true, then the inference from premises to conclusion is warranted.

Intuitively, reason-giving uses of arguments figure in rationally persuading addressees of something and figure in rationalizing one's believing (or doing) something. To rationally persuade an addressee to believe something involves inducing them to believe it in light of the reasons one advances as premises for it. In Chapter 6, I draw on Pinto (2001c) and say that an interlocuter R is directly persuaded by your reason-giving use of an argument only if R performs the inference that you invite. The inference your reason-giving use of argument invites is the one expressed by the argument as you use it. R performs the inference expressed by the argument so used only if R believes that the premises are reasons—in the sense you intend—for believing the conclusion. The content of the linking belief of R's inference is that of your inference-claim belief associated with your reason-giving use of argument. The persuasive force of your reason-giving use of argument for R is registered in terms of R performing the inference expressed by the argument as you use it.

As previously indicated, the book countenances a variety of types of reason-giving uses of arguments, each distinguished by the type of reasons the premises are intended to represent for believing the conclusion. This motivates the view that the type of rationality your reason-giving use of an argument secures for your believing the conclusion turns on the type of reasons your premises are for believing the conclusion. Chapter 7 develops this view by advancing an understanding of argumentative rationality along two dimensions: objective and subjective.

To briefly explain, suppose that you use an argument in a reason-giving way by advancing its premises as reasons *you have to believe the conclusion*. Accordingly, you believe that your premises are such reasons, since you believe your inference claim and this is what it says. If your inference-claim belief is true, then your believing the conclusion is *objectively rational*. If this claim is false because, unbeknownst to you, your premises are merely reasons for you to believe the conclusion and so not reasons you have to believe it, then your believing the conclusion is *subjectively rational*. I argue in Chapter 7 that if you believe a claim in light of reasons you believe are reasons you have to believe it, then your believing the claim is rational even when you are wrong because, unbeknownst to you, your reasons are merely reasons for you to believe it. In such a case, your believing the claim is subjectively rational.

By the lights of the book's understanding of reason-giving uses of arguments, an ingredient of intellectual honesty is essential to such uses of arguments and the inferential reasoning the arguments express when so used. Plausibly, your use of an argument to make a case for its conclusion displays intellectual honesty only if you intend and believe that the premises you advance are reasons for believing the conclusion. Since you use an argument in a reason-giving way only if you have this intention and belief, one's case-making counts as a reason-giving use of argument only if it satisfies this necessary condition for intellectual honesty. Relatedly, intellectual honesty is baked into the reflective inferences expressed by arguments used in a reason-giving way to the extent that a linking belief and associated argumentative intention are necessary features of the corresponding reflective inference. If inferential self-deception is possible here and you wrongly think that you believe the premises of your inference are reasons for believing the conclusion, then your inference isn't intellectually honest and so is not a reflective inference.

To help set expectations regarding what's included in the book and what's left out, I now say something about my general approach to developing the book's conception of reason-giving uses of argument. I then speak to what I take to be the significance of reason-giving uses of arguments so construed. I end by giving a chapter-by-chapter summary. The discussion of my general approach to the topics the book engages is intended to provide background for the chapter summaries that follow.

My thinking about reason-giving uses of arguments has been heavily influenced by Stephen Toulmin's *The Uses of Arguments* (1958, 2003) and John Dewey's *How We Think* (1933). Each has prompted my attention to reason-giving uses of arguments as conceived here, and both have influenced the book's approach to theorizing about such uses of arguments. I take Toulmin and Dewey in these books to consider reason-giving uses of arguments in everyday contexts of justification and inquiry, respectively. I now elaborate in order to clarify the book's approach to reason-giving uses of argument. I start with Toulmin.

Toulmin develops his account of the structure of arguments in the context of justification. In such contexts, arguments are used to justify their conclusions (2003, p. 89). Accordingly, one advances the premises as reasons for one to believe the conclusion. For example, when you assert that something is true to an interlocuter, you are on the hook for defending the truth of what you assert. Toulmin uses touch points of critical inquiry from an interlocuter to identify the components of your fully developed argument for what you assert.

To briefly illustrate borrowing from Toulmin (2003, pp. 90–98), you make an assertion and an imaginary interlocuter asks, "What do you have to go on?" In response, you supply premises in support of your assertion. The interlocuter then asks how you got from your premises to conclusion. In effect, the interlocuter asks you to supply what Toulmin calls a warrant, which is a principle or generalization that justifies your inferring the conclusion from your premises. Other components of your argument are generated in your responses to further critical queries from your imaginary interlocuter regarding your support for your initial assertion. On Toulmin's model of argument, an arguer A intends their premises to be reasons A has to believe the conclusion. On my view, arguer A's warrant grounds A's corresponding inference claim that the premises are such reasons. Accordingly, on Toulmin's picture of arguments, being deliberate in arguing for a conclusion involves one's believing that the premises one advances are (good) reasons one has to believe the conclusion. I take Toulmin's idealization of argument to reflect the book's conception of a reason-giving use of an argument.

I differ from Toulmin in two crucial respects. First, I take arguments to consist only of premises and a conclusion. Second, I liberalize the notion of *reasons for believing the conclusion* that premises may represent. Again, one may argue from one's interlocuter's beliefs (in which case one may intends one's premises to be reasons for one's interlocuter to believe the conclusion) or from suppositions (in which case one intends one's premises to be suppositional or hypothetical reasons to believe the conclusion). In a nutshell, what I draw from Toulmin is that the development of one's argument for a conclusion rises to the status of reason-giving when one intends and so believes one's claim that the premises one advances are reasons for believing the conclusion. Whether this involves believing that one's premises are true depends on the operative sense of *reasons for belief.*

Dewey's *How We Think* (1933) has also had a positive influence on my thinking about reason-giving uses of arguments. The type of ordinary thinking that is of interest to Dewey is what he calls reflective thinking. Dewey characterizes such thinking as "active, persistent, and careful consideration of a belief or supposed form of knowledge in light of the grounds which support it and the further conclusions to which it tends" (1933, p. 9). According to Dewey, reflective thinking is triggered by our desire to decide what to do or believe in order to resolve a perplexity.

The many examples Dewey uses to illustrate various dimension of reflective thinking are taken from ordinary, everyday contexts in which folks are deciding what to do or believe (see Hitchcock 2020 for a useful summary of Dewey's examples). The import of Dewey's focus on ordinary, everyday thinking is to highlight how enhancing our capacity for reflective thinking in such contexts and inculcating our motivation to so think are important factors in enabling our success in navigating the trials and tribulations of day-to-day living. This motivates Dewey's view that these should be among the primary educational goals in secondary and higher education.

Reflective thinking that resolves one's perplexity essentially involves using an argument in a reason-giving way. That is, a person S's reflective thinking essentially involves S's using an argument in a reason-giving way. There is premise gathering and then S draws a conclusion from the premises that S intends to be (good) reasons S has to believe the conclusion. S thereby believes the claim that the premises are reasons S has to believe the conclusion. S's belief that the premises are reasons S has to believe the conclusion is an essential element of S's reflective inference expressed by the corresponding argument S uses in a reason-giving way.

Toulmin and Dewey are discussed in greater detail in Chapter 4, where I develop my account of reflective inference. What I am pointing to here is that I take the book's conception of a reason-giving use of argument to figure in Toulmin's account of argument and Dewey's account of reflective thinking. Toulmin's account of argument, developed in an argumentative context of justification, suggests that when using an argument to give reasons one has to believe the conclusion one intends and believes that the premises are such reasons. This isn't merely to believe that the premises are true, but to believe that they support in some way the truth of the conclusion. The associated warrant, if true, justifies this belief, which is belief of the associated inference claim.

Dewey's account of reflective thinking in contexts of inquiry suggests that if you resolve a perplexity by reflectively inferring its solution from premises that you have previously gathered, then you intend the premises to be reasons you have to believe the conclusion and so believe the claim that this is so. Again, this is to regard the premises as not merely true, but as support for your conclusion-belief. Accordingly, an essential element of the reflective inference expressed by your reason-giving use of the corresponding argument is that you believe that the premises are reasons you have to believe the conclusion. Generalizing the notion of reasons for belief, an essential element of the inferential reasoning expressed by one's reason-giving use of an argument is the linking belief that the premises are reasons for believing the conclusion in the sense one intends.

In a nutshell, both Toulmin (2003) and Dewey (1933) conceive of our reason-giving practices in the contexts of justifying what we believe and of inquiry to decide what to believe, respectively, as essentially involving the possibly mistaken belief that the premises we advance are reasons for us to believe the conclusion, i.e., are normative reasons for us to believe that the conclusion is true. I move beyond Toulmin and Dewey by acknowledging reason-giving uses of arguments according to which the premises are not advanced as normative reasons to believe that the conclusion is true. In Chapter 3, drawing on an architectonic of *reasons for belief* (e.g., in Audi 1993), I discuss a variety of reason-giving uses of arguments not all of which demand that one think that the premises are true.

Toulmin generates his account of the structure of arguments in an ordinary context of justifying one's assertion in response to an interlocuter's critical queries. I develop my conception of reason-giving uses of arguments considering uses of arguments in ordinary, everyday contexts. I do not in this book apply this account to analyze reason-giving practices in specific fields of inquiry, such as in the sciences, or in a specialized area of argumentation, such as in the field of law. This accords with my Dewey-inspired approach to conceiving of the inferences expressed by arguments used in a reason-giving way according to which they are instances of *ordinary reasoning* (as discussed in Kuhn 1991; Perkins 2002), i.e., inferences that take place in the town square or in private life, not in more formal settings such as an academic journal or in a courtroom.

I have tried to write a book accessible to an audience at the advanced undergraduate/graduate student level consistent with its being of interest to relevant scholarly audiences. I avoid technicalities wherever possible, use everyday examples of reason-giving to illustrate key points, and develop my conception of reason-giving uses of arguments from what I take to be straightforward, accessible, and non-controversial starting points. Many sections in each chapter end with a summary, and arguments for key points are presented in standard format to make them more easily identifiable.

Again, the book focuses on reason-giving uses of arguments according to which the user intends the premises advanced to be reasons for believing the conclusion, claims as much, and believes what they claim. Furthermore, an essential element of the inferential reasoning expressed by an argument so used is believing the associated inference claim. I now discuss the import of this conception of reason-giving uses of arguments first to a general audience and then to scholarly literatures in informal logic and argumentation, philosophy of logic, psychology of reasoning, and rationality.

Over twenty years ago, in her book *The Argument Culture: Stopping America's War of Words*, the linguist Deborah Tannen questioned "the ubiquity, the knee-jerk nature, of approaching almost any issue, problem, or public person in an adversarial way" (1999, p. 8). Tannen uses the word *agonism*, which derives from the Greek word for "contest," *agonia*, to mean "an automatic warlike stance—not the literal opposition of fighting against an attacker or the unavoidable opposition that arises organically in response to conflicting ideas or actions" (1999, p. 8). For Tannen, an agonistic response "is a kind of programmed contentiousness—a prepatterned, unthinking use of fighting to accomplish goals that do not necessarily require it" (1999, p. 8). Drawing on examples from media, politics, litigation, and education, Tannen highlights throughout her book the harm inflicted on people and the damage done to public discourse from the prevalence of knee-jerk agonistic responses of attack and counterattack.

It is not hard to see that at present the argument culture in the United States is still in a sorry state. Issues of public concern such as gun control, abortion, immigration, and election integrity are framed as battles in which the goal of winning or losing in defense of one's side of the issues predominates. The resulting polarization fractures community and demonizes dissent. In such an adversarial setting, making the case for a point of view is weaponized to the point that it needn't involve using an argument in a reason-giving way as understood in this book. After observing that when the average person hears talk of an argument, what comes to mind immediately is a dispute or quarrel, Johnson notes the wide gulf between the entertainment value of arguing and its rational value (2000, p. 18). I believe that its rational value brings into play reason-giving uses of argument as characterized here.

If democracy begins in conversation, as John Dewey once said, then the intense polarization in public discourse derails it as a starting point for democracy.[2] Echoing Tannen (1999, pp. 8–9), we need to promote ways of arguing that result in better understanding and solving problems. Happily, there are accessible texts that address this need and the importance of satisfying it (e.g., Aikin and Talisse 2019). Toward this end, this book promotes a view of arguing according to which it is a practice of using an argument in a reason-giving way as conceptualized and discussed in the chapters that follow. Case-making counts as a *reason-giving use of argument* in this sense only if you intend the premises to be reasons for believing the conclusion

---

[2] I take Hook (1954, pp. 12–13), who was writing during the heyday of McCarthyism, to describe an agonistic method of controversy that diminishes the importance of case-making being genuine reason-giving: "Discussion is the lifeblood of the democratic process, and, wherever discussion flourishes, controversy is sure to arise. Certain methods of controversy, however, poison instead of refreshing the lifeblood of democracy. . . . They seek to discredit persons rather than to consider problems. They ignore or suppress relevant evidence. They aim to create a mood of refusal to listen to views challenging some favored or dominant notion. Instead of exposing, confronting, reconciling or negotiating the conflicts of interest and opinion, one interest is fanatically identified with the common interest, and one opinion with the loyal opinion."

and sincerely claim that this is so. No doubt, moving polarizing debate and echo-chamber thinking to meaningful dialogue and reflective thinking is a complex task that involves more than ensuring that our case-making counts as a reason-giving use of argument so understood. For example, part of the picture of how we should argue brings into play intellectual virtues such as intellectual humility, open-mindedness, and fair-mindedness.

I would add intellectual honesty to this list. Intuitively, when we argue well, our arguing is intellectually honest. This book contributes to a model of arguing that displays intellectual honesty by appealing to its conception of reason-giving uses of arguments. Arguing displays intellectual honesty only if the arguer intends the premises they advance to be reasons for believing the conclusion of the sort that is called for by the relevant argumentative context and believes their claim that they are such reasons. Hence, case-making that is a reason-giving use of an argument displays intellectual honesty.

Using an argument in a reason-giving way rules out ways of being dishonest in arguing and thinking. For example, as I discuss in Chapter 8, it rules out bullshitting when an arguer doesn't intend to be offering reasons for believing a conclusion when making a case for it. The bullshitter is not trafficking in reasons for believing the conclusion that they argue for. Here case-making does not involve claiming that the premises advanced are reasons for believing the conclusion even if an audience regards the premises as such. This doesn't matter in bull sessions; it does matter in conversational contexts where trafficking in reasons for belief is called for.

In Chapter 2, I motivate the idea that when you state an argument, p so q, that you use in a reason-giving way, you claim that p is a reason for believing q. Intellectual honesty demands that you believe what you claim. Since you don't genuinely use the argument to advance p as a reason for believing q unless you believe this claim, reason-giving uses of arguments rule out being intellectually dishonest by not believing this claim. Case-making in response to why one believes something is bluffing if one advances reasons one takes to be reasons for one to believe it, but are not the reasons for which one believes it, i.e., are not reasons which sustains one's belief. As clarified in Chapter 8, bluffing may qualify as intellectually honest, but it lacks intellectual integrity.

To avoid misunderstanding, the book's central theses do not motivate monopolizing the sense of *argument* and *argumentation*, which I initially take to be a conversational exchange that deploys arguments (Dutilh Novaes

2021), so that they necessarily involve reason-giving. For example, following Hoffman (2016, p. 371) Kim and Roth's claim that "argumentation involves at a minimum two ideas that are confronted" (2014, p. 302) could be understood as if "giving reasons" is not a necessary condition for arguments. This suggest that any set of conflicting positions or ideas would count as an argument. In the well-known Monty Python sketch, "Argument Clinic," the customer claims after many "No, you didn't—yes, I did": "This isn't an argument, it is just contradiction." Mere contradiction may be *argument* in some sense, but it isn't *argument* in my sense of a *reason-giving use of argument*, which is perhaps the sense of argument the customer in the Argument Clinic has in mind.

In sum, "Public discourse requires *making* an argument for a point of view, not *having* an argument—as in having a fight" (Tannen 1999, p. 4). I take the operative sense of "*making* an argument for a point of view" to be a reason-giving use of argument. Accordingly, increased understanding of reason-giving uses of arguments is a public good. Of course, motivation to make our practices of case-making more aligned with the practice of using an argument in a reason-giving way is critical. However, being aware of what exactly is involved in using arguments to give reasons for believing their conclusions is necessary in order to consistently argue well.

A first step toward improving one's practice of reason-giving by means of using arguments is to understand what, exactly, this practice involves. Hence, the motivation for an understanding of reason-giving uses of arguments accessible to a wide audience. My development of what I take to be a plausible conception of reason-giving uses of arguments aims to deepen our understanding of the argument-centric dimension of our practices of reason-giving in everyday contexts. I now say something about the book's scholarly significance, which I take to be its model of reason-giving uses of arguments, and the use of this model to discuss connections between such uses of argument and the topics of formal validity, rational persuasion, argumentative rationality, and intellectual honesty and integrity.

The intuitive notion of an inference claim associated with an argument used to advance its premises as reasons in support of the conclusion is the claim to the effect that the premises in some way support the conclusion. This notion of an inference claim is implicit in typical textbook characterizations of arguments (e.g., Barker 2003; Copi and Cohen 2005; Govier 2010; Scriven 1976; et al.), and serves as a starting point for theoretical accounts of their content in the scholarly literature in informal logic and argumentation theory (e.g., Bermejo-Luque 2011a; Hitchcock 2011; Groarkes 2002).[3] With few exceptions (Freeman 1988, p. 20), what I am calling an inference claim is not taken to be a component of arguments. I am unaware of anyone in print who construes an inference claim as a (perhaps, implicit) premise of the associated argument. Good thing since to construe inference claims as additional premises brings Carroll's paradox into view. This raises the question of how, exactly, an inference claim is associated with an argument.

With the distinction in mind between arguments conceived of as products of arguing and arguments conceived of as processes of arguing, I conceive of arguments as products of arguing (i.e., as premise-conclusion complexes of propositions) and associate inference claims with uses of arguments so conceived. In particular, I associate inference claims with reason-giving uses of arguments. This motivates developing the content of the intuitive notion of an inference claim so that it says, put loosely, that the premises of the associated argument are reasons for believing the conclusion.

I deploy a standard understanding of *reasons for belief* in clarifying the specific contents of the inference claims associated with reason-giving uses of arguments. When you use an argument to advance its premises as reasons for believing the conclusion, your inference claim is, in effect, that the premises are such reasons. The novel move here is my use of what I take to be a plausible account of *reasons for belief* (as sketched in Audi 1998 and Bondy 2017) to fix the content of inference claims. This move not only highlights the richness of the variety of reason-giving uses of arguments, but also clarifies how the content of inference claim determines the type of the reason-giving use of argument associated with it. Inference claims are associated with reason-giving uses of arguments and not with arguments per se. While it may be overreach to think of my conception of a reason-giving use of argument as capturing the notion of an argument as a process of arguing, it is closer to this notion than the notion of an argument as a product of arguing.

Besides this story about the content of inference claims, another novel dimension of the book's model of reason-giving uses of arguments is idea that the rationality of the argumentative intention, essential to reason-giving

---

[3] Hitchcock (2007a, 2; 2011, 210) sees the thesis to the effect that every argument makes an assumption or "implicit inference claim" that the premises suffice as support for the conclusion as going back to ancient Stoic logicians, who held, according to Diogenes Laertius, that the argument-indicator term 'since' appearing at the beginning of a sentence, e.g., since it is daytime, it is light, proclaims both that the second thing follows from the first and that the first is really a fact" (*Lives of Eminent Philosophers*, VII.71), http://www.perseus.tufts.edu/hopper/text?doc=Perseus%3At ext%3A1999.01.0258%3Abook%3D7%3Achapter%3D1.

uses of arguments, grounds the association of an inference-claim belief with a reason-giving use of argument. That is, when one uses an argument in a reason-giving way, one must believe that the premises are reasons for believing the conclusion given that one's argumentative intention satisfies the aforementioned doxastic requirement for being rational. Again, whether this involves one believing that the premises are true depends on the type of reason for belief operative in one's inference claim.

The import of this way of connecting reason-giving uses of arguments with inference claim beliefs turns on taking argumentative intentions to be essential to reason-giving uses of arguments. On my view, intending one's premises to be reasons for believing the conclusion distinguishes genuine from pseudo reason-giving uses of arguments. Accordingly, given that one genuinely uses an argument in a reason-way and that one's argumentative intention is rational, one must believe one's associated inference claim.

A third novel dimension of the book's model of reason-giving uses of arguments is the idea that the reasoning expressed by arguments so used is what I call reflective inferential reasoning, which I take to be a type-2 cognitive process, e.g., it is first-person, slow, and perhaps cognitively demanding. Reason-giving uses of arguments are at the core of reflective inferential reasoning. If you use an argument in a reason-giving way, then it expresses your reflective inference. Also, if you perform a reflective inference, then you use the corresponding argument in a reason-giving way. A key feature of the relationship between a reason-giving use of an argument and the expressed reflective inference is that the inference-claim belief associated with the reason-giving use of argument is the linking belief of the corresponding reflective inference. Of course, not every type of inference has an accompanying linking belief whose content is that the contents of the premise-beliefs are reasons for believing the content of the conclusion-belief. An associated linking belief is a distinguishing feature of reflective inferences.

The book's model of reason-giving uses of arguments, given in Part I, serves as a conceptual framework for exploring connections in Part II between such uses of arguments and the topics of formal validity, persuasion, argumentative rationality, as well as intellectual honesty and intellectual integrity. Specifically, I respond to the following four questions. How, if at all, does the fact that an argument is formally valid, or (more broadly) demonstrative, matter to whether a reason-giving use of it is good? What must an interlocuter believe in order to be rationally persuaded by your reason-giving use of an argument? How, if at all, does one's reason-giving use of an argument bear on whether it is rational for one to believe the conclusion? What is required for one's reason-giving use of an argument to be intellectually honest and have intellectual integrity? In order to prepare the reader for my responses given in Part II, I briefly elaborate.

How, if at all, is logical consequence normative for deductive reasoning has received much attention in the philosophical logic literature (e.g., Field 2009; Harman 1986; MacFarlane 2004; Sainsbury 2002; Steinberger 2016). Clarifying the operative sense of deductive reasoning matters to the plausibility of responses. For example, how does logical consequence matter to reflective inferences that are deductive? In Chapter 5, I ask, how is the fact that an argument is formally valid or demonstrative relevant to whether a reflective deductive inference that it expresses passes normative muster? My response follows those who understand norms for deductive reasoning in terms of the norms operative in the contexts that occasion such reasoning (e.g., Dutilh Novaes 2015).

For example, the use of an argument that is not demonstrative to advance its premises as conclusive reasons falsifies the associated inference claim, which says, roughly, that the premises are conclusive reasons for believing the conclusion. A reason-giving use of an argument is not good unless the associated inference claim is true. I defend this claim appealing to what I call pragmatic, doxastic, and dialectical norms that guide reason-giving uses of arguments. In short, the validity of an argument has a normative bearing on a deductive reflective inference the argument expresses, because it figures in whether the corresponding reason-giving use of the argument is good.

Turning to rational persuasion, Mercier and Sperber (2017) claim that a primary function of reasoning is to rationally persuade others of the truth of one's claims. Intuitively, if you aim to induce an interlocuter's belief in your conclusion in light of the premises you advance for it, then you use an argument in a reason-giving way. Reason-giving uses of arguments are a means of rationally persuading an audience of their conclusions. The persuasion attempted counts as rational in that it is an attempt to induce belief of the conclusion in light of premises advanced as reasons for believing the conclusion. Of course, not all such attempts at persuasion are successful.

Drawing on Pinto's (2001c) notion of *invitations to inference*, one's attempt at such persuasion is successful only if one's addressees perform the inference that one invites by means of one's reason-giving use of an argument. What determines whether an addressee's inference is so invited? Using the book's model of reason-giving uses of argument, my response is that the addressee's linking belief associated with their inference must be the belief of the associated inference claim. Your reason-giving use of an argument as an instrument of *rational* persuasion is not successful unless you and your addressee both believe the inference claim you convey in stating your argument. In this way, rational persuasion by means of reason-giving uses of arguments turns on agreement between speaker and addressee regarding the truth of the operative inference claims.

Turning to the topic of argumentative rationality, in Chapter 7 I use the book's model of reason-giving uses of arguments to shed light on how one's reason-giving use of an argument rationalizes one's believing the conclusion. Drawing on (Foley 1993), I distinguish between believing something being subjectively rational versus it being objectively rational. One's reason-giving use of an argument makes one's believing the conclusion subjectively rational when the premises one advances as reasons one has to believe the conclusion are, in fact, merely reasons for one to believe the conclusion and not reasons one has to believe it. One's reason-giving use of an argument make S's believing the conclusion objectively rational when the premises one advances as reasons one has to believe the conclusion are, in fact, such reasons.

I take this understanding of argumentative rationality in terms of subjective and objective rationality to motivate abandoning a univocal standard of argumentative rationality according to which one's use of an argument rationalizes one's believing the conclusion just in case the argument so used is good. A bad reason-giving use of an argument may nevertheless rationalize (subjectively or objectively) one's believing the conclusion. As sketched below in my summary of Chapter 7, this informs my take on the debate between the objective epistemic approach to argumentation (e.g., Siegel and Biro 2008, 2010) and the pragma-dialectic approach (e.g., Garssen and van Laar 2010) over the nature of the argumentative rationality each takes good arguments to engender for believing their conclusions.

In Chapter 8, the final chapter, I use the book's conception of reason-giving uses of arguments to understand when such uses of arguments are intellectually honest and when they have intellectual integrity. I distinguish between a reason-giving use of argument being intellectually honest and its having intellectual integrity in terms of features of the reasons that are advanced as premises for believing the conclusion. For example, the intellectual integrity of your reason-giving use of argument requires that your premises be reasons for which you believe the conclusion. That is, your premises must be reasons that sustain your conclusion-belief. However, this is not necessary for your reason-giving use of an argument to be intellectually honest. Intellectual honesty demands that you believe your inference claim to the effect that the premises are reasons for believing the conclusion in intended sense. Such reasons needn't sustain your believing the conclusion. Accordingly, that a reason-giving use of an argument is intellectually honest does not suffice for its having intellectual integrity.

Intuitively, intellectual honesty subsumes intellectual integrity in the sense that if a reason-giving use of an argument has intellectual integrity, then it is intellectually honest. I advance support for this claim in Chapter 8, appealing to what I identify as necessary conditions for reason-giving uses of arguments to be intellectually honest and have intellectual integrity. My account of these necessary conditions makes essential use of the book's conceptual framework for understanding reason-giving uses of arguments. This makes the discussion apt as a means of summarizing the framework laid out in previous chapters. I now summarize each chapter, starting with Chapter 2.

Chapter 2 develops a baseline conception of a reason-giving use of an argument from three starting points. First, I consider ordinary uses of "argue" and "argument" by reviewing their dictionary definitions in *Merriam-Webster* and *Oxford English Dictionary*. From this review, I identify what I label an argument-argue link: one argues, in the sense of *give reasons for or against something*, if and only if one produces a corresponding argument in the sense of *a coherent series of reasons, statements, or facts intended to support or establish a point of view*. I take this link to motivate a notion of *arguing* according to which it is essentially intentional in the sense that when one so argues, one intends what one advances (e.g., claims) to be reasons for or against something.

I then consider various textbook characterizations of *argument* in informal logic and argumentation theory. I extrapolate from these characterizations what I call the *informal logic notion* of an argument according to which a group of propositions doesn't qualify as an argument unless some of them *are or have been used* at a point in time to support in some way the truth of a further one. I take such arguments to be dialectical arguments. This suggests two general types of arguments, *abstract* and *dialectical*. An *abstract argument*, i.e., an argument in the abstract, is simply a collection of propositions in which the premises are distinguished from the conclusion structurally. A *dialectical argument* is an argument whose premises are offered or advanced as reasons for believing that the conclusion is true.

Extrapolating from several of the reviewed textbook characterizations of argument, a person S presents a dialectical argument only if S claims, in effect, that *the premises are reasons for believing that the conclusion is true.* Drawing from the argumentation theory of van Eemeren and Grootendoorst (2004) and the argument-argue link mentioned above, I say that one's dialectical argument is a reason-giving use of an argument only if one intends the premises one advances to be reasons for believing the conclusion.

The third starting point of the development of Chapter 2's baseline conception of a reason-giving use of an argument is the formal logician's notion of argument. Based on my commentary of several initial characterizations of *arguments* in formal logic textbooks, I articulate a rationale for the role played by arguments in conducting the business of formal logic. The book understands arguments as an ordered pair of a set of premises and a conclusion, premises and conclusion taken to be propositions. This is the notion of an argument in the abstract as opposed to the notion of a dialectical argument, which is an argument in use.

Pulling these three threads together, Chapter 2 conceives of a dialectical argument as the use of an abstract argument to advance premises collectively as reasons for believing the conclusion. Furthermore, one must claim in effect that the premises, collectively, are reasons for believing the conclusion. Dialectical arguments are reason-giving uses of arguments as I understand them only when in addition one believes what one claims, i.e., one believes that the premises one advances are reasons for believing the conclusion. Accordingly, in order for a dialectical argument to qualify as a reason-giving argument so understood, the operative argumentative intention must satisfy the previously mentioned inference-claim belief requirement for being rational.

I do not take myself in Chapter 2 to be advancing a theory of argument or a theory of argumentation, which includes much more than what I say in the book about arguments and argumentation.[4] Instead, I take it that any worthwhile theory of argument or argumentation should accommodate the model

---

[4] For example, according to Govier (2018a, pp. 21–22), among other things "a theory of argument would discuss the nature and purpose of argument and specify and defend standards for the appraisal of arguments. It would specify how many different types of arguments there are and what standards are appropriate to assess each type. It would explain when and why it is reasonable to read into discourse claims that are not explicitly stated, and whether and how the personalities and beliefs of arguers and audiences logically affect the merits of argumentation." For useful discussion of Govier and adequacy conditions for theories of argument and argumentation, see Johnson 2000, chap. 2.

of a reason-giving use of argument introduced in this chapter and developed later in the book.

There are several well-known theories of argument, such as pragma-dialectical theories (e.g., van Eemeren and Grootendorst 2004), epistemological theories (e.g., Lumer 2005), and pragmatic theories (e.g., Walton 1996). Ignoring terminological distinctions, I take these theories of argument to picture the premises of an argument to be reasons for believing that the conclusion is true (see Pinto 2019 for a similar observation). Understanding the premises of arguments as reasons given for believing the conclusion is widespread in informal logic and argumentation theory (Govier 2018c; Jackson 2019; Hoffman 2016; Pinto 2019; Walton 1990; Johnson 2000; Lumer 2005, among many others). In this book, I take such uses of argument to be intentional acts, where the operative intention is the argumentative intention that has the aforementioned doxastic import.

I follow those who take using an argument to be intentional (Pinto 2010; Hoffman 2016). Specifically, when you use an argument in a reason-giving way, you intend the premises to be reasons of some sort for believing the conclusion. Pinto (2010) maintains that an arguer's intentions matter to whether the rhetorical effect of one's argument is direct or oblique. For example, if I unintentionally persuade you of the conclusion of my argument, then this is an oblique rhetorical effect of my communication of the argument. If I communicate the argument intending to persuade you of the conclusion and you are so persuaded by virtue of performing the invited inference, then this is a direct rhetorical effect of my communication of the argument. This book advances an understanding of the intentionality connected with using an argument that makes it integral to whether it is a reason-giving use of it as opposed to whether its rhetorical effect is direct or oblique. Again, I focus on argumentative intentions that are rational insofar as they satisfy the inference-claim belief requirement.

This conception of a reason-giving use of an argument is developed along two dimensions. In Chapter 3, I say that what is believed is a specific kind of argument claim, which I call an inference claim (borrowing from Hitchcock 2007a, 2011) that is conveyed by means of an assertion made when stating an argument one uses in a reason-giving way. In Chapter 4, I characterize the inferences expressed by arguments so used as reflective inferences. The content of the inference-claim belief associated with a reason-giving use of an argument is the linking belief of the inference the argument as used expresses. I now elaborate, starting with Chapter 3.

As a means of clarifying the variety of reason-giving uses of arguments, Chapter 3 gives an account of the content of inference claims in three steps. First, I appeal to the notion *of a reason for belief* to interpret the argument claims, introduced in Chapter 2, that are associated with dialectical arguments. The import of these claims put in a course-grained way is that *the premises support in some way the conclusion.* In Chapter 3, I articulate the import of such claims, now inference claims, as *the premises are reasons for believing the conclusion.* Second, I use Audi's account of reasons for belief (1993) to fix the content of an inference claim relative to a particular reason-giving use of argument. For example, if you use an argument to advance premises as reasons for your interlocuter to believe the conclusion, then you thereby claim that they are such reasons. Third, another typical element of the content of inference claims is the intended epistemic import of the reasons to believe one advances for the conclusion. For example, your inference claim may be that your premises are *conclusive* (as opposed to *inconclusive*) reasons your interlocuter possesses for believing the conclusion. Accordingly, your inference claim expresses not only the operative sense of reason for belief, but may also express the intended epistemic import of the premises as such reasons.

The question arises how inference claims are conveyed in stating arguments. Specifically, when you use an argument in a reason-giving way, the abstract argument that is used must be stated. How is one's inference claim conveyed when one states the argument? In Chapter 3, I consider four options: one implies the inference claim, one implicates it conversationally or conventionally, or one asserts it. I argue that when one states an argument that one uses in a reason-giving way, one asserts the inference claim. I argue that the other means of communicating inference claims do not appropriately communicate that the inference claim is believed. Assertion, conceived of as an expression of belief (following Williams 2002 and Owens 2006), does appropriately communicate that the inference claim is believed.

It is worth emphasizing that I don't take the bulk of what I say about reasons for belief to be new or controversial. As Audi notes (1993), in general reasons to believe something are one or another kind of ground for believing it. Some grounds provide evidence for a belief; others merely motivate believing it; some are consciously known, others not. Walton takes the pragmatic dimension of argument to be the arguer's claim that the premises support in some way believing the conclusion (1990, p. 409). To account for the pragmatic dimension of argument, the key move in Chapter 3 is to use a standard framework of reasons for belief to interpret the content of the arguer's (inference) claim.

The two primary tasks in Chapter 4 are to characterize what I call reflective inferences, and then to argue that reason-giving uses of arguments are at the core of reflective inferences. Obviously, the second task is trivialized by just defining straightaway reflective inferences as the inferences that correspond to arguments used in a reason-giving way. The strategy deployed in Chapter 4 for characterizing reflective inferences is to draw on the literature on the nature of critical thinking.

Broadly speaking, I take critical thinking to be reflective thinking. This motivates the view that an inference that qualifies as critical thinking is a reflective inference. As the literature is fairly diffuse and contentious (for a good review, see Davies 2015), in order to isolate essential features of reflective inferences I focus on the well-known characterizations of critical thinking advanced by Dewey (1933), Lipman (2003), and Facione (1990), among select others (e.g., Bailin et al. 1999; Kuhn 1991; Siegel 1988).

In a nutshell, a reflective inference is active (e.g., conscious), persistent, purposeful, and criterial in the sense that the inferer thinks the inference fulfills standards of adequacy appropriate to the inference. Not every reflective inference so understood is critical thinking. If, in addition, a reflective inference is reasonable in the sense that it fulfills relevant standards to some minimal threshold level, then it qualifies as critical thinking (drawing on Bailin et al. 1999).

Using this characterization of reflective inferences, Chapter 4 makes the case for thinking that reason-giving uses of arguments are at the core of reflective inferences. Specifically, I argue that if you use an argument in a reason-giving way, then your corresponding inference is active, persistent, purposeful, and criterial. Also, if you perform such an inference, then you use the corresponding argument in a reason-giving way.

Chapters 5–8, which constitute the second part of the book, use the model of reason-giving uses of argument given in the first part of the book (Chapters 2–4) to discuss connections between reason-giving uses of arguments so conceived and formally valid and demonstrative arguments (Chapter 5), rational persuasion (Chapter 6), argumentative rationality (Chapter 7), and intellectual honesty and integrity (Chapter 8). I now summarize each chapter, starting with Chapter 5.

In Chapter 5 I ask, how, if at all, does your argument being demonstrative matter to whether your reason-giving use of it is good? This raises the question of what are the norms that explain when an argument being demonstrative matters to whether a given reason-giving use of it is good. Chapter 5 starts by clarifying terminology that I use in my responses.

I apply the deductive vs. inductive and demonstrative vs. ampliative distinctions to both arguments and reflective inferences. When we use arguments to advance the premises as reasons for believing their conclusions, we occasionally advance the premises as conclusive reasons for believing the conclusion. Arguments so used are deductive because we claim, in effect, that the premises if true rule out the possibility of the conclusion being false. If this claim is true, I say that the arguments used are demonstrative. Otherwise, they are not demonstrative. All formally valid arguments are demonstrative, but, controversially, on my view the converse fails. For example, the following demonstrative argument is formally invalid: *that is red, so that is colored*. Your argument is inductive if you claim, in effect, that the premises if true make it more likely than not that the conclusion is true without ruling out the possibility that it is false. If this claim is true, then your argument is ampliative.

Your reflective inference is a deductive inference only if your linking belief is that the premises of your inference are conclusive reasons for believing the conclusion. Your reflective inference is an inductive inference only if your linking belief is that the premises of your inference are inconclusive reasons to believe the conclusion. Demonstrative and ampliative inferences correspond to demonstrative and ampliative arguments, respectively.

With the relevant conceptual terrain set, I highlight that not all formally valid or demonstrative arguments can be used in a reason-giving way because not all such arguments correspond to reflective inferences. I take this to matter to the adequacy of a logic for evaluating reflective inferences. Specifically, drawing on Woods (2002), I make the case that it is not a problem for such a logic if an argument it judges as formally valid does not correspond to an intuitively good reflective inference as long as it does not correspond to a possible reflective inference. For example, classical logic's endorsement of *ex falso quodlibet*, literally from the false anything (follows), rules it out as a logic of reflective inferences only if there are possible reflective inferences that correspond to *ex falso quodlibet*.

I raise doubts that such reflective inferences are possible with the aim of arguing that classical logic's endorsement of *ex falso quodlibet* does not problematize it as a logic of reflective inference. As I explain in Chapter 5, what's questionable is the capacity of an *ex falso quodlibet* argument to be used to advance its premise(s) as reasons for believing the conclusion. Of course, this is compatible with classical logic being ruled out as a logic of reflective inference for other reasons.

I then sharpen Chapter 5's central question to the following. How is the fact that a deductive argument is formally valid or demonstrative germane to whether a reason-giving use of it passes normative muster? In response I argue for GOOD from claims (A) and (B).

GOOD: If your reason-giving use of an argument is *good*, then the corresponding inference claim is true, i.e., the premises you advance are reasons for believing the conclusion in the sense you intend.

(A) If your reason-giving use of an argument is *good*, then it satisfies pragmatic, doxastic, and dialectical norms.

(B) If your reason-giving use of an argument satisfies these norms, then the corresponding inference claim is true.

I defend claims (A) and (B) appealing to the following three norms, each discussed in detail in Chapter 5.

Pragmatic norm: if you intend the premises of the argument you use to be reasons of a certain sort for believing the conclusion, then the premises should be such reasons for believing the conclusion.

Doxastic norm: your inference-claim belief associated with your reason-giving use of argument should be true.

Dialectical norm: if you accept that the premises of an argument you use in a reason-giving way are reasons to believe the conclusion, then it is prima facie wrong for one to deny the conclusion.

Given GOOD, if your reason-giving use of a deductive argument is good, then the argument used should be demonstrative. The norms guiding reason-giving uses of arguments are ipso facto norms for corresponding reflective inferences.

The central idea discussed in Chapter 6 may be put as follows. Whether or not addressees accept the inference claim associated with your reason-giving use of argument registers the persuasive force it has for addressees in different ways. You are *directly* persuaded by my reason-giving use of an argument to accept the conclusion just in case you perform the inference that it invites (drawing on Pinto 2001c). If you perform the invited inference, then your inference is expressed by the argument as used by me. Here I distinguish between an inference that merely corresponds to an argument and one that is expressed by it, which brings into play how it is being used. Your inference is expressed by the argument I use in a reason-giving way only if your associated linking belief is the belief that, in effect, my inference claim is true. Accordingly, your being directly persuaded by my reason-giving use of an argument turns on our agreement about the associated inference claim.

A reason-giving use of an argument may have persuasive force for you sufficient to elicit your belief in the conclusion even though you do not accept the associated inference claim (drawing from Sorenson 1991). In such a case, you are *indirectly* persuaded by a reason-giving use of argument, because you take the argument to provide at least one reason, perhaps among others, for you to believe the conclusion. Accordingly, indirect persuasion does not turn on agreement about the associated inference claim.

In sum, an addressee R is *directly* persuaded by S's reason-giving use of an argument to believe its conclusion only if R believes S's inference claim. An addressee R is *indirectly* persuaded by S's reason-giving use of an argument to believe its conclusion only if R believes the argument provides at least one reason, perhaps among others, R has to believe the conclusion, but R doesn't accept the associated inference claim. Of course, these claims do not exhaust what can be said about the nature of the persuasive force of an argument. Rather, they are intended to highlight that whether an addressee accepts the inference claim associated with a reason-giving use of argument registers its persuasive force in two different ways, directly and indirectly.

In Chapter 7, I consider the connection between a reason-giving use of an argument and the rationality of believing its conclusion. The idea that rationality is in some way central to argumentation is widely held (e.g., Biro and Siegel 1992; Blair 2012; Habermas 1981; Johnson 2000; Siegel 1988). For example, Biro and Siegel assert, "Rationality is thus at the heart of argumentation, and argumentation theory should be understood as being concerned with the ability of arguments to render beliefs rational" (1992, p. 97). Taking rationality as the basic evaluative ideal of argument makes it "a fundamental task of any theory of argument . . . to supply, by manufacture or import, some theory of rationality" (Godden 2015, p. 136). Following Godden, I will call these theories of *argumentative rationality*.

Argumentative rationality concerns the rationality of believing the conclusion of an argument in light of believing its premises. A theory of argumentative rationality tells us when a reason-giving use of argument rationalizes one's believing the conclusion. The central task of Chapter 7 is to advance a theory of argumentative rationality. Toward this end, I consider three approaches to argumentative rationality: epistemic, pragma-dialectic, and what I call pragma-epistemic.

An epistemic approach (e.g., see Biro and Siegel 1992; Lumer 2005; Feldman 1994) reduces argumentative rationality to what is commonly referred to as the standard picture of epistemic rationality (e.g., Rysiew 2008). According to this picture, believing that something is the case is epistemically rational just in case it is justified to so believe it. On the epistemic approach, your reason-giving use of argument rationalizes your believing the conclusion only if your premises justify your believing the conclusion. Accordingly, to get at argumentative rationality on the epistemic approach requires an account of epistemic justification.

On a pragmatic-dialectic approach (e.g., see Van Eemeren and Grootendorst 2004) argumentative rationality is reduced to procedural rationality. A reason-giving use of an argument in a dialogical exchange devoted to resolving a difference of opinion rationalizes the participants' accepting the conclusion just in case the use of the argument accords with the procedural rules that should be accepted by the participants and used by them to guide their exchanges. Hence, to understand argumentative rationality on this approach requires an account of the operative rules in an ideal dialogical exchange devoted to resolving a difference of opinion. On what I call the pragma-epistemic approach to argumentative rationality, your successful use of an argument to advance reasons you have to believe the conclusion suffices to rationalize your believing the conclusion independently of whether the premises justify your believing it and independently of whether your use of the argument is in accordance with ideal procedural rules for dialogues conducted to resolve a difference of opinion. On a pragmatic-epistemic approach, your reason-giving use of argument rationalizes your believing the conclusion because in so using the argument you intend and so believe, perhaps incorrectly, that your premises are reasons you have to believe conclusion. Here to get at argumentative rationality we need two things: first, an account of *reasons for belief* according to which believing that something is true in light of them suffices to rationalize believing it; second, a rationale for thinking that one possesses such *reasons for believing* the conclusion when one successfully uses an argument to advance its premises as reasons one has to believe the conclusion.

In Chapter 7, I make a case for the pragma-epistemic approach to argumentative rationality over the epistemic and pragma-dialectic approaches. A significant feature of this approach is that it allows that one's bad reason-giving use of argument may nevertheless rationalize one's believing the conclusion. In defense of this I make the case that the evaluation of a person S's reason-giving use of argument, positive or otherwise, counts toward an epistemic evaluation of S's believing the conclusion just in case the premises are reasons S possesses for believing the conclusion. For example, criticism of S's reason-giving use of argument doesn't count as rational criticism of S's believing the conclusion in light of the premises unless the premises are reasons for S to believe the conclusion.

In a nutshell, the pragma-epistemic approach reflects the centrality of rationality to argumentation in terms of the role argumentation plays as a means for the evaluation of beliefs. Norms, pragmatic or epistemic, used to evaluate your reason-giving use of argument serve to evaluate your believing the conclusion just in case your reason-giving use of the argument rationalizes your believing the conclusion as understood on the pragma-epistemic approach. The dimension of argumentative rationality in play turns on the operative type of reasons that your premises are for believing the conclusion.

As previously mentioned, I draw on Foley (1993) here. If one believes that a proposition p is true in light of reasons one has to believe p, then one's believing p is *objectively rational*. If one believes that p is true in light of reasons one believes are reasons one has to believe p, but which, in fact, are merely reasons for one to believe it, then one's believing p is *subjectively rational*. I borrow a quick example from Audi (1993, 235–36): that Paige has heard S give testimony that there is life elsewhere in the universe might be a reason for Paige to believe that there is. But such a reason might not be normative, i.e., might not be a reason Paige has to believe this, because it has no justificatory force, say, because S is obviously unreliable. In such a case, Paige's believing that there is life elsewhere in the universe in light of S's testimony may not be justified, but it is at least subjectively rational. Of course, that one's believing something is subjectively (or objectively) rational doesn't rule out that believing it is intellectually irresponsible, unintelligent, or unethical.

Using the account of reason-giving uses of arguments developed in Chapters 2 and 3, I highlight how objective and subjective rationality are two dimensions of argumentative rationality. If your use of an argument to give reasons you have to believe the conclusion makes your believing it objectively rational, then your inference-claim belief is true. If it makes your believing the conclusion subjectively rational, then your inference-claim belief isn't true because, unbeknownst to you, the premises of your argument are only reasons for you to believe the conclusion and not reasons you have to believe it.

Again, on the pragma-epistemic approach to argumentative rationality, a reason-giving use of an argument may rationalize one's believing the conclusion even though it is not a good use of the argument because one's associated inference claim is false. In such a case one's use of the argument rationalizes (subjectively) your believing the conclusion, because the premises are reasons for you to believe it. I take the plausibility of this to motivate abandoning a univocal standard of argumentative rationality according to which one's use of an argument rationalizes one's believing the conclusion just in case the argument so used is good.

I develop this motivation for abandoning such a standard of argumentative rationality into a case against the epistemic and pragma-dialectic approaches in a way that I believe informs the debate between proponents of these approaches over the nature of the argumentative rationality (e.g., Siegel and Biro 2008, 2010; Garssen and van Laar 2010). I understand the epistemic and pragma-dialectic approaches to endorse that one's use of an argument rationalizes one's believing the conclusion only if the argument so used is good. Since each approach acknowledges just one notion of *good argument* (as captured by the corresponding theory of argument), each countenances a univocal standard of argumentative rationality.

Chapter 8 concludes the book with a discussion of reason-giving uses of argument and intellectual honesty and integrity. More specifically, I consider two questions. When are your reason-giving uses of argument intellectually honest? When do they have intellectual integrity? My responses draw on essential facets of the reason-giving uses of arguments discussed in earlier chapters. The book's conception of reason-giving uses of argument is useful as a backdrop for distinguishing between intellectual honesty and intellectual integrity in a way that I think informs how both are realized in our practices of using arguments in reason-giving ways.

I consider intellectual honesty and intellectual integrity intellectual virtues, which is a standard view (e.g., see the introduction in Miller and West 2020). I distinguish between one's reason-giving use of an argument displaying intellectual honesty and intellectual integrity from an arguer possessing these virtues. Here I follow those who think attributing honesty and integrity to things other than people makes sense (e.g., Miller 2021, p. 4, and Halfon 1989, pp. 6–7, respectively).

Drawing from the literature on the virtue of intellectual honesty (e.g., King 2021; Miller 2017; and Byerly 2022), I argue that your reason-giving use of an argument is intellectually honest only if you are being truthful in stating your argument. If you are truthful in stating your argument, then you believe what you claim and you have taken care to ensure the accuracy of what you claim (borrowing heavily from Williams 2002). So your reason-giving use of argument displays intellectual honesty only if you believe what you claim and you have taken care to ensure the accuracy of what you claim. This highlights that what qualifies your reason-giving use of an argument as intellectually honest turns partially on what claim(s) you make in stating your argument. In stating an argument that you use in a reason-giving way, you make the associated inference claim. So your reason-giving use of an argument is intellectually honest only if you believe your inference claim and have taken care to ensure its accuracy.

Intellectual honesty subsumes intellectual integrity in the sense that if a reason-giving use of an argument has intellectual integrity, then it is intellectually honest. However, I do not take the converse to hold. In order for your intellectually honest reason-giving use of an argument to display intellectual integrity, the premises you advance must be reasons that sustain your believing the conclusion as a manifestation of your intellectual autonomy, i.e., as a manifestation of *your properly thinking for yourself*. My motivation for this idea is the connection between intellectual integrity and intellectual autonomy made in accounts of the former (e.g., Calhoun 1995; Scherkoske 2013, p. 8). If a reason-giving use of an argument has intellectual integrity, then your associated reflective inference is an instance of your *properly thinking for yourself*. So getting clear on intellectual integrity in the context of reason-giving uses of arguments involves getting clear on when one's reflective inference is an instance of *properly thinking for oneself*.

I argue that your reflective inference is not an instance of your properly thinking for yourself unless your corresponding reason-giving use of argument is integrated with your epistemic stance regarding the conclusion. It is so integrated only if (i) the premises are reasons for which you believe the conclusion, and (ii) your reasons taken together are indicative of the depth of understanding it is reasonable to expect you have of why the conclusion is true. By (i), your reflective inference is what I call a belief-inducing inference.

Your premise-beliefs sustain your believing the conclusion. Regarding (ii), the depth of understanding you should have of why the conclusion is true turns on the relevant subject-specific domain and the level of expertise it is reasonable to expect of someone relative to their various roles in their personal and professional life. Whether it is your business to understand a subject matter to a certain degree turns on your roles such as autonomous moral agent, citizen, parent, auto mechanic, professional philosopher, etc. In nutshell, your reason-giving use of an argument has intellectual integrity only if (i) and (ii) obtain.

This concludes my review of the chapters to follow. In his autobiography, Benjamin Franklin remarks, "So convenient a thing it is to be a reasonable creature, since it enables one to find or make a reason for everything one has a mind to do" ([1793] 2022, p. 33). Relatedly, being reasonable creatures enables us to successfully use arguments in reason-giving ways for everything that we have a mind to do. More broadly, a convenience of being a reasonable creature is that it enables our reason-giving uses of arguments to rationalize what we have a mind to do or to accomplish other aims. My story about reason-giving centered on using arguments draws on a variety of literatures such as argumentation theory and informal logic, philosophy of logic, philosophy of language, epistemology, and virtue theory. Such breadth highlights how multifaceted our reason-giving uses of arguments are. Being reflective and deliberative about finding or making a reason for everything that we have a mind to do is another convenience afforded by being reasonable creatures. I hope that what follows contributes in some way to readers' understanding of what they are doing when they use arguments to advance reasons for belief.

PART I

ARGUMENTS, INFERENCE CLAIMS, AND REFLECTIVE INFERENCE

2

Reason-Giving Uses of Arguments

2.1. Preamble

The main job of this chapter is to introduce the book's conception of uses of arguments to give reasons for believing that their conclusions are true, i.e., in short, reason-giving uses of arguments. This conception will be developed in Chapters 3 and 4, and then deployed to discuss connections between reason-giving uses of arguments so understood and formal validity, rational persuasion, argumentative rationality, and intellectual honesty and integrity in Chapters 5, 6, 7, and 8, respectively.

My aim here is to develop a baseline conception of reason-giving uses of arguments that can be accommodated by different approaches to argumentation such as epistemic, pragmatic, and pragma-dialectic approaches. Accordingly, I begin by considering dictionary characterizations of senses of the expressions *argument* and *argue* in section 2.2. In section 2.3, I sample textbook characterizations of *argument* in the fields of informal logic, argumentation studies, and formal logic. The discussions in sections 2.2 and 2.3 set the background for the book's conception of reason-giving uses of arguments given in section 2.4.

According to this conception, one so uses an argument only if one claims the premises are reasons for believing the conclusion. I call this claim an inference claim (borrowing from Hitchcock 2011). Specifically, an inference claim says, in effect, that the premises of the corresponding argument are reasons for believing that the conclusion is true. The content of inference claims may be distinguished in terms of the different notions of *reasons for belief* that are operative in them. In Chapter 3, I spell out both the content of inference claims and the connection between them and reason-giving use arguments.

Arguments and Reason-Giving. Matthew W. McKeon, Oxford University Press. © Oxford University Press 2024.
DOI: 10.1093/oso/9780197751633.003.0002

2.2. Arguing and Arguments

People have arguments, they give arguments, and are convinced by them to do or believe something. What is an argument? How are arguments related, if at all, to arguing? For example, if Mom and Dad are arguing, must their conversational exchange in some way involve an argument? Is one arguing— in some sense—when one presents an argument? In this section, I develop answers to such questions, starting from dictionary definitions of "argue" and "argument." Their dictionary definitions tell us how these expressions are ordinarily used. In section 2.3, I sample several characterizations of arguments from the fields of informal logic, argumentation theory, and formal logic. The notion of an argument is central to these fields, and it varies significantly between them. Section 2.4 introduces the notion of a reason-giving use of an argument, which incorporates the formal logician's notion of argument. The plausibility of this turns, in part, on making a distinction between arguments so construed and uses of them in order to accommodate discussion points from sections 2.2 and 2.3.

I'll make primary use of the *Merriam-Webster* dictionary, https://www.merriam-webster.com, to highlight various senses of "argue" and "argument," starting with the first. I'll also bring into play, where explicitly noted, the *Oxford English Dictionary*. While a dictionary is not the end-all and be-all of an analysis of a concept, checking the lexical definitions of expressions that involve it is a good place to see how the concept is ordinarily used by speakers of the relevant language, which in our case is English. This enables us to see how far technical and theory-laden definitions of arguments in informal logic, argumentation theory, and formal logic deviate from or extend ordinary usage. I'll number the different senses of an expression identified by the dictionaries, and use corresponding numerical subscripts to identify the operative sense of an expression (and its cognates) that is under discussion. I now begin.

2.2.1. Arguing

The expression "argue" may function as an intransitive or transitive verb. Here are two senses of *argue* as an intransitive verb.

(1) to give reasons for or against something: REASON. *Argue* for a new policy;
(2) to contend or disagree in words: DISPUTE. They're always *arguing* about money.

A difference between them is that when you argue$_1$ you necessarily give reasons for or against something. This is not necessarily the case when you argue$_2$ as contending or disagreeing in words doesn't necessarily involve giving reasons for or against something.

A: You promised that you would walk the dog, but you didn't. The dog has to be let out.
B: I did walk the dog. Get your facts straight before accusing me of not following through.

A and B argue$_2$, but neither provides reasons for or against something. Also, arguing$_2$ but not arguing$_1$ presupposes opposing viewpoints regarding some matter at hand. If you and I agree about something, then we can't argue$_2$ about it, but we can argue$_1$ for or against it. What are reasons for or against something?

As a start, they are reasons for or against doing something and reasons for or against believing something. To illustrate, consider the following three statements.

(a) Kelly, it is wrong to believe that Paige stole your bike. After all, *she is your best friend.*
(b) Kelly, Paige didn't steal your bike, because *the theft occurred on Saturday and Paige was out of state the entire day.*
(c) Kelly, you should study for the test instead of going to the party, because *you want to do well in your class, and you won't do well unless you study for the test.*

It is easy to imagine scenarios in which these statements are used to argue$_1$ so that what is italicized is offered as a reason for or against believing or doing something. What is offered in (a), appealing to loyalty, is a reason against Kelly believing that Paige stole her bike. However, the reason offered doesn't seem to be a reason that indicates that Paige didn't steal Kelly's bike, but only a reason for thinking that it would be bad of Kelly to think this about her best friend. In regard to (b), the reasons put forward are more clearly reasons for Kelly to believe that it is true that Paige didn't steal Kelly's bike. What is offered in (c) is a reason for doing something rather than believing something. Specifically, what is given is a reason for Kelly to study for the test rather than go to the party. Given Kelly's desire to do well in the class, that she won't do well in her class unless she studies is a reason for her to study for the test rather than go to the party.

A reason for or against believing something can involve a variety of attitudes beyond believing it true or believing it false. For example, one may advance reasons for worrying or fearing that something is true, or reasons for believing that a claim is plausible or helpful (following Pinto 2001b). Here I focus on reason-giving uses of an argument according to which the premises are advanced as reasons for believing that the conclusion is true. I'll have more to say about such reasons in Chapters 3 and 7.

When you argue$_1$, what, if any, cognitive attitude must you have with respect to what you argue for or against? For example, when you argue for something, must you support doing or believing what you provide reasons for? If you argue for a new policy, must you support the new policy? If you argue against something, must you reject it or not be in favor of doing what you provide reasons against? If you argue against Kelly driving during the storm, must you think that she shouldn't do this?

At the very least, argue$_1$ has the connotation that when one argues$_1$ for something by providing reasons for believing that it is true, one believes what one argues for. Correspondingly, when one provides reasons for believing that something is not true, there is at least the connotation that one doesn't believe what one argues against. Of course, in certain contexts both connotations may be appropriately canceled. Certainly, one may argue by giving reasons someone has to believe something, and so be arguing$_1$, i.e., without necessarily arguing for it. For example, suppose that an atheist argues as follows in making a case against a theist who believes that there exists a perfectly good God.

> I grant for the sake of argument your belief that there exists a perfectly good God. It follows that there doesn't exist pain and suffering in world that serves no purpose.

We may imagine that the atheist advances a reason for the theist to believe that there isn't useless pain and suffering in the world, even though we may suppose that the atheist rejects this and the reason the atheist offers for it. Even though the atheist puts forward a reason for believing that it is true that there is no useless pain and suffering, the atheist is not trying to prove this. Plausibly, what the atheist does think is that the premise is a reason for the theist to believe the conclusion.

In sum, one way of arguing$_1$ for something is to give one's reasons *for* doing or believing it. Also, one may argue$_1$ against something by giving one's reasons *for* not doing or believing it. Arguing$_1$ is an act of reason-giving. That one argues$_1$ for or against something sometimes suggests that one believes what one argues$_1$ for and rejects what one argues$_1$ against. However, arguing$_1$ does not always suggest this. As illustrated above, one may argue$_1$ by advancing reasons for an interlocuter to believe that a claim is true without believing that it is true oneself. Finally, arguing$_1$ does not presuppose arguing$_2$. For example, giving one's reasons *for* doing or believing something does not presuppose that one is engaged in a dispute about doing or believing something. I now consider *argue* as a transitive verb.

(3) to give evidence of: INDICATE. The facts *argue* his innocence.

The lightning and clouds argue impending rain as they constitute evidence that it will rain soon. *Arguing* in this sense doesn't require actors. Whether or not meteorological events argue$_3$ one thing rather than another is independent of any individual's act of arguing.

(4) to consider the pros and cons of: DISCUSS. *Argue* an issue.

"Pro" is a Latin root word meaning *for*. If you make a list of pros and cons, you are listing the reasons for doing something and the reasons not to, respectively. You may so argue, even if you are the only one arguing. For example, suppose that Kelly is deciding whether to buy a new car X or keep her old car Y.

Kelly argues$_4$ the issue of whether to buy X by considering reasons for and against each option. Kelly takes that X is safer than Y, gets better gas mileage, and has a bigger trunk to be reasons in favor of buying X. She takes having no car payments, lower insurance cost, and having a problem-free history to be reasons for keeping Y. To argue$_4$ is to consider reasons in favor of and against doing or believing something without necessarily arguing for or against doing or believing that thing. After gathering her pros and cons, to resolve the issue Kelly will then have to decide whether the reasons in favor of buying X outweigh the reasons for keeping Y.

> (5) to prove or try to prove by giving reasons: MAINTAIN. Asking for a chance to *argue* his case.

Arguing$_4$ doesn't necessarily involve arguing$_5$. For example, proof doesn't seem to be the immediate aim of Kelly's arguing$_4$. Also, one may argue$_1$ without arguing$_5$. Recall from above how the atheist argues. However, necessarily if one argues$_5$, then one argues$_1$. If one argues$_5$, then one argues *for* something. Accordingly, when one argues$_5$, the reasons one gives are one's reasons for believing what one argues for. In other words, if you advance reasons for a claim in order to prove that it is true, then you believe that it is true.

> (6) to persuade by giving reasons: INDUCE. Couldn't *argue* her out of going.

To persuade by giving reasons is a form of persuasion that I'll label *rational persuasion*. Note that arguing$_6$ needn't be *arguing for* something. That is, one needn't believe what one argues in order to be engaged in rational persuasion. Recall again the atheist's attempt to rationally persuade the theist of the atheist's conclusion.

2.2.2. Summary

A prevalent sense of *argue* is arguing$_1$, i.e., the giving of reasons for or against something. If one argues in senses 4, or 5, or 6, then one argues$_1$. Three types of arguing$_1$ may be distinguished by the nature of the reasons the arguer advances. One way of arguing$_1$ is by giving one's own reasons for or against something. Another way of arguing$_1$ is to give what one takes to be another's reasons for or against something. A third way of arguing$_1$ is to advance hypothetical reasons for or against something, as when one argues$_4$ in considering pros and cons for believing or doing something.

What prompts arguing$_1$? Obviously, disagreements can and, in fact, do prompt our arguing$_1$ especially when we think that it is both feasible and worthwhile to resolve the disagreement. Also, deciding what to believe or do (Dewey 1933) or having a belief challenged (Toulmin 2003) may trigger one's arguing$_1$. Furthermore, a desire to rationally persuade others (Mercier and Sperber 2017) motivates arguing$_1$.

For sure, my review of dictionary senses of *argue* leaves many good questions about arguing unanswered. For example, what's worth arguing$_1$ about? Under what circumstances, if any, are we obligated to argue$_1$? When is arguing$_1$ inappropriate or bad? Is there an ethics of arguing$_1$?

2.2.3. Argument

I leave these questions unanswered in order to now turn attention to dictionary definitions of "argument." I'll make connections between various senses of *argument* and the senses of *arguing* that we have considered, highlighting a link between arguing$_1$ and senses of *argument* we consider. This link will ground the claim that one argues$_1$ well only if the associated argument is good in some sense. I now begin my review of dictionary definitions of "argument."

(7) the act or process of arguing, reasoning, or discussing: ARGUMENTATION.

Argumentation is defined by *Merriam-Webster* as follows. (1) The act or process of forming reasons and of drawing conclusions and applying them to a case in discussion. (2) A reason or set of reasons given with the aim of persuading others that an action or idea is right or wrong. "There is a strong argument for submitting a formal appeal."

Accordingly, *argument$_7$* designates the act or process of arguing$_1$ in a discussion. Having an argument$_7$ is engaging in the process of providing reasons for or against something and applying this to a discussion. The reasons offered may aim to persuade others in the sense of inducing them to be for or against something. If so, then one is having an argument$_7$ and so is arguing$_6$.

(8) a coherent series of reasons, statements, or facts intended to support or establish a point of view: a defense attorney's closing *argument*.

I make four observations for emphasis. First, an argument$_8$ is composed of a coherent series of reasons, statements, or facts. Hence, arguments$_8$ do not include the statement of the point of view being defended. Second, that the series be coherent requires, among other things, that it be consistent.

So, no argument$_8$ can have as components a statement and its negation. Third, the series of reasons, statements, or facts is intended to support or establish a point of view. This necessarily links arguments$_8$ to intentional actors. That is, for there to be an argument$_8$, an agent must *intend* a coherent series of reasons, statements, or facts to support or establish a point of view. Fourth, such a series may support a point of view without establishing it.

Clearly, if one produces an argument$_8$, then one thereby argues$_1$. If one argues$_1$, does one thereby produce an argument$_8$? Yes, but only if arguing$_1$ is intentional, i.e., only if giving reasons for or against something is an intentional act. Plausibly, to be engaged in an act of reason-giving, one must intend that what one offers for or against something be reasons for or against it. However, to be careful let's say that reason-giving counts as arguing$_1$ only if one intends what one offers to be reasons for or against something. This takes arguing$_1$ to involve an intentional act of reason-giving. Arguing$_1$ so conceived leaves open whether all reason-giving is intentional. In short, your reason-giving counts as arguing$_1$ only if you *intend* the statements, facts, or whatever, you give to be reasons that support or establish an expressed point of view. Let's call this intention the *argumentative intention*.

When you merely report another's argument, you aren't arguing$_1$ because you aren't giving your reasons for or against something. In such a case, you don't intend the premises to be reasons for or against something. Similarly, arguments delivered on a stage by an actor playing a character are not acts of arguing$_1$ because the actor doesn't intend the premises to be reasons for the conclusion. Of course, someone in the audience may nevertheless be persuaded by the argument the actor gives. To further illustrate, consider the following sample conversational exchange.

SON: I can't find my wallet.
DAD: It's probably in your room, which is rather messy.
SON: I looked there and couldn't find it.
DAD: It must not be in your room, since you looked there and couldn't find it?
SON: Okay, I'll look again.
DAD: I'll help.

We needn't take Dad to be arguing$_1$ for believing that his son's wallet is not in his room. Rather, we may think that Dad is using an argument to highlight his son's reasoning, which he questions. So interpreted, Dad isn't arguing$_1$ for the wallet not being in the room because he doesn't intend the premise he offers to be a reason that supports believing this.

If we take a point of view to be a stance for or against something, then one produces an argument$_8$ if one argues$_1$. Let's label the following the argument$_8$-argue$_1$ link: one argues$_1$ if and only if one produces a corresponding argument$_8$. Merely arguing$_2$, e.g., two people disputing something, doesn't generate arguments$_8$, because there isn't any reason-giving. Also, that certain facts argue$_3$, i.e., indicate, that something is the case, doesn't seem to suggest the existence of a corresponding argument$_8$. This reflects the intuition that a fact can indicate that something is the case without anybody being aware of this.

Does the argumentative intention have doxastic import? Specifically, in order to *intend* the premises you give to be reasons for or against a point of view, must you believe that they are such reasons? Certainly, we ordinarily take the lack of such a belief to indicate the lack of the associated intention. To illustrate, consider the following.

KELLY: Where's Beth?
PAIGE: She is in the living room. She is listening to the stereo.

If Kelly takes Paige to be arguing$_1$ that *Beth is in the living room*, then Kelly takes, in effect, Paige to intend her second statement to be a reason in support of her first. If Kelly were to later learn that Paige didn't believe that her second statement is a reason to believe her first statement (perhaps Paige only wanted to be informative about what Beth was doing in the living room), then this is grounds for Kelly to think Paige didn't intend her second statement to be a reason in support of her first statement. This would in turn be grounds for Kelly to think that, contrary to her initial thought, Paige wasn't engaged in arguing$_1$.

Perhaps S not believing that the premises S advances are reasons for a standpoint doesn't necessitate that S doesn't *intend* the premises to be such reasons. Instead, it may only follow that S's intention isn't rational since S intends S's arguing to be reason-giving, but S doesn't believe that S's arguing is reason-giving. S's argumentative intention isn't rational if S intends the premises S advances to be reasons for a standpoint, but doesn't believe that they are such reasons. Compare: if you take a recent work acquaintance at his word when he tells you that he intends to take his motorcycle out for a spin after work, then your inference that he believes he has a motorcycle assumes that his intention is rational. Upon learning that he doesn't believe that he possesses a motorcycle, it is plausible to infer that your acquaintance didn't speak truly on the assumption that he wouldn't irrationally intend to take his motorcycle out for a spin if he believed that he doesn't have a motorcycle. My suggestion here is that if Kelly learns that Paige didn't believe that her second statement is a reason to believe her first, then this is grounds for Kelly to think Paige didn't intend her second statement to be such a reason, *assuming* that Paige's argumentative intention is rational.

(9) an angry quarrel or disagreement having an *argument* over/about money trying to settle an *argument*. An exchange of diverging or opposite views, typically a heated or angry one. "I've had an argument with my father."

Argument$_9$ connects with arguing$_2$. You are arguing$_2$ just in case you are having an argument$_9$. For example, Mom and Dad argued$_2$ about money; Mom had an *argument$_9$* with Dad about money.

(10) a reason given for or against a matter under discussion. They presented their *arguments* in favor of the proposal.

This is a sense of argument that links up with *arguing$_4$*, i.e., considering the pros and cons of believing or doing something. Arguments$_{10}$, may be in play when we argue from assumptions, or from our interlocuter's beliefs (e.g., in order to deduce something that we believe to be false). As with arguments$_8$, arguments$_{10}$ are explicitly identified with the reasons given for or against some matter under discussion. Thus construed, an argument doesn't include as a component what the offered reasons are for or against.

(11) a form of rhetorical expression intended to convince or persuade.

If the operative intention is to convince by giving reasons to rationally persuade, then arguments$_{11}$ are forms of expression that express arguments$_8$ or arguments$_{10}$. Accordingly, if one uses an argument$_{11}$, then one argues in senses 1 or 6. Plausibly, when one argues$_6$, i.e., one gives reasons in order to persuade, one uses at least one argument$_{11}$. Typically, forms of expression intended to convince or persuade include *illative* expressions such as "since," "for," "so," and "therefore," which are used to flag reasons and the standpoints they are advanced to support, respectively. *Illation* is the Latin word for inference, and the words used to indicate inferential direction are called *illatives*.

PAIGE: I don't know if I passed the class.
KELLY: The professor said that if you passed the final exam, you passed the class. You passed the final exam. So you passed the class.

Plausibly, what Kelly utters is an argument$_{11}$. Since illatives that occur in arguments$_{11}$ are components of them, the illative, "So," is a component of Kelly's argument$_{11}$. The illative flags the conclusion, *you passed the class*, which Kelly infers from the two previous statements. Kelly engages in argument$_7$, and Kelly's argument$_{11}$ expresses an argument in senses 8 and 10, which does not include the expressed illative as a component.

2.2.4. Summary

Our review of lexical definitions of *argue* and *argument* conveys the breadth of the various dictionary senses of these expressions. How is arguing connected with giving arguments? With respect to what we have discussed, for each sense of *argument*, there is a corresponding sense of *argue*. That is, if one presents an argument in any of the above senses, then one argues—in some sense. I highlighted the argument$_8$-argue$_1$ link: (i) if one argues$_1$, then one gives an argument$_8$; and if one gives an argument$_8$, one argues$_1$. Also, (ii) if one argues in senses 4, 5, or 6, then one argues$_1$. Therefore, from (i) and (ii), if one argues in senses 4, 5, or 6, then one gives an argument$_8$.

Both argue$_1$ and argument$_8$ are identified as senses of argue and argument in dictionaries other than *Merriam-Webster*. For example, both are captured by the *Oxford English Dictionary* (OED) respectively as follows.

Argue, intransitive. To bring forward reasons concerning a matter in debate; to make statements or adduce facts for the purpose of establishing or refuting a proposition; to discuss; to reason.

Argue, transitive. To bring forward the reasons for or against (a proposition, etc.); to discuss the pros and cons of; to treat by reasoning, examine controversially.

Argument (4). A connected series of statements or reasons intended to establish a position (and, *hence*, to refute the opposite); a process of reasoning; argumentation.

Argument (5a). Statement of the reasons for and against a proposition; discussion of a question; debate.

Taking an argument (4) to be a product of bringing forward reasons in support of a standpoint or position, motivates taking *arguing* in either OED sense to be an intentional act in that one intends what one brings forward to be reasons for or against something. Again, the argument$_8$-argue$_1$ link accords with the plausible idea that arguments$_8$ are products of arguing$_1$. Plausibly, an outcome of the act of giving reasons for or against something is the production or presentation of a coherent series of reasons, statements, or facts intended to support or establish a point of view.

This motivates thinking that arguing$_1$ is an intentional act in the sense that one intends what one advances to be reasons, evidence, or facts for or against something. Plausibly, if this intention operative in arguing$_1$, i.e., the *argumentative intention*, is rational, then it has doxastic import. Specifically, if one's argumentative intention is rational, then one believes that what one gives for a standpoint are reasons for believing it.

The process sense of argument, argument$_7$, is argument in the argumentation sense. An argument$_7$ is the act or process of forming reasons and drawing conclusions from them and applying them in a discussion with the aim of persuading discussants. Here the components of an argument are acts or relevant processes of forming reasons and drawing conclusions from them. If such acts or processes are intentional, then arguments$_8$, collections of reasons, statements, or facts intended as support for or against a point of view are products of arguments$_7$.

2.3. Arguments in Informal Logic, Argumentation Studies, and Formal Logic

The concept of an argument is central to the fields of informal logic, argumentation studies, and formal logic. I now sample textbook characterizations of *argument* in these areas of study, comparing them with ordinary usages of *argument*. I start with informal logic.

2.3.1. Arguments in Informal Logic

As noted by Groarke (2021), that there are informal-logic textbook accounts of argument that offer theoretical innovations accords with the fact that the move from the formal-logic notion of argument to accounts of argument provided by informal logic and the Critical Thinking Movement are tied to pedagogical attempts to teach students and learners how to reason well (also see Johnson 2000, pp. 2–4). My approach to developing a baseline conception of a reason-giving use of argument drawing on textbook and dialectical characterizations of arguments parallels Walton's use of such characterizations to develop his baseline conception of argument, which he takes to set course-grained parameters for his theorizing about arguments (1990, pp. 408–11, 1996, pp. 1–11).

There is no universally accepted account of the nature of arguments in the informal-logic and argumentation literatures. Here I sample several well-known textbook characterizations of arguments in order to highlight various dimensions of arguments that inform the book's characterization of reason-giving uses of arguments given below in section 2.4. The textbook characterizations I use are used by Walton (1996) to inform his theoretical characterization of argument. I now begin.

> (a) In logic, **argument** refers strictly to any group of propositions of which one is claimed to follow from the others, which are regarded as providing support for the truth of that one. (Copi, Cohen, and McMahon 2014, p. 6)

Accordingly, for a group of propositions to qualify as an argument, some individual S must *claim* at some point in time that one of the propositions, say *p*, follows from the others, which at that time S regards as providing support or grounds for the truth *p*. This raises the question of whether such a claim is a component of the argument.

> (b) An **argument** is a set of claims in which one or more of them—the premises—are put forward so as to offer reasons for another claim, the conclusion. An argument may have several premises, or it may have only one. . . . When we present arguments in speaking or writing we try to persuade by giving reasons or citing evidence to back up our claims. We may also construct and consider arguments as a means of reflecting on how we could justify a claim that we already believe. (Govier 2010, p. 1)

Four observations for emphasis. First, the elements of arguments are identified as claims. I interpret claims as propositions that are asserted, i.e., that are claimed to be true. Intuitively, a proposition is what a sentence may be used to express. Second, whether a set of claims counts as an argument turns on there being a point in time that some individual puts forward in an attempt to show that some further claim is true. Third, components of an argument are identified as premises (one or more) and a conclusion. The premises make up the evidence or reasons for the conclusion. I take this to be compatible with premises being insufficient evidence or bad reasons for the conclusion. Finally, two prominent uses for arguments that advance evidence or reasons for their conclusions are to persuade others and to justify our beliefs.

> (c) When we use the word *argument* in this book, we mean a message which attempts to establish a statement as true or worthy of belief on the basis of other statements. Persons putting forward arguments present certain claims, make certain assertions, which they expect or hope their audience will simply accept. They also put forward some further statement as being supported by these accepted claims. There is, thus, a further claim that because we accept the first statements, we should accept the latter. The former give evidence, justification, support for the latter. There are thus two radically different roles which a statement may play in an argument. A reason for some other statement is a *premise*. A statement defended by some other statement or statements is a *conclusion*. Arguments, then, involve these three factors: premises, conclusions, and a claim that the premises support the conclusions. (Freeman 1988, p. 20)

As with (a) and (b), (c) says that whether a group of claims constitutes an argument depends on whether a person S advances some, i.e., the premises, collectively as reasons or evidence for the conclusion. Reasons for the conclusion give evidence, justification, or support for the conclusion. As with (b), the premises and conclusion are claims made by S in putting forward the argument, which are clearly here taken to be assertions. Interestingly, (c) says that the claim referred to in (a) to the effect that the premises support the conclusion, i.e., that they are reasons for the conclusion, is a component of the associated argument along with its premises and conclusion.

(d) In the study of logic and critical thinking, *an argument is a group of truth claims intended or understood to provide support (evidence) for another truth claim. Truth claims*, as the term reminds us, are statements asserting something to be true. Depending on what is asserted, truth claims may be either true or false. Logicians use the terms *proposition*, *statement* and *assertion* when referring to truth claims. (Soccio and Barry 1998, p. 7)

Both (a) and (c) entail that a group of propositions or claims does not qualify as an argument unless it is claimed that some support the truth of another. Characterization (b) also entails this if we take a person S's act of putting forward premises as support for the conclusion as involving S making the claim that, in effect, the premises support the conclusion. According to (d), a group of truth claims doesn't count as an argument unless someone intends or understands some (the premises) to provide support for another (the conclusion). Plausibly, if someone presents or considers an argument intending or understanding the premises to provide support for the conclusion, then they claim this. That is, one claims that the premises provide support for the conclusion. However, as with (a) and in contrast with (c), this is compatible with not making such a claim a component of the argument.

Unlike (a)–(c), (d) explicitly appeals to intentions in characterizing arguments. The author of an argument intends the premises to serve as support for the conclusion. Plausibly, if one intends the premises to serve as support for the conclusion, then one understands them as such and so believes that the premises support the conclusion. This links up with (a)–(c) in the following way: if a group of truth claims is an argument, it is sincerely claimed by someone S at some point in time that the truth of one of them is supported by the truth of the others.

(e) We may define an *argument* as a sequence of statements together with a claim. The sequence is made up of two or more statements. The claim is that one of these statements, called the *conclusion*, is said to follow in some way from the other statements, called the *premises*. (Carney and Scheer 1980, p. 3)

By (e), a sequence of statements is not an argument unless it is claimed that one (the conclusion) follows in some way from the other statement(s) (i.e., the premise[s]). Accordingly, (e), as with (a) and (c), says that there is a claim associated with arguments made by arguers to the effect that their conclusions follow in some way from their premises. Both (e) and (c) say that this claim is a component of an argument in addition to its premises and conclusion. However, by the lights of (e) this is compatible with the arguer not claiming that the premises or conclusion are true. In this way, (e) differs from (a) and (c).

All the textbook definitions, (a)–(e), suggest that arguments are not standalone. What I mean is best explained quickly with a simple illustration. Suppose that you walk into an empty classroom, and you see the following sentences written on the board.

(i) No popular US president ever served just one term.
(ii) Donald Trump served just one term.
Therefore, (iii) Donald Trump was not a popular US president.

By the lights of (a)–(e), for you to determine whether an argument is expressed, you must determine whether (i) and (ii) were offered as reasons for (iii) or determine whether it was claimed that (iii) logically follows from (i) and (ii). Hence, features intrinsic to what is written on the board are insufficient to determine whether what is written expresses an argument. An argument is characterized as stand-alone if it is simply defined as a sequence of premises and a conclusion. A characterization of an argument as stand-alone is illustrated by (f).

(f) For our purposes an argument may be characterized as a sequence of sentences of which one—the conclusion of the argument—is marked off as following from the others—which are the premises of the argument. (Gustason and Ulrich 1989, p. 1)

Note that by (f) what you see written on the board does express an argument, taking *therefore* to mark off (iii) as following from (i) and (ii). This supposes that "therefore" has semantic import to the effect that the sentence that comes after it logically follows from the sentences that precede it.

(g) An **argument** consists of one or more sentences, the *premises* of the argument, offered in support of another sentence, the argument's *conclusion*. (Kahane 1984, p. 1)

As with (f), (g) says that premises and conclusion are composed of sentences rather than propositions, statements, or claims. However, unlike with (f), an argument is not simply characterized as a collection of sentences. Some must be offered in support of another. This is what makes some of the given sentences premises and one a conclusion. Accordingly, by the lights of (g), arguments are not stand-alone.

> (h) An argument, as it occurs in logic, is a group of statements, one or more of which (the premises) are claimed to provide support for, or reasons to believe, one of the others (the conclusion). (Hurley and Watson 2018, p. 2)

As with (a) and (c), (h) explicitly associates arguments with claims that, in effect, say that the premises support—in some way—the conclusion. Here the notion of support is associated with *reasons to believe*, which concurs with (b), (c), and (e) in taking the premises of an argument to be advanced as reasons for believing the conclusion. If there are a variety of types of reasons for belief as is commonly held (e.g., Audi 1993), then it seems useful to associate the nature of the support the premises of an argument are intended to provide for the conclusion with their intended status as reasons for believing the conclusion.

2.3.1.1. Summary

Let's start by using the discussion in section 2.3.1 to respond to the following two questions. (i) What are the components of arguments? (ii) What types of things are the components of arguments?

  (i) According to all the textbook characterizations except for (c), arguments are composed of just at least one premise and one conclusion. Characterizations (c) and (e) adds an argument claim to the effect that the premises support the conclusion or are reasons for believing the conclusion. The motivation for this is unclear. Even if we grant that a collection of claims doesn't count as an argument unless it is claimed by someone that some support a further one, this by itself doesn't warrant making such a claim a component of the argument in addition to its premises and conclusion. Here, I'll follow the other characterizations of arguments taking them to be composed of just at least one premise and one conclusion.

(ii) What types of things are the premises and conclusion of an argument? Both (f) and (h) say they are sentences; (c), (d), and (e) say that they are statements; propositions, according to (a) and (d); and according to (b), (c), and (d), premises and conclusions of arguments are claims, which I understand to be propositions that are asserted. Construing the components of arguments as sentences is implausible, because it entails that one and the same argument can't be expressed by different sentences. This is counterintuitive (e.g., see Vorobej 2006, p. 9). For example, the following two sentences can be used to express one and the same argument: "Not every Republican is rich, so some Republicans won't benefit from the tax cuts"; "some Republicans are not rich; consequently, not every Republican will benefit from the tax cuts." These are different arguments$_{11}$; however, they may express one and the same argument$_s$.

Construing premises and conclusions as claims understanding them to be assertions isn't promising because it is too restrictive. Here I assume that to assert something is to believe that it is true or at the very least be committed to its truth. However, as I have discussed, one may argue from assumptions or from an interlocuter's beliefs. In such cases, one isn't asserting the premise(s) and conclusion of one's argument.

Out of the options mentioned above, this leaves statements or propositions as the type of elements that compose arguments. I take propositions to be abstract, mind-independent entities. There is a process/product ambiguity with respect to "statement." For example, "statement" designates both the act of stating and what is stated. Say you state something meaningful to me. Your "statement" refers to your speech act of stating something, and the proposition that you state. In what follows, I'll let the sentential context disambiguate my uses of "statement."

I'll take an argument to be composed of propositions, one the argument's conclusion and the others its premises. To state an argument is to express its premises and conclusion. Drawing from my discussion of (a)–(h), I now make five points important to the conception of reason-giving uses of arguments given below in section 2.4.

First, according to what I shall call the *informal-logic notion* of an argument, a group of propositions doesn't qualify as an argument unless some of them *are or have been used* at some point in time to support the truth of a further one, or advanced as reasons for believing that a further one is true. When so used, some become premises, and one becomes a conclusion. Accordingly, the status of some propositions as premises turns on their being used at some point in time in one of the above ways. Correspondingly, the status of a proposition as a conclusion turns on premises being given or having been given in support of it or for believing it. Hence, according to the *informal-logic notion* of arguments, they are not stand-alone. However, intuitively, there are stand-alone arguments considered as premise-conclusion complexes of propositions.

This suggests two general types of arguments, *abstract* and *dialectical*. An *abstract argument*, i.e., an argument in the abstract, is simply a collection of propositions, according to which the premises are distinguished from the conclusion structurally. For example, arguments in the abstract may be conceived as ordered pairs, the first element being the set of premise propositions, the second the conclusion proposition. Or they may be thought of as finite lists of propositions, i.e., of premises, followed by a conclusion indicator, and ending with the conclusion-proposition. As we will see below, such notions of argument are akin to the formal logician's notion of argument. Abstract arguments are stand-alone, because their existence is independent of their being used to advance reasons for the conclusion. This is why some (e.g., Goldman 1994, p. 27) conceive of this notion of argument as an abstract notion of argument.

I'll take a *dialectical argument* to be an argument whose premises are given as reasons for believing the conclusion. If you give a dialectical argument, then you express an abstract argument whose premises you offer or advance as reasons for believing the conclusion. Dialectical arguments are abstract arguments in use (borrowing from Biro and Siegel 2006a). I take all the textbook characterizations of *argument*, except for (f), to reflect in different ways dialectical arguments. Dialectical arguments are not stand-alone.

Recall our empty-classroom argument. You walk into an empty classroom, and you see the following sentences written on board.

(i) No popular US president ever served just one term.
(ii) Donald Trump served just one term.
Therefore, (iii) Donald Trump was not a popular US president.

What's expressed is an argument in the abstract. Whether the abstract argument qualifies as a dialectical one depends on whether (i) and (ii) are or have been advanced as support for (iii) or as reasons for believing (iii). This leads directly to my first point, which is that there is a distinction between abstract and dialectical arguments.

My second point concerns the connection between dialectical arguments and their associated argument claims. Characterizations (a), (c), (e), and (h) suggest that if person S's argument is dialectical, S claims, in effect, that *the premises support the conclusion in some way.* I take the import of what is italicized to be *the premises are reasons for believing the conclusion.* In Chapter 3, I'll call such argument claims *inference claims,* and will clarify them in terms of the different types of reasons for belief that may be operative in inference claims.

My third point is that dialectical arguments, in contrast to abstract arguments, must be stated. If some propositions are being offered or advanced as support for another, then at least some of them must be stated, merely in thought, in writing, or in speech. An argument is stated when its conclusion is stated and at least one of its premises is stated. The premises that are stated are the argument's given premises. A premise not given is implicit. In putting an argument into standard form, all its premises must be stated and so given. However, as arguments are composed of propositions, an argument is distinguished from any one statement of it.

My fourth point concerns the connection between arguments$_g$ and dialectical arguments. Specifically, every argument$_g$ is a dialectical argument. That is, every argument$_g$ is used to advance reasons for believing the conclusion. Recall that an argument$_g$ is a coherent series of reasons, statements, or facts *intended* to support or establish a standpoint. Above, I labeled the operative intention the *argumentative intention.* I take arguments$_g$ to be dialectical arguments whose conclusions expresses the relevant standpoints. Therefore, given the argue$_1$-argument$_g$ link, when one gives a dialectical argument that is an argument$_g$, one argues$_1$. This is compatible with the possibility that one uses an argument to give reasons for believing its conclusion without intending the premises to be such reasons. In such a case, one's dialectical argument is not an argument$_g$.

The inherent intentionality with respect to dialectical arguments that qualify as arguments$_g$ is explicitly or implicitly captured by all the textbook characterizations of argument that reflect the notion of a dialectical argument. For example, characterization (b) says an argument is a set of claims in which one or more of them—the premises—are put forward so as to offer reasons for another claim, the conclusion. Presumably, if one puts forward premises so as to offer reasons for another claim, then one intends the premises one advances to be reasons for believing the other claim. For another illustration, (h) says that an argument, as it occurs in logic, is a group of statements, one or more of which (the premises) are claimed to provide support for, or reasons to believe, one of the others (the conclusion). Presumably, if one genuinely makes such a claim, then one intends the premises one advances to be support for or reasons for believing the conclusion. In short, that (b) and (h) characterize dialectical arguments that are arguments$_8$ turns on their implicit appeal to what I am calling the argumentative intention.

My fifth point draws on my fourth. One's dialectical argument involves arguing$_1$ only if the argumentative intention is in play, i.e., only if one *intends* the statements, facts, or whatever one gives as premises to be reasons that support or establish a point of view expressed by the conclusion. Recall that I take reason-giving by means of stating an argument to count as arguing$_1$ only if one intends what one offers to be reasons for or against something. So, given the argue$_1$-argument$_8$ link, if one's dialectical argument counts as arguing$_1$, then the argument used is an argument$_8$. In short, arguing$_1$ is intentional reason-giving and so whether one's dialectical argument counts as arguing$_1$ turns on whether one intends the premises to be reasons for believing the conclusion.

2.3.2. Argumentation Studies

The general subject matter of argumentation studies is argumentative discussions, which involve interactive social processes with two or more participants who advance claims in order to induce agreement regarding a standpoint toward an expressed opinion (Pinto 2001c, p. 32; van Eemeren and Grootendorst 1984, pp. 39–45). The Amsterdam school of argumentation initially characterizes argumentation in terms of arguing for a standpoint.

> Argumentation is a verbal, social, and rational activity aimed at convincing
> a reasonable critic of the acceptability of a standpoint by putting forward a constellation of propositions justifying or refuting the proposition expressed by the standpoint. (van Eemeren and Grootendorst 2004, p. 1)

Arguing for a proposition, construed along the lines of this notion of argumentation, is a complex speech act (van Eemeren and Grootendorst 1984, pp. 29–35). That is, arguing for a proposition (*pro-argumentation* as opposed to *contra-argumentation*, i.e., arguing against a proposition [1984, p. 9]) is reflected in a variety of argumentative moves that are speech acts such as stating an argument, arguing against a proposed refutation of an argument, and clarifying terminology (van Eemeren and Houtlosser 2003, p. 87; van Eemeren and Grootendorst 2004, pp. 52, 62ff.).

Drawing on van Eemeren and Grootendorst, in order to concretize this notion of argumentation, I'll consider the speech act of arguing for a conclusion in the context of a critical discussion, which I'll construe simply as a discussion between a protagonist (Pro) and an antagonist (Con) triggered by their desire to resolve their difference of opinion with respect to some claim (the standpoint).[1] The role of Pro in the discussion is to defend the standpoint; Con's role is to raise doubts about it (van Eemeren and Grootendorst 2004, pp. 60–61). Their aim is to resolve their difference of opinion. This is realized only when Pro and Con have reached agreement on the acceptability of the standpoint (pp. 57–58).

Suppose Pro argues for the standpoint by giving an argument, i.e., by advancing premises Pro intends to be reasons in support of the standpoint represented by the conclusion. What makes Pro's speech act of stating the argument count as an act of arguing for the conclusion? Van Eemeren and Grootendorst contend that Pro isn't arguing for the conclusion unless Pro aims to persuade Con of it (2004, p. 53, 1984, pp. 47–49).[2]

Following Searle's (1969) way of distinguishing types of speech acts, van Eemeren and Grootendorst advance a number of further conditions constitutive of arguing for a conclusion O by adducing premise-statements S_1, $S_2, \ldots, S_n$ (1984, pp. 39–45).

(1) The speaker has advanced an opinion O.

(2) The speaker has put forward a series of assertions $S_1, S_2, \ldots, S_n$.

---

[1] Van Eemeren and Grootendorst provide a theoretical model of the ontology of a critical discussion (2004, Ch. 3), as well as operative norms (2004, Ch. 8). A starting point for their theorizing is their intuitive characterization of a discussion between participants who aim to resolve a difference of opinion by exchanging arguments and advancing reasoned responses to criticisms (e.g., 1984, pp. 1–2, where critical discussions are referred to as "argumentative discussions"). For an alternative but related account of the speech act of arguing see Bermejo-Luque 2011b, chap. 3.

[2] Van Eemeren and Grootendorst approvingly note (1984, p. 36) Searle's remark, "'I am simply stating that *p* and not attempting to convince you' is acceptable and 'I am arguing that *p* and not attempting to convince you' is not" (1969, 66). I take Searle's remark to be compatible with acknowledging uses of arguments other than as instruments of persuasion, e.g., to figure out what to believe, to demonstrate that one has worked out an inference claim for a tutor. This turns on the plausible claim that such uses of argument do not constitute acts of arguing for their conclusions.

(3) Advancing $S_1, S_2, \ldots, S_n$ counts as an attempt by the speaker to convince the hearer O is acceptable.

(4) The speaker believes that the hearer does not already accept O, but will accept $S_1, S_2, \ldots, S_n$ as justification for O.

(5) The speaker believes that O and $S_1, S_2, \ldots, S_n$ are acceptable, and that $S_1, S_2, \ldots, S_n$ justify O.

I consider these conditions collectively to be a theoretical development of the dictionary sense *argument₂*, i.e., *argument* in the argumentation sense. Goldman calls this the *social sense of argument* (1994, p. 27). *Argument* so understood designates arguing$_6$, arguing with the aim of inducing one's interlocuter to accept one's stated opinion by providing reasons for it. Accordingly, what is produced is an argument$_8$. Recall that arguing$_6$ is arguing$_1$, i.e., the giving of reasons for or against something.

To elaborate, conditions (1)–(3) restrict what counts as arguing for a conclusion. In a conversational exchange (like a formal debate, between a protagonist and antagonist) if you state your opinion about something and back it up, but you don't aim to persuade your interlocuter, then you are not arguing—in the intended sense—for your opinion. Also, arguing in the intended sense, i.e., arguing$_6$, presupposes a disagreement regarding the matter at hand.

I take condition (4) to imply that the speaker believes that the premises advanced are reasons for the interlocuter to accept the conclusion, and that the speaker believes that the hearer will accept O on the basis of the given reasons, $S_1, S_2, \ldots, S_n$. In other words: the speaker believes that the S_i taken together are reasons that justify the interlocuter's acceptance of O, which we may regard as the speaker's conclusion.

This brings us to condition (5), which imposes a sincerity condition with respect to arguing for a conclusion. Specifically, the speaker believes that the series of assertions put forward, $S_1, S_2, \ldots, S_n$, are acceptable and believes that they *justify* O, the speaker's conclusion. Accordingly, if you don't believe what you assert or don't believe that what you assert supports your opinion, then your arguing is insincere.

By (5), Pro's speech act of stating the argument counts as an act of arguing *for the conclusion* since Pro takes the acceptability of the premises to justify the acceptability of the conclusion O. This is what we may call *a persona (from the person) argumentation*, i.e., arguing for the truth of a conclusion O by adducing premises the speaker believes constitute an acceptable justification of O.[3] By arguing for a conclusion in this sense,[4] one advances what may be labeled an *a persona* argument$_8$. In using an *a persona* argument$_8$ to argue for its conclusion, a speaker S advances the premises as S's reasons for believing the conclusion. Specifically, the premises of such an argument are among S's reasons for which S accepts the conclusion.

As we have discussed, there are other senses of "arguing" according to which one doesn't argue for the truth of the conclusion. Nevertheless, it is plausible to think that there is a sincerity condition for arguing, regardless of whether or not it constitutes *a persona argumentation*. I now elaborate.

Note that van Eemeren and Grootendorst motivate the sincerity condition as a constraint on the speech act of arguing for the conclusion. Again, your giving an argument for a standpoint doesn't count as the speech act of arguing for its conclusion unless you believe the premises you advanced are acceptable and that they justify believing that the conclusion is acceptable. However, as I pointed out above, a dialectical argument that qualifies as an argument$_8$ is essentially an *intentional* use of an argument to advance its premises as reasons for believing the conclusion. So, your argument isn't such a dialectical argument unless you intend the premises to be such reasons. I've called this intention the argumentative intention. It is not rational to intend to use an argument to give reasons for believing conclusion, but not believe that the premises are such reasons. So, if a person S's argumentative intention associated with the person's dialectical argument is rational, then S believes that the premises are reasons for believing the conclusion.

Recall that when one gives an argument$_8$, one argues$_1$. Therefore, if one's associated argumentative intention is rational, then one argues$_1$ sincerely since one believes that one's premises are reasons for believing the standpoint

---

[3] Van Eemeren and Grootendorst worry that the sincerity condition is too speaker-centered and so doesn't reflect the obligations of arguers when they don't believe that the premises they advance justify the conclusion. They think, in effect, that if a respondent R justifiably takes a speaker S to be arguing for a conclusion in a critical discussion, then R is entitled to hold S responsible for the inference claim even if S doesn't believe the inference claim (1984, p. 42). This puts S on the hook to defend the inference claim if challenged by R. This is compatible with granting that there is *a persona* argumentation.

[4] Clearly, this notion of arguing is not idiosyncratic. For example, according to Bermejo-Luque, a constitutive goal of a speaker S's arguing for a conclusion is to show that a target claim is correct (2011b, p. 53), and the corresponding sincerity condition requires, in effect, that S believes that the premises advanced are reasons to believe the conclusion. Also, Aiken and Talisse (2019, p. 11) take, as a starting point, an argument advanced by a speaker S to be S's attempt not only to make clear what S's reasons are for her conclusion-belief, but also to vindicate or defend what S believes by showing that her conclusion-belief is well supported by compelling reasons. I take it that, according to these notions, the premises S advances for the conclusion are among the reasons for which S believes it. This is the operative sense of arguing here.

encapsulated in the conclusion. So, if a person S argues insincerely, then either S lacks the argumentative intention and S's corresponding dialectical argument is not an argument$_8$, or it is and S's associated argumentative intention isn't rational. Accordingly, a sincerity condition is constitutive of arguing$_1$ that involves dialectical arguments associated with rational argumentative intentions.

2.3.2.1. Summary

Relying on van Eemeren and Grootendorst (1984, 2004), I have developed the dictionary definitions of arguing$_6$ and argument$_7$ by providing five conditions that must be satisfied in order for one to be sincerely arguing for a conclusion. Since one may present an argument and thereby argue without arguing for the truth of the conclusion, I generalized condition (5), which constrains just *a persona* argumentation, to a *sincerity condition* for your arguing$_1$: if you give a dialectical argument in the course of arguing$_1$, then if your associated argumentative intention is rational, your arguing$_1$ is sincere in that you believe that the premises you advance are reasons for believing the conclusion in the intended sense. In Chapter 3, I spell out *reasons for believing the conclusion* in a way that accommodates the idea that one may advance premises as reasons for believing the conclusion even though one does not believe that the premises are true. This will enable consideration of reason-giving uses of arguments beyond the confines of *a persona* argumentation.

As I noted in the summary in section 2.2.2, dictionary senses of *argue* do not tell us what it is to argue well. Neither do conditions (1)–(5), which are conditions that must be satisfied in order for one to be arguing for a conclusion. What is it for you to so argue well? This multifaceted topic that is addressed by van Eemeren and Grootendorst in other places (e.g., in 2004) cannot be pursued here. However, in order to convey something of what is involved and convey a connection with the above sketch of arguing$_1$ well, I sketch my view.

Briefly, my view is that to argue$_1$ well requires arguing at the right time (during Thanksgiving dinner?) with the right interlocuter (Is there enough common ground?), for the right reasons (e.g., What's the aim? Win a rhetorical battle? Change someone's mind? Get to the truth?), to the right extent (When do you stop?), and in the right way (e.g., Is there listening? Is one's communication effective for the intended audience?).

If you don't believe that the premises of your dialectical argument are reasons that support believing the conclusion, then your use of the argument lacks intellectual honesty. Intellectual honesty demands that we not only assume responsibility for what we offer as reasons for a conclusion being reasons for it, but also that we believe them to be such reasons. The honesty of your use of an argument to advance reasons for believing its conclusion honors the trust your interlocuters place in your arguing for the conclusion. I discuss intellectual honesty and reason-giving uses of arguments further in Chapter 8.

Note that one's insincere arguing$_1$ problematizes the operative argumentative intention, as one intends to advance premises as reasons that support the conclusion, but one doesn't believe that they are such reasons. In such a case, one's argumentative intention is not rational. Second, insincere arguing$_1$ lacks *intellectual honesty*, which I take to be bad arguing. If your arguing$_1$ for something is intellectually honest, then you believe that what you advance as reasons in support of a viewpoint are such reasons for it in the sense that you intend. That is, intellectual honesty in arguing$_1$ by means of dialectical arguments requires the rationality of one's associated argumentative intention so that one believes that one's premises are reasons for believing the conclusion in the sense that one intends.

2.3.3. Arguments in Formal Logic

Formal validity is a central topic of study in formal logic. As formal validity is a property of arguments, a notion of an argument is needed for theories of formal validity. Unlike with characterizations of arguments in informal logic and in argumentation theory, the formal-logic notion of an argument is an extension of ordinary uses of *argument* that divorces arguments from arguing. Accordingly, using an argument in the formal-logic sense does not automatically count as an act of arguing. This is reflected by the fact that the formal-logic notion of argument is a notion of argument in the abstract.

The rationale for this characterization of an argument in formal logic turns exclusively on the roles arguments play in the study of formal validity. We need to say enough about formal validity to justify operative senses of the expression *argument* as it's used in formal logic. Two predominant, initial characterizations of formal validity advanced in textbooks and handbooks are in terms of valid argument forms, and in terms of the concept of logical consequence. I now briefly discuss, starting with the first.

An argument is formally valid only if it has a valid argument form. An argument form is valid just in case for each argument with that form, it is necessary that if every premise is true, then the conclusion is also true. Sometimes this is put as an argument is valid when truth is necessarily preserved from premises to conclusion in virtue of its form. What is an argument form? To illustrate, consider the following two arguments. Premises and conclusion are separated by the horizontal bar.

All squares are rectangles	All whales are amphibians
All rectangles are figures with <u>four straight sides</u>	All amphibians are cold-blooded <u>animals</u>
All squares are figures with four straight sides	All whales are cold-blooded animals

We may say that these two arguments are valid because they instantiate this valid argument form.

All Xs are Ys
<u>All Ys are Zs</u>
All Xs are Zs

An instance of this form is any argument produced by uniformly substituting expressions for the variables X, Y, and Z in a way that generates meaningful statements. This argument form is valid because for any instance, it is impossible that all the premises are true with the conclusion false. The following argument form is not valid; i.e., it is invalid, because it has a counterexample (i.e., it has an instance with true premises and a false conclusion) an example of which is given to its right.

Some X are Y	Some siblings are daughters
<u>Some X are Z</u>	<u>Some siblings are sons</u>
Some Y are Z	Some daughters are sons

Formal logic develops techniques for deriving argument forms from arguments, and methods for determining whether a given argument form is valid. Loosely, the form of an argument is a function of (i) what so-called logical expressions, if any, occur in the argument (e.g., *all, some, not, or,* and *and*), and (ii) the pattern of the remaining nonlogical expressions. Both (i) and (ii) are determined independently of how an argument is being used. In particular, they are determined independently of whether its premises serve as reasons for believing the conclusion.

<u>Kelly is happy and it is not the case that Kelly is happy</u>	<u>P and not-P</u>
Kelly is happy	P

Plausibly, the argument form is valid; it has no instance with a true premise and false conclusion because it has no instance with a true premise.[5] This illustrates how the validity of an argument doesn't require the truth or acceptability of its premises or conclusion. Correspondingly, the validity of the argument is not sufficient to justify a use of it to advance its premise as a reason for believing the conclusion.

A second approach to characterizing formal validity is to bypass the notion of a valid argument form, and directly appeal to the concept of logical consequence. "An argument is valid iff [if and only if] its conclusion is a logical consequence of its premises" (Blanchette 2001, p. 115). Logical consequence is a type of relation between sets of sentences, statements, propositions. To elaborate, I'll appeal to propositions.

For example, for any set of propositions, say {All whales are mammals, Willy is a whale}, we can ask about its set of logical consequences, e.g., what logically follows from these propositions? To make the connection between validity and logical consequence clear it is useful to talk about logical consequence as a relation between a proposition σ and a set Γof propositions. Proposition σ is a logical consequence of Γ iff it must be the case that on the assumption that every member of Γ is true, σ is also true (Etchemendy 2015, p. 603). To illustrate, the proposition *Beth is a first responder* is a logical consequence of the two propositions *Nurses are first responders* and *Beth is a nurse* because it must be the case that on the assumption that *Nurses are first responders* and *Beth is a nurse* are true, *Beth is a first responder* is also true.

---

[5] Here and elsewhere in this section I discuss validity and logical consequence in the framework of classical logic. I don't believe that my adoption of this framework problematizes my discussion of the formal logician's notion of an argument. For example, taking arguments to be ordered pairs, the first element being the set of premise propositions, the second the conclusion proposition seems fairly neutral regarding which logic one uses to judge validity (although see note 8 below).

Accordingly, the following argument is formally valid; it is an instance of the valid argument form given to its right.

Nurses are first responders	All X are Y
Beth is a nurse	a is X
Beth is first responder	a is Y

The characterization of formal validity in terms of logical consequence requires a sense of "logical consequence" according to which σ logically follows from Γ solely in virtue of the meanings of any logical expressions (e.g., *all, some, or, and, not*) that occur, and the pattern of remaining nonlogical expressions. In this more restricted sense, we see that *Kelly is male* is not a logical consequence of *Kelly is a bachelor*, since to recognize the consequence relation here we must understand the operative meanings of the two nonlogical expressions *male* and *bachelor*. This reflects that the argument just below on the left is invalid. It has an invalid argument form, given in the middle. An instance with true premises and false conclusion is given on the right.

Kelly is male	a is X	Kelly is tall
Kelly is a bachelor	a is Y	Kelly is a teenager

A logical consequence relation is often expressed with the symbol "⊨", which is called the double turnstile. Using a double turnstile, we may express *σ logically follows from Γ* as follows.

$$\Gamma \vDash \sigma$$

This statement is called a sequent. The meaning of "⊨" is further refined by a theoretical characterization of the logical consequence relation. Accordingly, the truth of a particular sequent may be supported by a theory of logical consequence of which there are many (e.g., see Priest 2008). Important for our purposes, whether Γ ⊨ σ is true for a given set Γ of propositions and proposition σ does not turn on there being an argument with Γ as its set of premises and σ as its conclusion.

I now sample several textbook characterizations of arguments in formal logic. For each, I make some observations and provide commentary drawing on the above brief discussion of validity. My aim here is to get a sense of what arguments are taken to be in formal logic that will inform the notion of *argument* at work in the characterization of reason-giving uses of arguments advanced in the next section.

(a) By an *argument* we mean a system of declarative sentences (of a single language), one of which is designated as the *conclusion* and the others as *premises*. (Mates 1972, p. 5)

A system of sentences connotes something more than a mere list of them. Specifically, the sentences that make up an argument are interconnected in some way. Furthermore, the components of an argument are taken to be declarative sentences, which rules out interrogatives, imperatives, etc., as components of arguments. Why? Echoing Mates (p. 5), characteristic of declarative sentences is that they are true or false and validity is necessary truth-preservation in virtue of form. So, it is only these types of sentences that matter.

Mates favors allowing arguments to have infinitely many premises, although he acknowledges that doing so extends ordinary usages of *argument* (1972, p. 5). Briefly, he illustrates his rationale as follows. We may ask whether the sentence, *every positive integer is less than the number of stars* follows logically from the infinitely many sentences: 1 is less than the number of stars, 2 is less than the number of starts, 3 is less than the number of stars, etc. (p. 5). Presumably, according to Mates, this is to ask whether the corresponding argument is valid. This seems to presuppose (i).

(i) If σ is a logical consequence of Γ, then there exists a valid argument with Γ as its set of premises and σ as its conclusion.

Accordingly, a reason for considering arguments with infinitely many premises is, in effect, that for logical consequence to suffice for validity, there must be arguments with infinitely many premises, since infinite sets of statements have logical consequences (1972, p. 5).[6]

(b) An argument is a list of *statements*, one of which is designated as the conclusion and the rest of which are designated as the premises. (Skyrms 2000, p. 13)

---

[6] Of course, the compactness of a logic such as first-order classical logic doesn't rule out arguments with infinitely many premises. Rather, it's import is that if such an argument is valid, the conclusion logically follows from a finite number of the premises.

I take a statement here to be a meaningful declarative sentence, which is truth apt. A list of statements becomes an argument when one is designated as the conclusion and the rest are designated as the premises.

To illustrate, consider the following list of statements R → W, R, W, which abbreviate *if it is raining, then the streets are wet, it is raining,* and *the streets are wet,* respectively. Now consider the following three arguments, each composed just of statements from this list.

$$
\text{R} \rightarrow \text{W, R; therefore, R}
\qquad
\begin{array}{l}
\text{W} \\
\text{R} \\
\therefore \text{R} \rightarrow \text{W}
\end{array}
\qquad
\begin{array}{|l}
\text{W} \\
\text{R} \rightarrow \text{W} \\
\text{R}
\end{array}
$$

Note the conclusion indicators: *therefore,* the :therefore: symbol, and the Fitch bar, respectively. They serialize the list R → W, R, W in different ways by flagging one as the conclusion, signaling that the others are premises. We've been using the horizontal bar to (graphically) flag conclusions and thereby mark off the collection of premises. No stand-alone proposition qualifies as a conclusion. Rather, a proposition is a conclusion only in relation to a set of propositions designated as premises. The converse is also true. That is, a set of premises is such only in relation to another proposition designated as a corresponding conclusion.

> (c) An argument (in standard form) is defined as a sequence of statements, called assumptions, followed by the word *so* and a statement called the conclusion. (Packard and Faulconer 1980, p. 1)

Two observations. First, what (c) characterizes are arguments in standard from: a sequence of statements according to which assumptions (i.e., premises) are listed first and then "so" and that ends with a statement that serves as the conclusion. However, the conclusion indicator doesn't need to be "so." Accordingly, the above three arguments are all in standard from. Second, the assumptions don't necessarily represent reasons given for believing the conclusion.

> (d) An argument is an ensemble of sentences, of which one is designated as the conclusion by some such illative as *therefore, accordingly, so, thus,* and the rest are *premises,* alternatively a complex sentence in which the premisses are designated by some such illative subordinator as *as, since,*

because, and the main clause is the conclusion. (*Illation* is the Latinate word for inference, and the words used to indicate inferential structure or direction are therefore called *illatives*. As you will have noticed from this and the previous sentences, the same vocabulary has non-illative uses as well. (Jennings and Friedrich 2006, p. 8)

The use of an illative in presenting an argument does not signify that something is being concluded from the given premises, because arguments in formal logic are conceived independently of any use of them to argue (e.g., Bessie and Glennan 2000, pp. 2–3). Corcoran (1993, p. xx) emphasizes that an argument in this sense doesn't per se purport to show anything, and so it's misleading to say that the conclusion is based on the argument's premise set or that the premises are given for the conclusion. Corcoran remarks that his subsequent use of "∴" to present arguments is best not read as *therefore* but simply as *conclusion*.

(e) To facilitate discussion of reasoning, it will be useful to introduce a *standard form* in which any ordinary piece of reasoning can be represented. For this purpose, we introduce the notion of an argument. . . . Our usage of the term "argument" is a technical one abstracted from one of the ordinary meanings of the term. In our usage, an argument is a *sequence of propositions*. We call the last proposition in the argument the conclusion: intuitively, we think of it as the claim that we are trying to establish as true through our process of reasoning. The other propositions are *premises*: intuitively, we think of them as the basis on which we try to establish the conclusion. There may be any finite number of premises (even zero). (Smith 2012, p. 11)

In his prior discussion of what logic is (2012, pp. 3–4), Smith claims that knowing basic logic is essential to being able to reason well. One attempt to support this claim runs as follows. First, Smith agrees with the nineteenth-century logician Charles Peirce, a major player in the development of modern logic, about what makes reasoning good.

The object of reasoning is to find out, from the consideration of what we already know, something else which we do not know. Consequently, reasoning is good if it be such as to give a true conclusion from true premises, and not otherwise. (Peirce 1877, p. 7)

This is a sense of reasoning according to which good reasoning cannot lead from a true starting point to a false conclusion. Reasoning from true premises of a valid argument to its conclusion is good in the sense that it is necessarily truth-preserving. Accordingly, logic is usefully applied to reasoning because we want to avoid reasoning in ways that lead us from true starting points to false conclusions (Smith 2012, p. 4).[7]

Notice that Smith requires that the premises of an argument be finite in number. Does the applicability of logic to reasoning motivate ruling out infinitely many premises? It does only if for every piece of such reasoning there are finitely many starting points. This is suggested by Lambert and Van Fraassen (1972, p. 7). They stipulate that the number of statements composing an argument be finite since we are interested in appraising validity only insofar as the conclusion can be correctly inferred from the premises. This supposes that the premises of an inference must be finite in number and that an inferer must be capable of entertaining each premise simultaneously. As our minds are finite and bounded, our inferences must have finitely many starting points.

To see the motivation for allowing arguments with no premises, consider (ii).

(ii) If Γ is the set of premises and σ is the conclusion of a valid argument, and $\Gamma = \emptyset$, then σ is a logical truth.

The symbol "$\emptyset$" designates the empty set. Lambert and van Fraassen acknowledge in their textbook that most arguments are representations of patterns of reasoning used to prove the conclusion from the given premises (1972, p. 7). They then explicitly extend this notion of argument to include those with a conclusion but no given premises in order to reflect the truth of (ii) in accommodating their (standard) use of validity to define logical truth (p. 27). A sentence is logically true iff it is a logical consequence of the empty set of premises. So, given (i), an argument with the empty set of premises is valid iff its conclusion is logically true.

---

[7] It is widely espoused in texts, handbooks, and the scholarly literature that logic is the study of correct reasoning (e.g., Barker 2003, pp. 4–9; Epstein 2001, p. 2; Lambert and van Fraassen 1972, pp. 1–2; Priest 1999, p. 184; Shapiro 2002, p. 227; 2005, p. 651), or of "what makes good reasoning good" (Restall 2006, p. 9).

Jeffrey (1991, p. 14) uses (iii) to account for the use of classical validity as a consistency detector. A set Γof statements is inconsistent iff p & ~p is a logical consequence of Γ. This underwrites (iii) given (i).

(iii) If Γ is the set of premises and σ is the conclusion of a valid argument, and σ is of the form p and not-p, then Γ is inconsistent.

In short, there are two jobs for arguments considered merely as sequences of propositions. First, they are tools for representing reasoning, according to which the content of reasoning is a sequence of propositions, and the direction of the reasoning is from premises to conclusion. Such arguments are "bits of reasoning in language" (Barker 2003, p. 5; Bonevac 1999). However, not every argument, i.e., not every sequence of propositions, represents a piece of reasoning. This is motivated by the need to connect the concept of validity with other logical concepts such as logical consequence and truth, and consistency as reflected by (i)–(iii).

2.3.3.1. Summary

Whether or not something qualifies as an argument in formal logic is a separate matter from its potential use in arguing for its conclusion. Arguments in formal logic are arguments in the abstract. They are not dialectical arguments, since their existence doesn't turn on the premises having been used to advance reasons for believing the conclusion. What is the rationale for a notion of argument that makes it abstract in conducting the business of formal logic?

The rationale is threefold, concerning nature of validity, the reasoning that such arguments express, and the normative import of validity. First, the formal validity of an argument, i.e., that truth is necessarily preserved from premises to conclusion in virtue of form, is independent of whether the argument is dialectical. Second, the reasoning expressed by a valid argument, i.e., what inference from premises to conclusion is expressed, is independent of whether the argument is dialectical. This raises the question, engaged in Chapter 5, of how the reasoning expressed by an argument used to advance reasons for the believing the conclusion differs from the reasoning expressed by a valid, abstract argument. Third, the normative import of validity for reasoning, i.e., how the validity of an argument determines that the reasoning expressed is good, is independent of whether the argument is dialectical. I now briefly elaborate on the three rationales, starting with the first.

Given that arguments are considered in formal logic only in light of the fact that they are the bearers of validity, the first rationale motivates a notion of argument that is unconstrained by the ways that arguments are ordinarily used. Accordingly, the $argue_1$-$argument_8$ link isn't a determinant of what counts as an argument in formal logic. In practice, this motivates allowing them to have *any* number of premises.[8]

The second rationale is connected with the idea that the reasoning expressed by an argument is identified simply as the inference from its premises to its conclusion. Arguments aren't inferences, and the inferences they express consist of starting points expressed by the given premises, and an end point expressed by the conclusion. Accordingly, how the argument is being used is not determinative of the reasoning it expresses. Furthermore, the steps in reasoning one may take from initial starting points to conclusion aren't relevant to what reasoning the argument expresses.

The third rationale is motivated by the following. The validity of an argument determines that the reasoning the argument expresses is necessarily truth-preserving, because the argument necessarily preserves truth in virtue of its form. That reasoning is necessarily truth-preserving makes it good in the sense that it's reasoning that cannot lead from a true starting point to a false conclusion. Given the first rationale, whether the argument is dialectical is irrelevant to whether the reasoning expressed is necessarily truth-preserving.

Before leaving this section, I briefly consider the difference between a deduction and an abstract argument. A deduction is a stepwise derivation of a statement, sentence, or proposition from an initial set of given statements, sentences, or propositions. Deductions exhibit logical consequence in the sense that each step in the deduction is a consequence of a set of prior steps. However, arguments needn't so exhibit logical consequence. Arguments that don't are invalid. By appealing to the notion of the notion of logical consequence, we distinguish between deductions and arguments.

To illustrate another basis for distinguishing abstract arguments from deductions, consider the following valid argument and is form.

---

[8] In substructural logics, the order of premises may matter to the validity of the argument (e.g., see Restall 2000); in multiple-conclusion logic, an argument may have more than one conclusion (e.g., see Restall 2005).

<u>Kelly is happy and Paige is hungry</u>	<u>P and Q</u>
If it is not that case that Kelly is happy, then Beth is angry	If Not-P, then R

A deduction provides information regarding how to get to, i.e., derive, the conclusion from the premise(s) of a valid argument. An abstract argument provides no such information. Consider the following sketch of a deduction from the argument's premise to its conclusion.

(1) P and Q, given
(2) P, from (1)
(3) P or R, from (2)
(4) If not-P, then R, from (3).

Often, each step in a deduction identifies a principle that justifies that step. Obviously, unlike (1) and (4), the sentences at steps (2) and (3) are not components of the argument.

2.4. Reason-Giving Uses of Arguments

I now characterize the notion of a reason-giving use of argument that is operative in the remainder of the book. Recall that a dialectical argument is an abstract argument whose premises are or have been advanced by someone as reasons for believing the conclusion. Furthermore, if a person S's dialectical argument deploys an argument$_8$, then S intends the premises to be reasons for believing the conclusion and claims that this is so. What I call a reason-giving use of argument is a dialectical argument according to which the user intends the premises to be reasons for believing the conclusion. When you so use an argument and thereby argue$_1$, you intend the premises to be reasons for believing the conclusion and claim that they are such reasons. Assuming that the operative argumentative intention is rational, you believe what you claim.

Abstract arguments can be used in a variety of ways (Biro and Siegel 2006a; Blair 2004). To illustrate, consider the following.

A: Due to its form, it is not possible for an argument that is valid to have true premises and a false conclusion.
B: Can you give me an example of a valid argument?

A: Kelly is happy, so Kelly is happy.

B: That argument is valid, because it is not possible for one and the same proposition to be simultaneously true and false.

A: That's correct. For any proposition p, p is a logical consequence of p.

By uttering, "Kelly is happy, so Kelly is happy" person A gives an argument, an explicitly circular one. Since A and B are not quarreling and A doesn't advance the premise as a reason for believing the conclusion, the argument A gives isn't an argument in any of the dictionary definitions previously discussed. Furthermore, since A doesn't offer the premise as a reason that supports the conclusion or as a reason for believing the conclusion, A isn't claiming that their premise has either status. This rules out that A gives an argument as understood in most of the informal-logic textbook characterizations of argument previously sampled, as well as the previously discussed one in argumentation theory. In short, A gives an abstract argument, but not a dialectical argument and so does not use the argument in a reason-giving way.

A: The room is cold. I wonder why since I put the heat on low in the house.

B: The room's cold because it got very cold last night, and all the rooms' windows were left open.

It seems wrong to say that B is trying to support or justify that the room is cold since this is not at issue. Does B give an argument, put in standard form as follows?

It got very cold last night

All the windows in the room where left open

The room is cold

Yes: B gives an abstract argument. Plausibly, B is not arguing for believing that the room is cold given that this is not at issue. Rather, B intends the argument's premises to be reasons that explain why the conclusion is true and B claims that they are such reasons. If it is plausible to construe premises that are reasons that explain why the conclusion is true as (explanatory) reasons for believing that it is true, then it is plausible to think that B's dialectical argument is an argument used in a reason-giving way and that B is engaged in arguing$_1$.

A: Where's Beth? I thought that she was in the garage, but she's not there.
B: She told me that she was going to listen to the stereo. The stereo is in the living room. So, probably, Beth is in the living room.

B argues₁ by advancing (inconclusive) reasons for believing that Beth is in the living room. Accordingly, B gives the following abstract argument, put in standard form.

> Beth told me that she was going to listen to the stereo
> <u>The stereo is in living room</u>
> Beth is in the living room

B's dialectical argument seems to be a reason-giving use of it as B intends the premises to be (inconclusive) reasons for believing the conclusion. B's use of "So" suggests that B claims that the premises are such reasons.

In sum, what I am calling reason-giving uses of arguments are dialectical arguments since their premises are put forward by arguers as reasons for believing the conclusion. However, the argumentative intention is an essential feature of reason-giving uses of arguments, as understood here. One uses an argument in a reason-giving way only if one intends that one's premises are reasons for believing the conclusion. Furthermore, reason-giving uses of arguments are associated with argument claims. Specifically, if you use an argument in a reason-giving way, then you claim that the premises are reasons for believing the conclusion in the sense that you intend. I call this argument claim an inference claim. The content of inference claims associated with reason-giving uses of arguments is a primary topic of Chapter 3.

Using an argument in reason-giving way needn't involve believing that the conclusion is true. For example, the premises may be offered as reasons for believing that the conclusion is plausible, nontrivial, or possible in principle or as reasons to worry or fear that the conclusion is true. The drift of this chapter's discussion of dialectical arguments has focused on arguments whose premises are advanced as reasons for believing that the conclusion is true. I'll simply call such uses of arguments reason-giving uses of arguments with the understanding that my focus here is reason-giving centered on such reason-to-believe arguments.

In short, two essential features of a reason-giving use of an argument are the arguer's intention that the premises advanced are reasons for believing the conclusion, and the arguer's inference claim that the premises are such reasons. If the arguer's argumentative intention is rational, then the arguer's inference claim expresses the arguer's belief that the premises are reasons for believing the conclusion in the intended sense.

If you use an argument with the intention that its premises serve as reasons for believing the conclusion and you don't believe that they are such reasons, then your argumentative intention is irrational as it doesn't cohere with how you understand the status of the premises as reasons for believing the conclusion. It is irrational for one to act with the intention of doing X when one doesn't believe by so acting one is X-ing. It is irrational for a person S to use an argument with the intention of giving the premises as reasons for believing the conclusion when S doesn't believe that in giving the premises for the conclusion S is giving reasons for believing it. So, if you rationally intend the premises you advance to serve as reasons for believing the conclusion, then you believe, perhaps incorrectly, that they are such reasons. That is, one's argumentative intention is rational only if it is associated with one's inference-claim belief.

Let's say that an argumentative intention with the associated inference-claim belief satisfies the inference-claim belief requirement for being rational. An argumentative intention that satisfies the inference-claim belief requirement may not be rational for other reasons. Perhaps some arguments are so bad that it isn't rational to intend their premises to be reasons for believing their conclusions. Nevertheless, argumentative intentions that are rational insofar as they satisfy the inference-claim belief requirement ground a sincerity condition for arguing$_1$, i.e., for giving reasons for or against something.

When you argue$_1$, you use an argument in a reason-giving way. When you argue$_1$ sincerely, you believe that what you advance are reasons for believing it or reasons against believing it. If you use an argument in a reason-giving way and your argumentative intention satisfies the inference-claim belief requirement, then you believe that the premises are reasons for believing the conclusion in the sense you intend. So, when your arguing$_1$ is sincere, the argumentative intention associated with your reason-giving use of argument satisfies the inference-claim belief requirement for being rational. Sincere arguing$_1$ can't be associated with argumentative intentions that fail to be rational by virtue of not satisfying the inference-claim belief requirement.

My motivation for focusing on such reason-giving uses of arguments is twofold. First, I am interested in understanding genuine and not pseudo-reason-giving uses of arguments. A *genuine* reason-giving use of an argument minimally requires that the operative intention is the argumentative intention. If a person S uses an argument to make a case for the conclusion but doesn't intend the premises to be reasons for believing the conclusion, then S really isn't using the argument to give reasons for believing it. According to my intuitions, no argumentative intention, no reason-giving use of argument. To avoid misunderstanding, this is compatible with my understanding of a dialectical argument as the use of the argument to give reasons for believing the conclusion.

To elaborate, by means of one's dialectical argument one may pretend to give reasons for believing one's conclusion without intending one's premises to be such reasons. For example, one may (deceitfully) offer one's premises as reasons for believing one's conclusion even though one thinks that they are not such reasons. According to my intuitions, such dialectical arguments are not genuine reason-giving uses of arguments because of the absence of the argumentative intention.

My second motivation for focusing on reason-giving uses of arguments as conceived here is that we typically take a person S's reason-giving use of an argument to communicate that S believes that the premises one advances are reasons for believing the conclusion. For example, if I take you to be using an argument in a reason-giving way in order to justify believing the conclusion, rationally persuade me of its truth, or explain why you maintain the conclusion, I take it that you believe that your premises are reasons—in some sense—for believing the conclusion. If I learn that you do not have such a belief, then I would ordinarily think that in using your argument you are not thereby engaged in justification, rational persuasion, or rational explanation of your conclusion belief. This is because I would ordinarily think that your intentions in so arguing do not include what I am calling the argumentative intention. I am interested in reason-giving uses of arguments capable of justification, rational persuasion, and rational explanation. Accordingly, I focus on reason-giving uses of arguments whose associated argumentative intensions satisfy the inference-claim belief requirement for being rational. What this belief exactly involves depends on the operative sense of *reason for belief*.

Arguments are used in reason-giving ways to realize a variety of aims, such as (i) to communicate one's reasons for which one accepts the conclusion (Thomson 1967); (ii) to communicate hypothetical reasoning (Meiland 1989); and (iii) to persuade an addressee of the truth of the conclusion (Pinto 2001c). These different aims are reflected in the different types of reasons for believing the conclusion that the premises may be used to represent. For example, (i) concurs with the use of premises of an argument to represent reasons which ground or sustain the arguers' conclusion belief. With (ii), the premises are used to represent hypothetical reasons for believing the conclusion. In regard to (iii), the premises may be used to represent reasons for the addressees to believe the conclusion. This suggests that different types of reason-giving uses of arguments are determined by the types of reasons for believing the conclusion that the premises are intended to express.

In sum, a reason-giving use of an argument is a dialectical argument. That is, it is a use of an argument according to which the premises are advanced as reasons for believing the conclusion. When you use an argument in what I am calling a reason-giving way, you intend the premises to be reasons for believing the conclusion and you claim that the premises are such reasons. I focus on those reason-giving uses of arguments that are associated with argumentative intentions that are rational insofar as they satisfy the inference-claim belief requirement. So, a dialectical argument whose associated argumentative intention fails to satisfy the inference-claim belief requirement isn't a reason-giving use of an argument in the sense that is of concern here. Hereafter, unless explicitly indicted otherwise when I speak of reason-giving uses of arguments, I speak of reason-giving uses of arguments as just described.

It is worth emphasizing that the conception of reason-giving uses of arguments advanced here accommodates well-known theories of argumentation. For example, on an epistemic approach to argumentation, a good argument makes believing the conclusion rational by providing good reasons for believing it, which are reasons that justify believing it (e.g., see Siegel and Biro 1997, p. 278; Feldman 1994, p. 176). On a pragma-dialectic approach, a good argument makes believing the conclusion rational by providing good reasons for believing it, but here such reasons are claims that are acceptable to all interlocuters and are acceptable to all as reasons that justify their believing the conclusion (e.g., van Eemeren and Grootendorst 2004, pp. 3, 144). According to Johnson's pragmatic approach to argumentation (2000, p. 168), an argument whose aim is to persuade an interlocuter of the truth of its conclusion advances premises as good reasons for believing it true. Good reasons for believing the conclusion provide rational support for the interlocuter's believing that the conclusion is true in light of the given reasons (2000, p. 169).

According to these rough glosses, an argument used to advance its premises as reasons for believing the conclusion is good only if the premises qualify as good reasons for believing the conclusion. Each theory offers a story about what makes premises good reasons for believing the conclusion, which I leave undeveloped here. I understand *an argument used to advance its premises as good reasons for believing the conclusion* as an argument used in a reason-giving way.

The conception of a reason-giving use of an argument introduced here is compatible with these different understandings of what counts as *good* reasons for believing the conclusion. For example, suppose that we follow the epistemic approach and think that a person S's reason-giving use of an argument doesn't rationalize S's believing the conclusion unless the premises justify S's believing the conclusion. This is compatible with thinking that because S genuinely uses the argument in a reason-giving way, S's argumentative intention that the premises be (good) reasons for believing that the conclusion satisfies the inference-claim belief requirement for being rational, and thereby S believes that the premises are such reasons. This illustrates the theoretical innocence of the conception of reason-giving uses of arguments advanced here. It isn't determinative of a particular story about what makes argumentation good. I take this to be a plus.

2.4.1. Summary

There are three central, interrelated dimensions to the conception of reason-giving uses of arguments introduced in this section. First, a reason-giving use of an argument is essentially intentional. If you use an argument in a reason-giving way, then you intend the premises you advance to be reasons for believing the conclusion. I label this intention the argumentative intention. Second, when you use an argument in a reason-giving way, you claim that the premises are reasons for believing the conclusion. I call this claim an *inference claim*. Third, your argumentative intention satisfies the inference-claim belief requirement for being rational. So, you believe, perhaps wrongly, that your associated argument claim is true.

Here's one way these dimensions are interrelated. Essential to a person S's reason-giving use of argument is the corresponding argumentative intention. Given that S's argumentative intention satisfies the inference-claim belief requirement necessary to be rational, S's associated argument claim is an expression of S's belief to the effect that the premises are reasons for believing the conclusion. That is, the doxastic import of S's argumentative intention makes S's argument claim an expression of S's belief that the premises are such reasons.

2.5. Conclusion

Concepts, terminology, and themes introduced in Chapter 2 are utilized throughout the remaining chapters. I now briefly summarize the highlights from each section that inform the characterization of reason-giving uses of arguments introduced in section 2.4.

The $argue_1$-$argument_8$ link is highlighted in section 2.2. Specifically, there is $arguing_1$ if and only if there is a corresponding $argument_8$. In other words, you give reasons for or against something if and only if you give a coherent series of reasons, statements, or facts *intended* to support or establish a point of view. This supports the idea that when you $argue_1$, an $argument_8$ is a product of your $arguing_1$. According to this idea, your $arguing_1$ is intentional: you intend what you state to be reasons for a standpoint.

In section 2.3.1, I said that the *informal-logic notion of an argument* is the notion of an argument according to which the premises *are being offered or have been offered* to support the truth or rational acceptability of the conclusion. An argument so conceived is a dialectical argument, i.e., one whose premises are or have been advanced as reasons for the conclusion. Dialectical arguments are associated with inference claims which roughly say, in effect, that the premises are such reasons.

In section 2.3.2, *the argumentation theory* of $argument_7$ and $arguing_6$ stipulates a sincerity condition for arguing in order to persuade an interlocuter of something by giving an argument for it. I applied a sincerity condition to $arguing_1$. From section 2.3.1, when one $argues_1$ for a standpoint, one intends what one advances to be reasons for believing the standpoint. Given that one's argumentative intention is rational, one believes that what one advances are reasons for believing the conclusion. In short, the doxastic import of a rational argumentative intention includes the belief that what one advances are such reasons. To emphasize, what is in play is not the full-blown rationality of an argumentative intention, but only that it satisfies the inference-claim belief requirement.

The *formal-logic notion of argument*, discussed in section 2.3.3, is the notion of an abstract argument, understood here as a premise-conclusion complex of propositions taken to be an ordered pair of a set propositions that counts as the set of premises and a conclusion proposition. The existence of arguments so conceived does not turn on the premises serving as reasons in support of the truth of the conclusion. Accordingly, such arguments, unlike dialectical arguments, are stand-alone. I adopt the formal-logic notion of argument.

Finally, in section 2.4 I characterized reason-giving uses of arguments. A reason-giving use of an argument, understood in the formal logic sense, is a *dialectical argument* whose premises the arguer intends to be reasons for believing the conclusion and claims that the premises are such reasons. Drawing from section 2.2, if you use an argument in a reason-giving way, then you intend the premises to be reasons for believing the conclusion and, drawing from section 2.3.1, you claim that the premises are such reasons. Drawing on sections 2.3.2 and 2.4, given that your argumentative intention satisfies the inference-claim belief requirement necessary for being rational, you believe your argument claim. I call this argument claim an inference claim (borrowing from Hitchcock 2007a).

My consideration of reason-giving uses of arguments is doubly focused. First, it concerns only reason-giving uses of arguments according to which the premises are advanced as reasons for believing that the conclusion is true. Of course, uses of arguments that are truth-aiming in this way are typical. Second, my story about reason-giving uses of arguments assumes that the operative argumentative intentions are minimally rational in that they satisfy the inference-claim belief requirement.

In Chapter 3, I develop the notion of reason-giving use of an argument by giving an account of the content of inference claims. For simplicity of exposition, I'll focus on simple (as opposed to extended) arguments and so take an argument to be abstract, e.g., an ordered pair of a set of propositions (premises) and a conclusion-proposition. I'll argue that when you state an argument that you genuinely use in a reason-giving way, you assert your inference claim as opposed to merely implying or implicating it.

3

Inference Claims

3.1. Preamble

From Chapter 2, if you argue₁, i.e., if you give reasons for or against some-thing, then you use an argument in a reason-giving way and thereby claim that the premises are reasons for believing the conclusion. I call this claim an inference claim, borrowing from Hitchcock (2007a, p. 105; 2011, pp. 191–92). I take an inference claim to say, in effect, that the premises of the as-sociated argument are collectively reasons for believing the conclusion, i.e., for believing that it is true. Recall also from Chapter 2 that when you use an argument in a reason-giving way, you intend the premises to be reasons for believing the conclusion.

This argumentative intention, as I called it in Chapter 2, has cognitive import. Specifically, one is explicitly aware of one's use of the premises as reasons for believing the conclusion. Additionally, one believes the associ-ated inference claim. So if you use an argument to give reasons for believing the conclusion, you are aware that you are giving reasons for believing the conclusion and you explicitly believe the associated inference claim.

In Chapter 3, my aim is to deepen understanding of how an inference claim matters to a reason-giving use of argument. Toward this end, I defend two theses.

(I) A reason-giving use of argument isn't successful unless the corre-sponding inference claim is true.

(II) An inference claim is conveyed by one's statement of an argument by means of assertion as opposed to being merely implied or implicated.

By (I), a reason-giving use of an argument is successful only if the corre-sponding inference claim is true. To see the import of thesis (II), recall from Chapter 2 that if you use an argument in a reason-giving way, then you state the argument. When you state the argument, you convey the associated

Arguments and Reason-Giving. Matthew W. McKeon, Oxford University Press. © Oxford University Press 2024.
DOI: 10.1093/oso/9780197751633.003.0003

inference claim. Thesis (II) says that you assert the inference claim when stating the argument.

Looking ahead, Chapter 4 advances an account of the nature of the reasoning expressed by arguments used in a reason-giving way. Such reasoning is essentially reflective. Being reflective makes this type of reasoning representational in the sense that its starting points are represented by the reasoner as reasons for believing its conclusion. This isn't surprising given that such reasoning essentially involves believing the corresponding inference claim.

3.2. Argument Claims and Uses of Arguments

Recall that I take arguments to be abstract in that they are premise-conclusion complexes of propositions. Also, recall that any use of an argument so construed requires that it be stated, i.e., that it be expressed in writing, thought, or speech. To state an argument is to express it. If one asserts something or merely gives voice to it, then one expresses and so states it. To avoid misunderstanding, merely expressing an argument doesn't suggest that one endorses it. Also, I noted in Chapter 2 that an argument should be distinguished from any one statement of it. In this section, I introduce the notion of an *argument claim* and say something about the connection between argument claims and uses of the corresponding arguments. This will inform my discussion in the next section of inference claims, which are a type of argument claim.

Consider the following sentence.

If the street is wet, then it rained, the street is wet; therefore, it rained.

Suppose that someone utters this sentence in order to state an argument. Let's call the argument (A). We put (A) into standard form as follows.

If the street is wet, then it rained
The street is wet
It rained

All sorts of claims can be made about (A).

(i) An essential feature of (A) is that it has two premises.

(ii) The form of (A) is expressed by the following: If P, then Q, P $\therefore$ Q.

(iii) A's conclusion is a logical consequence of (A)'s two premises.

(iv) It is more probable than not that (A)'s conclusion is true, given that (A)'s premises are true.

(v) If we change (A) just by adding a premise, the resulting argument is valid.

Since (i)–(v) are about an argument, specifically argument (A), I call them argument claims (borrowing from Sainsbury 2001, p. 24). They are all true. The number of premises of an argument is an essential feature of it. No argument with just one premise or more than two is identical with (A). Argument claim (ii) is true as (A) instantiates a modus ponens argument form: any argument with a conditional and the statement of its antecedent as the premises and a statement of its consequent as the conclusion is a valid argument. Since this argument form is valid, (iii) is true. So (iv) is also true. Since it is a fact that a valid argument can't be turned into an invalid argument simply by adding premises, (v) is true.

Note that the truth of (i)–(v) turns exclusively on facts about argument (A) independently of how (A) might be used. Therefore, we don't need to know how (A) is being used in order to justify (i)–(v). However, the truth of other argument claims involving (A) does turn on how (A) is being used. For example, consider the following two claims.

(vi) (A) is a deductive argument.

(vii) (A) is an inductive argument.

Whether these argument claims are true depends on what the author of argument (A) claims, if anything, about how (A)'s conclusion follows from the premises. Specifically, a *deductive argument* is one that is stated with the possibly mistaken argument claim that the conclusion strictly follows from the premises. If this argument claim is true, then the argument used is valid. An *inductive argument* is advanced with the possibly mistaken argument claim that the conclusion is more likely than not given the truth of the premises even though the conclusion does not strictly follow from them. If this argument claim is true, then the argument is ampliative.

For example, consider the following.

Beth is a Republican, so probably didn't vote for the Democrat.

The implicit argument claim signaled by the conclusion modifier *probably* is that the truth of the premise makes the conclusion more likely than not even though the conclusion does not strictly follow from it. If the conclusion strictly follows, then something stronger than *probably* is warranted. This argument claim militates against filling out the enthymeme by adding *No Republican voted for the Democrat*. To put the argument into standard form in this way makes the argument claim signaled by the conclusion modifier, *probably*, misleading.

If argument (A) is given and neither claim is made, then both (vi) and (vii) are undetermined and so (A) is neither deductive nor inductive. Accordingly, whether an argument is deductive or inductive turns on the author's associated argument claim. This suggests that an argument is neither intrinsically deductive nor intrinsically inductive.

To illustrate, consider the following basic argument pattern of an appeal to popular opinion.

It is widely held among population P that p
∴ p is true

Suppose that for a given instantiation of P and p, Beth and Kelly both infer the conclusion from the premise. Beth claims that the conclusion strictly follows the premise. However, Kelly claims that the conclusion is more likely than not given the truth of the premises even though the conclusion does not strictly follow from them. Beth's claim seems mistaken since the argument doesn't seem valid. However, where the members of P are in a position to know about p, or when the best explanation of the prevalence of the belief that p among P is that p is true, Kelly's claim may well be true. In short, whether one's argument is deductive or inductive turns on whether one claims that the conclusion strictly follows from the premises or instead claims that the conclusion is more likely than not given the truth of the premises even though the conclusion does not strictly follow from them.

In sum, there are argument claims (e.g., (i)–(v)) whose truth or falsity turns on facts about the corresponding arguments that are independent of what claims their authors make about them. The truth or falsity of other argument claims (e.g., (vi) and (vii)) turns on what the authors of the associated arguments claim about their arguments. Typically, the rationale for an author's claim about their argument is connected with how they intend to use the argument.

Again, if you use an argument in a reason-giving way, then your argument is dialectical and so you claim that the premises are reasons for believing the conclusion. Suppose Kelly uses argument (A), repeated just below, to provide conclusive reasons for believing the conclusion.

If the street is wet, then it rained
The street is wet
It rained

Kelly's aim in using (A), to provide conclusive reasons for believing the conclusion, provides a rationale for why Kelly makes the argument claim to the effect that the premises are conclusive reasons for believing the conclusion.

Suppose Kelly wrote (A) on the chalkboard in order to provide an example of a valid argument to her class. Then her aim in presenting the argument does not provide a rationale for her making the argument claim that the premises are conclusive reasons for believing the conclusion. She may believe this, but her use of the argument does not commit her to believing it as in this scenario (A) is not a dialectical argument.

How do arguers' argument claims figure in whether their reason-giving uses of arguments are good? Toward developing a response, consider argument claim (viii).

(viii) Argument (A) is a good argument.

Obviously, whether (viii) is true turns on what counts as a *good argument*. What makes an argument *good*? The distinction made in Chapter 2 between arguments and uses of them motivates a teleological notion of *good*. That is, whether or not an argument is good is relative to how it's being used. On this view, "Argument (A) is good" is short for "(A) is good for X-ing." For example, (A) may be good for explaining one's justification for believing that it rained, or it may be good for persuading someone that it rained. It doesn't seem good for explaining why it rained or for illustrating an invalid argument.

Since there are many uses for arguments, what make an argument *good* varies from one use of it to another. We can speak of an argument being suitable for some uses and not suitable for others. One might think that an argument is intrinsically bad if it is not suitable for any use of it. However, this is impossible, because it can be appropriately used as an example of an argument that is not well suited for some use of it.

If an argument is not suitable for a given use of it, then the aim of so using the argument is not realizable, and so it isn't a good use of the argument. To illustrate, let's look at some quick examples. Obviously, argument (A) is ill suited for illustrating an invalid argument because argument claim (iii) (mentioned above) is true and so it is true that the conclusion strictly follows from the premises. Accordingly, this is not a good use of (A). It is appropriate to use (A) to explain why one believes it rained only if it is true that *the premises taken together are reasons for which one believes the conclusion.* Otherwise, this is a bad use of the argument since the aim of explaining why one believes it rained is not fulfilled.

It is suitable to use (A) to persuade an interlocuter that the streets are wet only if the interlocuter *should believe the premises.* (A) is ill suited to serve as a proof that it rained, unless *both premises are true.* These are good uses of (A) only if the interlocuter should believe the premises and both premises are true, respectively. If neither condition obtains, then such uses of (A) are not good as the expressed aims are not realizable.

In short, it is not arguments themselves that are good. Rather, it is arguments in use that are good. Relative to a given use of an argument, the argument is good just in case it is suitable for that use of it. If the argument is not suitable for a given use of it, then so using the argument will not be successful as the intended aim isn't realizable. Given the teleological notion of *good* that is operative here, to determine whether an argument is good, we need to understand its contents, how it is being used, and what must be true in order for the use of the argument so understood to succeed.

Taking seriously the distinction between arguments and uses of them and granting that there are all sorts of uses for arguments, the following argument is appropriate only relative to some particular use of it.

The earth is the third planet from the sun
The capital of Michigan is Flint or it is not

Since it isn't possible for the conclusion to be false, this argument is valid by the lights of the classical account of validity given in Chapter 2. Of course, the premise is true. However, it can't be successfully used in a reason-giving way, because the associated inference claim is necessarily false in the sense that there is no notion of "reason" according to which the premise is a reason for believing the conclusion. After all, the truth of the premise has no bearing on the truth of the conclusion. This is further developed in Chapter 5.

3.2.1. Summary

A given use of an argument is successful only if the argument used is suitable or appropriate for that use of it. If the argument used is appropriate for a given use of it, then relative to such a use it is a good argument. This reflects the fact that an argument in use isn't good unless the argument is suitable for that use of it. A successful reason-giving use of an argument succeeds in advancing the premises as reasons for believing the conclusion in the sense that one intends. If the premises are such reasons, then the argument is suitable for such a use of it. For example, suppose that you use the above argument (A) to persuade me that it rained. The argument is not suitable for this use of it unless the premises are reasons for me to believe the conclusion. If the argument is so suitable, then you have succeeded in advancing premises that warrant my believing the conclusion. Of course, your use of the argument may succeed in this sense, but not in the sense that I am persuaded by your argument to believe that it rained. Perhaps, unbeknownst to you, I already believed for other reasons that it rained.

3.3. The Connection between Inference Claims and Reason-Giving Uses of Argument

As stated in section 3.1, a central claim of Chapter 3 is (I) A reason-giving use of argument isn't successful unless the corresponding inference claim is true. Drawing on the discussion in section 3.2, the rationale for (I) runs as follows.

1. A reason-giving use of argument is successful only if the argument used is good.
2. If an argument used in a reason-giving way is good, then the associated inference claim is true.
   If a reason-giving use of an argument is successful, then the associated inference claim is true.

The conclusion is (I). By the lights of (I), inference claims are essential to reason-giving uses of arguments, because their truth is required for the success of the corresponding reason-giving uses of arguments.

From the discussion in section 3.2, (i) a reason-giving use of an argument is successful only if the argument used is suitable. The suitability of the argument so used turns on whether the premises are reasons for the believing the conclusion in the intended sense. If they are not, then the argument so used is not suitable. By the lights of a teleological notion of good argumentation, (ii) if the argument is suitable, then it is good (relative to the given reason-giving use of it). Premise 1 follows from claims (i) and (ii).

A rationale for premise 2 is as follows. If an argument used in a reason-giving way is good, then its premises are reasons for believing the conclusion. Since this is what the associated inference claim says, it follows that an argument used in a reason-giving way is good only if the associated inference claim is true. This is premise 2. For example, if you use the previously given argument (A) to advance reasons for me to believe that it rained, then this argument isn't good relative to this use of it unless the associated inference claim is true to the effect that the premises are reasons for me to believe that it rained.

To enhance the plausibility of the argument for (I), clarification is needed of the notion of *reasons for believing* that is operative in inference claims. This will deepen understanding of how inference claims matter to reason-giving uses of argument. In section 3.4, I turn to the matter of how, exactly, inference claims are conveyed by one's statement of an argument.

3.3.1. Inference Claims and Reasons for Believing

In Chapter 2, I sampled several informal-logic textbook characterizations of arguments that associated certain argument claims with arguments. These characterizations highlighted that a collection of claims, propositions, or what not, advanced by a person S doesn't count as an argument unless S makes what we are calling an inference claim that, in effect, singles out some (the premise[s]) as support—in some sense—for the truth of one of them (the conclusion).

It is commonly held in the scholarly literature that an inference claim to this effect is essential to arguments. However, the articulation of the connection between inference claims so construed and arguments varies. For example, the Groarkes say, "Every argument assumes that the premises warrant the conclusion . . . whether they are deductive or not" (2002, p. 51; also see Scriven 1976, p. 84; Grennan 1994, p. 187–88). This suggest that authors of arguments are merely committed to the claim that the premises warrant—in some way—the conclusion. Of course, one may not believe what one is committed to (e.g., one's commitments may be cognitively inaccessible to one).

Alternatively, a connection between inference claims and arguments is sometimes cast in terms of what arguers claim when presenting their arguments. For example, Vorobej states that essential to an argument is the claim that the conclusion follows in some fashion, from the non-empty set of premises (2006, pp. 8–9; also see Hitchcock 2011, p. 191; Bermejo-Luque 2011b, p. 90). Plausibly, if one sincerely claims that one's conclusion follows—in some sense—from the premises of one's argument, then one believes the claim.

As just illustrated, articulating a connection between arguments and inference claims involves characterizing in some way what inference claims say. Recall that some of the textbook characterizations of argument surveyed in Chapter 2 conveyed that the associated inference claim says, in effect, that the conclusion follows—in some way—from the premises (e.g., Copi, Cohen, and McMahon 2014, p. 6; Carney and Scheer 1980, p. 3). Freeman's characterization of arguments offered two different formulations of the associated argument claim: *because the audience accepts the premise(s), they should accept the conclusion*; and *the premises support the conclusion* (1988, p. 20). Also recall that according to Hurley and Watson's characterization of argument, inference claims say that *the premises provide support for the conclusion or are reasons to believe the conclusion* (2018, p. 3).

Any plausible formulation of what inference claims say must reflect that arguments are used in reason-giving ways to realize a variety of aims, such as (i) to communicate one's reasons for which one accepts the conclusion (Thomson 1967); (ii) to communicate hypothetical or, equivalently, suppositional reasoning (Meiland 1989); and (iii) to persuade an addressee of the truth of the conclusion (Pinto 2001c). Accordingly, it is desirable to construe inference claims in a generic way so as to make them relevant across the various types of reason-giving uses of arguments.

To illustrate, suppose that following is uttered in a conversational exchange.

> Suppose that you are right that lying is always wrong. Then the lie you told your father was wrong.

The speaker S argues from the interlocuter's beliefs and so uses an argument to give a reason for their conclusion without necessarily claiming that it constitutes evidence for the truth of the conclusion. The argument may be put into standard form as follows.

> Lying is always wrong.
> The lie you told your father was wrong.

Since S uses the argument, considered in the abstract, in a reason-giving way and S is arguing that the premise is a reason for the interlocuter to believe the conclusion, S claims this; i.e., S claims that the premise is a reason for the interlocuter to believe the conclusion. This is compatible with the speaker's rejecting both the premise and conclusion. For example, it is coherent for the speaker to think that because the interlocuter accepts the premise, the interlocuter should accept the conclusion, but not claim that the premise supports the conclusion in the sense that it is a reason to believe the conclusion.

To see another example of a reason-giving use of an argument according to which the speaker does not claim that either the premise or conclusion is true, consider the following suppositional reasoning.

> Suppose (1) Kelly has two oranges. Then (2) Kelly has some fruit. So, (3) if Kelly has two oranges, then Kelly has some fruit.

The reasoner R believes that (2) follows from (1) because R thinks that (1) is a hypothetical or suppositional reason for believing (2). The inference claim associated with the argument from (1) to (2) is that (1) is a hypothetical reason for believing (2). To believe this inference claim commits one to believing that if (1) were true, then it would be a reason to believe (2). The inference claim may be thought of as serving as a premise from which (3) is concluded.

These illustrations suggest that there are different types of reason-giving uses of arguments distinguished by the different types of reasons the premises are intended to be for believing the conclusion. A plausible account of what inference claims say should accommodate this. Hence, there is motivation for taking inference claims to be claims that, in effect, say that the premises are reasons for believing the conclusion. Understanding inference claims this way reflects a connection between inference claims and different types of reason-giving uses of arguments in virtue of the fact that there are varieties of reasons for belief that underwrite the different types of reason-giving uses of arguments.

I now elaborate by discussing types of reasons for believing something, which distinguish various reason-giving uses of argument. A type of reason-giving use of argument is determined by the type of reasons for believing the conclusion the premises are intended to represent. Drawing heavily on Audi (1993, pp. 235–37), I now outline several varieties of reasons for belief.

Reasons for believing

1. *Reasons to believe* are objective and normative: if p is a reason to believe q, then p is evidence that makes it more likely than not that q is true; i.e., p is evidence qua indicator or sign of the truth of a statement *beyond itself*. So p can't be a reason to believe p.

2. *Reasons a person S has for believing* are subjective and normative. If p is a reason a person S has for believing q, then S believes p or should believe p and p is a reason to believe q. From 1, if p is a reason to believe q, then p is evidence that provides some justification for S's believing q regardless of whether or not S believes p or believes q.

3. *Reasons for a person S to believe* are subjective and non-normative.

4. *Reasons for which a person S believes* are reasons that sustain S's belief.

A paper bag contains five apples. This is a reason to believe that it contains at least three. Is it a reason Kelly has for believing that the bag contains at least three? It is only if Kelly also believes or should believe given the information available to her that the paper bag contains five apples. Suppose Kelly correctly believes that it's Paige's bag of apples and Paige communicates to Kelly her erroneous belief that the bag contains four apples. Given Paige's testimony, that the bag contains four apples is a reason for Kelly to believe that it contains at least three. If Kelly believes this, say because she believes what Paige communicated, then that the bag contains four apples is a reason for which Kelly believes that it contains at least three.

Whether a person S's argument is suitable for S's reason-giving use of it depends on the type of reasons the premises are intended to be for the conclusion. An argument used to advance reasons to believe the conclusion is suitable only if the premises are reasons to believe the conclusion. An argument used to advance reasons a person S has for believing the conclusion is suitable only if S believes or should believe the premises and they are reason to believe the conclusion. An argument used to advance reasons for a person S to believe the conclusion is suitable only if S believes the premises or should believe them given the information available to S, and the conclusion follows from them in some way. An argument used to advance reasons for which a person S believes the conclusion is suitable only if S believes the conclusion because S believes the premises.

Suppose that you use an argument to advance its reasons for the conclusion in order to persuade an interlocuter of the conclusion. Accordingly, you intend the premises to be reasons for believing the conclusion. In order for one to judge the suitability of the argument you use, one needs to understand the type of reasons for believing the conclusion that you intend to advance. For example, are you advancing the premises as reasons the interlocuter has for believing the conclusion or as reasons for the interlocuter to believe the conclusion? If the former, then the argument is not suitable for your reason-giving use of it unless the interlocuter believes or should believe the premises and they are reasons to believe the conclusion. If the latter, then the argument is not suitable unless the interlocuter believes the premises or is at least committed to them.

Suppose that you use an argument to explain why you believe something. Such an explanation is (i) *causal* and (ii) *normative* (e.g., see Wright 2001): (i) you give reasons for which you believe the conclusion; and (ii) you give reasons you think you have to believe the conclusion. In order for this reason-giving use of the argument to be successful, the premises must represent both types of reasons for belief.

Across these four varieties of reasons for belief, reasons for belief may be conclusive or non-conclusive. For example, conclusion and inconclusive reasons to believe something may be described as follows.

p is a conclusive reason to believe q just in case p is true and its truth (perhaps along with operative background conditions) rules out the possibility of q being false.

p is an inconclusive reason to believe q just in case p is true and its truth (perhaps along with operative background conditions) makes the truth of q more likely than not without ruling out it being false.

Also, reasons for believing something may be hypothetical or suppositional. For example, we characterize a hypothetical reason to believe as follows.

p is a hypothetical reason to believe q just in case p is merely possibly true and if it were true, it would be a reason, conclusive or otherwise, to believe q.

I'll say that the epistemic import of a reason for believing something is whether it is conclusive, inconclusive, or hypothetical.

With respect to a person S's reason-giving use of an argument, what the associated inference claim specifically says turns on the type of reasons and their epistemic import S intends the premises to be for the conclusion. Let's say that for a given reason-giving use of an argument the *proto-inference claim* says is, in effect, that the premises are reasons for believing the conclusion. A proto-inference claim is indeterminate with respect to both the type of reasons for believing the conclusion that the premises are and their epistemic import. That is, it does not specify the operative type of reason for belief or the epistemic import of the reasons advanced. Accordingly, a proto-inference claim can be instantiated across two dimensions: the type of reasons for believing the conclusion that premises are, and their epistemic import.

How the proto-inference claim is instantiated with respect to a person S's reason-giving use of an argument bears on the particular inference claim S makes in so using the argument. The specific inference claim S makes is a function of what S intends, if anything, regarding the type of reasons the premises are intended to be, as well as their epistemic import.[1] To illustrate, suppose the following three scenarios display reason-giving uses of argument.

(I)   Kelly: Is Beth home?
      Paige: Certainly. Her car is in the driveway.
(II) Kelly: Where's Beth?
      Paige: She might be listening to music on the stereo. If so, then she may be in the living room.

---

[1] Of course, there are occasions when you give an argument you are communicating more than this, for example, that you're representing all the relevant accessible evidence. In particular, you may be communicating that you are not holding back undercutting evidence and that you've not avoided finding undercutting evidence. Such information may be pragmatic implicatures of the assertion of an inference claim that are derived, in part, using relevant contextual clues. More than what is expressed by the content of one's inference claim can be communicated regarding the status of one's reasons when presenting an argument that one uses in a reason-giving way. Thanks to a reviewer for prompting this footnote.

(III) Kelly: Why do you think that there is life after death?
       Paige: There is life after death since there is a God who promises that
       there is life after death.

In each of these conversational exchanges, we take Paige to be engaged in
dialectical argument and so to be claiming that the premise is a reason for
believing the conclusion. To illustrate with respect to (i), the argument that
Paige gives may be put into standard form as follows.

<u>Beth's car is in the driveway</u>
Beth is home from work

Paige uses the argument dialectically because, at minimum, she makes the
proto-inference claim to the effect that Beth's car is in the driveway is a reason
for believing the conclusion. Her use of the argument is genuinely reason-
giving only if she intends the premise to serve as a reason for believing the
conclusion and thereby believes the proto-inference claim.

Whether Paige believes a particular instantiation of the proto-inference
claim turns on what type of reason for belief and its epistemic import that
Paige intends the premise to represent. Admittedly, (i)–(iii) are a bit thin as
examples of reason-giving uses of arguments and so it isn't obvious what the
operative inference claims are beyond the generic one to the effect that the
premise is a reason for believing the conclusion. Here are three hypotheses
regarding Paige's inference in conversational exchanges (i)–(iii).

(i)   Paige claims that Beth's car is in the driveway is a *conclusive* reason to
      believe that Beth is at home.
(ii) Paige claims that Beth listening to music on the stereo is a *hypothet-
      ical, non-conclusive* reason to believe that Beth is in the living room.
(iii) Paige claims that there is a God who promises that there is life after
      death is a reason for which she believes that there is life after death
      that is also a reason she has to believe this. Perhaps, Paige doesn't in-
      tend the reason to be conclusive or non-conclusive.

In a nutshell, whether any of Paige's reason-giving uses of argument is successful turns on Paige's aim(s) relevant to determining the particular inference claim that must be true. What inference claim Paige makes in using
an argument in a reason-giving way is a function of what she *intends* the

premises to be as reasons for believing the conclusion. This calls upon the notion of an argumentative intention introduced in Chapter 2. Let's briefly review it.

I take reason-giving to be an intentional activity. When you are X-ing intentionally you are aware that you are X-ing. So when you are giving reasons for believing something intentionally you are aware of what you are doing; i.e., you are aware that you are giving reasons for believing something. If you are aware that you are giving reasons for believing something, then you believe that what you give are reasons for believing it.

However, your awareness of being engaged in reason-giving needn't involve believing that the premises are a particular type of reason for believing the conclusion. Furthermore, one might believe that the premises are reasons to believe the conclusion, i.e., that they constitute evidence for the truth of the conclusion, but have no belief regarding whether or not such evidence is conclusive. Plausibly, the more sophisticated the arguer the more likely it is that the arguer will intend the premises to be a particular type of reason for believing the conclusion and intend that they have a particular epistemic import.

In sum, the content of your inference-claim belief required for your use of an argument to count as reason-giving is derived from your argumentative intention. If you intend the premises you advance to be reasons of a certain type for the conclusion and have a certain epistemic import, then your inference-claim belief is that they are reasons of that type for the conclusion with that epistemic import. The content of the inference-claim belief that reflects the operative argumentative intention may merely be the proto-inference claim or an instantiation of it. Again, what is believed signifies the intention behind the reason-giving use of the argument.

To illustrate, consider the following conversational exchange.

KELLY: Assuming that we only have 5K in our savings account in July, if we pay off the car that month, then we won't have enough to pay for a vacation in July.

PAIGE: No. We would still have enough for a vacation, a weekend getaway somewhere local.

Since Kelly is advancing a reason for something, Kelly is arguing$_1$. By the argue$_1$-argument$_8$

link from Chapter 2, Kelly presents an argument$_s$. That is, Kelly presents a coherent series of reasons, statements, or facts intended to support or establish a point of view. An argument used in a reason-giving way is an arguments$_s$. We may put the argument$_s$ that Kelly uses into standard form as follows.

<u>We have 5K in our savings account in July</u>
If we pay off the car in July, then we won't have enough for a vacation in July

To present a coherent series of reasons, statements, or facts intended to support or establish a point of view is to present reasons for believing a statement that expresses the point of view. As Kelly uses this argument to give a reason for its conclusion, Kelly intends the premise to be a reason for believing the conclusion. Therefore, Kelly believes, at minimum, the associated inference claim to the effect that the premise is a reason for believing the conclusion. Kelly's inference-claim belief signifies her argumentative intention.

We look to what Kelly expresses, to contextual clues, and other background information to determine if possible the type of reason that Kelly intends the premise to be for believing the conclusion. I have engineered the example to make it plausible that Kelly intends the premise to be a hypothetical reason for believing the conclusion. She draws her conclusion from her assumption regarding their savings. Paige's response registers her rejection that the premise is such a reason for believing the conclusion. Different ideas about what a July vacation looks like are in play in the disagreement between Kelly and Paige.

For another simple illustration of the connection between argumentative intentions and inference-claim beliefs, I use an example from Chapter 2.

THEIST: There exists a perfectly good God.
ATHEIST: It follows that there doesn't exist useless pain and suffering in the world. However, this is clearly false.

One plausible way of reconstructing the atheist's case is as follows. The atheist argues$_1$ by virtue of putting forward what the theist claims as a reason for the point of view expressed by the statement that *there doesn't exist useless pain and suffering in the world*. Accordingly, the argument$_s$ the atheist presents may be put as follows.

There exists a perfectly good God
∴ There doesn't exist pain and suffering in the world that serves no purpose

Since the atheist uses the (abstract) argument in a reason-giving way, the atheist intends the premise to be a reason for believing the conclusion. Accordingly, the atheist believes that the premise is some sort of reason for believing the conclusion. Background information regarding the atheist's belief set suggests that the atheist rejects the premise. So it is implausible to think that the atheist intends the premise to be a reason the theist has for believing the conclusion. Rather, the atheist intends the premise to express a reason for the theist to believe conclusion, which commits the theist to the truth of the conclusion.

As the atheist thinks the conclusion is false, this counts as a criticism of the theist's premise-belief. Given the atheist's argumentative intention, the atheist's inference-claim belief is that the premise is a reason for the theist to believe the conclusion. The argument the atheist uses isn't suitable for this use unless the associated inference claim is true. For example, the theist may reject the inference claim by arguing for a concept of God according to which although perfectly good, God is not capable of preventing useless pain and suffering. If this is the theist's conception of God and the theist has no beliefs incompatible with it, then the premise is not a reason for the theist to believe the conclusion. In such a case, the operative inference claim is false and the atheist's argument is not good.

This highlights the subjective dimension of *reasons for a person S to believe*. In order for a statement p to be a reason for S to believe something, S must believe p. This contrasts with *reasons to believe*, which are not subjective in this way. If p is a reason to believe something, e.g., it is evidence for the truth of the belief, then it is so regardless of whether anybody believes p. This difference between subjective and objective reasons for believing something matters to how inference-claims beliefs are justified.

As we've seen, the atheist is not entitled to claim that the premise is a reason for the theist to believe the conclusion unless the atheist's understanding of the theist's premise-belief warrants thinking that it commits the theist to the conclusion. In contrast, suppose Paige, in conversation with Kelly, advances the premise that Beth's car is in the driveway as a reason to believe that Beth is at home. The truth of Paige's inference-claim belief turns exclusively on Beth's car being in the driveway counting as evidence for the truth that she is at home. Accordingly, what Kelly believes is irrelevant to the truth of Paige's inference-claim belief. However, again, what the theist believes is quite relevant to the truth of the atheist's inference-claim belief.

3.3.2. Summary

As noted by informal logicians (e.g., Blair 2004, p. 139), defining arguments in terms of just one type of use of them is problematic because it rules out as arguments other uses of premise-conclusion complexes that intuitively qualify as arguments. Informal logic is the field that studies what must be true in order for uses of arguments to be successful and so studies what makes arguments appropriate or inappropriate relative to various uses of them. The need to accommodate different uses of arguments motivates following those who construe arguments in terms of abstract objects, distinguishing between arguments and their uses (e.g., Biro and Siegel 2006a, p. 92; Goldman 1994, p. 27). Two prominent object-based ontologies for arguments are illocutionary-act type complexes and propositional complexes (for discussion see Grennan 1997, chap. 1). In Chapter 2, I took arguments, considered in the abstract, to be premise-conclusion complexes of propositions.

Hitchcock advances an initial conception of arguments in their reason-giving sense according to which an argument is a type of discourse in which the arguer expresses a point of view (encapsulated in the conclusion) and offers one or more reasons (the premise[s]) in support of the conclusion (2007a, p. 103).[2] Arguments so construed are what I have been calling reason-giving uses of arguments. Accordingly, I take the premises of an argument so used to be advanced as reasons for believing the conclusion, i.e., for believing that the conclusion is true. I construe such reasons as truth bearers, and take truth bearers to be propositions, or, equivalently, statements.[3]

---

[2] In a recent postscript to his 2007a, Hitchcock remarks that he now thinks that this characterization of argument is too narrow since it rules out arguments whose premises are advanced as reasons against a claim or as hypothetical support of a claim (2017, p. 519). It isn't obvious to me that the characterization given above is so narrow. For example, reasons advanced against a claim are reasons for its negation, and the premise-reasons of a piece of cogent hypothetical reasoning must support—in some sense—the conclusion. Also, I am happy not to automatically count a derivation of a statement from others as an argument. I don't have space to elaborate.

[3] Hitchcock (2007a) holds that arguments are composed of illocutionary act-types and takes the premises of an argument to be instantiations of such types (assertions, suppositions, guarded assertions, etc.). Such "reasons" would be true or false, either directly or derivatively from the truth-value of their propositional content.

Different *reason-giving* uses of arguments are distinguishable by the type of reasons the premises are. In this book, I primarily focus on theoretical reasons and ignore practical, pragmatic, or explanatory reasons. Taking theoretical reasons for something to be reasons for believing it, I distinguish theoretical reasons across two dimensions: the type of reasons for believing the conclusion the premises are, and their epistemic import.

Hitchcock remarks, "What is crucial to an argument is the claim that the reasons offered collectively support the conclusion" (2007a, p. 105). Hitchcock calls such a claim an "inference claim."[4] Taking Hitchcock's remark to be about reason-giving uses of arguments and understanding *reasons offered that collectively support the conclusion* as *reasons offered for believing the conclusion*, I explain why Hitchcock's remark is true as follows.

Inference claims are crucial to reason-giving uses of arguments in two ways. First, a person S is not using an argument in a reason-giving way unless S believes the proto-inference claim to the effect that the premises, collectively, are reasons for believing the conclusion. Whether or not what S believes is an instantiation of the proto-inference claim turns on S's argumentative intention, i.e., turns on what type of reasons and their epistemic import S intends the premises to be for the conclusion. Second, in order for an argument to be suitable for a reason-giving use of it, the associated inference claim must be true. That is, if the inference claim isn't true, then the argument isn't suitable for the reason-giving use of it and so that use of the argument isn't good and is, therefore, unsuccessful.

3.3.3. Dialectical Arguments and Reason-Giving Uses of Arguments

Recall from Chapter 2 that a dialectical argument is an argument used to advance the premises as reasons for believing the conclusion. Such a use of an argument *commits* the arguer to the inference claim that says, in effect, the premises are reasons of some sort for believing the conclusion. Also, recall

---

[4] In conjunction with his most recent, expanded version of the "reason-giving sense of argument," Hitchcock now initially characterizes an inference claim as saying in effect that the reasons cited would if true or otherwise acceptable support (attack) the target (2017, p. 529). I believe that Hitchcock's 2007a characterization is more basic than this updated one. For example, an argument used to advance reasons that attack a target claim is defective unless it is true that *the reasons collectively support the negation of the target claim*. The italicized claim reflects Hitchcock's 2007a characterization of inference claims.

from Chapter 2 that all reason-giving arguments are dialectical arguments, but not all dialectical arguments are reason-giving uses of arguments. The rationale for this is twofold. One's dialectical argument *merely commits* one to the truth of the associated inference claim. However, if one uses an argument to give reasons for the conclusion, then one *believes* that the associated inference claim is true.

In short, I distinguish dialectical arguments from reason-giving uses of arguments by appealing to the notion of an argumentative intention that is rational insofar as the associated inference claim is believed. One's use of an argument to advance its premises as reason for believing the conclusion isn't an act of reason-giving unless one intends the premises to be such reasons. You are not engaged in giving reasons for believing something unless you intend what you offer to be reasons for believing it and so believe that they are such reasons. I now elaborate by means of three scenarios intended to illustrate dialectical arguments that do not involve using arguments to give reasons for their conclusions.

> *Deceptive.*[5] Husband wants to join an HMO by signing over their Medicare benefits to save money. Wife objects because it would mean she could no longer see the doctor she knew and trusted. In arguing her point of view, she says, "I like Dr. B. He knows me, he's interested in me. He calls me by my first name." Husband's knee-jerk response parries the last point: "I don't like that. He's much younger than we are. He shouldn't be calling us by first name." Husband does not believe that their age rules out the propriety of Dr. B's address. He just wants to score points in order to win the argument.

Of course, Husband's response is a distraction as it does not address Wife's concern. Nevertheless, Husband is engaging in dialectical argument. He uses an argument to advance a reason for believing its conclusion. The argument may be construed as follows: Dr. B is much younger than we are; therefore, he shouldn't be calling us by first name. Since Husband advances the premise as a reason for believing the conclusion, he is committed to the inference

---

[5] This example is adapted from the one given by Tannen (1999, p. 9) to illustrate what she takes to be our all too typical aims in arguing with those who we are closest with: listening for weaknesses in logic to leap on, points you can distort to make the other person look bad and yourself look good. "Sometimes you know, on some back burner of your mind, that you're doing this—that there's a kernel of truth in what your adversary is saying and a bit of unfair twisting in what you're saying" (p. 9).

claim that says, in effect, the premise is a reason for Wife to believe the conclusion. However, although Husband is on the hook for defending this claim, he doesn't believe it. Accordingly, he is not using the argument he presents to give reasons for the conclusion.

Perplexed.[6]

Student is presented with the sentence L: *This sentence is false*, and asked by their logic teacher to determine its truth-value. Student reasons as follows.
(1) If L is false, then it is true, given what it says.
(2) If L is true, then it is false, since it says that it is false.
(3) L is true or false.
So, (4) it is both true and false.
Student believes (1)–(3). Furthermore, Student believes that (4) follows from (1)–(3) as Student draws (5) L is true if and only if L is false from (1) and (2), and draws (4) from (3) and (5). However, Student refuses to accept (4).

Student is perplexed as a result of reflection on their dialectical argument with (1)–(3) as premises and (4) as the conclusion. Student's perplexity is sustained by their awareness that they are committed to the inference claim that (1)–(3) are reasons for them to believe (4), which they reject. Also, it is sustained by their temporarily being unable to justify their rejection of the inference claim that they are committed to. In short, Student's rejection of the inference claim they are committed to that, in effect, says that (1)–(3) are reasons for them to believe (4) make the corresponding argument paradoxical and engenders Student's state of perplexity. Since Student rejects the inference claim, their dialectical argument does not count as a reason-giving use of argument.

---

[6] I craft this illustration drawing on Sainsbury (2009, sec. 6.2) and utilizing his understanding of a paradox: "an apparently unacceptable conclusion derived by apparently acceptable reasoning from apparently acceptable premises" (p. 1). *Perplexed* instantiates this understanding of paradox in terms of the notion of *reasons for one to believe*. That is, an argument is paradoxical for a reasoner S if S is committed to the inference claim that the premises are reasons S has to believe the conclusion, but S rejects the inference claim. Resolving the state of aporia resulting from S's realization that an argument is paradoxical for S involves either eliminating the commitment to the inference claim by rejecting a premise, rejecting the reasoning, or accepting the inference claim and accepting the conclusion.

Unreflective.[7] Joey is playing hide-and-seek with Mom. Joey is looking for Mom, who is hiding somewhere in the house. Joey hears a noise in the up-stairs bedroom. He says to himself, "That's Mom!" and infers that she is hiding in the bedroom. He goes upstairs to search the bedroom.

Joey *takes* that there is a noise in the bedroom to be a reason he has to believe that Mom is hiding in the bedroom. However, being only seven years old, Joey is oblivious to the fact that he is engaging in reason-giving. His inference is automatic and unreflective. His *taking* that there is a noise in the bedroom to be a reason he has to believe that Mom is hiding in the bedroom in no way involves an awareness that he is engaged in the practice of reasons-giving. Joey doesn't believe that *there is a noise in the bedroom* is a reason he has to believe that Mom is hiding there, as Joey lacks understanding of *reasons for belief.* Although he is committed to the inference claim that the noise in the bedroom is a reason he has to believe that Mom is hiding in the bedroom, Joey does not believe it.

Husband, Student, and Joey are engaged in dialectical argument. Each advances premises as reasons for a conclusion, but they are not engaged in arguing$_1$; i.e., they do not engage in reason-giving. Since they do not be-lieve the associated inference claims, they do not intend their premises to be reasons for believing the conclusion. Accordingly, their dialectical arguments are not reason-giving uses of arguments. We may say that Husband, Student, and Joey are committed to the truth of the proto-inference claims associated with their arguments, but as they don't believe these commitments, they do not use their arguments in reason-giving ways.

3.3.4. Summary

An inference claim is essential to a reason-giving use of an argument in two ways. First, from Chapter 2, one isn't using an argument to give reasons for its conclusion unless one believes the corresponding inference claim. Second, from section 3.2, the inference claim must be true in order for the argument

---

[7] Here I borrow from Boghossian (2014, pp. 6–7), who uses a hide-and-seek example to illustrate that children perform inferences even though they lack meta-beliefs about the relations between their premise judgments and their conclusions. For example, seven-year-olds typically lack the normative concept of one belief justifying another. As expressed just below, this militates against construing Joey's believing the noise in the bedroom to be a reason for him to believe that Mom is hiding in the bedroom.

to be suitable and so good for the corresponding reason-giving use of it. That is, if the inference claim isn't true, then the argument isn't suitable for this particular reason-giving use of it. In such a case, so using the argument will not be successful. This reflects the obvious point that one doesn't succeed in advancing premises as reasons for believing the conclusion in the sense one intends unless the premises are such reasons.

A dialectical argument counts as a reason-giving use of argument only if the user believes the associated proto-inference claim to the effect that the premises taken together are reasons for believing the conclusion. Again, there are two ways that one may not believe the inference claim: (a) one disbelieves it (e.g., Husband and Student), or (b) one is not being intentional about one's arguing and one is simply unaware of one's inference-claim commitment (e.g., Joey). Regarding (b), your dialectical use of an argument may evolve into a reason-giving use of it upon further reflection given that you have the wherewithal. For example, your dialectical argument meets criticism. In response, you defend the associated inference claim and thereby come to explicitly believe it. In this way, responding to criticism of our dialectical arguments can deepen our understanding of the status of the premises we advance as reasons for believing the conclusion.

3.4. How, Exactly, Are Inference Claims Conveyed by One's Statement of an Argument?

I have said in Chapter 2 that to use an argument in a reason-giving way, one must state the argument (simply to oneself or to others) and thereby convey an inference claim to the effect that the premises are reasons of some sort for believing the conclusion. How, exactly, is the inference claim conveyed? Is it merely implied, implicated in some way, or asserted? In this section, I develop a response. Specifically, I make the case that when one uses an argument in a reason-giving way, one asserts the associated inference claim as opposed to merely implying or implicating it. My case for this draws on the following three theses.

(*Belief*) If you express an inference claim by your statement of an argument that you use in a reason-giving way, then you believe the inference claim.

(*Value*) If the statement of an argument used in a reason-giving way is true or acceptable, then so too is the inference claim it conveys.

(*Primary*) Expressing the inference claim is a primary point made by the statement of an argument used in a reason-giving way, not a secondary one.

I now support each, starting with *Belief*.

From Chapter 2, (1) your statement of an argument counts as an act of arguing$_1$, i.e., an act of reason-giving, only if you state an argument$_a$. That is only if you state an abstract argument that you use in a reason-giving way. Therefore, (2) if your statement of an argument counts as an act of arguing$_1$, then you intend the premises to be reasons for believing the conclusion and so you believe that they are. Here I assume that the rationality of the involved argumentative intentions insofar as it satisfies the inference-claim belief requirement. Accordingly, (3) you don't express an inference claim to the effect that the premises are reasons for believing the conclusion unless you believe this claim.

How do we get to (3) from (2)? If you use an argument to give reasons for the conclusion, then you express the associated inference claim, because you believe it. Again, you believe it because you (rationally) intend the premises to be reasons for believing the conclusion. If you don't intend this, then you aren't using the argument to give reasons for the conclusion. This constitutive connection between a reason-giving use of an argument and believing the corresponding inference claim is reflected by *Belief*.

If you don't believe the inference claim, then you aren't using the argument you state in a reason-giving way and, by *Belief*, you don't express the inference claim in stating the argument; i.e., you don't express the claim that the premises are reasons for believing the conclusion, although you could certainly be taken to be expressing this. After all, you are committed to the inference claim. What it is to count as an act of arguing$_1$ is interestingly ambiguous in this way, just like promising—between whether it is *really* that or just *appears to be and so is taken to be*. In short, *Belief* grounds a pragmatic criterion that S's statement of an argument must satisfy in order for the use of the argument to qualify as reason-giving.

Toward a defense of *Value*: recall from section 3.2, that (1) in order for an argument to be suitable for a reason-giving use of it, the associated inference claim must be true. That is, if the inference claim isn't true, then the argument isn't suitable for this particular reason-giving use of it and so such a use isn't successful. Intuitively, (2) the statement of an argument used to advance its premises as reasons for the conclusion is true or acceptable only if the argument that is stated is suitable for how it is being used. *Value* is implied by (1) and (2).

By the lights of *Value*, an argument being suitable as a means of giving reasons for the conclusion bears on whether a statement of it is true or acceptable. Furthermore, if S is justified in believing that their statement of an argument is true or acceptable, then *Value* enables the transference of this justification to S's belief that the inference claim is also true or acceptable. Given that a statement of an argument doesn't count as a *good* act of arguing₁, i.e., a *good* act of reason-giving, unless (1) and (2) (just above) obtain, *Value* underwrites the idea that a speaker's act of arguing for a conclusion by stating an argument is *good* only if the statement of the argument is true or acceptable. This idea is intuitively plausible.

Turning to *Primary*, one doesn't state an argument that one uses in a reason-giving way unless one's statement conveys an associated inference claim. Intuitively, when using an argument in a reason-giving way, a speaker's primary point is to express an inference claim. This motivates *Primary*. *Primary* reflects a connection between a primary point in stating an argument and a primary aim in using its premises as reason for believing the conclusion. For example, if speaker S's primary aim in stating an argument in a critical discussion is to persuade a conversant of the conclusion, then the primary points conveyed by S's statement of an argument are what the addressee must accept in order to be persuaded by S's argument.

The addressee must accept the inference claim in order to be so persuaded. Hence *Primary*. Alternatively, one may take the primary aim of a reason-giving use of argument to be showing that the conclusion is true. If so, then the primacy (the non-derivativeness) of expressing the inference claim is a consequence. That is, if a primary aim of S's in stating an argument in a critical discussion is to justify acceptance of the conclusion to the addressees, then expressing the corresponding inference claim is a primary point made by the statement of the argument.

Our question in this section may be put as follows: with respect to a person S's use of an argument to give reasons for its conclusion, how, exactly, is S's inference claim conveyed by S's statement of the argument? *Belief*, *Value*, and *Primary* constrain adequate responses. First, S must believe the inference claim. Second, the truth of S's statement suffices for the truth of the inference claim that is conveyed. Third, expressing the inference claim is a primary point of S's statement of the argument. More generally, the manner in which an inference claim is expressed by the statement of an argument used to give reasons for its conclusion must satisfy *Belief*, *Value*, and *Primary*. For ease of reference, I repeat them.

> (*Belief*) If you express an inference claim by your statement of an argument used in a reason-giving way, then you believe the inference claim.
> (*Value*) If the statement of an argument used in a reason-giving way is true or acceptable, then so too is the inference claim it conveys.
> (*Primary*) Expressing the inference claim is a primary point made by the statement of an argument used in a reason-giving way, not a secondary one.

Appealing to these theses, I now make the case that if a speaker S uses an argument in a reason-giving way, then S thereby asserts the corresponding inference claim as opposed to merely implying it, conversationally implicating it, or conventionally implicating it. The case turns on the speech act of assertion fairing best in satisfying *Belief*, *Value*, and *Primary* out of these alternatives. The below scorecard summarizes the following discussion.

	(Belief)	(Value)	(Primary)
Mere implication	No	Yes	Yes
Conversational implicature	No	No	Yes
Conventional implicature	No	No	No
Assertion	Yes	Yes	Yes

As the table indicates, *Belief* alone establishes that if a speaker S uses an argument in a reason-giving way, then S thereby asserts the corresponding inference claim. *Value* and *Primary* are worth discussing as a means of shedding further light on the connection between inference claims and reason-giving uses of arguments. I now justify the entries, starting with mere implication.

3.4.1. Mere Implication

I label the position that an inference claim is *merely* implied by what is expressed in stating the corresponding argument as *mere implication*. I understand the notion of implication semantically. Accordingly, I take mere implication to hold that an inference claim is implied by virtue of the meaning of one or more expressions that occur in the statement of the argument.

For example, I take Hitchcock (2007a, 2011) to hold that a speaker's statement of an argument in arguing for its conclusion implies the corresponding inference claim. His rationale is threefold. First, an inference claim "can be marked linguistically by means of an illative expression (e.g., 'therefore', 'since') governing the conclusion or reason" (2007a, p. 106). Second, in order for a statement of an argument to express an inference claim, it must contain, explicitly or otherwise, an illative expression, which is in sync with Hitchcock's view that the components of arguments include illative expressions (2007a, pp. 106–7). Third, the inference claim is an analytical implication of the meaning of the illative expression contained (perhaps, implicitly) in the statement of the argument. For example, "the word 'so' when used inferentially implies, as part of its meaning and not as some pragmatic implicature of its ordinary use, that the statement preceding it is relevant to the statement following it . . . in the sense that it helps to establish the truth of the conclusion" (2011, p. 214).

Mere implication moves beyond Hitchcock in being explicit that an inference claim is *merely* implied by the meaning of an illative expression that occurs, implicitly or otherwise, in what is expressed by the statement of an argument. If an inference claim may be conveyed by the statement of an argument even though an illative is not expressed, implicitly or otherwise, then this problematizes mere implication. At any rate, mere implication does not satisfy *Belief*, because implication is simply a relation between propositions that obtains regardless of a speaker's beliefs.

That is, the logical connection doesn't depend on your believing the implication. You say to me, "Beth is in the living room." "Beth is in the living room or in the kitchen" being an implication of the proposition you state doesn't depend on your believing the implication. Furthermore, on my view, belief is not closed under implication. Since what is implied by what you utter is independent of whether or not you believe what is implied, implication fails *Belief*.[8]

---

[8] Of course, this doesn't rule out connections between the relation of implication and stating an argument. One might argue that stating an argument is undermined if you aren't prepared to at least defend the implications of that statement.

Mere implication satisfies *Value* because it preserves truth values. For example, if p implies q and p is true, then q must be true. Also, mere implication seems to satisfy *Primary*. Consider *he is either very smart or very silly, and he isn't very smart* uttered in order to convey that *he is very silly*. This shows that you *can* intend the implication of what you express. In stating an argument, you may imply an inference claim in order to convey your belief of the inference claim. However, implication can't satisfy *Belief* this way because, again, believing the implication of what you express is not necessary for the implication to obtain.

Before turning to conversational implicature, it is worth briefly discussing the meaning of illative expressions highlighted by mere implication. The use of illative expressions (e.g., "since," "therefore") to express that a relation of support holds between premises and a conclusion is widely acknowledged by informal logicians (e.g., Hamblin 1970, pp. 228–30; Epstein 2002, p. 23), and appealed to in critical thinking texts to explain to students why the occurrence of such expressions indicates the presence of arguments (e.g., see Sinnott-Armstrong and Fogelin 2010, p. 51; Govier 2010, p. 3). We may think that there are two independent roles for "therefore" and its cognates: mere conclusion designator (e.g., Corcoran 1993) and the expression of a relation of support between premises and conclusion (e.g., Epstein 2002; Hamblin 1970; Hitchcock 2007a). As was highlighted in Chapter 2, this suggests that the *therefore* of informal logic differs from the formal-logic *therefore*, because only informal logic considers arguments in their dialectical and reason-giving senses.

However, in stating *p therefore q* in order to advance *p* as a reason for *q* a speaker conveys that *p* is reason on behalf of *q* (for textbook explications of this use of *therefore* see Govier 2010, p. 3, and Sinnott-Armstrong and Fogelin 2010, p. 51). In this way, the use of a *therefore* to state an argument in its reason-giving sense is different from its use as mere conclusion designator in the presentation of an argument in what I've called in Chapter 2 its abstract sense. This suggests that one's statement of an argument is truth evaluable only relative to a reason-giving use of it.

The primary point here is that your use of an illative expression in stating an argument can signal that you intend the premises taken together to be support—in some sense—for the conclusion. I understand the support that the premises are intended to provide for the conclusion in terms of the intention that the premises serve as reasons for believing the conclusion. I've called such an intention the *argumentative intention*. Since, as discussed above, there are a variety of reasons for believing the conclusion with varying epistemic import, the exact nature of the support relation between premises and conclusion expressed by an illative expression will vary from one reason-giving use of an argument to another.

This brief discussion of the import of expressions used as illatives highlights that there are different layers of inference-claim theorizing. Claims such as "*q* follows from *p*" or "*p* supports *q*" may be regarded as first-step characterizations of the inference claim associated with an argument *p, so q*. We may even take "so" used as an illative to express that, say, the conclusion follows—in some way—from the premise(s). My appeal to the notion of *reasons for belief* in my section 3.2 account of inference claims develops these first-step characterizations of them. In order to separate my account of inference claims in terms of reasons for belief from the issue of how they are conveyed by statements of arguments, unless otherwise specified, in what follows I will take the import of an inference claim associated with an argument to merely be that the conclusion follows from the premise(s). Of course, if the premises are reasons for believing the conclusion, then the conclusion follows from them in some sense.

3.4.2. Conversational Implicature

Does an arguer's statement of an argument in a critical discussion conversationally implicate the corresponding inference claim?[9] An affirmative response is derivable from Bermejo-Luque's account (2011a, 2011b) of how inference claims are communicated when arguers argue for their conclusions by adducing premises in support of them. To illustrate, suppose that in the course of arguing for a claim *q* in a critical discussion, Pro utters *p so q* in order to persuade Con, who disbelieves *q*, that *q* is true.

---

[9] My discussion of conversational and conventional implicatures aims to present the elements of Grice's view of implicatures relevant to answering the primary question of this section, stated at the start. Toward this end, I draw from Grice's 1967 publications "Logic and Conversation" and "Further Notes on Logic and Conversation." I rely on their reprints in Grice 1989. I also draw on the following sources that critically survey Grice's account of implicatures: well-known textbooks on linguistic communication (Levinson 1983; Bach and Harnish 1979); handbook and encyclopedia articles (Horn 2004; Korta and Perry 2020); review articles (Neale 1992; Potts 2007); and Bach's oft-cited critical discussions of Gricean implicatures in his 1994 and 1999 publications.

Following Bermejo-Luque (2011b, p. 64), Pro thereby implicitly asserts the material conditional, if p then q, represented as $p \supset q$. Bermejo-Luque thinks this is the inference claim (2011b, p. 62).[10] Bermejo-Luque contends that Pro's intention to communicate that q follows from p is conveyed as a conversational implicature of Pro's implicit assertion that $p \supset q$.[11] By virtue of believing that Pro abides by the cooperative principle and the conversational maxims guiding the critical discussion, Con is entitled to think that in asserting $p \supset q$, Pro conveys as a conversational implicature that q follows from p (2011a, p. 64; 2011b, p. 335).

Conversational implicatures are essentially calculable.[12] Borrowing from Bach and Harnish (1979, p. 169), Levinson (1983, pp. 113–14), and Neale (1992, p. 527), I illustrate how Con's reasoning might run in calculating the conversational implicature, *q follows from p*, of Pro's statement *p so q*.

(1) Pro says *p so q* and thereby implicitly asserts p $\supset$ q;
(2) There is no reason to suppose that Pro is not observing the conversational maxims and cooperative principle that guide the critical discussion;
(3) Only if Pro thinks that *q follows from p* is Pro's saying $p \supset q$ consistent with the presumption that Pro is observing the maxims and cooperative principle;[13]

---

[10] Critics have pointed out that construing the content of inference claims in terms of the material conditional drains the normative force from them (e.g., Pinto 2011a). In response Bermejo-Luque's highlights the pragmatic aspect of the normative force of inference claims (2011a, p. 335; 2011b, p. 175). For example, arguing that *Donald Trump likes asparagus, so 2 < 3*, is problematic (it's hardly imaginable!), because even though *Donald Trump likes asparagus* $\supset 2 < 3$ is true by virtue of the truth of its consequent, it is not appropriate, by Grice's Maxim of Quantity, to assert it solely on the basis of knowledge of the consequent. Hence, arguing as above is pragmatically flawed. However, Bermejo-Luque's response doesn't register why so arguing is epistemically flawed.

[11] This requires that $p \supset q$ be part of what is said in stating the argument. The requirement is motivated by Grice's view that a conversational implicature is derived from what, if anything, is said by an utterance. On Grice's strict conception of what is said, what is said by an utterance must correspond to "elements of [the sentence uttered], their order, and their syntactic character" (1989, p. 87). Following others (e.g., Bach 1999, p. 335), this does not mean that what is said must be made fully explicit. For example, one can say that $p \supset q$ is communicated by a speaker's utterance *p so q* by virtue of a correspondence between $p \supset q$ and "so." This suffices for making $p \supset q$ implicitly asserted and so (implicitly) stated by the statement of the corresponding argument. A fuller account would spell out the nature of the correspondence between $p \supset q$ and the conclusion indicator.

[12] "The presence of a conversational implicature must be capable of being worked out; for even if it can be intuitively grasped, unless the intuition is replaceable by an argument, the implicature (if present at all) will not count as a conversational implicature" (Grice 1989, p. 31).

[13] That *q follows from p* is simply introduced at step (3) without explanation. One explanation is that in order to think that Pro's assertion that $p \supset q$ advances Pro's aim of stating *p so q*, i.e., advances Pro's arguing for *q*, Pro should think that *q* follows from *p*.

(4) Pro knows (and knows that I know that Pro knows) that I can see that Pro thinks the
supposition that Pro thinks that *q follows from p* is required;

(5) Pro has done nothing to stop me thinking that *q follows from p*.

So, from (1) to (5), (6) Pro intends me to think, or is at least willing to allow me to think that *q follows from p*.

So, from (6), (7) Pro has implicated that *q follows from p*.

Steps (1)–(7) reflect three speech-act moves Pro makes in arguing for *q*: (i) stating, *p so q*, thereby (ii) (implicitly) asserting, $p \supset q$, and (iii) conversationally implicating that *q follows from p*. Con's reasoning, embodied in (1)–(7), reflects Con's belief that Pro's (implicit) assertion that $p \supset q$ is not sufficiently informative in the context of Pro's arguing for *q*. So the conveyance of *q follows from p* requires Con's inference from the supposition that Pro wouldn't have said $p \supset q$ if Pro hadn't meant something more than that, i.e., hadn't also meant *q follows from p*. I now make several comments, (a)–(c), that inform my evaluation of conversational implicature as the mechanism by which inference claims are expressed.

(a) Step (5) registers the cancelability of conversational implicatures (following Grice 1989, p. 44). This makes the pragmatic inferences that arise from such implicatures defeasible. In this way, they are more like inductive inferences than deductive ones (see Levinson 1983, pp. 114–16). However, *p so q, but q doesn't follow from p*, seems problematic when the argument stated is an argument in its reason-giving sense. This suggests that the follows-from claim is either a part of what is said in uttering *p so q* used in a reason-giving way or is a conventional implicature of this utterance which isn't cancelable (as described below). Either way, this intuition counts against treating *q follows from p* as a conversational implication of $p \supset q$, assuming that $p \supset q$ is implicitly asserted in stating a reason-giving argument *p so q*.

(b) Con's reasoning in calculating the implicature of Pro's assertion of $p \supset q$ is cogent even if Pro doesn't believe that *q follows from p*. This is because failing to fulfill a maxim (or the cooperative principle) may nevertheless give rise to implicatures. Following Bach and Harnish (1979, p. 167), one may quietly and unostentatiously fail to fulfill a maxim, which is likely to mislead. In such a case, Pro's assertion that $p \supset q$ is

infelicitous, precisely because it implicates that *q follows from p*, which
Pro does not believe.

(c) Since an implicature is not part of what is said by the utterance from
which the implicature is inferred, it may be neither true nor acceptable while what is said is true or acceptable. For example, $p \supset q$, may
be true even though *q* does not follow from *p*. Not satisfying *Value*
distinguishes implicatures (both conventional and conversational)
from implication.

Conversational implicature does not satisfy *Belief*. Suppose that Pro states
an argument, *p so q*, and thereby conversationally implicates that *q* follows
from *p*. Conversational implicature satisfies *Belief* only if it is necessary that
Pro believe that *q* follows from *p* in order for Pro to implicate this. Given
point (b) above, this isn't the case. Hence, conversational implicature fails
Belief. Certainly, Pro's saying $p \supset q$ as part of stating the argument while not
believing that *q* follows from *p* is *infelicitous* since Pro is on the hook for
defending if not believing that *q* follows from *p*. However, this is insufficient
for conversational implicature satisfying *Belief*. Assuming responsibility for
believing the follows-from claim is short of believing it. If we suppose that
Pro doesn't believe that *q follows from p*, it is nevertheless expressed as an
implicature of Pro's utterance since Pro did not explicitly opt out of following
the maxims (or cooperative principle).

Given point (c), conversational implicature doesn't satisfy *Value*. For example, what you utter may be true even though what you implicate by your
utterance is false. However, conversational implicature satisfies *Primary*.
Consider an utterance, *I am on a diet*, made in response to the question *Would
you like dessert?* Plausibly, a primary aim of the speaker's utterance is to convey
as a conversational implicature that the speaker does not want dessert.

3.4.3. Conventional Implicature

According to Grice (1989), the statement of an argument that explicitly uses an
illative expression (e.g., "since," "therefore") conventionally implicates the corresponding inference claim.[14] Bach defines conventional implicature as follows.

---

[14] In an oft-cited passage, Grice introduces the notion of conventional implicatures in his well-
known "Logic and Conversation" in order to distinguish them from conversational implicatures,
which is his main concern.

A proposition is a conventional implicature of an utterance just in case (a) the speaker (speaking seriously) is committed to the truth of the proposition, (b) which proposition that is depends upon the (or a) conventional meaning of some particular linguistic device in the utterance, but (c) the falsity of that proposition is compatible with the truth of the utterance. (1999, p. 331)

Condition (b) grounds the fact that conventional implicatures are not cancelable. Horn puts this as, "[they are] not CANCELABLE without contradiction" (2004, p. 4). This accommodates the intuition that there is something always wrong in uttering *p so q, but q doesn't follow from p*, when the argument is being used in a reason-giving way. Also, an illative has to occur in what is uttered in order for the corresponding inference claim to be conventionally implicated. So, if statements of arguments convey inference claims as conventional implicatures, then they must contain, explicitly or otherwise, an illative expression.

The expressions "therefore" and "but" are often used to illustrate conventional implicatures (but see Bach 1999, discussed below). Suppose (i) and (ii) are uttered in ordinary conversations.

(i) Beth is listening to music, but she is in the living room.
(ii) Beth is listening to music; therefore, she is in the living room.

The descriptive meaning of utterances (i) and (ii), what Grice identifies with what is said, is the same: (iii) Beth is listening to music and she is in the living room. If either conjunct in (iii) is false, then so are (i) and (ii). Sample conventional implicatures of utterances (i) and (ii) are CI_i—*Beth is not usually listening to music in the living room*; CI_{ii}—*Beth is in the living room* follows from *Beth is listening to music*. The CIs illustrate conventional meanings of utterance (i) and (ii) in typical conversational settings.

In some cases the conventional meaning of the words used will determine what is implicated, besides helping to determine what is said. If I say (smugly), *He is an Englishman; he is, therefore, brave,* I have certainly committed myself, by virtue of the meaning of my words, to its being the case that his being brave is a consequence of (follows from) his being an Englishmen. But while I have said that he is an Englishman, and said that he is brave, I do not want to say that I have *said* (in the favored sense) that it follows from his being an Englishman that he is brave, though I have certainly indicated, and so implicated, that this is so. I do not want to say my utterance of this sentence would be, *strictly speaking,* false should the consequence in question fail to hold. So *some* implicatures are conventional, unlike the one (a conversational implicature) which I introduced this discussion of implicature (1989, pp. 25–26).

Pro utters *p, so q* in a critical discussion. Treating the inference claim, *q follows from p*, as an implicature of Pro's utterance takes it to be a meaning of the utterance that is not part of what Pro says. Accordingly, in stating *p, so q*, Pro is not saying *q follows from p*. If the inference claim is a conversational implicature of Pro's utterance, then it is a pragmatic meaning that arises from the interaction between the communicative goals of Pro and Con in their critical discussion, and the conversational maxims guiding rational communication. In contrast, if *q follows from p* is a conventional implicature of Pro's utterance *p so q*, then it is a conventional meaning of Pro's utterance that stems entirely from the conventional meaning of "so." However, the meaning of "so" does not contribute to what Pro says and so does not affect the truth or falsity of what Pro says.[15]

Conventional implicature does not satisfy *Belief*, because conventional implicature stems entirely from the conventional meanings of lexical items or grammatical constructions occurring in the sentence uttered. If my utterance of *p so, q* conventionally implicates that *q follows from p*, then it does so regardless of whether or not I believe my commitment to the inference claim. Therefore, conventional implicature fails *Belief*.

According to Grice, the meaning of a conventional implicature does not contribute to the truth-conditional content of the statement that has the conventional implicature. Accordingly, conventional implicature does not satisfy *Value* since, like conversational implicature, it does not necessarily preserve acceptability or truth. For example, what is uttered may be true even though what is conventionally implicated by the utterance is false. The oddity of treating the value of the inference claim as irrelevant to the value of the argument's statement can be brought out by considering a clearly invalid argument with true premises and a true conclusion, such as the argument: "Some politicians are men and some politicians are corrupt, so some men are corrupt." Would it be coherent to say: "That's true, but your conclusion doesn't actually follow from the reasons you give"? If the correct response is affirmative, then Grice's position is vindicated. If the correct response is negative, as I think, then Grice's position is refuted.

---

[15] As is commonly noted (e.g., see Korta and Perry 2020), an internal tension in Grice's view of conventional implicatures results from Grice maintaining that (i) a conventional implicature is a conventional meaning of an utterance, (ii) the conventional meaning of an utterance contributes to the truth-conditional content of what is said, and (iii) the meaning of a conventional implicature does not contribute to the truth-conditional content of the corresponding utterance. Claims (i)–(iii) are prima facie incompatible.

Moving to *Primary*, it is standard to think that the proposition expressed by a conventional implicature is secondary to the main assertion of a declarative sentence (e.g., see Abbott 2006; Potts 2007). Following Potts (2007, p. 667), at the discourse level we find if one objects to an assertion of, say, (i) above, one is not construed as having objected to CI_i, which is liable to slip quietly to the common ground, unless the objector is explicit that they object to the CI_i-content as well. This illustrates what Potts calls the assertoric inertness of conventional implicatures (2007, p. 672). That conventional implicatures are assertorically inert is a reason to think that they do not satisfy *Primary*.

Before turning to assertion, it is worth considering Bach (1999, pp. 338–43), who argues that conventional implicatures do not exist. Obviously, if this is correct then this counts against construing an arguer's inference claim as a conventional implicature of the statement of the argument. Bach deploys what he calls the IQ-test (the indirect quotation test) to make the case that conventional implicatures are not distinguished from the descriptive meaning of utterances and so are part of what is said in the sense of Grice. To illustrate, between (ii) and (iii), which is an accurate paraphrase, using indirect quotation, of what S uttered?

S: (i) Beth is listening to music on the stereo and therefore Beth is in the living room.
  (ii) S said that Beth is listening to music on the stereo and therefore Beth is in the living room.
  (iii) S said that Beth is listening to music on the stereo and that Beth is in the living room.

According to Bach, it's (ii). Statement (iii) leaves out the contribution of "therefore"; unlike (ii), it does not report S's statement of an argument. If (ii) is true, which seems right, then what S says is (i). If S had just said that Beth is listening to music on the stereo and that Beth is in the living room, then (ii) would be partly untrue.

3.4.4. Assertion

As some have noted (e.g., Bach 1999, p. 330), Grice's example of "therefore" as a device of conventional implicature is unfortunate since that q follows from *p* seems to be required for the truth of what is stated by uttering *p*, *therefore q*. This suggest that, contra Grice, *q follows from p* is part of what is said in stating *p, therefore q*. Hitchcock remarks that in stating an argument—in its reason-giving sense—"[t]he arguer *implicitly claims* that the conclusion . . . follows from the reason or reasons from which it is drawn" (2011, pp. 191–92). Accordingly, by stating an argument in its reasoning giving sense a speaker claims, i.e., asserts, the corresponding inference claim.

What distinguishes assertion from other types of speech acts?[16] I favor an expressive account of assertion (for challenges see MacFarlane 2011). Briefly, your utterance counts as an assertion only if it expresses your belief of the propositions stated (Searle 1979, p. 12; Bach and Harnish 1979, p. 42). Expressions of belief are caused by the beliefs they express (Williams 2002, pp. 73–75; Owens 2006). As noted by Williams (2002, p. 74), since only sincere assertions can express beliefs in this direct way, insincere assertions are assertions in a parasitic sense.[17] Since you express an inference claim by means of sincerely asserting it only if you believe it, (sincere) assertion satisfies *Belief*.

Assertion satisfies *Value*. In arguing for a conclusion by stating an argument, a speaker S performs the speech acts of asserting the premises, the conclusion, and the corresponding inference claim. Drawing on Bach (1999), Potts labels the phenomenon of an individual sentence that is uttered expressing multiple meanings *semantic multidimensionality* (2007, pp. 674–76). Construing the meaning of a sentence as the proposition it expresses, semantic multidimensionality is instantiated by a one-sentence-potentially-many-propositions semantics. This enables the analysis of the meaning of a speaker S's utterance, *p, so q*, in terms of two propositions expressed by the sentence S utters: *p and q, q follows from p*. Here, what is expressed comprises more than one proposition. Since part of what is expressed in stating an argument is the inference claim asserted, the inference claim must be true if what is stated in the statement of the argument is true. Finally, assertion accommodates *Primary* by the fact that the

---

[16] For useful overviews of the many different accounts of assertion developed in response, see Brown and Cappelen 2011b and Pagin 2016.

[17] According to Williams, "[T]he standard conditions of A's asserting that P are that A utters a sentence 'S,' where 'S' means that P, in doing which either he expresses his belief that P, or he intends the person addressed to take it that he believes that P" (2002, p. 74). The second disjunct, which accommodates acts of insincere assertion, expresses what I take to be the sincerity condition for A's act of conversationally implicating that P by uttering "S." Again, as previously suggested, A conversationally implicating that P does not require that A believe P.

inference claim is asserted, and what is asserted in an utterance is a primary point of the utterance.

In sum, S's assertion *p, so q* by means of uttering it asserts that *q follows from p*, which is among the propositions expressed by S's utterance. Since S doesn't utter *q follows from p*, the question arises what determines whether the assertion of the inference claim by means of uttering *p, so q* is implicit or explicit. Here I follow Grice in understanding what is *explicitly* expressed by an utterance strictly in terms of what is said by means of the utterance. Defense of this substantive claim is beyond the scope of this chapter. Briefly, by stating an argument you explicitly assert the corresponding inference claim only if you utter an illative expression in stating the argument. Otherwise, the inference claim is implicitly asserted.[18]

I've said that statements of arguments in their reason-giving sense are truth evaluable. However, as Bach notes (1999, p. 354), a sentence that expresses more than one proposition, rather than a conjunction of them, does not have a unitary truth condition. If my utterance expresses several propositions all true except for one, is what I say false? Without addressing this question directly, we can say that what is uttered by stating an argument is true if every proposition that is expressed is true.

That assertion satisfies *Belief, Value,* and *Primary* provides a rationale for a central thesis of this chapter. By stating an argument used to give reasons for its conclusion a speaker S *asserts* the associated inference claim. Before concluding this section, I now sketch my responses to two objections to this thesis.

One form of pushback questions the belief condition, which I have labeled *Belief.* This criticism says that when one argues for a conclusion *one necessarily represents oneself as believing* that the conclusion follows from the premises given in its support. Of course, merely representing oneself as believing *p* isn't to believe *p*.

My response appeals to the operative argumentative intention in reason-giving. If one argues for a conclusion by giving reasons for it, then one intends the premises to be reasons for believing the conclusion. If one intends the premises to be reasons for believing the conclusion, then one believes that the conclusion follows from them in some sense. So, if one engages in

---

[18] I distinguish between implicit assertions and mere implications. Taking S to be implicitly asserting an inference claim construed as a mere implication of her statement of the argument threatens to erase what many take to be an intuitive and useful distinction between what is asserted and what is merely implied (e.g., MacFarlane 2011, p. 80).

dialectical argument and thereby *represents oneself as believing* that the conclusion follows from the premises given in its support without believing this, then there is a pretense of using an argument in a reason-giving way, but one isn't really so using the argument to give reasons for believing the conclusion.

Another form of pushback undercuts motivation for the above thesis by advancing either an alternative plausible story about mere implication or a neo-Gricean account of implicature that satisfies *Belief, Value,* and *Primary.* For example, regarding mere implication, one might follow Harman (1986) and argue that one believes what is easily inferable from what one expresses. Harman distinguishes between explicit and implicit belief. Briefly, you believe something explicitly if your belief involves an explicit mental representation whose content is the content of that belief (1986, p. 13). You believe something only implicitly if it is not explicitly believed, but, for example, is easily inferable from one's explicit beliefs (1986, p. 13). Given that you explicitly believe that Beth has at most four children, you can easily infer that Beth does not have five children, that Beth does not have six, and so on. So, all these propositions are things that you believe implicitly.[19] In response, I say that one give reasons for a conclusion unless one explicitly believes the associated inference claim, i.e., unless one possesses, in a belief-like way, a representation with that content. Development of this response is a job for Chapter 4, where I discuss the reasoning expressed by arguments in reason-giving ways.

3.4.5. Summary

In order to use an argument in a reason-giving way, one must state the argument. By stating the argument, one conveys the associated inference claim. How must the inference claim be conveyed? I've motivated the conditions *Belief, Value,* and *Primary* using the connection between reason-giving uses of arguments and their associated inference claims. Of the alternatives considered here, I have argued that assertion best satisfies *Belief, Value,* and *Primary* as opposed to mere implication and implicature. Accordingly, when stating an argument in order to give reasons for its conclusion, one asserts the corresponding inference claim as opposed to merely implying or implicating it.

---

[19] For other ways that something can be merely implicitly believed see Harman 1986, pp. 13–14.

Left open here is the question of how one's statement of an argument that is a dialectical argument conveys the associated inference claim when one doesn't believe it. Again, I take assertions to be essentially expressions of belief. On my view, when one states an argument whose premises one advances as reasons for believing the conclusion and one doesn't believe that they are such reasons, then one does not assert the associated inference claim. The assertion of an inference claim in the statement of an argument is symptomatic of the distinction between using an argument to advance its premises as reasons for the believing the conclusion and actually using the argument to give reasons for believing the conclusion.

3.5. Conclusion

The two central claims of Chapter 3 are (I) a reason-giving use of argument isn't successful unless the corresponding inference claim is true; and (II) an inference claim is conveyed by one's statement of an argument used to give reasons for its conclusion by means of assertion as opposed to being merely implied or implicated. One way (I) and (II) are related is as follows.

According to (II), when you state an argument in order to give reasons for believing the conclusion, you thereby express your belief that the premises are reasons for believing the conclusion. From (I), your reason-giving isn't successful unless the inference-claim belief you express is true, i.e., unless the premises are reasons for believing the conclusion in the intended sense. Hence if your reason-giving use of an argument is successful, your inference-claim belief, which you express in stating the argument, is true.

4

Reflective Inferences

4.1. Preamble

A theoretical inference is reflective only if the inferer performs the inference because they believe that the premises are reasons for believing the conclusion in one of the senses discussed in Chapter 3.[1] J. S. Mill is right: "To draw inferences has been said to be the great business of life" (1875, p. 8). However, not all inferences are reflective.[2] An essential feature of reflective inferences is that they are accompanied by a linking belief, i.e., the belief that the inference's premises are reasons of some sort for believing the conclusion. For example, returning from her walk Paige wonders whether Beth is at home. She sees and so believes that Beth's car is in the driveway. She then infers and thereby believes that Beth is home, because she takes Beth's car in the driveway to be a reason to believe that Beth is at home. Paige's inference is reflective only if her *taking* that Beth's car is in the driveway to be a reason to believe that Beth is at home involves her *believing* this.

Reflective inferences are connected to reason-giving uses of arguments in the following two ways.

(I) If you perform a reflective inference, then you use the corresponding argument in a reason-giving way.

(II) If you use an argument in a reason-giving way, then you have performed a reflective inference from its premises to conclusion.

---

[1] The conclusion of a theoretical inference concerns what to believe, whereas the conclusion of a practical inference is about what to do. In this chapter, I consider reflective inferences in terms of theoretical inferences.

[2] "Humans . . . cannot spend a minute of their waking life without making inferences. On the other hand, they can spend hours or even days without ever engaging in reasoning" (Mercier and Sperber 2017, p. 55). As I clarify below, reflective inference qualifies as "reasoning" in their sense because, loosely, it is "extracting new information from available information attending to reasons" (2017, p. 55).

Arguments and Reason-Giving. Matthew W. McKeon, Oxford University Press. © Oxford University Press 2024. DOI: 10.1093/oso/9780197751633.003.0004

The central business of Chapter 4 is identifying distinguishing features of reflective inferences in order to ground theses (I) and (II) in a way that accounts for why reflective inferences are necessarily accompanied by a linking belief. Toward this end, I'll consider what qualifies an inference as an episode of critical thinking. From this I will generate my conception of a reflective inference. It will turn out that if an inference counts as episode of critical thinking, then it is a reflective inference. However, not all reflective inferences count as critical thinking.

My defense and elaboration of (I) and (II) starts by asking, what features must an inference have for it to qualify as instance of critical thinking? To answer this question, I consider the nature of critical thinking as understood by philosophers, higher-education theorists, and cognitive psychologists. To be sure, there is no universally accepted definition in the large and diffuse interdisciplinary literature on critical thinking (for good reviews see Davies 2015; Fisher 2019; and Hitchcock 2020). My aim here is to draw on this literature to develop a plausible understanding of critical thinking that is robust enough to extrapolate essential features of reflective inference that I appeal to in defending (I) and (II).

Looking ahead, in Chapter 5 I ask: What are the norms guiding reason-giving uses of arguments that make the formal validity of an argument germane to whether a given reason-giving use of it is good? My general strategy for developing a response is as follows. First, I take formally valid arguments to be demonstrative arguments and I explain what makes an argument demonstrative. Then I identify the norms guiding reason-giving uses of arguments that make an argument's being demonstrative matter to whether certain reason-giving uses of it are good. I develop my response to Chapter 5's question in a way that clarifies when and how the formal validity of an argument is relevant to whether a corresponding reflective inference is good.

4.2. Critical Thinking

It is widely considered among philosophers and education theorists that a primary goal of secondary and higher education is to develop students into lifelong critical thinkers (e.g., Dewey 1933, chap. 2; Kuhn and Dean 2004, pp. 268–69; Willingham 2008, p. 21; Davies and Barnett 2015, pp. 2–3, 21–23; Siegel 1988, p. 2; Hitchcock 2017a, pp. 488–89). Reviews of the critical-thinking literature acknowledge the widespread disagreement about the nature of critical thinking and how best to define it so that it informs curriculum and pedagogy in elementary, secondary, and higher education (e.g., see Bailin et al. 1999; Davies 2015; Davies and Barnett 2015; and Hitchcock 2020).

I consider critical thinking not to defend a particular conception of it, but rather to isolate commonly accepted features relevant to understanding what makes the performance of an inference count as an act of critical thinking. Accordingly, my discussion will be strategic. Its central focus is on three well-known characterizations of critical thinking (Dewey 1933; Facione 1990; Lipman 2003). Working primarily from these sources, I isolate essential features of critical thinking that an inference must have for it to be critical thinking. This will generate my understanding of reflective inference according to which reflective inferences are active, purposeful, persistent, and criterial, as explained below.

4.2.1. Baseline Characterizations of Critical Thinking

A typical philosophical account of critical thinking has four components: (i) a baseline characterization of critical thinking; (ii) specification of core critical-thinking skills; (iii) specification of character traits or habits of mind definitive of critical thinkers; and (iv) a specification of the various phases of critical thinking.[3]

Baseline characterizations of critical thinking are commonly considered to be stipulative (Ennis 1991, pp. 6–7; Johnson 2014, p. 205). They motivate and set the parameters for developing (ii)–(iv). The rationale for (ii) is that since critical thinking is a skillful activity, an account of such thinking needs to highlight core critical-thinking skills. Since good critical thinkers use their critical-thinking skills well, a proper critical-thinking curriculum must induce the necessary affective and cognitive dispositions that trigger and regulate the exercise of critical-thinking skills. Hence, the rationale for (iii). Borrowing from Davies (2015, p. 44), (iii) captures the individual (i.e., personal) dimension of critical thinking. Component (iv) uncovers the structure of critical thinking, which I touch on below. Proper development

---

[3] For example, the accounts of critical thinking advanced by Ennis 1991; Facione 1990; Bailin et al. 1999; Hitchcock 2017b. To quickly illustrate, Ennis gives a baseline characterization of critical thinking (1991, p. 6), which provides a rationale for his list of critical-thinking dispositions and critical-thinking abilities (pp. 8–9). Ennis describes the phases of critical thinking (p. 7) and then illustrates them with an example based on real-life critical thinking (pp. 10–20). Taken together, this constitutes what he calls a streamlined conception of critical thinking.

of (i)–(iv) should generate a concrete picture of both critical thinking and critical thinkers. My discussion of critical thinking concentrates on (i), only briefly engaging with (ii)–(iv). I start with Dewey.

4.2.1.1. Dewey, *How We Think* (1933)

It is widely acknowledged that Dewey's book-length discussion of reflective thinking offers the first explicit characterization in print of what later came to be called critical thinking (e.g., Fisher 2019, p. 7; Hitchcock 2017a, p. 478; Lipman 2003, p. 35). Here I sketch Dewey's influential views expressed in 1933 regarding what constitutes reflective thinking, what triggers such thinking, and its intended aim.

Dewey's baseline characterization of reflective thinking is as follows.

> Reflective thinking is active, persistent, and careful consideration of a belief or supposed form of knowledge in light of the grounds which support it and the further conclusions to which it tends. (1933, p. 9)

Before addressing how reflective thinking is active, persistent, and careful, it is worth noting for my later characterization of reflective inference that Dewey's characterization picks out what I call forward and reverse reflective reasoning.[4] *Forward reflective reasoning* is the active, persistent, and careful consideration of a belief or supposed form of knowledge in light of the further considerations to which it tends. I now schematically illustrate such reasoning aimed at deciding what to believe.

A person S draws a conclusion p (about what is the case or what one should do) because S takes p to follow from their beliefs. S then deliberates about whether to believe p, because (i) S takes themself to be committed to the truth of p and because (ii) S takes the issue of whether to accept p to be important. Both (i) and (ii) motivate S to decide whether to accept p. Two possible outcomes: (+) S decides that their beliefs constitute good reasons to accept p; i.e., S decides that they support the truth of p; or (–) S decides that their beliefs do not constitute good reasons to accept p. Outcome (+) induces S's belief that p is true. On the other hand, outcome (–) induces S's disbelief

---

[4] Walton also acknowledges the directionality of reasoning. "Reasoning normally has a direction. Most often, as already mentioned, it moves 'forward' from the premise toward the conclusion. Directionality of reasoning depends, however, on how it is being used in a context of argument. There can be 'backward' reasoning in some instances—for example in a kind of case where a conclusion is known and the reasons (premises) supporting the conclusion are sought out. Backtracking of this sort is not always reasoning, but it can be a kind of reasoning in some cases" (1990, p. 404).

of a formerly held belief (i.e., (−) induces S to reject a formerly held belief or become agnostic and refrain from accepting it or rejecting it).

I now consider *reverse reflective reasoning* in terms of active, persistent, and careful consideration of a belief in light of the grounds which support it. In developing his conception of reflective thinking, Dewey emphasizes the difference between believing that something is the case and being reflective in so believing. Consider the thoughts we by happenstance pick up from others and unreflectively accept.

> Such "thoughts" grow up unconsciously. They are picked up—we know not how. From obscure sources and by unnoticed channels they insinuate themselves into our mind and become unconsciously a part of our mental furniture. Tradition, instruction, imitation—all of which depend upon authority in some form, or appeal to our own advantage, or fall in with a strong passion—are responsible for them. Such thoughts are prejudices; that is, prejudgments, not conclusions reached as the result of personal mental activity, such as observing, collecting, and examining evidence. Even when they happen to be correct, their correctness is a matter of accident as far as the person who entertains them is concerned. (1933, p. 7)

For sure, in my cognitive history there are many examples of such "thoughts." Here's a quick one. In grade school I had to memorize the names of the planets. As an adult, I was certain that Earth is a planet. Learning that Pluto's status as a planet was controversial made me realize that I didn't have a clue about what counts as a planet. Therefore, I was unable to personalize my justification of my belief that Earth is a planet. My desire to assume responsibility for sustaining this belief motivated me to learn the criteria of planethood from NASA's website. This enabled me to personally justify that Earth is a planet and understand why Pluto's status as a planet is controversial.

The starting point of your *reverse reflective reasoning* is one of your beliefs. Generally, the aim of such reasoning is to justify your belief by becoming aware of the grounds for its truth. Your reasoning doesn't generate your belief of the conclusion since you already believe it. Rather, it is confirmative. The support you identify sustains your belief in a way that enables you to play an active part in maintaining it. A motivation for engaging in such reasoning is a desire to think for oneself and draw one's own conclusions.

Turning to another topic, Dewey says that reflection implies belief on evidence.

Reflection thus implies that something is believed in (or disbelieved in), not on its own direct account, but through something else which stands as witness, evidence, proof, voucher, warrant; that is, as *ground of belief.* (1933, p. 11)

For example, borrowing from Dewey, we distinguish between your believing that it is raining, because you see that it is raining, and your inferring that it rained from seeing the wet streets. Dewey holds that if you infer something through something else that you see, then this counts as reflective thinking only if "the seen thing is regarded as in some way *the ground or basis of belief* in the suggested thing; it possesses the quality of *evidence*" (1933, p. 10). To illustrate what I take Dewey to be driving at, consider scenarios (A) and (B).

(A) Paige is vacuuming the couch. She finds a pen between the cushions. She recognizes it as the pen Paige gave Beth for a past birthday, and so believes this. Paige next thinks that Beth's birthday is next week.

(B) Paige is returning from her walk. She sees a car in the driveway. She recognizes it as Beth's car and so believes that Beth's car is in the driveway. Paige next thinks that Beth is at home.

What would qualify one of these series of beliefs as the performance of an inference? It is hard to imagine that Paige's mental transition in (A) counts as the performance of an inference, because it is hard to imagine that somebody would count that Beth's pen was between the cushions as evidence that her birthday is next week. On the other hand, it is plausible to think that in scenario (B) Paige performs an inference because it is imaginable that Beth's car being in the driveway counts as evidence that Beth is at home.

What triggers reflective thinking? Paraphrasing Dewey, [R]reflective thinking originates in a state of doubt, hesitation, perplexity, or mental difficulty and involves searching, hunting, or inquiring to find material that will resolve the doubt, settle and dispose the perplexity (1933, p. 12). "Demand for the solution of a perplexity is the steadying and guiding factor in the entire process of refection" (p. 14). Hence, "The nature of the problem fixes the end of thought, and the end controls the process of thinking" (p. 15).

There are two features, cognitive and affective, of typical triggers of reflective thinking. First, there is a disruption in belief maintenance (a challenge to maintaining a belief, e.g., something is experienced that raises doubt that one's belief is true); or a difficulty in belief acquisition (deciding what to indirectly believe in challenging contexts, e.g., answering questions for oneself with non-obvious answers) that isn't resolvable solely by observation or quick thinking. Second, there is a desire to believe for oneself about what is the case that is strong enough to induce an attempt to form a judgment that resolves the experienced perplexity. In short, the aim of reflective thinking is the resolution of a perplexity or state of wonder that results in a judgment.

Dewey gives numerous examples of reflective thinking. (See Hitchcock 2020 for a useful review and discussion of Dewey's many examples.) I start with two homegrown examples, and then use two of Dewey's examples.

> *Home.* Kelly arrives home in the later afternoon after work and wonders whether someone is at home. She hears a noise upstairs, but then thinks that it might be the cat. She hears music from the alarm/clock radio in Paige's bedroom, but recalls that Paige often forgets to shut the alarm off. Kelly thinks that it might have been playing since this morning. She then notices the teapot being heated on the stove and sees a nearby empty cup with a teabag. She knows that Mom is the only one in the home that drinks tea. She concludes that Mom is home.

Kelly's thinking is triggered by wondering who else if anybody is at home. Her thinking, aimed at settling this, is informed by experience (e.g., it is only Mom that drinks tea; tea-loving friends, relatives, or strangers never let themselves in), and relevant general knowledge (e.g., unlike alarm clocks, their oven doesn't turn on automatically; the cat, unlike the aquarium fish upstairs, can make noises). Kelly's thinking concludes with a judgment based on reasoning from evidence.

> *Knights/knaves.* In logic class, Paige's teacher presents the following puzzle: knaves always lie and knights always tell the truth. Every native is either a knight or a knave. Two natives approach you, and one says, "We are not both knights." Can you determine the identity of the two natives? This triggers Paige's thinking. The thought pops into her head that the native that speaks is a knave. To test this idea, Paige supposes it is true and infers that what the native says true. However, she thinks that this can't be right because what knaves say is never true. Since every native is either a knight or a knave, she infers that the native that speaks is a knight. Since knights always speak the truth and what the knight says is "We are not both knights,"

she infers that the other native is a knave. She concludes that the speaker is a knight and the other native is a knave.

The initial material for resolving the problem is given and so, unlike in the first scenario, evidence gathering is unnecessary. Reflective thinking is conscious and effortful. If Paige's conclusion just popped into her head from her subconscious, as sometimes happens when solving puzzles, then her thinking wouldn't qualify as reflective. That both Kelly and Paige think in order to decide what to believe illustrates the inherent intentionality of reflective thinking.

As illustrated by *Home*, background knowledge guides evidence gathering and drawing conclusions. Dewey's many examples of reflective thinking illustrate the various ways background knowledge matters to reflective thinking in ordinary, everyday contexts. Consider *Burglary*.

> [*Burglary*.] A man who has left his room in order finds it upon his return in a state of confusion, articles being scattered at random. Automatically, the notion comes to his mind that burglary would account for the disorder. . . . The state of the room is a *fact*, certain, speaking for itself; the presence of the burglars is a possibility that may explain the facts. (1933, 166–67)

A little afterward, Dewey comments on the importance of hypotheses as guides to gathering evidence.

> The real problem is: What facts are *evidence* in this case? The search for evidential facts is best conducted when some suggested *possible* meaning is used as a guide in exploring facts, especially in instituting a hunt for some fact that would point to one explanation and exclude all others. (1933, 168)

Besides the possibility of burglary, the man entertains the possibilities that a member of the family had an urgent need to find something and didn't clean up afterward, and that children in the family are responsible. Clearly, the man's background knowledge is operative here: he'll only consider initial possibilities that are real to him, e.g., "[T]he children are not above mischief on occasion" (p. 168). Before searching for facts that would explain the disorder, the man infers from each conjectured possibility what follows if it's what happened. For example, if it is burglary, then an article is missing. The man checks and finds jewelry missing. Also, he observes damage to some items. Give his background knowledge, he takes these observations to rule out all other hypotheses but burglary. Given his knowledge of the entry points to the room, he concludes that burglary would imply a forced entry into the room. He then examines the window and sees that it has been tampered with—"a fact consistent only with the action of a burglar" (p. 168). He concludes that burglary best explains the disorder.

In the following scenario, "[N]either the problem nor mode of solution would have occurred except to one with some prior scientific training" (1933, p. 94).

[*Tumblers.*] In washing tumblers in hot soapsuds and placing them mouth downward on a plate, bubbles appeared on the outside of the mouth of the tumblers and then went inside. Why? The presence of bubbles suggests air, which I note must come from inside the tumbler. I see that the soapy water on the plate prevents escape of the air save as it may be caught in bubbles. But why should air leave the tumbler? There was no substance entering to force it out. It must have expanded. It expands by increase of heat, or by decrease of pressure, or both. Could the air have become heated after the tumbler was taken from the hot suds? Clearly not the air that was already entangled in the water. If heated air was the cause, cold air must have entered in transferring the tumblers from the suds to the plate. I test to see if this supposition is true by taking several more tumblers out. Some I shake so as to make sure of entrapping cold air in them. Some I take out holding mouth downward in order to prevent cold air from entering. Bubbles appear on the outside of every one of the former and on none of the latter. I must be right in my inference. Air from the outside must have been expanded by the heat of the tumbler, which explains the appearance of the bubbles on the outside. But why do they then go inside? Cold contracts. The tumbler cooled and also the air inside it. Tension was removed, and hence bubbles appeared inside. To be sure of this, I test by placing a cup of ice on the tumbler while the bubbles are still forming outside. They soon reverse. (1933, pp. 93–94)

The protagonist uses his background knowledge of established scientific fact and principles to infer the explanation of the movement of water in the form of bubbles from the outside to the inside of the tumbler (1933, p. 95). He verifies his explanation by placing a cup of ice on the tumbler and observes that bubbles behave as they should if the explanation is correct. Dewey intentionally models the structure of reflective thinking on the scientific method of inquiry (1933, pp. 171–78).

This brings us to my next point. Reflective thinking, which aims to resolve a question or intellectual problem, takes the form of an inquiry. Simplifying Dewey's account of the reflective-thinking process, such an inquiry if successful typically has three phases, considered in a general way as follows.[5] First, material relevant to resolving the question is gathered or if already at hand brought into focus for consideration. Second, this material is evaluated as evidence that justifies an answer to the initial question or intellectual problem that triggered the inquiry. Third, based on the evaluation, an inference is performed from some of the material considered as evidence to a judgment that resolves the operative question or intellectual problem. If one's judgment that p is an outcome of reflective thinking, then one believes p in light of reasons. Specifically, one believes p because one believes that one has reasons to believe that p is true.

Dewey emphasizes the importance to being a reflective thinker of habits of mind that regulate critical thinking (e.g., open-mindedness, wholeheartedness, intellectual responsibility [1933, pp. 28–33]), and affective dispositions that increase the likelihood that reflective thinking is triggered (e.g., curiosity [1933, pp. 36–40]). For Dewey, reflective thinkers are curious and actively desire that their beliefs be reasonably generated and sustained. In short, a reflective thinker has an appropriate desire for truth, knowledge, and understanding, is actively committed to believing reasonably in satisfying this desire, and possesses the necessary skill sets to conduct the associated inquiries.

As noted earlier, Dewey's baseline characterization of reflective thinking says that it is *active, persistent*, and *careful*. The previous illustrations exemplify these features of reflective thinking. I now conclude my discussion of Dewey's baseline characterization of reflective thinking by briefly considering each.

That reflective thinking is *active* signifies its personal dimension. Dewey's concept of reflective thinking is an agential concept of thinking. Reflective

---

[5] Dewey describes five phases of reflective thought (1933, pp. 107–15): (1) *suggestions*, in which the mind leaps forward to a possible solution; (2) an intellectualization of the difficulty or perplexity into a *problem* to be solved, a question for which the answer must be sought; (3) the use of one suggestion after another as a leading idea, or *hypothesis*, to initiate and guide observation and other operations in collection of factual material; (4) the mental elaboration of the idea or supposition as an idea or supposition (*reasoning*, in the sense on which reasoning is a part, not the whole, of inference); and (5) testing the hypothesis by overt or imaginative action.

thinking is not a sub-personal, automated process (e.g., like the visual processing of information) or mental transition. It is intentional. That is, reflective thinking is thinking done in order to decide what to believe or do based on evidence. Accordingly, it is appropriate to hold you responsible for your reflective thinking.

Reflective thinking is *persistent* because, in part, it takes the form of an effortful inquiry and thus extends over the period needed for its phases to run their course. Ideally, the inquiry ends with a judgment that resolves the question, intellectual challenge, or mental difficulty that triggered it. A reflective thinker engaged in reflective thinking is persistent in maintaining the intellectual stamina and focus needed to resolve what triggered the thinking in the first place. This involves enduring the tension induced by perplexity so as to not jump to conclusions and involves suspending final judgment until all the evidence is gathered.

Finally, one's reflective thinking is *careful*, because for one to think reflectively one must think conscientiously; i.e., one's thinking is contemporaneous with being mindful of the operative norms and rules that one believes should guide one's thinking. Put in another way: reflective thinking is careful in part by being self-regulating. In his discussion of Dewey, Lipman puts it this way.

> *Reflective* thinking is thinking that is aware of its own assumptions and implications as well as being conscious of the reasons and evidence that support this or that conclusion. Reflective thinking takes into account its own methodology, its own procedures, its own perspective and point of view. Reflective thinking is prepared to recognize the factors that make for bias, prejudice, and self-deception. It involves *thinking about its procedures* at the same time it involves *thinking about its subject matter*. (2003, p. 26)

Intellectual carefulness is an excellence partly because the intellectually careful person habitually understands what must be attended to and when in order to successfully accomplish their intellectual tasks. Since reflective thinking more or less requires substantive effort, there is a realistic possibility of getting things wrong. Accordingly, being careful requires thinking that considers its own methodology, its own procedures, its own perspective and point of view. This implies knowing what would qualify in the operative context as evidence sufficient for justifying a belief. I now turn to Lipman's characterization of critical thinking.

4.2.1.2. Lipman, *Thinking in Education* (2003)

Critical thinking is thinking that (1) facilitates judgment because it (2) relies on criteria, (3) is self-correcting and (4) is sensitive to context (Lipman 2003, pp. 211–12)

Starting with (1), I now discuss each of the four facets of Lipman's characterization. I won't spend much time on (4).

(1) Critical thinking is thinking that facilitates judgment. Like Dewey's notion of *reflective thinking*, Lipman's conception of critical thinking makes it essentially purposeful. It is widely accepted that critical thinking is thinking aimed at forming a judgment in service of some purpose or end, "such as answering a question, making a decision, solving a problem, resolving an issue, devising a plan, or carrying out a project" (Bailin et al. 1999, p. 287).

Accordingly, it is thinking that has an intended terminus, which is a judgment that resolves the matter at hand. Compare: in logic class you construct a random deduction. This qualifies as "thinking" in some sense, but it isn't "critical thinking" unless it serves an intended aim. Mindless application of a set of logical principles "as an exercise" does not suffice as purposeful thinking—likewise with idle musing, daydreaming, and associative thinking. You see Beth's pen on the couch, which reminds you that it is Beth's birthday next week, which, in turn, leads you to remember the movie you two saw last week. This is merely associative thinking and so doesn't qualify as critical thinking because it isn't conducted by you in order to serve a purpose.

(2) Why and how does critical thinking *rely* on criteria? I first address the why and then the how. Lipman believes that critical thinking is skillful thinking and so cannot be understood without the operative criteria by means of which an episode of critical thinking can be evaluated. So, "[C]ritical thinking is reliable [i.e., skillful] thinking that both employs criteria and can be assessed by appeal to criteria" (Lipman 2003, p. 212).

Not all activities have performance standards.[6] Compare doodling to writing English or daydreaming to reciting a poem. Lipman illustrates the essential connection between criteria and skillful practice.

---

[6] Lipman distinguishes between meta-criteria and mega-criteria (2003, p. 215). He says that criteria for judging that something is the case are reasons that provide a warrant for the judgment. Meta-criteria are the criteria for selecting reasons for judgment such as reliability, strength, relevance, coherence, precision, and consistency. The deployment of meta-criteria seems to involve what Kuhn (1999) calls second-order cognition (discussed below). Also, Lipman distinguishes between standards and criteria. "Standards represent the degree to which a given criterion must be satisfied" (2003, p. 217). Age is a criterion for legally drinking; a US standard for legally drinking is age twenty-one.

Thus, architects will judge a building by employing such criteria as *utility*, *safety*, and *beauty*; magistrates make judgments with the aid of such criteria *legality* and *illegality*; and critical thinkers rely upon such time-tested criteria as *validity*, *evidential warrant* and *consistency*. Any area of practice—like the examples just given of architectural practice, judicial practice, and cognitive practice—should be able to cite the criteria by which that practice is guided. (2003, p. 213)

Every area of intelligent human inquiry and practice, such as science, art, and medicine, embodies within it practices of criticism by which judgments regarding what to believe or how to act are tested, criticized, and revised. The cognitive practices of critical thinking (e.g., gathering evidence, evaluating evidence, drawing conclusions) essentially admit of criteria by which they are guided. Bailin et al. claim that critical thinking essentially satisfies operative standards.

[T]hinking about what to believe or do must meet appropriate *standards* if it is to be regarded as critical thinking. Moreover, these standards cannot be met merely by accident or happenstance. If someone were inadvertently to fulfil relevant standards in their thinking, but had not intentionally attempted to fulfil them, they would not generally be regarded as having engaged in critical thinking. To be engaged in critical thinking one must be aware that there are such standards and must be striving to fulfil them. This is not to say, of course, that a person engaged in thinking critically is necessarily able to state or verbally explicate the relevant standards. (1999, p. 287)

They note that fulfilling the standards is not an all-or-nothing affair. "We sometimes talk about good or poor critical thinking to indicate the degree of fulfillment of the relevant standards" (p. 287).

How does critical thinking rely on criteria? At least in the following two ways: (a) cognitively and (b) constitutively. Specifically, (a) the thinker is *trying* to fulfill standards of adequacy appropriate to the thinking; (b) the thinking *fulfills* the relevant standards to some threshold level. I now elaborate, starting with (a).

Hitchcock (1983) sees critical thinking as thinking that uses the standards of reason to decide what to believe and what to do. For example, one uses standards of reason in judging the probability of a sampling error, establishing a control group, standardizing procedures for evidence gathering, or using reliable measurements. Since critical thinking is thinking that is done in conformity with the relevant standards, those who think critically do so in full knowledge and awareness of the expected standards of thinking (even if they cannot verbalize these "standards").

Regarding (b), taking critical thinking to be necessarily reliant on criteria makes critical thinking essentially normative, i.e., makes critical thinking constitutively normative. Critical thinking is necessarily good thinking by virtue of meeting adequate standards. As noted by Bailin et al. (1999, p. 45), this makes the quality of thinking determinative of whether it qualifies as critical thinking. For example, fallacious thinking is contrary to critical thinking. Using questionable evidence, failure to assess sources, and relying on dubious authority isn't thinking critically (1999, p. 45). In short, critical thinking is necessarily good thinking by virtue of satisfying operative standards.

Both (1) and (2) of Lipman's characterization of critical thinking concur with Ennis's well-known baseline characterization of critical thinking. "Critical thinking is reasonable, reflective thinking focused on deciding what to believe or do" (1991, p. 6). Re (1): critical thinking is done for the purpose of making up one's mind about what to believe or do. This makes it active, first-person thinking. Re (2): (a) the thinking is reflective in that the thinker is trying to fulfill standards of adequacy appropriate to the thinking; and (b) critical thinking is reasonable in the sense that it fulfills relevant standards to some minimal threshold level.

That critical thinking is essentially criterial, understood in terms of (a) and (b) taken together, is reflected in Siegel's well-known characterization of critical thinking.

To be a critical thinker is to be appropriately moved by reasons. To be a rational person is to believe and act on the basis of reasons. There is then a deep conceptual connection, by way of the notion of reasons, between critical thinkers and rational persons. Critical thinking is best conceived, consequently, as the educational cognate of rationality: critical thinking involves bringing to bear all matters relevant to the rationality of belief and action; and education aimed at the promulgation of critical thinking is nothing less than education aimed at the fostering of rationality and the development of rational persons. (1988, p. 32)

Siegel conceives of critical thinking as a form of rational thinking and thereby makes critical thinking essentially normative in conformity with (b). For Siegel, critical thinking is necessarily good thinking because it is necessarily rational thinking, and all rational thinking is good thinking in the sense of satisfying operative standards. What is it to be "appropriately moved by reasons"? For example, if you judge that p, then what must be true of your act of judging if it is to be "appropriately moved by reasons"? Working from Siegel, I develop a response in three steps.

First, Siegel remarks that a "critical thinker is one who appreciates and accepts the importance and convicting force of reasons" (1988, p. 33). This reflects (a). Second, the critical thinker's appreciation and acceptance of the convincing force of reasons manifests itself in their acts of "assessing claims, making judgments, evaluating procedures, or contemplating alternative actions" (1988, p. 33). Third, how, exactly, is this manifested in such acts? By their success! A critical thinker's appreciation and acceptance of the convincing force of reasons is evidenced by their successful search of (good) reasons on which to base their "assessments, judgements, and actions" (1988, p. 33). Importantly, "To seek reasons, moreover, is to recognize and commit oneself to principles, for, as R.S. Peters put it, 'principles are needed to determine the relevance [and strength] of reasons'" (1988, p. 33).

Let's tie this together in response to the question, what is it to be "appropriately moved by reasons"? If you judge that p, then for your act of judging to be appropriately moved by reasons you have the *true belief* that you have good reasons in support of your judgment that p and *this belief is justified* by your recognition of and commitment to a principle whose truth grounds your support for your judgment that your reasons to believe p are *good*.

Siegel quotes Scheffler approvingly with a passage that starts with "[R]eason is always a matter of abiding by general rules or principles." Given my response to the question posed at the start of the previous paragraph, "abiding" is not merely "reasoning in agreement with general rules or principles," but rather "accepting in a way that involves believing general rules or principles" or "acting intentionally in accordance with general rules or principles," which involves believing the operative general rules or principles. To illustrate the cognitive import of judging that is appropriately moved by reasons, let's use Siegel's example that he uses to illustrate the connection between reasons, consistency, and principles.

Johnny's teacher keeps him after class one day for throwing spitballs. The teacher explains to his parents that the reason why Johnny stayed after was for being disruptive in class. "For this belief to properly count as a reason, the teacher must be committed to some principle which licenses or backs that reason, i.e., establishes it as a bona fide reason, e.g., all disruptive student behavior warrants keeping students after class" (1988, p. 33). If the teacher does not consistently apply this principle, then her putative reasons for keeping Johnny after class, i.e., Johnny's disruptive behavior, does not constitute a genuine reason. For example, "by noting that Mary, who also threw spitballs, was not kept after class, Johnny might well say: 'Since you don't apply any relevant principle consistently, you have no reason to keep me after class. If throwing spitballs is not a reason for detaining Mary, it cannot be a reason for detaining me either.'" (1988, p. 33)

After acknowledging the possibility of mitigating circumstances, Siegel remarks that "the point remains that the teacher's putative reason is rightly regarded as a reason, which warrants or justifies her behavior, only if it is backed by some principle which (can itself be justified and) is consistently applied in relevantly similar cases" (1988, p. 34). The teacher believes that Johnny was disruptive in class. For this to be a reason that warrants the teacher's judgment that Johnny should be kept after class, the teacher must be committed to some principle such as *all disruptive student behavior warrants keeping students after class*. If the teacher's reasoning from her belief (i) that Johnny behavior in class was disruptive to her judgment that (ii) Johnny should be kept after class counts as critical thinking, then the teacher's commitment to the operative principle is *doxastic*. That is, the teacher recognizes the force of the principle and *believes* that the principle is true.

Accordingly, the teacher believes that (i) is a reason to believe (ii). This illustrates the twofold cognitive import of one's judging that p being appropriately moved by a reason, say q, to believe p. One must believe that q is a reason to believe p and one must recognize and thereby believe a principle by virtue of which q is a reason to believe p. Furthermore, the teacher's reasoning counts as critical thinking only if her belief that q is a reason to believe p is true and she can justify this in terms of the operative principle.

In short, Siegel's characterization of critical thinking satisfies (a) and (b) as follows.

Regarding (a): the thinker is *trying* to fulfill standards of adequacy appropriate to their reasoning by virtue of abiding by the operative principle(s), which involves recognizing and committing to the principle(s). Regarding (b): critical thinking *fulfills* the relevant standards to some minimal threshold since it is principled thinking (Siegel 1988, p. 34) in the way exemplified in the above *Spitball* scenario. Schematically, "p is a reason for q only if some principle r renders p a reason for q, and would equally render p' a reason for q' if p and p' and q and q' *are* relevantly similar" (p. 34). Ignoring complexities such as explaining the relation of relevant similarity, this reflects (b) taking the operative principle to be the operative standard.

In sum, an episode of critical thinking is essentially reliant on criteria at least in the following two ways: (a) the thinker is *trying* to fulfill standards of adequacy appropriate to the thinking; and (b) the thinking *fulfills* the relevant standards to some threshold level. Thesis (a) provides a rationale for why critical thinking is an "intellectually disciplined process" (Scriven and Paul 1987). Thesis (b) accounts for why critical thinking is essentially normative. It is good thinking in the sense that it necessarily fulfills the operative standards to some minimum threshold. Thesis (a) suggests that there must be some kind of meta-cognitive awareness when one thinks critically (e.g., see Mulnix 2012, p. 465). This brings us to the next feature of critical thinking in Lipman's characterization.

(3) *Critical thinking is self-correcting*, i.e., *self-regulative* (e.g., Facione 1990, p. 3). We sometimes think about our thinking. For example, sometimes we ask: Should I gather more evidence before deciding what to believe? Should I change my mind regarding my opinion? Are my beliefs consistent? Is this the best strategy for my thinking about this problem? When people ask such questions, they are adopting a regulative stance to their thinking. Roughly, *self-regulation* is understood to mean

> [s]elf-consciously to monitor one's cognitive activities, the elements used on those activities, and the results educed, particularly by applying skills in analysis, and evaluation to one's own inferential judgments with a view toward questioning, confirming, validating, or correcting one's reasoning or one's results. (Facione 1990, p. 22)

In his historical review of baseline characterizations of critical thinking, Fisher (2019, p. 12) acknowledges as typical the importance of "thinking about one's thinking" to thinking critically. For example, consider the following characterization.

> Critical thinking is that mode of thinking—about any subject, content or problem—in which the thinker improves the quality of his or her thinking by skillfully taking charge of the structures inherent in thinking and imposing intellectual standards upon them. (Paul, Fischer, and Nosich 1993, p. 4)

It is widely acknowledged that thinking critically involves exercising competencies with respect to imposing relevant standards upon one's thinking (see Davies 2015; Halonen 1995; Halpern 1998; Hitchcock 2017b; Kuhn and Dean 2004; Martinez 2006; Swartz and Perkins 2017, among many others). This involves a capacity for recognizing what standards are relevant, and understanding those that are relevant to help ensure that they are correctly applied. Notice how this connects with the criterial dimension of critical thinking, discussed just above. For example, we said that (a) the critical thinker is *trying* to fulfill standards of adequacy appropriate their thinking. This brings into play competencies with respect to imposing relevant standards upon one's thinking so that it is more likely than not that (b) the thinking *fulfills* the relevant standards to some threshold level.

Thinking about thinking is second-order thinking. Looking for evidence to determine whether Beth is at home is first-order thinking. Thinking about whether your belief that Beth's car is in the driveway warrants believing that Beth is at home is second-order thinking. In order to sharpen our understanding some of the competencies for second-order thinking germane to critical thinking, I now consider work from the educational psychologist Deanna Kuhn.

Kuhn identifies three such competencies, which she labels *meta-knowing* competencies: *meta-strategic*, *meta-cognitive*, and *epistemological* competencies (1999, p. 18). A unifying dimension of the development of these meta-knowing competencies is "that of thought becoming increasingly aware of itself and under the individual's control" (1999, p. 23). I first sketch these *meta-knowing* competencies and then connect them to critical thinking.

Meta-strategic competency is competency in selecting thinking strategies and effectively monitoring their application. It is associated with a procedural understanding of one's thinking. Roughly, it is knowing how to think in order to realize a particular cognitive aim. In tackling a variety of thinking tasks, we sometimes deploy meta-strategic, e.g., how-to cues to guide our thinking process. For example, consider a Wordle strategy that says to start with a word that has the most vowels, or the crossword strategy that says first do the easiest clues, e.g., the fill-in-the-blank clues. Being meta-strategic in engaging challenging intellectual tasks involves regularly stepping back mentally "to appraise and rework plans by asking such questions as, what am I trying to accomplish? What are the most promising pathways? Is my strategy working?" (Martinez 2006, p. 697).

Meta-cognitive competency refers to an understanding of one's own knowledge state, being aware of what one knows and how one knows it. "To be competent and motivated to 'know how you know' puts one in charge of one's knowing, of deciding what to believe and why and of updating and revising those beliefs as one deems warranted" (Kuhn 1999, p. 23). Think about being asked if you can name the first ten US presidents in order. You either can do so or you cannot. But your honest answer to the question might be yes or no in either case. That is, you can be accurate or inaccurate in your appraisal of your own knowledge. In a nutshell, being meta-cognitively competent is to have achieved a high degree of Socratic wisdom, which involves a recognition of the extent of one's own ignorance. Socratic folly, on the other hand, is the meta-cognitive error of believing one knows when, in fact, one does not (Martinez 2006, p. 698).

The development of *meta-cognitive* competency is essential to critical thinking because critical thinking involves reflection on what is known and how that knowledge is justified. "Individuals with well-developed meta-cognitive skills are in control of their beliefs in the sense of exercising conscious control of their evolution in the face of external influences. They *know* what they think and can *justify* why" (Kuhn 1999, p. 23). The generality of meta-cognitive competency is acknowledged in a seminal article on meta-cognition.

> The skills of metacognition do appear to have recognizable counterparts in "real-world," everyday life situations. Checking the results of an operation against certain criteria of effectiveness, economy, and commonsense reality is a metacognitive skill applicable whether the task under consideration is solving a math problem, memorizing a prose passage, following

a recipe, or assembling an automobile. Self-interrogation concerning the state of one's own knowledge during problem solving is an essential skill in a wide variety of situations, those of the laboratory, the school, or everyday life. (Brown 1978, pp. 80)

Kuhn conceives of *epistemological competency* in terms of having a conception of knowledge that includes an understanding of attendant notions such as truth and justification. This accords with Siegel's idea of the epistemology that underlies critical thinking.

> As long as there is a reason assessment component to critical thinking, so that critical thinking is conceived as thinking that is appropriately guided by reasons, then critical thinking must be understood as requiring an epistemology which does justice to the central notions of reasons and rationality. (Siegel 1992, p. 104)

There is much to say here in defending and explaining Siegel's view of the connection between epistemology and critical thinking. Here I must be brief. The complex of epistemic theses that do justice to *reasons* and *rationality* in grounding reason assessment is threefold. First, rational justification is a fallible indicator of truth. Second, truth is independent of rational justification. Third, the goodness of reasons and rational justification is not relative to persons, times, cultures, and so on (Siegel 1992, p. 104).

A thinker's adoption of this epistemology puts her at the top of Kuhn's hierarchy of levels of epistemic understanding that bear on the development of critical-thinking skills. Kuhn summarizes these levels as follows.

> The core dimension underlying and driving the progression in epistemological understanding is the coordination of the subjective and objective components of knowing. The absolutist sees knowledge in largely objective terms, as located in the external world and knowable with certainty. The multiplist becomes aware of the subjective component of knowing, but to such an extent that it overpowers and obliterates any objective standard that would provide a basis for comparison or evaluation of opinions. Only the evaluativist is successful in integrating and coordinating the two, by acknowledging uncertainty without forsaking evaluation. (1999, pp. 22–23)

The four levels of epistemological understanding are summarized by Kuhn (1999, p. 23) in Table 4.1. Kuhn claims that developing into a critical thinker is contingent upon developing one's epistemological understanding from a Realist understanding, predominant among very young children, to an Evaluativist understanding, which is more common among adults. A case can be made that the epistemology Siegel thinks underlies critical thinking reflects the Evaluativist level of epistemological understanding in Kuhn's hierarchy. I will not develop this here. Instead, I briefly illustrate how Kuhn's three second-order competencies connect with other cognitive elements of critical thinking.

Table 4.1 Levels of Epistemological Understanding

Level	Assertions	Reality	Knowledge	Critical thinking
Realist	Assertions are **copies** that represent an external reality.	Reality is directly knowable.	Knowledge comes from an external source and is certain.	Critical thinking is unnecessary.
Absolutist	Assertions are **facts** that are correct or incorrect in their representation of reality (possibility of false belief).	Reality is directly knowable.	Knowledge comes from an external source and is certain.	Critical thinking is a vehicle for comparing assertions to reality and determining their truth or falsehood.
Multiplist	Assertions are **opinions** freely chosen by and accountable only to their owners.	Reality is not directly knowable.	Knowledge is generated by human minds and is uncertain.	Critical thinking is irrelevant.
Evaluative	Assertions are **judgments** that can be evaluated and compared according to criteria of argument and evidence.	Reality is not directly knowable.	Knowledge is generated by human minds and is uncertain.	Critical thinking is valued as a vehicle that promotes sound assertions and enhances understanding.

Source: Kuhn 1999, p. 23.

Davies spells out the cognitive element of critical thinking in terms of "a composite of the following related, but quite different, skills and abilities" (2015, p. 53).

- Analyzing arguments, claims, or evidence (Ennis 1985; Facione 1990; Halpern 1998; Paul 1992)
- Judging or evaluating arguments (Ennis 1985; Facione 1990; Lipman 1988; Tindal and Nolet 1995)
- Making decisions or problem-solving (Ennis 1985; Halpern 1998; Willingham 2008)
- Drawing inferences using a variety of standard reasoning patterns such as induction and deduction (Ennis 1985; Facione 1990; Paul 1992; Willingham 2008)
- Predicting (Tindal and Nolet 1995)
- Reasoning verbally (Halpern 1998)
- Interpreting and explaining (Facione 1990)
- Identifying assumptions (Ennis 1985; Paul 1992)
- Defining terms (Ennis 1985)
- Asking questions for clarification (Ennis 1985)

I now cherry-pick from these elements of critical thinking to illustrate how *meta-strategic, meta-cognitive,* and *epistemological* competencies figure in critical thinking.

A meta-strategic competency benefits decision-making and problem-solving. For example, checklists provide meta-strategic guidance with respect to thinking critically in making decisions or problem-solving. Monitoring one's thinking in deciding what to do or believe in accordance with a checklist that organizes the deployment of relevant skills and attitudes is second-order, meta-strategic thinking. For example, Ennis (1991, p. 20) uses the acronym FRISCO for his checklist.

1. Identify the FOCUS: the main point or main problem.
2. Identify and evaluate the relevant REASONS.
3. Judge the INFERENCES.
4. Attend to the SITUATION: aspects of the setting, which provide meaning and rules.
5. Obtain and maintain CLARITY in what is said.

6. Make an OVERVIEW of what you have discovered, decided, considered, learned and inferred.

The following scenario illustrates meta-strategic thinking.

Paige must decide which college she wants to attend. She first thinks about what her decision process should look like. She thinks that she needs to start by asking: What are my criteria for deciding? (e.g., cost, quality of programs, location, safety, campus life, academic support and career services, athletics, extra-curricular opportunities). She then thinks that she will need to clarify the operative criteria by deciding on corresponding standards. For example, what overall cost is prohibitive? What counts as a safe environment? What matters with respect to location? (E.g., away from home? Out of state?) Furthermore, she will need to decide how these are ranked. (E.g., is cost a more important factor than location?) Paige acknowledges that after selecting criteria and standards for her decision, she must set aside some time to do some research and she strategizes about how best to collect the needed data on the colleges.

I won't try to explicitly correlate elements of Paige's thinking with elements of Ennis's FRISCO. Paige's episode of strategizing about her decision-making process exemplifies meta-strategic thinking. The importance of being meta-strategic with respect to such a complex and significant decision goes without saying. I now illustrate a connection between meta-cognitive thinking and inference making.

Recall that *meta-cognitive competency* involves a competency to correctly judge what one knows, and a competency to justify how one knows. Think about times when you quickly, automatically inferred something from given information based on a gut feeling without consciously reasoning in support of your inference. Such an inference may be so intuitively compelling that you do not check your inference or do so only to rationalize it. For example, consider the following cognitive reflection test, well known in cognitive psychology, as given by Evans (2017, p. 109).

If it takes 5 machines 5 minutes to make 5 widgets, how long would it take 100 machines to make 100 widgets?

Evans reports that many people, even of high IQ, intuitively infer from the given information, 100 minutes, which comes straight to mind without any reflective understanding of why they infer this (2017, p. 109). However, this inference is incorrect. From the given information it follows that each machine takes 5 minutes to make a widget. Therefore, 100 machines would take 5 minutes to make 100 widgets.

People who correct their initial intuitive response to the test engage in more careful, meta-cognitive reasoning. Research in cognitive psychology has been devoted to determining when such a meta-cognitive intervention will occur and when it is successful (e.g., see Thompson 2009). By nature, people are cognitive misers and will expend effort on meta-cognitive reasoning devoted to checking their intuitively sound inferences only if they are motivated and disposed to do so (Stanovich 2011).

As Davis notes (above), a cognitive element of critical thinking is judging or evaluating arguments. Evaluating an argument used to advance its premises as reasons for believing the conclusion involves evaluating whether the premises are reasons for believing the conclusion. Plausibly, the epistemology underlying the reason-assessment dimension of critical thinking involves understanding the variety of reasons for believing and their epistemic import, as discussed in Chapter 3.

For example, recall the distinction between reasons a person has for believing something and reasons for a person to believe something. *Reasons a person S has to believe* are subjective and normative. If p is a reason S has to believe q, then S believes p or should believe p and p is a reason to believe q. However, *reasons for S to believe* are subjective and non-normative. Even though what you believe may provide you with a reason for you to believe something else, it may not be a reason to believe it. To assess whether something is, say, a reason a person S has to believe something or a reason for S to believe it are different assessments. Accordingly, in accordance with Siegel (as discussed above), critical thinking must be understood as requiring an epistemology which does justice to the notion of *reason for belief*.

Furthermore, drawing further on Chapter 3, the epistemological understanding underlying reason assessment requires understanding the notion of epistemic import across the varieties of reasons for belief. The epistemic import of a reason for believing something is whether it is a conclusive, inconclusive, or hypothetical reason for believing something. For example, p is a conclusive reason to believe q just in case p is true and its truth (perhaps along with operative background conditions) rules out the possibility of q being false; p is an inconclusive reason to believe q just in case p is true and its truth (perhaps along with operative background conditions) makes the truth of q more likely than not without ruling out it being false. Recall from Chapter 3 that p is a hypothetical reason to believe q just in case p is merely possibly true and if it were true, it would be a reason, conclusive or otherwise, to believe q. In short, epistemic competence underlying reason assessment requires understanding the epistemic import of reasons.

I now wrap up discussion of the *self-regulative* feature of critical thinking. That critical thinking is self-regulative makes it a form of thinking that essentially involves what is generally referred to as meta-cognition, what Kuhn (1999) calls second-order thinking. Put loosely, meta-cognitive thinking is thinking about thinking, i.e., attending to one's reasoning in order to realize one's intellectual goals (e.g., deciding what to believe or do). I used Kuhn's framework of *meta-knowing* competencies to illustrate meta-cognition's connection with critical thinking. Meta-cognition, understood as the awareness and effective management of one's own thought (Kuhn and Dean 2004, p. 270), is essential to critical thinking because recall that when one thinks critically one is trying to fulfill a standard or standards of adequacy appropriate to the thinking. Being attuned to the alignment between one's thinking and operative standards requires adopting a meta-cognitive standpoint with respect to such thinking.

I now turn to the final element in Lipman's characterization of critical thinking. (4) Critical thinking is thinking that is sensitive to context. Lipman spells this out in terms of thinking that involves recognition of the following (2003, pp. 219–20).

1. *Exceptional or irregular circumstances.* For example, we normally examine statements for truth or falsity independently of the character of the speaker. But in a court trial, the character of a witness may become a relevant consideration.
2. *Special limitations, contingencies, or constraints wherein normally acceptable reasoning might find itself prohibited.* An example is the rejection of certain Euclidean theorems, such as that parallel lines never meet, in non-Euclidean geometries.
3. *Overall configurations.* A remark taken out of context may seem to be flagrantly in error, but in the light of the discourse taken as a whole it can appear valid and proper, or vice versa. [Instead of Lipman's long

example, I simplify with my example. *If not A, then B* may be valid in a context of just *A or B*, but seems flagrantly in error when taken out of context and there are other options besides *A* and *B*.]

4. *The possibility that evidence is atypical.* An example is a case of overgeneralizing about national voter preferences based on a tiny regional sample of ethnically and occupationally homogeneous individuals.

5. *The possibility that some meanings do not translate from one context to another.* There are terms and expressions for which there are no precise equivalents in other languages and whose meanings are therefore wholly context-specific.

Here I'll be brief as this element of Lipman's characterization of critical thinking is less significant than the others to my account of reflective inference given below. Given that critical thinking is thinking that is sensitive to context in the ways highlighted above by Lipman, we cannot property assess an episode of thinking as *critical thinking* without knowing the context in which it occurs. A central question of Chapter 5 may be put as follows: How is formal logic, with its acontextual subject matter and methods, applicable to the determination that an inference as an instance of critical thinking, when critical thinking is sensitive to context?

4.2.1.3. Facione, *Delphi Report* (1990)

In 1998 the American Philosophical Association asked Peter Facione to investigate what critical-thinking skills and dispositions are in order to clarify how to teach and assess critical thinking in secondary and higher education. Using the Delphi Method,[7] Facione invited forty-six experts in critical thinking from a variety of fields to develop a consensus view of a baseline characterization of critical thinking and an associated account of critical-thinking skills and dispositions. The following is the consensus baseline characterization.

We understand critical thinking to be purposeful, self-regulatory judgment which results in interpretation, analysis, evaluation, and inference, as well

---

[7] Participants individually responded to Facione's queries, which were then summarized and anonymized by Facione and shared for further confidential feedback. Altogether there were six rounds of consultation. Among participants, 52 percent were from philosophy, 22 percent from education, 20 percent from the social sciences, and 6 percent from physical science.

as explanation of the evidential conceptual, methodological, criteriological, or contextual considerations upon which that judgment was based. Critical thinking is essential as a tool of inquiry. Critical thinking is a pervasive and self-rectifying human phenomenon. The ideal critical thinker is habitually inquisitive, well-informed, trustful of reason, open-minded, flexible, fair-minded in evaluation, honest in facing personal biases, prudent in making judgments, willing to consider, clear about issues, orderly in complex matters, diligent in seeking relevant information, reasonable in selection of criteria, focused in inquiry and persistent in seeking results which are as precise as the subject and circumstances of inquiry permit. (Facione 1990, p. 3)

Here we have explicit characterizations of both *critical thinking* and *ideal critical thinkers*. Critical thinking is purposeful in that its aim is the formation of a judgment that is an outcome of various critical-thinking activities, i.e., activities that result "in interpretation, analysis, evaluation and inference." Also, critical thinking is self-regulatory. Accordingly, judgments that are outcomes of critical thinking are made in accordance with operative standards recognized by the thinker. This second-order recognition of the operative standards enables the thinker's capacity to explain "the evidential conceptual, methodological, criteriological or contextual considerations upon which that judgment was based."

Critical thinkers are characterized in terms of the possession of dispositions that trigger critical-thinking skills (e.g., "habitually inquisitive") and regulate their exercise skills (e.g., "well-informed, honest in facing personal bias"). To be a critical thinker, one must be disposed to exercise critical-thinking skills to judge in accordance with the relevant standards of good thinking. In addition, one must be motivated by a fundamental commitment to truth and rationality, i.e., by a fundamental commitment to believe only what is true and to act responsibly. Passmore (1972) characterizes the possession of these dispositions or character traits as having a "critical spirit." The attitudes and habits of mind constituting the "critical spirit" have been defined in a variety of ways (see Bailin et al. 1999 for a summary). Siegel offers a sketch.

The critical spirit component includes a cluster of attitudes, dispositions, and character traits, many of which could equally well be thought of as intellectual virtues. Among them are (1) the dispositions to seek reasons and evidence, to demand reasons and justifications for claims advanced, to query and, when appropriate, to investigate proffered but unsubstantiated claims, and to engage in open-minded and fair-minded reason assessment; (2) a willingness and inclination to conform belief, judgment, and action to epistemic principle, especially those concerning the proper normative evaluation of reasons and evidence; (3) a cluster of related attitudes and character traits, including a rejection of partiality and arbitrariness, a commitment to the objective evaluation of relevant evidence and to the sympathetic and impartial consideration of interests, and the valuing of good reasoning, intellectual honesty, justice to evidence, objectivity of judgment, and impartiality with respect to epistemic evaluation generally, even when it runs counter to self-interest; and (4) habits of mind consonant with all these. They overlap in complex ways, and I do not presume any sharp distinctions among the mentioned attitudes, dispositions, character traits, and habits of mind. The critical spirit involves, fundamentally, caring about reasons and their quality, reasoning, and living a life in which they play a fundamental role. (2017, p. 96)

A critical thinker's tendency to fulfill the standards and principles of good thinking cannot be mindless or simply the result of habituation. It must be based on a recognition of the value of critical thinking to fostering true beliefs and responsible action (Siegel 1988, p. 40).

Unlike with Dewey's and Lipman's baseline characterizations of critical thinking, the *Delphi Report* explicitly characterizes both critical thinking and critical thinkers. This raises the question of the connection between them (see Siegel 1988 for discussion). Being a critical thinker requires being disposed to skillfully exercise the cognitive elements of critical thinking (summarized by Davies above) when appropriate. Accordingly, to explain what makes a person a critical thinker requires accounting for and explaining the fact that critical thinkers think critically in appropriate occasions, at the appropriate time, with the appropriate people, for the appropriate reasons.

Must one be a critical thinker in order to think critically? An affirmative response seems unlikely since one may be skilled at critical thinking but not have the critical spirit (following Siegel 2017). For example, Dewey's *Burglary* example of reflective thinking is a plausible example of critical thinking. However, obviously it doesn't provide enough information to determine whether the protagonist possesses the critical spirit as characterized by Siegel just above.

4.2.2. Summary

Critical thinking is multifaceted. It can take place when one is thinking privately to oneself or in an argumentative context such as when one is trying to argue for something to someone else. My discussion has isolated four essential features. Critical thinking is essentially active, persistent, purposeful, and criterial.

Critical thinking is active reasoning in that it is conscious thinking. You are aware of your thinking, i.e., you are aware of your thinking as something that you are doing. For example, you are aware that you are gathering evidence, weighing pros and cons, inferring a conclusion, judging that something is true, deciding what to do, and so forth. That critical thinking is persistent connotes that it is slow and cognitively demanding. Critical thinking is triggered in order to realize an aim, e.g., to decide what to do or believe. The thinker is conscious of the aim and desires to satisfy it.

Critical thinking is criterial in two ways. First, when thinking critically one is *trying* to fulfill a standard or standards of adequacy appropriate to the thinking. It is thinking that is intended to conform to operative standards, which if satisfied makes the thinking good. Accordingly, critical thinking is self-regulating, and so has a second-order cognitive dimension. This reflects the slogan that meta-cognition is essential to critical thinking and borrows from Dewey's idea that reflective thinking is careful. Critical thinking is *careful* because for one to think critically one must think conscientiously, i.e., one's thinking is contemporaneous with being mindful of the operative norms and rules that one believes should guide one's thinking. Put in another way: reflective thinking is careful in part by being self-regulating.

Second, critical thinking is criterial in the sense that it *fulfills* the relevant standard(s) to some threshold level. Critical thinking is essentially good thinking in the sense of meeting operative standards. The cognitive elements of critical thinking as well as the context in which it occurs trigger the operative standards. For example, interpreting an opponent's argument should be guided by the principle of charity. It is legit to draw a conclusion about a population from a sample only if the sample is representative of the population. Circular definitions are typically bad because they are typically useless. Generally, critical-thinking texts (e.g., Govier 2010) review standards guiding cognitive elements of thinking across a variety of domains of inquiry.

4.2.3. Inference and Critical Thinking

In this section, I highlight three related facets of the connection between critical thinking and inference that inform my characterization of reflective inference given in section 4.3. First, I identify the acts of inferring that typically occur in critical thinking. Second, I identify the features that an act of inferring must possess in order to count as an episode of critical thinking. Third, I end by discussing how reason-giving uses of arguments figure in critical thinking.

All sorts of mental acts occur during typical episodes of critical thinking (Hitchcock 2017a and Davies 2015), including acts of inference. Dewey remarks that no reflective thinking occurs without the performance of at least one inference (1933, p. 95). Generally, inferential abilities are recognized as critical-thinking abilities (Davies 2015, p. 53; Glaser 1941, p. 6; Facione 1990, 9; Ennis 1991, pp. 6, 9; Fisher and Scriven 1997, pp. 99, 111; Halpern 1998, p. 452; Hitchcock 2020; 2017a, pp. 485, 487; and Mulnix 2012, p. 464).

Acts of *inferring* typically occur during critical thinking in the following two ways. One works out what would be the case if something else was assumed (e.g., in *Burglary*, the protagonist thinks: if it was a burglary, then an article is missing); or one draws a conclusion once sufficient relevant evidence is gathered. That is, one makes a judgment based on accumulated evidence and reasoning (e.g., in *Home*, Kelly judges that Beth is home). These acts of inferring correspond to two different types of inferences: *hypothetical or suppositional* and *a persona*.

With an *a persona (from the person) inference*, the premises are the reasoner R's reasons for which R believes the conclusion. With a *hypothetical inference*, the premises of the inference are regarded by the reasoner R as hypothetical reasons for the conclusion in the sense that R regards them as merely possibly true and thinks that they would support the conclusion if true. Recall *Knights/knaves*: Paige performed both *hypothetical* and *a persona* inferences. She reasoned from the supposition that the native speaker is a knave. She also judged that the speaker is knight based on the given that natives are either knights or knaves and her judgment that the speaker is not a knave. Again, the thinking illustrated by *Burglary* involved the protagonist performing hypothetical inferences when inferring from conjectured possibilities regarding the cause of the disorder in his room. As was discussed, these inferences played a vital role in the evidence gathering that led to his *a persona*-inference-based-judgment that his room had been burglarized.

What qualifies an act of inferring as an episode of critical thinking? In response, we don't want to reason as follows: if a mental act occurs as part of one's episode of critical thinking, then it must have the properties that essentially characterize critical thinking. This commits the fallacy of composition. In general, it's false that what is true of the whole must be true of its parts. Instead, we should allow that one's act of inferring may occur as a part of one's critical thinking without itself being critical thinking.

I use the following syllogism as a template to organize my thinking in response to the question posed at the start of the previous paragraph.

(1) All critical thinking possesses features A, B, C, . . .
(2) Some acts of inferring qualify as critical thinking
   So, some acts of inferring possess A, B, C, . . .

What are A, B, and C, . . .? Well, we've said that critical thinking is essentially *active, persistent, purposeful,* and *criterial.* Accordingly, it follows, given (2), that some acts of inferring are essentially active, persistent, purposeful, and criterial. Let's spell this out drawing on my development in section 4.2.1 of these essential features of critical thinking. I speak to (2) below in section 4.3. My aim here is to clarify what exactly is an act of inferring that is essentially active, persistent, purposeful, and careful.

The concept of an inference that is *active* is an agential, i.e., personal, concept of inference. It is an inference that is conscious. You are aware of what you are doing; you are *aware* that you infer a conclusion from premises, and you are aware of the premises and the conclusion you draw from them. Two cognitive aspects of a personal inference are as follows. First, the inference is intentional in that the inferer S intends the premises to be reasons of some sort for believing the conclusion that S draws. Second, S believes that they are such reasons. In sum, your inference is active only if it is intentional and so entails a corresponding inference-claim belief.

The operative inference-claim belief accounts for the different cognitive import of *a persona* and hypothetical inferences. You perform a hypothetical inference only if you believe the inference claim to the effect that the premises are hypothetical reasons for believing the conclusion. You perform an *a persona* inference only if you believe, perhaps mistakenly, that the premises are reasons you have to believe the conclusion. Accordingly, your performance of a hypothetical inference indicates that you regard the premises as merely possible. On the other hand, you perform an *a persona* inference only if you regard the premises as actually true, not merely possibly true. This explains why the two types of inferences have different cognitive import.

An inference that is persistent is one that is deliberative and cognitive demanding. These features are not true of the inferences which we perform on autopilot. Think of the quick, effortless inferences involved in facial recognition or in interpreting an interlocuter's utterance. A deliberative inference is one that the inferer consciously decides to perform.

An *active* inference that is *purposeful* is an inference that is performed in order to realize an aim that the inferer is explicitly aware of. The aim of an active inference is realized only if the premises are reasons in the intended sense for the conclusion. That is, the inference serves its intended purpose only if the associated inference-claim belief is true, i.e., the premises are reasons—in the intended sense—for believing the conclusion.

For example, you are deciding whether to believe q. In service of this aim, you perform an inference from p to q. Suppose this is active inferential reasoning. Your associated inference-claim belief is that p is a reason for believing q in the intended sense. Your inference serves its intended purpose only if your corresponding inference-claim belief is true. I now illustrate.

Kelly wants to know whether Beth is at home. She sees Beth's car in the driveway. She infers that Beth is at home. Kelly's inference serves its intended purpose (i.e., knowing whether Beth is at home) only if that Beth's car is in the driveway is reason Kelly has to believe that Beth is at home.

Note that Kelly may legitimately draw many conclusions from her belief that Beth's car is in the driveway. It is legit for her to infer that *it is false that there is not a car in the driveway*, that *there is a car in the driveway*, or that *Beth's car is in the driveway or Beth is at home*. However, drawing any of these conclusions does not serve Kelly's aim of determining whether Beth is home. Given Kelly's aim, if she takes Beth's car's being in the driveway to support that Beth is home, then this will suffice for her to infer that Beth is at home.

Kelly wakes up after a night's sleep and wonders whether Beth is a home. She reasons that if Beth's car is not in the driveway, then Beth isn't home. She then moves to the window to see whether Beth's car is in the driveway. Kelly's reasoning doesn't serve its intended purpose (i.e., knowing whether Beth is at home) unless Beth's car not being in the driveway is a hypothetical reason for believing that Beth isn't home.

Paige says that Beth is at home. Kelly disagrees. Kelly communicates her reasoning to Paige as follows: if you think that Beth is at home, then you should think that Beth's car is in the driveway; but Beth's car is not in the driveway. Kelly draws the conclusion that Beth's car is in the driveway from the premise that Beth is at home in order to show Paige that she is committed to believing what is false. Kelly's inference does not realize her aim unless that Beth is at home is as reason for Paige to believe that Beth's car is in the driveway.

In short, an inference that is an episode of critical thinking is purposeful in the sense that it is performed in order to realize an aim. Its aim is not realized unless the premises are reasons—in the intended sense—for believing the conclusion. Accordingly, the inference performed must meet the appropriate standards by which the premises are reasons for believing the conclusion. This brings us to the next feature that must be true of an inference for it to count as critical thinking.

An inference that qualifies as critical thinking is criterial in the following ways. The inference is warranted by a standard, the inferer is cognizant of this standard, and believes that it warrants their inference. Hume remarks, "I am uneasy to think I approve of one object, and disapprove of another; call one thing beautiful, and another deformed; decide concerning truth and false-hood, reason and folly, without knowing upon what principles I proceed" ([1739] 1978, p. 271). The criterial dimension of critical thinking determines that such judgments are not the outcomes of inferences that qualify as critical thinking unless the one who judges knows upon what principles they proceed.

To perform an inference *carefully* requires being conscientious, i.e., being mindful of the standards that one is trying to meet. Attunement to the operative standards normative for one's inference is necessary for the inference to count as critical thinking. Here's an illustration of how these features figure in determining whether an inference counts as an episode of critical thinking.

> Beth's car keys are not on the key rack near her workbag. She panics as she is late for work. Beth thinks (1) that they are in the kitchen or in the family room. After looking in the kitchen, she believes (2) that they are not in the kitchen. Beth infers (3) that they are in the family room. She looks there.

What must be true about Beth's inference from (1) and (2) to (3) for it to count as an episode of critical thinking? *First*, she must be aware that she performs the inference, i.e., she is cognizant of the fact that she draws the conclusion (3) from her premise-beliefs (1) and (2). Also, Beth intends (1) and (2) to be reasons she has to believe (3). Accordingly, she believes that they are such reasons. Furthermore, Beth knows why she performs the inference (e.g., to find her car keys). *Second*, Beth's inference is purposeful. As just indicated, she performs the inference in order to arrive at a judgment about the location of her keys so that she can get to work. *Third*, Beth is aware, at least tacitly, of the principle that she believes warrants or licenses her inference. For example, for any propositions p, q: necessarily, if p or q and not p, then q.

An inference that qualifies as critical thinking corresponds to an argument whose premises and conclusion are the contents of the premise and conclusion of the inference. When you perform such an inference, you use the corresponding argument in a reason-giving way. That is, you use the premises as reasons for believing the conclusion.

An aim of an inference performed in a context of inquiry such as problem solving is to decide what to believe. A person S's inquiry is successful when S performs an inference that results in S acquiring a belief whose truth resolves the perplexity or problem that triggered the inquiry in the first place. The premises of the corresponding argument are reasons for which S believes its conclusion. S uses, perhaps implicitly, the corresponding argument in a reason-giving way in order to realize the aim of the associated inquiry.

To illustrate quickly, recall that in *Knights/knaves* Paige inferred that that the speaker is a knight from the given that natives are either knights or knaves and her judgment that the speaker is not a knave. Her *a persona* inference was from her premise-beliefs that natives are either knights or knaves and that the speaker is not a knave to her conclusion-belief that the speaker is a knight. By virtue of performing the inference, Paige uses the corresponding argument, which may be displayed as follows, in a reason-giving way.

> Natives are either knights or knaves
> The speaker is not a knave
> The speaker is a knight

Of course, Paige needn't have used a "therefore." That is, Paige needn't have explicitly expressed her inference in the format of an argument. She nevertheless uses the argument to advance reasons for her believing the conclusion. If asked to explain why she thinks the speaker is a knight, Paige might give the above argument in response. The argument that expresses your inference is the one that you use in a reason-giving way by virtue of drawing the conclusion from the premises. By virtue of what does an argument express an inference is a topic of discussion in Chapter 6. The point here is that for Paige to have used this argument to advance reasons for the conclusion she needn't have established her conclusion-belief by the explicit production of the argument even if she uses the argument to publicize her reasoning.

However, there are contexts in which one's inferential reasoning is facilitated by the explicit production of an argument. Kuhn labels this "thinking as argument" (1991, pp. 2–5).[8] For example, consider inferential reasoning one performs in response to an interlocuter's demand to justify a belief that one happens to hold unreflectively. The production of an argument in response to the interlocuter facilitates the reasoning performed to justify the belief. To develop this picture, I draw on Toulmin (2003) and the textbook by Toulmin, Rieke, and Janik (1979).

Toulmin's well-known account of the structure of arguments focuses on their uses as instruments of justification (2003, p. 12). He asks, "What, then, is involved in establishing conclusions by the production of arguments?" (2003, p. 89). In response, Toulmin develops his account of arguments in steps. Each step corresponds to a phase of the development of an argument, which Toulmin conceives heuristically in terms of the author's responses to an interlocuter's critical challenges to their proffered support for their belief (2003, pp. 89–100). In Toulmin, Rieke, and Janik (1979), arguments are initially characterized as chains of reasoning (pp. 11, 13). For the creation of an argument so conceived to count as critical thinking the involved reasoning must be active, purposeful, and careful. I sketch Toulmin's phases of argument production with the aim of illustrating how inferential reasoning that qualifies as critical thinking is facilitated by the explicit production of a fully developed argument in order to argue for its conclusion.

Phase 1: S asserts that q and thereby expresses S's belief that q. This puts S on the hook to defend q. An interlocuter asks, what have you got to go on? In response, S asserts that p. In Toulmin's terminology, p is presented as a datum that serves as S's basis or foundation for the conclusion q. More generally, premises used to justify a conclusion comprise a particular set of data for the

---

[8] Kuhn distinguishes between rhetorical and dialogical arguments (1991, pp. 12–13). A rhetorical argument is simply an assertion with accompanying justification. A dialogical argument is an argument "that is a dialogue between two people who hold opposing views. Each offers justification for his or her own view; in addition (at least in a skilled argument), each rebuts the other's view by means of a counterargument" (p. 12).

conclusion (2003, p. 90). Toulmin displays an argument at this initial phase of its development schematically as follows.

D ⟹ C

"D" represents the data given for the conclusion, and "C" represents the conclusion. Unless S's assertion is entirely baseless and, therefore, illegit, S is cognizant of their reasons in support of their assertion that q. Toulmin is clear that the phase-1 development of an argument is an argument. S uses the argument, p so q, in response to the interlocuter to advance S's reason for believing q. Accordingly, S uses the argument p so q in a reason-giving way.

According to Toulmin, the next phase of the argument's development is prompted by S's justification of the step from D to C. For example, an interlocuter asks S: How did you get to q from p? Toulmin takes such a question in this context to serve as a request for justification of S's step from the initial data, i.e., the given premise(s), to the conclusion (2003, pp. 90–91). What he calls a warrant ("W") grounds the direct justification of the step from D to C. A warrant is an appropriate generalization of the conditional corresponding to the argument in its phase-1 development (2003, pp. 91–92).[9]

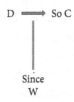

For Toulmin, the warrant, which is not a premise, is a component of the argument in its phase-2 development. Its truth justifies the step from D to C. So an arguer's phase-2 development of their argument requires that they be cognizant of the warrant whose truth is necessary for the legitimacy of the inferential step from D to C. To illustrate, consider Toulmin's toy example of an argument in its phase-2 development, which he pictures as follows (2003, p. 92).

---

[9] Toulmin is incautious in his discussion of warrants, sometimes describing them in terms of inference licenses (or rules) (2003, p. 91), and at other times expressing them as generalizations (2003, p. 94). For purposes here, I take them to be generalizations and so capable of being true.

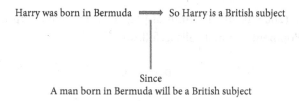

The given warrant is a generalization of the conditional corresponding to the argument in its phase-1 development, *If Harry was born in Bermuda, then Harry is a British subject.* That is, the warrant corresponds to *For every person x, if x was born in Bermuda, then x is a British subject.* The warrant expresses the standard according to which that Harry was born in Bermuda is a reason to believe that Harry is as British subject.

I now pause my discussion of Toulmin to consider the inference expressed by an argument at these first two phases of its development. I draw on the terminology and conceptual apparatus previously discussed in this and prior chapters, and so depart from Toulmin. Recall that with respect to the first phase of a reasoner S's production of an argument, S uses the argument in a reason-giving way. So S believes the inference claim associated with the argument in its phase-1 production; i.e., S believes that p is a reason S has to believe q, and so believes p is a reason that supports the truth of q.

However, at this phase of the production of the argument S needn't be cognizant of support for S's inference-claim belief. This is because one needn't be cognizant of the warrant, i.e., the corresponding generalization of the conditional associated with the argument. Crucial here is that the inference claim, *p is a reason that supports q,* isn't true unless the inferential step from p to q is justified. That is, what is required to justify the inferential step is necessary for the truth of the corresponding inference claim. Hence, the operative warrant grounds the inference claim; i.e., the truth of the inference claim turns on the truth of the warrant. Accordingly, one's belief that an inference claim is true doesn't count as knowledge unless the accompanying warrant is true.

To illustrate, S asserts that Harry is a British subject. When challenged, S claims in response that Harry was born in Bermuda. S uses the argument (1) *Harry is a British subject, so* (2) *Harry was born in Bermuda* to advance a reason in support of the conclusion. Hence, S believes the associated inference claim; S believes that (1) is a reason S has to believe (2). So S believes that (1) is evidence for the truth of (2). Accordingly, S is committed to the warrant that justifies this claim. However, S need not explicitly believe the associated warrant at this phase of the development of S's argument for (2). This echoes Toulmin idea that at this phase of the development of S's argument for (2), the warrant is an implicit element of the argument.

S's inference-claim belief is not justified for S unless S recognizes the associated warrant. S's phase-2 development enables this awareness of the warrant that S is committed to by virtue of their inference from (1) to (2). Accordingly, this is the minimal level of the development of an argument for the corresponding inference to count as an episode of critical thinking. The argumentative reasoning is obviously active (the reasoner consciously authors an argument), purposeful (in order to justify a belief), and careful (the reasoner is attentive to the inference's license).

Suppose that in an email conversation you state an opinion on a controversial topic. Your conversant responds that you are wrong, and you feel the need to defend your belief. After thinking for a time (you want to present the best possible case for your opinion) you articulate reasons in support of your opinion that now sustain it. You email your argument to your conversant. The argument that you email you use in a reason-giving way. It expresses your inference, which is a form of reverse inferential reasoning as the corresponding argument is developed starting from your opinion-belief. Whether your reasoning counts as critical thinking turns on how developed your argument is. For example, are you aware of the warrant that licenses your inference?

Toulmin conceptualizes reasoning done to justify a belief in terms of the explicit production of an argument. Elements of the argument produced correspond to the elements of the reasoning. This motivates Toulmin's picture of arguments according to which they include more than premise(s) and a conclusion.

For Toulmin, the elements of a fully developed argument include backing for the warrant, a qualifier modifying the conclusion indicator, and conditions of rebuttal (2003, p. 97). Backing justifies the truth of the warrant, and conditions of rebuttal ground the applicability of the warrant to legitimatizing the step from data to conclusion. Toulmin says that typically in producing an argument only the conclusion and the premises (i.e., the data) from which it is drawn are explicitly given. The other elements are implicit and, therefore, touchpoints of critical challenges to the inference. They are made explicit in responding to relevant critical challenges. Toulmin schematically diagrams an argument with these extra elements added as follows.

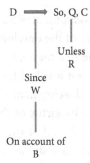

Key

D = Data, premise(s)	B = Backing; support for W
C = Conclusion	Q = Qualifier
W = Warrant, links D to C	R = Conditions of rebuttal; qualify the applicability of W

The greater the development of one's argument, the more reflective is the reasoning that it expresses, i.e., the more aware one is of the dimensions of one's associated reasoning. Toulmin illustrates further development of the previously given toy example of an argument as follows.

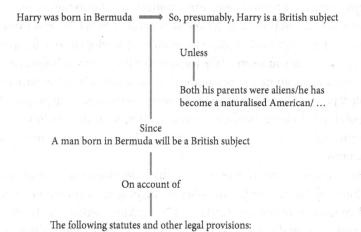

In sum, on Toulmin's picture of arguments they are at minimum composed of premises and a conclusion. Recall from Chapter 2 that on my view these are the only components of an argument. I take the other components Toulmin identifies to be concerned with how the argument is being used and the justification of this use. For example, the qualifier indicates whether the premises are being offered as conclusive reasons for believing the conclusion. The warrant and the associated backing justify the associated inference claim, which I do not take to be a component of the argument.

According to Toulmin, a reasoner's fully developed argument for a conclusion makes explicit the dimensions of the reasoner's inferential reasoning intended to justify their conclusion-belief. At what point in the development of an argument in Toulmin's sense is the corresponding inference from premises to conclusion an act of critical thinking? The phase-2 development of your argument requires your recognition of the operative standard, construed as a warrant, which guides your inference from premises to conclusion. The warrant is your justification for your associated inference-claim belief to the effect that the premise are reasons for you to believe the conclusion. If the warrant legitimizes your inference making your inference-claim belief true, then your inference counts as critical thinking.

4.2.4. Summary

I have drawn on the critical-thinking literature to characterize inferences performed in contexts of inquiry or justification that count as episodes of critical thinking. For an inference to qualify as critical thinking it must be (i) active, (ii) persistent, (iii) purposeful, and (iv) criterial. The inference is criterial in that (a) the inferer is *trying* to fulfill appropriate standards of adequacy; and (b) the inference *fulfills* the relevant standards to some threshold level. Condition (a) reflects the idea that such inferences are intended to satisfy what the inferer thinks are appropriate standards even if the inferer is unable to adequately verbalize them. Condition (b) makes inferences that qualify as critical thinking normative in that they satisfy the operative standards to some minimal threshold. Obviously, clarifying the normativity requires identifying this threshold.

I now use this characterization of inferences that are episodes of critical thinking to characterize the inferences associated with reason-giving uses of arguments. I call such inferences *reflective inferences*. In the next section, I characterize this class of inferences and then clarify their association with reason-giving uses of arguments.

4.3. Reflective Inferences and Reason-Giving Uses of Arguments

A reflective is an inference for which just (i)–(iii), and (iv-a) hold. That is, a reflective inference is (i) active, (ii) persistent, (iii) and purposeful, and (iv-a) the inferer is *trying* to fulfill appropriate standards of adequacy.[10] However, as a reflective inference may not fulfill appropriate standards of adequacy, (iv-b) fulfillment is not an essential feature of them. The premises of some reflective inferences taken together are not good reasons (in the intended sense) for believing the conclusion. Failing (iv-b), such inferences do not qualify as critical thinking. However, all inferences that count as critical thinking are reflective inferences. Hence, if an inference isn't reflective, then it isn't an episode of critical thinking.

Recall theses (I) and (II) given in the preamble to this chapter.

(I)   If you perform a reflective inference, then you use the corresponding argument in a reason-giving way.

(II)   If you use an argument in a reason-giving way, then you have performed a reflective inference from its premise(s) to conclusion.

Together, (I) and (II) indicate that reflective inferences have reason-giving uses of arguments at their core. I now articulate the rationales for (I) and (II), starting with (I).

---

[10] I take reflective inference so conceived to instantiate what in the psychology of reasoning is called type-2 or system-2 inferential reasoning, which is explicit, conscious, and effortful in a way that involves the inferer being conscious of their rationale for thinking that their inference is warranted (Evans 2017, esp. chap. 7; 2020, esp. chaps. 1 and 5; Stanovich 2011). Such inferential reasoning contrasts with type-1 or system-1 inferential reasoning, which is quick, effortless, often subconscious, and is not accompanied by any meta-cognitive awareness of the principle(s) upon which the inference proceeds (e.g., Thompson 2009). Also, my notion of a reflective inference as associated with reasoning-giving uses of argument in the manner described by theses (I) and (II) (just below) resembles what Mercier and Sperber refer to as reflective inferences (2009), which they characterize in terms of their model of the mind as massively modular rather than bifurcated into type-1 and type-2 systems (2017). Very roughly, on their view the argumentation module of the mind is responsible for reflective inferences, according to which inputs (i.e., starting points) are represented as premise-reasons for believing the output, which is represented as a conclusion. A non-premise input is the representation of the premises as reasons for believing the conclusion that taken together warrants inferring the conclusion (2017, pp. 153–61). Further discussion is worthwhile about how the course-grained picture of reflective inference drawn here relates to full-blown accounts of inferential reasoning in the literature on the philosophy and psychology of reasoning as a means of illustrating that my picture of reflective inferences is fairly ecumenical among competing accounts of inferential reasoning in this rather substantial literature (for a good, quick introduction, see Evans 2017). Unfortunately, I don't have the space here for such discussion, which is worthy of another book devoted to it.

Suppose that you perform a reflective inference from p to q. The argument corresponding to your inference is p *so* q. Since you perform a reflective inference, you intend that p serve as a reason of some sort for believing q, and thereby believe that p is such a reason for believing q. So, when you draw q from p you use the corresponding argument, p *so* q, in a reason-giving way. Generalizing, if one performs a reflective inference, one intends the inferential premises to be reasons for believing the conclusion and so believes the inference claim associated with the corresponding argument. Accordingly, you use the corresponding argument in a reason-giving way as understood in this book.

My rationale for (II) is more involved than my rationale for (I). It involves two central claims, which I label (a) and (b).

(a) If you use an argument in a reason-giving way, then you infer the conclusion from your premises, because you believe that they are reasons (in the intended sense) for believing the conclusion.

(b) If you believe that your premises are reasons (in the intended sense) for believing the conclusion and you draw the conclusion from them because you believe this, then you perform a reflective inference.

Thesis (II) follows from (1) and (2). I now briefly elaborate, drawing on my characterization of reflective inference and the account of reason-giving uses of arguments given in Chapters 2 and 3.

My rationale for (a) is as follows. If you use an argument in a reason-giving way, then you intend your premises to be reasons for believing the conclusion and so you believe that they are such reasons. This assumes that your argumentative intention is rational by virtue of satisfying the inference-claim belief requirement. Because you believe that the premises are reasons of the kind you intend for the conclusion, you infer the conclusion. That is, given that you use an argument in a reason-giving way in order to realize some aim, your believing that the premises are reasons of the intended sort for believing the conclusion causes you to perform the associated inference. Your inference is motivated by your aim in using the associated argument in a reason-giving way. Compare: suppose that you believe that Beth is at work, and you believe that Kelly is home. Of course, this alone doesn't motivate you to draw the conclusion that *Beth is at work and Kelly is home*, even if you believe such an inference is warranted unless it serves some purpose. Your inference-claim belief is the linking belief of your inference associated with your reason-giving use of argument.

Why is (b) true? Because, if you believe that your premises are reasons for believing the conclusion and you draw the conclusion from them because you believe this, then your inference is active, purposeful, and at least somewhat careful. It is active (e.g., intentional), it is purposeful (e.g., you perform the inference in service of your aim(s) in using the corresponding argument to advance reasons for its conclusion), and it is somewhat careful (e.g., you appeal, perhaps implicitly, to a standard that is your justification of your inference-claim belief). Accordingly, it is a reflective inference.

To elaborate, when you use an argument in a reason-giving way, you intend the premises to be reason for believing the conclusion. Therefore, the corresponding inference is active. You represent the premises of your inference as reasons for believing the conclusion of your inference. Your reason-giving use of an argument is purposeful. For example, you use an argument to advance reasons for its conclusion in order to persuade an interlocuter, weigh pros and cons, or to justify one's judgment that the conclusion is true. You perform the corresponding inference in service of such aims. Finally, your inference is careful in the sense that you think that your inference is warranted, i.e., you believe that your inference meets standards that you may be unable to verbalize. If you didn't think this, you wouldn't have performed the inference since in such a case you wouldn't think that your reason-giving use of argument serves your aim(s).

In sum, theses (I) and (II) speak to the connection between reflective inferences and reason-giving uses of arguments. You perform a reflective inference just in case you use the corresponding argument in a reason-giving way. Whether believing that the conclusion is true is an outcome of such an inference depends on the type of reasons for belief that you take the premises to be.

4.4. Conclusion

To conclude, I now summarize the central claims of Chapter 4. A reflective inference is an inference that is essentially active, purposeful, and careful in the sense that the reasoner is *trying* to fulfill standards of adequacy appropriate to the inference. Because such inferences are active and careful, they are necessarily accompanied by a linking belief to the effect that the premises are reasons for believing the conclusion. The linking belief must be true for the inference to serve its intended purpose.

My view of reflective inference was generated from my discussion of critical thinking. Reflective inferences are related to critical thinking in the following two ways. First, only good reflective inferences qualify as critical thinking. Second, if an inference qualifies as critical thinking, then it is a reflective inference.

Together (I) and (II) indicate that reflective inferences have reason-giving uses of arguments at their core.

(I)   If you perform a reflective inference, then you use the corresponding argument in a reason-giving way.

(II) If you use an argument in a reason-giving way, then you have performed a reflective inference from its premises to conclusion.

The inference-claim belief associated with a reason-giving use of an argument is the linking belief of the corresponding reflective inference.

Reason-giving uses of arguments are essentially *deliberative* in the sense that they involve the user's judgment that the premises, collectively, are reasons—in some sense—for believing the conclusion. Accordingly, the reasoning expressed by arguments so used is essentially *reflective* in the sense that the reasoner R reasons from the premises to the conclusion, because R judges that the premises are reasons for believing the conclusion. A speaker's reason-giving use of an argument being essentially deliberative explains why their reasoning from premises to conclusion is essentially reflective. This explanatory connection motivates a normative connection: norms that guide reason-giving uses of arguments generate norms that guide the reasoning that the arguments express. This normative connection is developed in Chapter 5.

PART II

FORMAL VALIDITY, RATIONAL PERSUASION, ARGUMENTATIVE RATIONALITY, INTELLECTUAL HONESTY, AND INTELLECTUAL INTEGRITY

5

Reason-Giving Uses of Arguments, Formally Valid Arguments, and Demonstrative Arguments

5.1. Preamble

Suppose that you use a formally valid argument in a reason-giving way. Your argument is demonstrative because it is impossible for the premises to be true and the conclusion false. So the conclusion is implied by the premises. Why, if at all, does your argument being demonstrative matter to whether your reason-giving use of it is good? After all, there are good reason-giving uses of arguments that are not demonstrative. This raises the question of what are the norms that explain when an argument being demonstrative matters to whether a given reason-giving use of it is good.

This explanation has the potential for shedding some light on how formal validity matters to good reasoning. Peirce's remark, "It is foolish to study logic unless one is persuaded that one's own reasonings are more or less bad" (1955, p. 126), presupposes that logic can be used to identify good and bad reasoning. The question of how, if at all, the formal validity of arguments is normative for reasoning has received much attention in the philosophical logic literature (e.g., Field 2009; McFarlane 2004; Sainsbury 2002; Steinberger 2016). Some are skeptical that formal validity has any normative implications for reasoning (e.g., Harman 1986, 2002). However, the plausibility of such skepticism turns on the operative notion of reasoning.

Recall two points from Chapter 4. First, the inference-claim belief associated with a reason-giving use of argument is the linking belief of the corresponding reflective inference. Second, a reflective inference is good only if the linking belief is true. Taken together, these claims suggest that developing a response to the question posed at the start is relevant to clarifying how formal validity can matter to whether a reflective inference is good.

Arguments and Reason-Giving. Matthew W. McKeon, Oxford University Press. © Oxford University Press 2024.
DOI: 10.1093/oso/9780197751633.003.0005

I begin by reviewing the distinction between deductive and inductive arguments introduced in Chapter 3. I then distinguish between demonstrative and ampliative arguments. Next, I distinguish between formally valid and demonstrative arguments. All formally valid arguments are demonstrative arguments, but not every demonstrative argument is formally valid. The formal validity of an argument is germane to whether a reason-giving use of it is good only because formally valid arguments are demonstrative arguments. I then make a case for thinking that some (classically) formally valid arguments do not correspond to reflective inferences and so cannot be successfully used to advance their premises as reasons for their conclusions. I show how this fact matters to whether a formal logic such as classical logic is adequate for judging reflective inferences.

In the penultimate section, I identify three norms, pragmatic, doxastic, and dialectical, that I take to guide reason-giving uses of arguments. I use these three norms to explain when a deductive argument used to advance reasons for believing its conclusion should be demonstrative. This will explain when an argument being demonstrative matters to the legitimacy of the corresponding reflective inference.

In Chapter 6, I discuss what is required for an argument used in a reason-giving way to express an inference. An argument used to advance reasons for its conclusion may correspond to an inference that it does not express. This figures in whether attempts to persuade are successful. For example, whether your inference is expressed by your interlocuter's argument or merely corresponds to it matters to whether you are persuaded by argument your interlocuter gives to accept its conclusion. More specifically, you are so persuaded only if your inference not only corresponds to the interlocuter's argument but is expressed by it.

5.2. Deductive Arguments, Demonstrative Arguments, and Reflective Inferences

In this section, I review what deductive and demonstrative arguments are by appealing to two distinctions: demonstrative vs. ampliative arguments and deductive vs. inductive arguments. My discussion draws on Chapter 3, section 3.2. Next, using the notion of the epistemic import of reasons introduced in section 3.3.1, I characterize arguments used in a reason-giving way that are deductive and those are demonstrative. Much of this rehearses discussion from Chapter 3 and so hopefully is familiar. This discussion is extended to reflective inferences by characterizing deductive and demonstrative reflective inferences.

A *demonstrative argument* is one that has premises such that if they are all true, they guarantee the truth of the conclusion, i.e., if true they rule out the possibility—in some sense—of the conclusion being false. This guarantee obtains just in case the conclusion is implied by the premises. To illustrate, consider arguments (A) and (B).

(A)
Everybody over six feet tall is
over five feet tall
Matthew is over six feet tall
Matthew is over five feet fall

(B)
Some over five feet fall are over
six feet tall
Matthew is over five feet tall
Matthew is over six feet tall

(A) is demonstrative, (B) is not. Recall from Chapter 3 that a *deductive argument* is an argument that is advanced with the claim that the conclusion is implied by the premises, even if this claim is mistaken. If it is mistaken, then the deductive argument is not demonstrative. The demonstrative argument (A) is a deductive argument relative to a use of it according to which the user claims that the conclusion is implied by the premises. Argument (B) is deductive if it is used with the mistaken claim that the conclusion is implied by the premises.

In Chapter 3 I said that an *ampliative argument* is one with premises such that if they are all true, they render the conclusion probable in the sense that they make the truth of the conclusion more likely than not, while not guaranteeing its truth. Accordingly, ampliative and demonstrative arguments are mutually exclusive types of arguments. The following is an example of an ampliative argument.

(C)
90 percent of the philosophy faculty at State U are males
Shannon's sibling is a philosophy faculty member at State U
Shannon's sibling is probably a male

Adding the premise "Shannon's sibling is named *Olivia*" results in a non-ampliative argument given that it is unlikely that a male would be named *Olivia*. From Chapter 3, an *inductive argument* is an argument advanced with the claim that the premises if true make the conclusion more likely than not without ruling out the conclusion being false. So whether argument (C) is inductive depends on whether the user of the argument is claiming that if the premises are all true, taken together they make the truth of the conclusion probable, while not guaranteeing its truth.

The two distinctions, demonstrative vs. ampliative arguments and deductive vs. inductive arguments, highlight two points. First, whether an argument is deductive or inductive turns on what its user claims regarding the premise-conclusion link. Second, this is not the case with respect to whether the argument is demonstrative or ampliative. That is, whether an argument is demonstrative or ampliative is independent of users' claims regarding the premise(s)-conclusion link. I now elaborate, starting with the first point.

Matthew asserts that nobody who likes heavy metal music likes jazz music. Shannon disagrees. She quickly responds by arguing as follows.

> Most of my friends like heavy metal music. Most of them like jazz music.
> So, probably I have a friend who likes both heavy metal and jazz music.

Shannon's argument may be displayed as follows.

(D)
Most of Shannon's friends like heavy metal music
Most of them like jazz music
Shannon has a friend who likes both heavy metal and jazz music

Shannon's use of "probably" signals that she claims that the truth of (D)'s premises taken together make the truth of the conclusion more likely than not without guaranteeing it. Accordingly, argument (D) as used by Shannon is inductive. However, Shannon's claim is, in fact, false. (D) is a demonstrative argument since the conclusion is implied by the premises. Taking *Most As are Bs* to mean that *more than half of the As are Bs*, it is not possible for the premises to be true and the conclusion false. If (D) is used in conjunction with the correct claim that the conclusion is implied by the premises, then (D) is a deductive argument.

The moral here is that whether an argument is deductive or inductive turns on whether its user claims, in effect, that the conclusion is implied by the premises. That is, whether an argument is deductive or inductive turns on how its user regards the premise(s)-conclusion link. However, whether an argument is demonstrative or ampliative is independent of what a user claims regarding the premise(s)-conclusion link. That (A) and (D) are demonstrative arguments, that (C) is an ampliative argument, and that (B) is neither are all facts that are independent of the arguments status as deductive or inductive.

I now apply the *demonstrative vs. ampliative* and *deductive vs. inductive distinctions* to reason-giving uses of arguments. This calls upon my earlier discussion in Chapter 3 of the epistemic import of reasons. I articulate a link between the *deductive vs. inductive* distinction and reason-giving uses of arguments that grounds a distinction between deductive and inductive reflective inferences. I now briefly review the notion of the epistemic import of reasons.

Some uses of arguments advance the premises as *conclusive* as opposed to *inconclusive* reasons for believing the conclusion. A proposition p is a *conclusive* reason for believing proposition q just in case p is a reason—in some sense—for q, and, in addition, if p is true, then this rules out the possibility of q being false. For example, in arguing for a conclusion, one's inference claim may be that the premises are conclusive reasons to believe the conclusion. In such a case, one believes both that the premises are reasons to believe the conclusion and that their truth rules out the possibility of the conclusion being false. If one argues from an interlocuter's assumptions, one's inference claim may be that the premises are conclusive reasons for the interlocuter to believe the conclusion. Accordingly, one believes that the premises are reasons for the interlocuter to believe the conclusion and that if true, they rule out the possibility of the conclusion being false.

By using an argument to advance the premises as *inconclusive* reasons for believing the conclusion one does not thereby believe that the premises rule out the possibility of the conclusion being false. A proposition p is an *inconclusive* reason for believing proposition q just in case p is a reason—in some sense—for q, and, in addition, if p is true, then this makes it more likely than not that q is true without ruling out the possibility of q being false.

If you use an argument to advance its premises as conclusive reasons for believing the conclusion, then your inference claim is, in effect, that the premises are such reasons. Accordingly, the argument so used is deductive, as you claim, in part, that the conclusion is implied by the premises. If the argument is not demonstrative, then this claim is false and so too is the inference claim.

If you use an argument to advance its premises as inconclusive reasons for its conclusion, then your inference claim is, in effect, that the premises are inconclusive reasons for believing the conclusion. Hence, the argument used is inductive, since you claim, in part, that the premises if true make the truth of the conclusion more likely than not without guaranteeing it. If the argument is not ampliative, then this claim is false and so too is the inference claim.

In short, whether the argument you use to advance reasons for the conclusion is deductive or inductive turns on what, if anything, your associated inference claim says about the epistemic import of the reasons the premises represent for the conclusion. If you claim and so believe that the premises represent conclusive reasons for the conclusion, then the corresponding argument is deductive. If you claim and so believe that the premises represent inconclusive reasons for the conclusion, then the corresponding argument is inductive. Of course, you may use an argument in a reason-giving way without being cognizant of the epistemic import of the reasons you advance for the conclusion. In such a case, your argument is neither deductive nor inductive although it is ampliative, demonstrative, or neither.

Recall from Chapter 4 that if you perform a reflective inference, then you possess the corresponding linking belief; i.e., you believe that the premises of your inference are reasons for believing the conclusion. If you believe that they are conclusive reasons for the conclusion, then your reflective inference is deductive. Alternatively, if you believe that they are inconclusive reasons for the conclusion, then your reflective inference is inductive.

Also recall from Chapter 4 that you perform a reflective inference just in case you use the corresponding argument in a reason-giving way (this combines theses (I) and (II) from Chapter 4). You perform a deductive/inductive reflective inference just in case the argument you use in a reason-giving way is deductive/inductive. Whether a reflective inference is deductive or inductive turns on what the inference's associated linking belief involves regarding the epistemic import of the premises as reasons for the conclusion. The linking belief is the inference-claim belief associated with the corresponding reason-giving use of argument. Accordingly, it is determinative of whether the argument so used is deductive or inductive.

I apply the demonstrative vs. ampliative distinction to reflective inferences. An inference is demonstrative just in case the corresponding argument is demonstrative. An inference is ampliative just in case the corresponding argument is ampliative. An argument corresponds to an inference just in case its given premises are the propositional contents of the initial premise-beliefs of the inference and the conclusion is the propositional content of the conclusion-belief. An argument may correspond to an inference that hasn't been performed. In such a case, it corresponds to a type of inference, whose possible instances are inferences, deductive or otherwise, from its premises to conclusion.

5.2.1. Summary

When we use arguments to advance the premises as reasons for believing their conclusions, we occasionally advance the premises as conclusive reasons for believing the conclusion. Arguments so used are deductive because we claim that the premises if true rule out the possibility of the conclusion being false. If this claim is true, the argument so used is demonstrative. Otherwise, it isn't demonstrative. Your argument is inductive if you claim that the premises if true make it more likely than not that the conclusion is true without ruling out the possibility that it is false. If this claim is true, then your argument is ampliative.

Suppose that you walk into an empty classroom and see what you take to be an argument written in standard form on the board. Given the needed know-how, you may determine whether it is demonstrative or ampliative based on your understanding of the premises and conclusion. However, this understanding does not suffice for determining whether it is deductive or inductive, which requires knowing how the author of the argument intended, if at all, to use the argument. Being demonstrative or ampliative are features of what I called in Chapter 2 stand-alone arguments. Being deductive or inductive are features of arguments in use.

I apply the deductive vs. inductive and demonstrative vs. ampliative distinctions to both arguments and reflective inferences. Your reflective inference is a deductive inference only if your linking belief is that the premises of your inference are conclusive reasons for believing the conclusion. Your reflective inference is an inductive inference only if your linking belief is that the premises of your inference are inconclusive reasons for believing the conclusion. Demonstrative and ampliative inferences correspond to demonstrative and ampliative arguments, respectively.

5.3. Formally Valid Arguments and Demonstrative Arguments

What's the connection between formally valid arguments, as discussed in Chapter 2, and demonstrative arguments? Every formally valid argument is a demonstrative argument. However, I will not assume that every demonstrative argument is formally valid. In this section, I explain how some demonstrative arguments are not formally valid. Then I illustrate how demonstrative arguments used in a reason-giving way that are not formally valid are reducible to formally valid arguments. My discussion of formal validity presupposes the brief discussion of it in Chapter 2.

All formally valid arguments are demonstrative arguments. Recall from Chapter 2 that an argument is formally valid only if it has a valid argument form. An argument form is valid just in case for each argument with that form, it is necessary that if every premise is true, then the conclusion is also true. Sometimes this is put as an argument is valid when truth is necessarily preserved from premises to conclusion in virtue of its form. If truth is necessarily preserved from premises to conclusion in virtue of its form, then the conclusion is implied by the premises. However, some demonstrative arguments are not formally valid. Consider argument (E).

(E)

Matthew is taller than Shannon	x is taller than y
Shannon is not taller than Matthew	y is not taller than x

Some resist taking the form on the right as determinative of the formal validity of (E), because *taller than* is not a logical expression (e.g., Quine 1986, pp. 28–29, 95; but see Etchemendy 2008). For example, *taller than* lacks the topic neutrality typical of logical expressions such as *or, not, and, all, some,* etc. (Tarski [1941] 1995, pp. 18–19). Alternatively, we may treat (E) as having a suppressed premise that when made explicit and added to (E) generates a formally valid argument. For example, if we add *if a person x is taller than y, then y is not taller than x* as premise, then (E) so amended is formally valid.

I will assume that not all demonstrative arguments are formally valid arguments. I take (E) to be a formally invalid argument that is a demonstrative argument. Argument (E) is formally invalid because its form, displayed below on the left, has an instance, on the right, with a true premise and false conclusion.

| xRy | 3 is less than or equal to 2+1 |
| not yRx | 2+1 is not less than or equal to 3 |

However, (E) is a demonstrative argument because *if a person x is taller than y then y is not taller than x* is a necessary truth. Given this, it is not possible for (E)'s premise to be true and its conclusion false. So (E) is a formally invalid argument that is nevertheless a demonstrative argument. Whether a formally invalid argument is a demonstrative argument turns on whether the generalization that links premise(s) and conclusion is necessarily true.

(F)	(G)
Shannon lives in the capital of Indiana	$3 > 4$ and $4 > 5$
Shannon lives in Indiana	$3 > 5$

Argument (F) is demonstrative only if it is necessarily true that one who lives in the capital of a state lives in the state. Argument (G) is demonstrative only if it is necessarily true that the less-than relation is transitive (i.e., for all numbers x, y, z, if $x > y$ and $y > z$, then $x > z$). Argument (F) may be demonstrative as the corresponding generalization is a geopolitical necessary truth. Likewise, (G) seems demonstrative since its corresponding generalization is a mathematical necessary truth. Note that if we add the respective generalizations to (F) and (G), we generate formally valid arguments. This indicates that demonstrative arguments used in a reason-giving way that are not formally valid are reducible to formally valid arguments by adding as a premise the truth(s) by which the premises are *conclusive* reasons for believing the conclusion. I now illustrate using an example from Chapter 4.

Recall the *Spitball* scenario Siegel uses to illustrate the connection between reasons, consistency, and principles that I discussed in Chapter 4. Teacher explains to Johnny's parents that her reason why she was right in keeping Johnny after class was that his behavior in class was disruptive. Accordingly, she uses an argument in a reason-giving way to give her reason for why keeping Johnny after class was right. The argument may be displayed as follows.

(H)
(1) Johnny's class behavior was disruptive
(2) Keeping Johnny after class was warranted

Suppose that Teacher advances (1) as a conclusive reason she has to believe to (2), which makes (H) a deductive argument. Since Teacher uses (H) in a reason-giving way, we suppose that Teacher believes that associated inference claim; i.e., she believes that (1) is a conclusive reason she has to believe (2). This is her inference-claim belief. Teacher's inference-claim belief is false unless the argument is demonstrative. What's the operative principle, as Siegel calls it, which makes (1) a conclusive reason Teacher has to believe (2)? Following Siegel, suppose the teacher appeals to (P).

(P): a student's disruptive behavior in class warrants keeping the student after class.

Accordingly, argument (H) is demonstrative only if this is necessarily true. Johnny's parents might wonder whether there are degrees of disruptive behavior that do not warrant keeping students after class. Or they may wonder whether a warning should precede the action of keeping the student after class. If Teacher made (P) explicit and added it as a premise to her argument (H), the result would be formally valid argument.

The *Spitball* scenario highlights the potential use of a formally invalid argument to communicate a demonstrative inference. Another example: the inference from Matthew is drinking water to Matthew is drinking H_2O is demonstrative even though the corresponding argument, *Matthew is drinking water; therefore, Matthew is drinking H_2O*, is formally invalid. Adding the necessary truth that water is H_2O as a premise to the argument corresponding to the inference generates a formally valid argument. The following argument is formally valid: *Matthew is drinking water, water is H_2O; therefore, Matthew is drinking H_2O.*

Given that some demonstrative arguments are not formally valid, what's the advantage of using formally valid arguments instead of formally invalid demonstrative arguments to advance conclusive reasons for believing their conclusions? One advantage is that it makes explicit the principle or necessary truth by which the conclusion of your inference is implied by the premises of your inference. This facilitates the communication of your inference by making it more transparent. For example, the principle that makes the inference corresponding to (E) demonstrative is, in effect, that *if a person x is taller than y, then y is not taller than x*. As previously mentioned, when added to (E) as a premise, the resulting argument is formally valid. Also, using a formally valid argument to express your demonstrative inference facilitates the confirmation that it is demonstrative since there are effective procedures for determining the formal validity of the corresponding argument.

Furthermore, a formally valid argument may be used to identify the operative contingent principle that if true make one's premises inconclusive reasons for believing one's conclusion. For·example, uttering, "Matthew's friend is a Republican, so probably Matthew's friend voted for the Republican nominee" plausibly indicates that the speaker advances the premises as an inconclusive reason for the conclusion, which makes the argument so used inductive. A candidate for the operative principle is a general truth such that adding it as a premise to the above argument results in a formally valid argument. For example, adding, *a person who is a Republican voted for Trump* results in a formally valid argument. Suppose that this is the principle the speaker appeals to. Then, since the original argument is inductive, the speaker doesn't take this to be necessarily true. Rather, the speaker takes the generalization to be more likely true than not.

For another example, recall Toulmin's toy argument from Chapter 4.

(1) Harry was born in Bermuda. So, presumably, (2) Harry is a British subject.

Suppose that a person S uses this argument to advance (1) as a reason to believe (2). The conclusion modifier, in Toulmin's terminology the *qualifier*, indicates that S believes that (1) is an inconclusive reason to believe that (2). Recall that Toulmin gives the following generalization as S's warrant, i.e., the principle, grounding the link between (1) and (2).

(P): A man born in Bermuda will be a British subject.

Given S's conclusion modifier, S does not take (P) to be a necessary truth. This is suggested by S's recognition that (P) fails if it should turn out that relevant possibilities, mentioned by Toulmin, should obtain such as both of Harry's parents are aliens, or he has become a naturalized American. Certainly, adding (P) as a premise to the toy argument generates a formally valid argument. However, this doesn't make the toy argument demonstrative since plausibly (P) is not necessarily true. Given that S's argument is inductive, what matters to its evaluation is whether the argument is ampliative. This turns on whether (P) is more likely true than not.

5.3.1. Summary

Every formally valid argument is a demonstrative argument, but some demonstrative arguments are not formally valid. Certainly, ampliative arguments are not formally valid since no ampliative argument is demonstrative. When you use an argument to advance its premises as reasons with a certain epistemic import, i.e., as conclusive or otherwise, you appeal to a generalization, which I have loosely called a principle, according to which the premises qualify as reasons for believing the conclusion in the intended sense. Taking the principle to be necessarily true is required for you to advance the premises as *conclusive* reasons for believing the conclusion. Taking the principle to be more likely true than not but not necessarily true is required for you to advance the premises as *inconclusive* reasons for believing the conclusion.

I said in Chapter 4 that a reflective inference is criterial in the sense that the inferer is *trying* to fulfill a standard or standards of adequacy appropriate to the inference, which if satisfied makes the inferer's thinking good. If your inference is deductive, then a standard that you intend to meet is that the corresponding argument is demonstrative. If the corresponding argument is not formally valid, then this standard is not met unless the principle that links your premise(s) and conclusion is necessarily true. If your inference is inductive, then a standard that you intend to meet is that the corresponding argument is ampliative. This standard is not satisfied unless the principle that links your premise(s) and conclusion is more likely true than not, but not necessarily true.

5.4. Formally Valid Arguments and Reason-Giving Uses of Arguments

Some formally valid arguments do not correspond to reflective inferences and so cannot be successfully used to advance their premises as reasons for their conclusions. This is not surprising since, as discussed in Chapter 2, formal validity is a property of arguments in the abstract and so whether an argument so conceived is formally valid is independent of its suitability to be used in a reason-giving way. More generally, this is also true of demonstrative arguments. That an argument is demonstrative does not by itself make it suitable as a means of advancing reasons for believing the conclusion.

In this section, I sample some formally valid arguments and make a case that they do not correspond to reflective inferences. I appeal to a distinction between deductive reflective inferences that are belief-inducing and those that are not. My discussion addresses two related topics: (i) the connection between formally valid arguments and reason-giving uses of arguments; and (ii) judging the adequacy of a formal logic for evaluating deductive reflective inferences.

Regarding (i), certainly, a reason-giving use of a formally valid argument may be a bad, because the premises are not *good* reasons to believe the conclusion (e.g., say a premise is obviously false). Furthermore, a formally valid argument may not be suitable for a reason-giving use of it because it does not correspond to a reflective inference, good or otherwise. Such arguments can't be successfully used to advance their premises as reasons for believing the conclusion. This leads to topic (ii).

It isn't a problem for a formal logic to endorse that an argument, p *so* q, is formally valid even though it isn't good reasoning to infer q from p, if it is impossible to infer q from p. For example, it is said that classical logic is inadequate because it incorrectly endorses inferring anything you like from an explicit contradiction (e.g., Read 1995, pp. 42–33), and inferring any logically necessary truth from anything you like (e.g., Priest 1979, p. 297). Since incorrect reasoning is nevertheless reasoning, these criticisms assume a characterization of inferential reasoning according to which it is possible to perform these inferences. Below, I question that these criticisms impugn the use of classical logic to judge reflective inferences, by questioning that such reasoning qualifies as reflective inference. Toward this end, I now turn to a distinction between belief-inducing and non-belief-inducing reflective inferences.

Your reflective inference is belief-inducing if it induces your belief that the conclusion is true. Such inferences are either generative or confirmative. That is, the premise-beliefs of your belief-inducing inference either generate your conclusion-belief or increase your degree of certainty of your conclusion-belief acquired by some other means. If your reflective inference is non-belief-inducing, then it is neither generative nor confirmative. Accordingly, it does not induce your belief in the conclusion. I now elaborate, starting with reflective inferences that are belief-inducing.

Shannon is serving dessert and she wonders whether she should cut Beth a piece of pie. She then recalls both that (i) that Beth drank a beer just before dinner and that Beth has told her in the recent past (ii) that if she drinks a beer just before a dinner, she doesn't want dessert afterward. Shannon infers and comes to believe that (iii) that Beth does not want dessert after dinner, because she believes that (i) and (ii) are conclusive reasons for her to believe (iii). Taken together, (i) and (ii) reasons *for which* Shannon believes (iii). Shannon's inference is belief-inducing. It's what I called in Chapter 4, an *a persona* inference. Accordingly, Shannon's inference exemplifies a transfer of certainty from her acceptance of the premise to the conclusion. When Matthew asks Shannon why she isn't cutting Beth any apple pie, Shannon communicates an argument equivalent with the below formally valid argument, whose form is displayed on the right.

If Beth drank a beer just before a dinner, then she doesn't want dessert afterward	$A \to B$
Beth drank a beer just before dinner	A
She doesn't want dessert afterwards	B

Because belief-inducing inference results in believing-for-a-reason, it is distinguishable from non-belief-inducing reasoning in terms of its cognitive import. For example, only the former can be generative or confirmative; e.g., the premise-beliefs of your belief-inducing inference either generate your conclusion-belief (as with Shannon's inference) or increase your degree of certainty of it acquired by some other means (e.g., the example of reverse reasoning in Chapter 4). So reasoning can't be belief-inducing unless there is a transfer of a degree of certainty from given premises to the conclusion. Call this the *credence feature* of a reflective belief-inducing inference.

Belief-inducing reflective inferences are mental transitions between beliefs that are consciously entertained. With respect to such inferences, a reasoner's acceptance of the premises induces their acceptance of the conclusion. Call this the *acceptance feature* of belief-inducing reflective inferences. Here I appeal to a notion of acceptance according to which one's acceptance that p necessitates one's assenting to and so believing that p. In this sense of "acceptance," one accepts that p at time t if and only if at t one is consciously attending to one's belief in the sense that one judges that or assents to p. The acceptance feature accords with the idea that reflective inferences are a type of reasoning that includes what Broome (2013, sec. 13.1) calls active, belief reasoning, which is theoretical reasoning that concludes in one believing something and which is conscious in the sense that the reasoner is conscious of, i.e., explicitly aware of, the contents of the given premise- and conclusion-beliefs of the inference.

In short, *acceptance* and *credence* are essential features of belief-inducing reflective inferences. Are they essential features of non-belief-inducing reflective inferences? Toward a response, I simplify and regard non-belief-inducing reflective inferences as suppositional or (hypothetical) reflective inferences.[1] So our question becomes: Are *acceptance* and *credence* essential features of suppositional reflective inferences? *Credence* is not, but a version of *acceptance* is an essential feature of suppositional reflective inferences. I now elaborate.

Recall Dewey's *Burglary* example of reflective thinking, given in Chapter 4. The protagonist P reasons from the hypothesis that his room has been burglarized. So P thinks that it is possible (i) that the room has been burglarized. If P didn't think this, P wouldn't be considering (i) given P's aim of figuring out why his room is disheveled. P reasons from (i) to (ii) that an article is missing. P performs a suppositional reflective inference, because P believes both that (i) is merely (relevantly) possible and that (ii) follows from (i). P's suppositional inference motivates P to check his belongings to see if anything is missing.

I assume that P performs a reflective inference, and so I assume that he uses the following argument to advance its premise as a conclusive suppositional reason for believing its conclusion.

The room has been burglarized
An article in the room is missing

---

[1] Of course, reflective inferences are belief-inducing or not. My simplification here amounts to taking non-belief-inducing reflective inferences to be suppositional in the sense that to perform such an inference the inferer must at minimum regard the premises at least as merely possibly true, and think that the conclusion follows from them in some way. Accordingly, reflective inferences are either belief-inducing or (-exclusive) suppositional in this sense. This is plausible. If you perform a reflective inference, then you believe that the premises of your inference are reasons for believing the conclusion. Given the account of reasons for belief in Chapter 3, if you believe that the premises of your reflective inference are reasons for believing what you infer so understood, then your reflective inference is either belief-inducing or suppositional. This parallels the observation in Chapter 4 that inferences occurring in the process of critical thinking *are a persona* (and so belief-inducing) inferences or suppositional. Chapter 7's discussion of reasons for belief and rationality lends support to the idea that reflective inferences are either belief-inducing or suppositional.

This makes the argument deductive. It is necessarily true that a room that has been burglarized has an article missing from it. Accordingly, the argument is demonstrative and so too is P's corresponding inference.

P's linking belief associated with his inference is, in effect, that (i) is a conclusive, suppositional reason for believing (ii). This linking belief seems true in the context of *Burglary* because (i) is possibly true, and if true would be a conclusive reason to believe (ii). However, prior to determining whether an article is missing, P believes neither (i) nor (ii). As with all suppositional reflective inferences, *credence* and *acceptance*—as related to belief-inducing inferences—are not features of P's inference. This makes it a non-belief-inducing inference. While P does not accept that (i) is true, P does accept that (i) is merely possible. Again, if P thought it was impossible for the room to have been burglarized, then P wouldn't have performed the inference given his aim of accounting for why the room was a mess.

Let's label P's acceptance that (i) is merely possible *suppositional acceptance* to distinguish it from *belief-inducing acceptance*. If your acceptance that *p* is suppositional, then you accept that *p* is merely possibly true. Suppositionally accepting that *p* does not invoke a commitment to the truth of *p*. However, your belief-inducing acceptance that *p*, i.e., your acceptance that p is true, obviously does invoke a commitment to the truth of *p*.

To summarize, I break down reflective inferences into those that are belief-inducing and those that are suppositional. Both *acceptance* and *credence* are essential features of reflective inferences that are belief-inducing. Accordingly, an inference that lacks either isn't a belief-inducing reflective inference. *Suppositional acceptance* is a necessary feature of suppositional reflective inferences, but *credence* is not.

Drawing on what we said about how arguments correspond to inferences at the end of section 5.2, an argument corresponds to a reflective inference just in case its premises are the propositional contents of the premise-beliefs, and the conclusion is the propositional content of the conclusion-belief. An argument may correspond to a reflective inference that hasn't been performed. In such a case, it corresponds to a type of reflective inference, whose instances are reflective inferences, deductive or otherwise, from its premises to conclusion.

To see why not every formally valid argument may correspond to a deductive reflective inference, consider the following three arguments.

(I)

<u>Matthew is 6′3″ and it is not the case that Matthew is 6′3″</u>   A & ~ A
Paige lives in Maryland   B

(J)

If Shannon is an artist, then Shannon is artistic   A → B
<u>Shannon is an artist</u>   <u>A</u>
Shannon is astute or it is not the case that Shannon is astute   C v ~ C

(K)

<u>Paige lives in Maryland</u>   <u>A</u>
Paige lives in Maryland   A

I understand these arguments to have forms as displayed to their right, using "&," "→," and "~" to symbolize the expressions "and," "if . . . then," and "it is not the case," respectively. These expressions are commonly considered as logical expressions. In displaying the argument forms, I use A, B, and C as proposition placeholders. For example, replacing A in (K)'s argument form with any proposition will generate an argument that instantiates the same form, such as the following.

<u>If Shannon is an artist, then Shannon is artistic</u>
If Shannon is an artist, then Shannon is artistic

Note that (I), (J), and (K) are demonstrative arguments since for each it is impossible for the premise(s) to be true and the conclusion untrue. I will assume classical formal logic, according to which (I), (J), and (K) are formally valid. For each, there is no argument that instantiates its form that can have true premise(s) and a false conclusion. This is clearly so with respect to (K). With respect to (I), every argument that instantiates its form has a premise that is necessarily false. So, for such arguments it is not possible for the premise to be true and the conclusion false. No argument that instantiates (J)'s form has a conclusion that is possibly false. So, for each such argument it is not possible for the premise to be true and the conclusion false.

There are good philosophical grounds for questioning that (I) and (J) are indeed formally valid. It is hard to understand how exactly (I)'s premise if true nontrivially guarantees the truth of the conclusion when it is impossible for the premise to be true. With respect to (J), how is it that (J)'s premises if true guarantee the truth of the conclusion when the necessary truth of the conclusion seems independent of the truth of the premises? That is, how does the truth of (J)'s conclusion follow *from* the supposition that the premises are true?

There is much more to say regarding how a formal logic that makes arguments (I) and (J) formally valid may be a problem for the logic (e.g., see Read 1995 and Priest 1999). I now turn to the topic of whether (I)–(K) correspond to deductive reflective inferences, taking these to be either belief-inducing or suppositional. If they do not, as I argue below, then that a logic judges (I) and (J) as valid does not problematize its use to assess reflective inferences.

For any of (I), (J), and (K), if you draw its conclusion from the premise(s), what must be true about your inference for it to qualify as a deductive reflective inference? Earlier I said that if your reflective inference is deductive, then you advance the premises of the corresponding argument as *conclusive* reasons for the believing the conclusion. From Chapter 4, for an inference to be reflective it must be active, persistent, purposeful, and criterial. I now briefly review to set up my case that none of the three arguments correspond to those reflective inferences that are belief-inducing or suppositional.

If your inference is active, then you are cognizant of the contents of your premise- and conclusion-beliefs. For example, with respect to argument (I) you are aware that by virtue of your premise-belief you accept that an explicit contradiction is true. If your inference is persistent, then it is a mental transition from premise(s) to conclusion between thoughts that is slow and cognitively demanding. Your inference is purposeful in that you draw the conclusion from the premises to serve your aim(s) in using the corresponding argument in a reason-giving way. For example, for your inference corresponding to (J) to be purposeful you must infer the tautology, *Shannon is astute or it is not the case that Shannon is astute*, from (J)'s premises in order to serve your aim(s) in using (J) in a reason-giving way. Finally, a reflective inference must be criterial in the sense that the inferer R must think that their inference meets the standard(s) by which it is warranted; i.e., R must believe that their inference is good. This connotes that R performs a reflective inference carefully in that R believes that they correctly judge that the premise are reasons of the relevant sort for believing the conclusion.

It is far from obvious to me that (I), (J), and (K) correspond to deductive reflective inferences understood as either belief-inducing or suppositional.

If not, then none can be successfully used in a reason-giving way. Of course, this presupposes that only those arguments that correspond to reflective inferences can be successfully used to advance their premises as reasons for believing the conclusion. I consider each argument in turn, starting with (I).

For an inference from (I)'s premise to its conclusion to be a reflective inference, either *belief-inducing acceptance* or *suppositional acceptance* must be a feature of it. Suppose argument (I) corresponds to a reasoner R's deductive reflective inference that is belief-inducing. Then *acceptance* obtains. That is, R explicitly accepts and so believes the explicit contradiction serving as the premise of R's inference. Furthermore, since R's reflective inference is essentially active reasoning, R is explicitly aware of the content of R's premise-belief and so aware that they accept as true an explicit contradiction.

It is one thing to acknowledge that anyone can have inconsistent beliefs, it is quite another to say that one can accept and so assent to what one takes to be an explicit contradiction. If one can't assent to what one believes to be an explicit contradiction (following Foley 1986; Goldstein 1988; Marcus 1981; and Smiley 1993; but see Priest 1993), then argument (I) does not correspond to a reflective belief-inducing inference.

Following Smiley (1993, p. 20) and Price (1990, p. 224), a primary function of one's use of a negation is to register rejection. If you sincerely and truthfully claim that it is not the case that Matthew is tall, you communicate your rejection that Matthew is tall. Correspondingly, if you believe that it is not the case that Matthew is tall, then you reject that Matthew is tall. Acceptance and rejection are commonly regarded as mutually exclusive cognitive attitudes (e.g., Sainsbury 2009, p. 154; Smiley 1993, p. 20; Priest 1993, p. 39). Accordingly, it is not possible to simultaneously accept and reject a proposition.

Given that negation registers rejection, it follows that it is not possible to accept an explicit contradiction. Suppose otherwise, e.g., suppose that one accepts an explicit contradiction, $p \mathbin{\&} \sim p$. Then one accepts p, and one accepts $\sim p$. If one accepts $\sim p$, then one rejects p. But then one accepts and rejects p, which is psychologically impossible. Therefore, contrary to our supposition, one can't accept $p \mathbin{\&} \sim p$.

One may object by arguing that when one accepts $p \mathbin{\&} \sim p$ one isn't using negation to register one's rejection of p (e.g., see Priest 1993). Rather, one is using negation to merely register one's acceptance that p is false. A *dialethia* is a proposition such that both it and its negation are true. Given that a negation is true just in case what is negated is false, if there are *dialethias*, then there are propositions that are both true and false. If one accepts that there are *dialethias*, one thinks that truth doesn't exclude falsehood.

For example, consider the Liar paradox. Let proposition p be *this proposition is false*. Proposition p is either true or false. Suppose that p is true. Then what it reports is the case. Hence, p is false as well. Suppose that p is false. Then since this is what p reports, p is true as well. Therefore, p is both true and false (Priest 2008, p. 129). This makes true (and false) the explicit contradiction, $p \ \& \sim p$. Clearly, the cost of this resolution of the Liar paradox is that it deviates from the ordinary use of negation to register rejection. Given that there are other plausible responses to self-reference paradoxes which do not bring *dialethia* into play (for discussion see Sainsbury 2009, chap. 7; Read 1995, chap. 6), one might think that this cost is too high.

Plausibly, the ordinary use of negation is to register rejection. This pragmatic observation seems supported by the following. Intuitively, if you find yourself having inconsistent beliefs you don't thereby accept an explicit contradiction. Rather, finding out that you have inconsistent beliefs is always sufficient reason to suspend judgment and re-examine the basis of the beliefs that got you there. Since this is so obvious, no reasoner can perform a reflective belief-inducing inference from her acceptance of an explicit contradiction to her acceptance of the conclusion. Hence, reasoning in a belief-inducing, reflective way from an explicit contradiction is impossible.

Suppose that argument (I) corresponds to a reasoner R's deductive reflective inference that is suppositional and so non-belief-inducing. Then R believes that (I)'s premise is a conclusive suppositional reason for believing the conclusion. Accordingly, R accepts two claims: (i) that the premise is merely possibly true and (ii) that R's inference is demonstrative. Since by hypothesis, R regards (I)'s premise as a suppositional reason for the conclusion, R accepts (i). Since R thinks that the premise is a *conclusive* reason for the conclusion, R accepts (ii). Since R's reasoning is careful by virtue of being a reflective inference, R judges that argument (I) is demonstrative. Therefore, R judges that (I)'s premise is impossible, and so R rejects (i). But it is not possible for R to accept and reject (i). Therefore, our initial supposition is false. (I) does not correspond to a reasoner R's suppositional reflective inference.

Let's turn to argument (J), which has as premise patterns $A \rightarrow B$ and A, and $C \lor \sim C$ as the pattern of the conclusion. Consider Broome's example of the connection between rule-following in performing an inference and the inferential act seeming right to the inferer.

When you infer $r \vee {\sim}r$ from p and $p \rightarrow q$, this will seem right relative to the rule of inferring a tautology but not right relative to the *modus ponens* rule. When you infer q from p and $p \rightarrow q$, this will seem right relative to the *modus ponens* rule, but not relative to the rule of inferring a tautology. (Broome 2014, p. 22)

Roughly, Broome characterizes rule-following to consist in acting in accordance with a simple disposition to act in a particular way and for your act to seem right to you relative to a rule.

In contrast to the reasoning guided by a modus ponens rule, the given premises are explicitly superfluous to the use of the rule of inferring a tautology to reach the conclusion. A premise is *explicitly superfluous* to a formally valid argument if a derivation of the conclusion from the set of premises does not deploy a rule that uses the premise to derive the conclusion. Since $r \vee {\sim}r$ is a tautology, and, therefore logically necessary, any argument with it as a conclusion is demonstrative. Accordingly, inferring $r \vee {\sim}r$ "from" p and $p \rightarrow q$ appealing to the rule of inferring a tautology does not use p and $p \rightarrow q$. This makes the premises explicitly superfluous to drawing the conclusion (e.g., $r \vee {\sim}r$ may be drawn using the rule of inferring a tautology with the negations of p and $p \rightarrow q$ as premises).

Suppose that you knowingly use the rule of inferring a tautology to infer and so believe (J)'s conclusion. This makes your inference criterial. Further suppose that your inference is reflective. Accordingly, you are aware that the premises are explicitly superfluous to your use of the rule. Furthermore, since you perform your inference carefully, you recognize that your use of the rule of inferring a tautology nullifies the status of the premises as reasons for believing the conclusion. Your explicit appeal to the rule of inferring a tautology to warrant your inference means that you accept that *Shannon is astute or it is not the case that Shannon is astute* because it is a tautology and not because you take the premises to be reasons for believing it. But then, contrary to what we supposed, your inference isn't reflective. So it doesn't correspond to an argument whose premises are reasons for believing the conclusion.

This accounts for why following the rule of inferring a tautology doesn't involve a transfer of the reasoner's credence that the premise is true to their credence that the conclusion is also true. Argument (J) corresponds to no belief-inducing reflective inference. As using the rule of inferring a tautology to infer (J)'s conclusion from premises that are explicitly superfluous discounts the inference as a reflective inference, it also discounts the inference as a suppositional reflective inference.

I now turn to explicitly circular argument (K). (K) is explicitly circular because its conclusion and premise are one and the same proposition. Its corresponding conditional, *if Shannon lives in Maryland, then Shannon lives in Maryland*, instantiates the pattern, *if A then A*, which is often referred to as the (logical) law of identity (e.g., Detlefsen, McCarty, and Bacon 1999, p. 62). Obviously, any instance is tautologous and so is necessarily true. Relatedly, (K) is clearly demonstrative, and unlike the classical logician's judgment that (I) and (J) are formally valid, the assessment that (K) is formally valid is not controversial.

Does (K) correspond to a reflective inference? Perhaps the simplest way to see that it does not is to observe that the inference corresponding to (K) is not persistent. That reflective inferences are persistent requires that they are mental transitions from one thought to another. That is, a reflective inference involves a period of changing from one mental state to another. Since (K) is explicitly circular, the argument corresponds to no inference that is persistent. For example, a belief-inducing reflective inference is persistent because it requires a *transition* from premise-belief(s) to conclusion-belief, which presupposes that the conclusion-belief isn't a premise-belief. This explains why any inference from (K)'s premise to conclusion lacks the credence feature. How could it possess *credence* when the premise and conclusion are one and the same?

That a suppositional inference is persistent suggests that the corresponding linking belief is nontrivial, which indicates that the inference is cognitively demanding. However, your belief that *Paige lives in Maryland* is a suppositional reason for believing that *Paige lives in Maryland* requires believing that *if it is true that Paige lives in Maryland, then this is reason for me to believe that Paige lives in Maryland*. This is trivial, which makes it hard to see how an inference corresponding to (I) serves the purposes of deciding what to believe or do.

In short, I think that there are good reasons for denying that (I)–(K) correspond to reflective inferences. Does this suggest that any logic that judges them formally valid such as classical logic should not be regarded as a logic of reflective inferences? Let's consider affirmative and negative responses in turn.

If yes, then this rules out any logic such as classical logic being a logic of reflective inference. According to Gabbay and Woods (2005, p. 20), the *consequence-attenuation approach* to the connection between logical consequence and a type of reasoning restricts the formal validity of arguments to those that correspond to the reasoning. By this approach, formal validity needs to be conceptualized so that formally valid arguments necessarily correspond to reflective inferences.

The consequence-attenuation approach motivates various logics for various types of reasoning. For example, on this approach (I), (J), (K) would not be formally valid according to a logic of reflective inferences. While shaping a notion of formal validity and the related logical consequence relation to fit a particular type of reasoning may serve to recover formal logic's place as a theory of reasoning (Gabbay and Woods 2005, p. 18),[2] it seems to rule out the traditional conception of formal validity as a priori determinable and a necessary feature of arguments (as reflected in their different ways by Tarski [1936] 1983; Etchemendy 2008; and Hanson 1997). For example, the consequence-attenuation approach makes whether (K) is formally valid depend on the nature of the inferences it is used to judge, which is an empirical matter. There may be good reasons to follow Gabbay and Woods (2005), as well as others (e.g., van Benthem 2008), and think so much the worse for the traditional conception of logical consequence.

Again, the question that I am considering is as follows. If a logic endorses (I)–(K) as formally valid, should it thereby not be considered a logic of reflective inferences? A rationale for a negative response put simply runs as follows. A logic such as classical logic that makes arguments (I)–(K) formally valid may nevertheless be regarded as a logic of reflective inferences given that these arguments do not correspond to reflective inferences. If correct, this rationale motivates restricting the class of arguments to those that correspond to reflective inferences in order to use an appropriate logic, classical or otherwise, to logically judge reflective inferences. One way of so fixing the class of abstract arguments is to impose structural constraints on them so that they correspond to reflective inferences, ensuring that every formal valid argument corresponds to a reflective inference. This strategy loosely reflects Aristotle's use of syllogisms to mediate a connection between formal validity and syllogistic reasoning. I now elaborate, drawing heavily on Woods (2002).

Aristotle initially defines a syllogism as a kind of deduction with the following features.

---

[2] They develop a conception of logic that they characterize as the practical turn in logic, which counters the standard picture of mathematical logic as a theory of reasoning (2005, p. 17).

> [A] deduction [*syllogismos*] rests on certain statements such that they in-
> volve necessarily the assertion of something other than what is stated,
> through what has been stated. (*On Sophistical Refutations* 1, 165ᵃ 1–3)

Woods remarks that Aristotle uses a notion of syllogistic reasoning to restrict the class of arguments so that they correspond to syllogistic reasoning. Aristotle's developed account of syllogisms construes them as finite
sequences of propositions terminating with a conclusion, the preceding
members being its premises (Woods 2002, pp. 46–47). Woods notes that
scholars agree that the following are necessary features of syllogisms.

(1) Its premises jointly necessitate the conclusion.
(2) It does not contain idle premises.
(3) Its conclusion does not repeat a premise.

Condition (1) blocks a valid argument from being a syllogism if it's valid
just because its conclusion is a logical truth or *just* because one of its premises is inconsistent. While condition (2) makes the property of *syllogosity*
non-monotonic. That is, adding a premise to a syllogism may not result in
a syllogism. Compare: adding any premise to an abstract argument results
in another abstract argument. Condition (3) makes it incompatible with explicit circularity. Woods says that analysis of the structure of syllogisms gives
reason to think that additional constraints apply:

> that syllogisms must be consistently premissed; that syllogisms can have at
> most one conclusion (and, in some accounts, at most) two premises; that a
> logical truth cannot be the conclusion of a syllogism; that the premises of a
> syllogism must be relevant to the conclusion; and so on. (2002, p. 47)

As Woods acknowledges (2002, p. 50), Aristotle aligns valid arguments with
syllogistic reasoning by restricting valid arguments in terms of constraints
on their structure rather than by adopting the consequence-attenuation approach. Recall that on this approach, instead of constraining what counts as
a valid *argument*, the logical consequence relation is constrained in order to
use the associated logic to judge a class of inferences. For example, in accordance with the consequence-attenuation approach one could follow the relevance logician and restrict logical consequence so that no argument is valid
just because it has an inconsistent premise and constrain valid deductions to

those that must use every premise (e.g., see Mares 2002). Of course, the relevance logician thinks that validity and deduction so unconstrained aren't genuine. Woods remarks that

> Aristotle need not say this and almost certainly doesn't believe it. By his lights, unconstrained deductions from premises are valid. What they aren't is *syllogisms*. Readers may wish to ponder whether we have here a difference that makes a difference. (2002, p. 51)

We do indeed have a difference that makes a difference. Borrowing from Wood's commentary on Aristotle, we may impose constraints on the class of arguments so that each corresponds to a reflective inference. Call such arguments reflective-inference arguments. Obviously, what counts as a reflective-inference argument turns on the nature of reflective inferences and so is empirically determined. The key idea here is that the use of a conceptually adequate account of formal validity to judge deductive reflective inferences is mediated by a restriction of the associated class of abstract arguments to reflective-inference arguments.

A logic such as classical logic that makes (I)–(K) formally valid may nevertheless be regarded as a logic of reflective inferences, if we take the logic to judge not mere abstract arguments, but reflective-inference arguments, i.e., abstract arguments that correspond to reflective inferences. Plausibly, (1)–(3) are conditions that constrain what counts as a reflective-inference argument. If so, condition (1) rules out (I) and (J) as reflective-inference arguments. Conditions (2) and (3) rule out (J) and (K) as reflective-inference arguments. Argument (J) is ruled out twice.

Chapter 2's distinction between abstract and dialectical arguments favors the Aristotelean approach to the connection between formal validity and reflective inferences over the consequence-attenuation approach. Recall that in Chapter 2 I distinguished between abstract and dialectical arguments. My rationale for the distinction is that abstract arguments, the formal logician's notion of argument, are needed to define formal validity and logical consequence. For example, abstract arguments can have infinitely many premises or none. But dialectical arguments cannot, i.e., arguments used to advance their premises as reasons for believing the conclusion. Whether an abstract argument is formally valid is independent of its feasibility as a dialectical argument. An abstract argument needn't correspond to a reflective inference, but a dialectical argument that is a reason-giving use of argument must (recall theses (I) and (II) from Chapter 4).

To be clear, for a given formal logic a restriction of the class of associated arguments[3] to those that correspond to reflective inference does not suffice for the conceptual adequacy of the logic's account of formal validity. For example, nothing said so far entails that classical logic is correct about what arguments count as formally valid. If classical logic isn't correct about formal validity, then it isn't adequate as a logic for judging reflective inferences. What my discussion in this section highlights is that the plausibility of arguing that a logic is inadequate for judging reflective inferences because it has some formally valid arguments that correspond to intuitively logically incorrect reflective inferences presupposes that those arguments correspond to reflective inferences. If this presupposition fails, then so too does the criticism.

Classical logic's endorsement of *ex falso quodlibet*, literally from the false anything (follows) and *ex quolibet verum*, i.e., from the truth anything (follows), is controversial. Typically, *ex falso quodlibet* is taken to endorse that an arbitrary proposition follows from a necessarily false proposition such as an explicit contradiction. *Ex quolibet verum* is typically taken to endorse that a necessarily true proposition follows from an arbitrary proposition. More than a few logicians reject both principles (see Read 1995, chap. 2; Priest 1979; and Hitchcock 2011, among many others). Rejecting *ex falso quodlibet* rules out accepting that a proposition q follows from a proposition p just because p is necessarily false. Rejecting *ex quolibet verum* rules out accepting that that a proposition q follows from a proposition p just because q is necessarily true. The intuitive rationale for both rejections is that the mutual relevance between p and q is necessary for one to follow from the other.

Consider the following scenario used by Mares (2002, p. 609) to illustrate the implausibility of *ex quolibet verum*. Suppose that a classical logician addressing a conference of fellow number theorists uses the following argument for Fermat's Last Theorem, as expressed by (2).

(1) The sky is blue

∴ (2) There is no integer n greater than or equal to 3 such that for any non-zero integers x, y, and z, $x^n = y^n + z^n$

---

[3] The class of such arguments are the arguments composed of sentences from the language L associated with the logic; i.e., the logic defines logical consequence and validity for L.

Both (1) and (2) are true. Since (2) is a mathematical necessity, it is impossible for (1) to be true and (2) false. Accordingly, I take the argument to be demonstrative. Nevertheless, the classical logician's reason-giving use of this argument is clearly problematic. As Mares correctly notes, the classical logician's reasoning is a non sequitur. The truth of (1) has nothing to do with the truth of (2). Mares takes this to suggest that intuitively (2) does not follow from (1) and so the classical logician's reasoning corresponding to the argument is logically incorrect. If so, then the argument shouldn't be demonstrative. This suggests, following Mares, that the classical-logic account of validity is conceptually inadequate. For example, not every argument with a logical necessity as its conclusion (as with argument (J) above) is formally valid.

However, thinking that the classical logician's reason-giving use of the argument is unsuccessful doesn't automatically suggest the inadequacy of the classical account of validity. One might think that the classical logician's reason-giving use of the argument is unsuccessful not because the corresponding reflective inference is logically incorrect, but because the argument used does not correspond to a reflective inference from (1) to (2). Therefore, the argument doesn't correspond to a reflective inference that is a non sequitur, because it doesn't correspond to a reflective inference.

Consider the following passage from Priest in which he appeals to intuitions regarding logically correct reasoning to criticize the orthodox (i.e., classical) account of validity for overgenerating.

> For the notion of validity that comes out of the orthodox account is a strangely perverse one according to which any rule whose conclusion is a logical truth is valid and, conversely, any rule whose premises contain a contradiction is valid. By a process that does not fall far short of indoctrination most logicians have now had their sensibilities dulled to these glaring anomalies. However, this is possible only because logicians have also forgotten that logic is a normative subject: it is supposed to provide an account of correct reasoning. When seen in this light the full force of these absurdities can be appreciated. Anyone who actually reasoned from an arbitrary premise to, e.g., the infinity of prime numbers, would not last long in an undergraduate mathematics course. (1979, p. 297)

Following McFarlane's reading of Priest here (2004, p. 4), Priest seems to assume that if an argument is formally valid, then it is always correct to reason from its premises to its conclusion. So it should always be logically correct to reason from an arbitrary premise to the infinity of primes, which Priest emphasizes is problematic. Priest doesn't characterize the type of reasoning that we may use formal validity to judge and so it is unclear what is the nature of the reasoning from, say, *Shannon is an artist* to *There are infinitely many prime numbers*. Plausibly, it isn't reflective inferential reasoning. Accordingly, Priest's criticism does not automatically impugn the use of classical logic to logically evaluate reflective inferences.

5.4.1. Summary

Recall from Chapter 2 that I take arguments to be abstract. It is not controversial to claim that the mere fact that an argument so construed is formally valid doesn't make it correspond to a human psychological process of drawing an inference from its premises to conclusion (e.g., see Walton 1990; Cherniak 1986, chap. 4). After all, arguments can have a huge number of premises or premises that are syntactically complex, but the human psychological process of drawing an inference is essentially constrained by time and by finite cognitive resources. Generally, to understand how knowledge of formal validity facilitates inferential reasoning, we need to know that arguments correspond to inferences.[4]

The central point of this section is that the formal validity of an argument serves as a guide for your performance of a deductive reflective inference only if it corresponds to a deductive reflective inference. I have illustrated the import of this point taking reflective inferences to be either belief-inducing or suppositional. I think the point generalizes to all demonstrative (and ampliative) arguments. A demonstrative argument can't be used to advance reasons for its conclusion unless it corresponds to a reflective inference. Accordingly, the fact that an argument is demonstrative is relevant to whether a reason-giving use of it satisfies norms for reason-giving uses of arguments only if it corresponds to a reflective inference.

---

[4] This turns Harman's (1984) inquiry into the connection between logic and reasoning on its head: "So I thought I might be able to understand how argument and calculation facilitate reasoning if I could understand how the appreciation of implication can facilitate reasoning" (pp. 112–13). The view that I have advanced suggests that to understand how the appreciation of implication can facilitate reasoning, one must first understand how arguments facilitate reasoning by virtue of understanding how they correspond to episodes of such reasoning.

5.5. Demonstrative Arguments and
Reason-Giving Uses of Arguments

When should the argument that one uses to advance its premises as reasons for believing the conclusion be demonstrative? My response appeals to pragmatic, doxastic, and dialectical norms for reason-giving uses of arguments. Before addressing these norms specifically, I first say something briefly about norms in general, and then speak to the function of norms in determining when a reason-giving use of argument is good.

Railton (1999, p. 321) traces the etymology of the English expression *norm* to the Latin *norma*, which refers to a builder's square. A *norma* is used by those in the know (e.g., carpenters) as a guide in, say, making square one's cut in a board. Carpenters consult such tools to guide themselves in making square cuts and judging whether their work "measures up." Railton appeals to this concrete example of the "action-guidingness" and associated "standard of correctness" of a *norma* to highlight the regulative function and applicability conditions of norms.

The regulative function of a *norma* is manifested in one's treating any gaps between actual cuts and the square to show that there is something to be "corrected" in the cut rather than in the tool (Railton 1999, p. 321). However, the tool itself does not guide carpenters in judging when their cuts should measure up to the *norma*. That is, the *norma* itself offers no guidance regarding its applicability. The applicability of a *norma* as a guide for making cuts turns, in part, on the nature of the desired cut. For example, if a compound curve is needed, then the cut can't be guided by a *norma*. More exactly, the applicability of the *norma*, and so the relevance of its regulative function to the activity of making a cut, turns on the carpenter's aims in making a cut square.

Norms that guide reason-giving uses of arguments are regulative. They measure whether such uses of arguments measure up. So these norms are applicable to your use of an argument only if you use the argument to advance what you believe to be reasons for believing the conclusion. Suppose a spokesperson S for a US presidential administration advances an argument in defense of its position on immigration in response to a reporter's criticism. Further suppose that S doesn't believe a word of their defense and so doesn't believe the associated inference claim. Then S's act of defending the administration isn't using an argument to give reasons for the conclusion. Whatever else S might be doing, S is not genuinely giving reasons for the conclusion of the argument that S presents even if S's audience takes them to be doing so. In the terminology of Chapter 2, S's dialectical argument does not amount to giving reasons for the conclusion. Accordingly, the norms that guide reason-giving uses of arguments do not apply to S's use of their argument. Applying such norms would be like trying to use a builder's square to guide a compound curve. Of course, other norms may apply to S's use of argument, which as pictured is intellectually dishonest.

Your reason-giving use of an argument is *good* only if the premises are reasons—in the sense you intend—for believing the conclusion. If the premises are not such reasons, then your use of the argument does not amount to giving reasons—in the intended sense—for believing the conclusion even if unbeknownst to you they are reasons of some sort for believing the conclusion. In the remainder of this section, I aim to identify three norms that ground the link between a reason-giving use of argument being *good* and the truth of the associated inference claim. More specifically, I identify three norms that figure in the support for GOOD.

GOOD: If your reason-giving use of an argument is *good*, then the corresponding inference claim is true, i.e., the premises you advance are reasons—in the sense you intend—for believing the conclusion.

GOOD follows from (A) and (B).

(A) If your reason-giving use of an argument is *good*, then it satisfies pragmatic, doxastic, and dialectical norms.
(B) If your reason-giving use of an argument satisfies these norms, then the corresponding inference claim is true.

I now elaborate by defending (A) and (B) for each of the three norms I consider. Also, I use each norm to explain when and why an argument used in a reason-giving way should be demonstrative. To avoid misunderstanding, I do not take these argumentation norms to be exhaustive. Again, I discuss them in order highlight the role played by true inference claims and true inference-claim beliefs in regulating good reason-giving uses of arguments. I start by discussing a pragmatic norm.

A pragmatic norm guiding reason-giving uses of arguments may be put as follows.

Pragmatic norm: if you intend the premises of the argument you use to be reasons of a certain sort for believing the conclusion, then the premises should be such reasons for believing the conclusion.

Recall that we sort reasons for believing something by type, e.g., suppositional reasons, reasons someone has to believe etc., and by epistemic import, e.g., conclusive or otherwise. By *Pragmatic norm*, if you intend the premises of an argument you use to be *conclusive* reasons to believe conclusion, then they should, in fact, be such reasons for believing the conclusion. That is, they should be conclusive reasons to believe the conclusion. If you intend the premises to be *non-conclusive* reasons someone has for believing the conclusion, then by *Pragmatic norm* this should be so. In either case, *Pragmatic norm* is not satisfied by your reason-giving use of an argument unless the corresponding inference claim is true. This is because if *Pragmatic norm* is satisfied, then the premises you use as reasons for believing the conclusion are reasons for believing the conclusion in the sense you intend. Since the content of the associated inference claim is a function of this argumentative intention, if *Pragmatic norm* is satisfied, the associated inference claim is true.

To quickly illustrate, suppose that you use an argument, *p so q*, to advance *p* as a conclusive reason for your interlocuter R to believe *q*. Then you intend *p* to serve as a conclusive reason for R to believe *q*. Accordingly, you believe the inference claim: *p is a conclusive reason for R to believe q*. If the argument you use is not demonstrative, then the premise is not a *conclusive* reason for R to believe the conclusion. In such a case, there is mismatch between the intended epistemic import of the premise and the epistemic import it, in fact, has. This violates *Pragmatic norm* and thereby falsifies your inference claim. Also, if your argument is demonstrative, but R doesn't believe *p*, then *p* is not a reason for R to believe *q*. In such a case, there is a mismatch between the sort of reason the premise is intended to be and its being such a reason. This violates *Pragmatic norm* and thereby falsifies your inference claim.

Pragmatic norm speaks to the alignment of one's intention to use the premises of one's argument as reasons of a certain sort for believing the conclusion and the sort of reasons the premises qualify as for believing the conclusion. If you intend the premises of the argument you use to be reasons of a certain sort for believing the conclusion, then in order for the argument to be suitable for your use of it, the premises should be such reasons for believing the conclusion. Otherwise, your reason-giving use of the argument isn't successful because the argument is unsuitable for your use of it.

In a nutshell, if your reason-giving use of an argument fails *Pragmatic norm*, then it is thereby pragmatically flawed since your use of the argument fails to give reasons for believing the conclusion in the sense that you intend. I now advance support for GOOD, given above, appealing to *Pragmatic norm*.

GOOD: If your reason-giving use of an argument is *good*, then the corresponding inference claim is true, i.e., the premises you advance are reasons— in the sense you intend—for believing the conclusion.

The schematic versions of (A) and (B) given above instantiated in terms of *Pragmatic norm* are as follows.

(A): If your reason-giving use of an argument is *good*, then your reason-giving use of the argument satisfies *Pragmatic norm*.

(B): If your reason-giving use of the argument satisfies *Pragmatic norm*, then the corresponding inference claim is true.

As expected, GOOD follows from (A) and (B). I now give the rationale for these instantiations of (A) and (B), starting with the first.

In support of thesis (A), consider the following. (1) If your reason-giving use of an argument is good, then you have succeeded in advancing premises that are reasons for believing the conclusion in the sense that you intend. (2) If you have so succeeded, then the argument you use is suitable for your use of it. (3) If your argument is suitable for your use of it, then your reason-giving use of the argument satisfies *Pragmatic norm*. (A) follows from (1)–(3).

Claim (1) highlights the pragmatic dimension of what makes reason-giving uses of arguments good. For example, if you have not succeeded in advancing your premises as reasons for believing the conclusion in the sense that you intend, then your use of the argument is pragmatically flawed. It is pragmatically flawed, because the argument that you use is not suited for your use of it as the premises are not reasons for believing the conclusion in the sense that you intend. Hence, it isn't a good reason-giving use of the argument.

Regarding (2), recall from Chapter 3 (section 3.2) that if an argument is suitable relative to certain reason-giving use, then the premises are reasons for believing the conclusion in the intended sense. If the premises are such reasons, then your argument is good relative to your use of it. This connects the pragmatic dimension of good reason-giving uses of arguments with the arguments themselves being good. Specifically, if your reason-giving use of an argument is good, then the argument you use is good relative to your use of it.

Finally, the rationale for claim (3) is two-fold. First, (a) if your argument is suitable for your use of it, then the premises are reasons for believing the conclusion in the sense that you intend. This reflects, as discussed in Chapter 3, what is required for an argument to be suitable for a reason-giving use of it. For example, if you use an argument in a reason-giving way intending to be arguing from your interlocuter's beliefs and your interlocuter, in fact, rejects a premise, then the argument you use is not suitable for your use of it. Second, (b) if the premises are reasons for believing the conclusion in the intended sense, then your use of the argument satisfies *Pragmatic norm*. This reflects the content of the norm. Claim (3) follows from (a) and (b).

Defense of claim (B) is more straightforward. If your reason-giving use of an argument satisfies *Pragmatic norm*, then the premises you advance are reasons in the sense that you intend for believing the conclusion. If the premises are such reasons, then your associated inference claim is true. Hence, (B). I now turn to a doxastic norm guiding reason-giving uses of arguments.

A doxastic norm is a norm exclusively concerned with the quality of one's act of believing something or one's belief state. A doxastic norm guiding reason-giving uses of arguments may be put as follows.

Doxastic norm: your inference-claim belief associated with your reason-giving use of argument should be true.

The rationale for *Doxastic norm* is multi-faceted. I highlight two rationales. First, in general it is wrong to believe true what is, in fact, false, since truth is the aim of belief (for discussion, see Chan 2013). Learning that one's belief is false calls for giving it up. Second, recall from Chapter 4 that an inference-claim belief is the linking belief of the reflective inference that corresponds to the argument used in a reason-giving way. Therefore, a false inference-claim belief is a false linking belief. A false linking belief makes the associated reflective inference epistemically defective. For example, if you infer q from p on the grounds of your false belief that p is a reason you have to believe q, then your inference is unwarranted and thereby epistemically defective. Insofar as an inference is epistemically defective, it shouldn't be performed.

If you advance the premises of your argument as conclusive reasons for believing the conclusion, then by the lights of *Doxastic norm* the argument you use should be demonstrative. If it isn't, then your associated inference-claim belief is false, which violates *Doxastic norm*. Satisfying *Doxastic norm* matters to whether a reason-giving use of an argument is good.

The *Doxastic norm* versions of (A) and (B) together support GOOD. Regarding (A), your reason-giving use of an argument is good only if it is epistemically sound. If it is epistemically sound, then your reflective inference is correct. It isn't correct unless your use of the argument satisfies *Doxastic norm*. So, (A) if your reason-giving use of an argument is good, then your reason-giving use of the argument satisfies *Doxastic norm*. Regarding (B), it is obvious that if your reason-giving use of an argument satisfies *Doxastic norm*, then the corresponding inference claim is true. After all, true inference-claim beliefs require true inference claims.

By *Doxastic norm*, when one's inference-claim belief is that the premises of one's argument are conclusive reasons for believing the conclusion, then one's argument should be demonstrative. Otherwise, one's inference-claim belief is false, which violates *Doxastic norm*. Therefore, with respect to reason-giving uses of arguments, *Doxastic norm* demands that one's argument should be demonstrative if one believes that one's premises are *conclusive* reasons for believing the conclusion. I now turn to what I refer as a dialectical norm for reason-giving uses of arguments.

A dialectical norm guiding reason-giving uses of arguments may be put as follows.

> *Dialectical norm*: if one accepts that the premises of an argument you use in a reason-giving way are reasons to believe the conclusion, then it is prima facie wrong for one to deny the conclusion.

Why is it prima facie wrong for one to deny the conclusion if one accepts that the premises of an argument that you use in a reason-giving way are reasons to believe the conclusion? To sharpen the question, suppose that you accept that the premises of an argument are true and that taken together they support the truth of the conclusion.[5] Unless you possess stronger reasons for denying the conclusion, you should not deny it. Why? Because otherwise your denial is not coherent, and it is prima facie wrong to incoherently deny the truth of a claim. If your denial (or acceptance) of a claim is incompatible

---

[5] Recall that a reason p to believe a proposition q is a truth that is indicative of the truth of q. I take this to mean that p *supports believing that q is true* and so the truth of q follows from p and p *is true*. I elaborate in Chapter 7.

with what you take to be evidence in support of its truth, then it is incoherent and so not rational for you to deny the claim.

Suppose that you are aware that 98 of the 100 balls in the paper bag are blue. Without further information, this problematizes your rejecting that the ball you pull out will be blue. In light of your evidence, it is not coherent to reject out of hand that you will pull out a blue ball. *Dialectical norm* speaks to the coherence of belief in light of what one takes to be evidence for the truth of the belief.

For example, suppose that you accept that p is a conclusive reason you have to believe q, but you deny q. Since you deny q, you believe *not-q*. Since you accept that p is a conclusive reason you have to believe q, you are committed to the truth of q. Without further information, you are committed to the truth of an impossibility, q and *not-q*. It is wrong to have beliefs that commit you to the truth of an impossibility for the obvious reason that impossibilities can't be true. So, it is wrong for you to accept that the premises of an argument taken together are conclusive reasons you have to believe the conclusion, but deny the conclusion. This accords with the claim that it is prima facie wrong to simultaneously deny the conclusion of an argument one correctly believes to be demonstrative and accept the premises (e.g., see Streumer 2007, e.g., p. 253; Beall and Restall 2006, p. 16; Sainsbury 2002, p. 4).[6]

The *Dialectical norm* versions of (A) and (B) in support of GOOD are as follows.

(A) If your reason-giving use of an argument is good, then it satisfies *Dialectical norm*.

---

[6] The import of prima facie *wrong* in this claim may be illustrated with the paradox of the preface, which is a well-known problem for anyone who takes formal validity to be a normative constraint on belief (see Beall and Restall 2006, pp. 16–18 for useful discussion that lays out the problem). Here's how the paradox arises. I am committed to each of the propositions $p_1, \ldots, p_n$ that I assert in this book. However, being prone to error I accept that not everything that I say is correct, i.e., I accept, in effect, the proposition $\sim(p_1 \&, \ldots, \& p_n)$. Correspondingly, the following list [C] registers my commitments: $p_1, \ldots, p_n, \sim(p_1 \&, \ldots, \& p_n)$. A logical consequence of [C] is the conjunction $(p_1 \&, \ldots, \& p_n) \& \sim (p_1 \&, \ldots, \& p_n)$, which is an explicit contradiction. I certainly do not believe this conjunction. I reject it. Hence the paradox. Following Beall and Restall's advice (2006, p. 17), I reject $(p_1 \&, \ldots, \& p_n)$ even though I accept each conjunct and I accept that any argument is valid whose conclusion is a conjunction and whose premises include each conjunct. [C] registers my incoherent set of commitments, which I do not take to involve my endorsement of a particular explicit contradiction. According to the picture Beall and Restall (2006) paint, "In an important sense, [I] ought not to accept $p_1, \ldots, p_n$, while simultaneously rejecting their conjunction" (p. 17). Accordingly, it is *wrong* to do so. "However, if one has good grounds to reject that conjunction, and one has good grounds for each of the conjuncts, it seems that one has good grounds for having an incoherent set of beliefs. The normativity of logical consequence remains, even if in this circumstance it is trumped by other norms." Accordingly, my acceptance of $p_1, \ldots, p_n$ while simultaneously rejecting their conjunction is merely prima facie wrong.

(B) If your reason-giving use of an argument satisfies *Dialectical Norm*, then the associated inference claim is true.

GOOD follows from (A) and (B). I now defend (A) and (B), starting with (A).

If your reason-giving use of an argument is good, then it is rationally compelling. If it is rationally compelling, then it satisfies *Dialectical norm*. Hence (A). A *good* reason-giving use of an argument is *rationally compelling* only if it is prima facie wrong for one to accept that the premises are reasons to believe the conclusion and deny the conclusion. That a reason-giving use of an argument is rationally compelling so understood underwrites it as a means of rationally persuading an audience of its conclusion, justifying one's belief in the conclusion, and rationally explaining why one believes the conclusion.

For example, asked to explain why he believes (1) *that Beth is not at home*, Matthew responds by reporting his belief (2) *that Beth's car is off the property*. This rationally explains why Matthew believes (1) only if we think that the corresponding reason-giving use of argument satisfies *Dialectical norm*, in which case it is prima facie wrong for him to accept (2) and deny (1). In short, Matthew's reason-giving use of the argument from (2) to (1) rationally explains why he believes (2) only if *Dialectical norm* is satisfied.

Suppose that Matthew justifies his believing (1) by reporting that he believes (2). His believing (2) does not justify his believing (1) unless the there is a true general claim that Matthew at least implicitly accepts that makes his belief of (2) a reason he has to believe (1). No true generalization qualifies as such unless it makes it prima facie wrong for Matthew to accept (2) and deny (1). For example, suppose that Matthew accepts that (3) that most of the times when Beth's car is off the property, Beth is not at home. If (3) is true, then (2) is an inconclusive reason for him to believe (1). Accordingly, it would be prima facie wrong for him to accept (2) and deny (1). In short, Matthew's reason-giving use of argument from (2) to (1) justifies his believing (1) only if *Dialectical Norm* is satisfied, i.e., only if it is prima facie wrong for him to accept (2) and deny (1).

Suppose that Matthew attempts to rationally persuade Paige that Beth is not at home by advancing the argument with (2) as the premise and (1) as the conclusion. The success of Matthew's dialectical aim of rational persuasion turns on Paige's accepting the inference claim to the effect that (2) is a reason she has to believe (1). If Paige is rationally persuaded by Matthew's argument to accept (1), then this is, in part, because it would be prima facie wrong for Paige to accept the inference claim and deny (2). In short, Matthew's argument has rational persuasive force for Paige only if *Dialectical Norm* is satisfied, i.e., only if it is prima facie wrong for Paige to accept (2) and deny (1).

In short, a *good* reason-giving use of an argument is *rationally compelling* for a person S only if it is prima facie wrong for S to accept the premises as reasons to believe the conclusion, but deny the conclusion. This explains why the *Dialectical norm* version of (A) is true. Furthermore, this helps explain why good reason-giving uses of arguments are appropriate as a means of rationally persuading an audience of its conclusion, rationally explaining why one believes the conclusion, and rationally justifying one's belief in the conclusion. I now turn to (B)

(B) If your reason-giving use of an argument satisfies *Dialectical norm*, then the associated inference claim is true.

Why is (B) true? (1) If a reason-giving use of the argument satisfies *Dialectic norm*, then one's believing that the premises are reasons to believe the conclusion rationally motivates believing the conclusion in light of them. The idea here is that believing that the premises are reasons to believe the conclusion rationally motivates believing the conclusion if it is prima facie wrong for one to deny the conclusion given that one thinks the premises are such reasons. (2) If believing the conclusion in light of the premises is rationally motivated, then the associated inference claim is true. Why? Because your believing the conclusion in light of your premises beliefs rationally motivates believing the conclusion only if the conclusion follows—conclusively or otherwise—from the premises and the premises are true. It follows that the associated inference claim is true. That is, it follows that the premises are reasons you have to believe the conclusion and so they are reasons to believe it. Recall that the premises are not reasons to believe the conclusion unless they are true, and the conclusion follows from them. [B] follows from (1) and (2). Here I appeal to a notion of rational motivation according to which if your reason-giving use an argument so motivates your believing the conclusion, then it makes your believing the conclusion in light of the given premises objectively rational. In Chapter 7, I discuss objective rationality as a dimension of argumentative rationality.

5.5.1. Summary

I have appealed to the *Pragmatic, Doxastic,* and *Dialectical norms* to argue for the following two claims. (1) If your reason-giving use of an argument is *good*, then it satisfies these three norms. (2) If your reason-giving use of an argument satisfies such norms, then the corresponding inference claim is true. GOOD follows from (1) and (2).

> GOOD: If your reason-giving use of an argument is *good*, then the corresponding inference claim is true; i.e., the premises you advance are reasons—in the sense you intend—for believing the conclusion.

Intuitively, if you use an argument in a reason-giving way to advance its premises as conclusive reasons for believing the conclusion, then the argument you use should be demonstrative. GOOD accounts for why. Briefly, if you use an argument in a reason-giving way to advance its premises as conclusive reasons believing for the conclusion, then your inference claim says that this is so. By GOOD, this claim should be true. It is true only if the argument you use is demonstrative, formally valid or otherwise. Therefore, given GOOD, if you use an argument in a reason-giving way to advance its premises as conclusive reasons for the conclusion, the argument should be demonstrative.

Recall the argue$_1$-argument$_8$ link from Chapter 2. If you argue$_1$, then you give an argument$_8$; i.e., you give reasons for believing the conclusion. You don't argue$_1$ well unless your reason-giving use of argument is good. So, you argue$_1$ well only if the associated inference claim(s) is(are) true. Accordingly, to know that you argue$_1$ well is to know that the involved associated inference claim(s) is (are) true.

To be sure, for you to argue$_1$ well requires more than that your reason-giving uses of argument satisfy the *Pragmatic, Doxastic,* and *Dialectical norms.* For example, to argue$_1$ well is to argue for the right reason, with the right people, at the right time, and to the right extent. I only bring this up to point out that to argue$_1$ well brings more into play than the truth of one's inference claims. Relatedly, there are norms guiding reason-giving uses of arguments other than the three discussed. My focus on these three norms is motivated by the fact that they explicitly make the truth of an inference claim as discussed in Chapter 3 matter to a reason-giving use of an argument being good. This is illustrated by my discussion of how these norms function as support for GOOD.

5.6. Conclusion

The central question of Chapter 5 may be put as follows. Why, if at all, does your argument's being demonstrative matter to whether your reason-giving use of it is good? In order to develop my response, I engaged a variety of related topics. To conclude, I summarize the chapter's primary claims.

Whether an argument is deductive or inductive depends on how it is being used. For example, if you use an argument to advance its premises as conclusive reasons for believing the conclusion, then the argument is deductive relative to this use of it. If you use it to advance its premises as inconclusive reasons for believing the conclusion, then relative to this use the argument is inductive. Conclusive reasons for a conclusion rule out the possibility of its being false. Inconclusive reasons for a conclusion make its truth more likely than not without ruling out the possibility that the conclusion is false.

Whether an argument is demonstrative, ampliative, or neither is independent of whether it is deductive or inductive. An argument is demonstrative when its premises if true rule out the possibility of the conclusion being false. The conclusion of a demonstrative argument is implied by the premises. An ampliative argument is one with premises such that if they are all true, they render the conclusion probable, i.e., they make the truth of the conclusion more likely than not, while not guaranteeing its truth. Accordingly, ampliative and demonstrative arguments are mutually exclusive types of arguments. That an argument used in a reason-giving way is demonstrative or ampliative matters to the epistemic import of its premises as reasons for the conclusion. The premises are not *conclusive* reasons for believing the conclusion unless the argument is demonstrative. If the premises are *inconclusive* reasons for believing the conclusion, then the argument is ampliative.

The appropriate logic for judging arguments used in reason-giving ways is a logic for judging the reflective inferences expressed by arguments so used. That an argument is valid by the lights of a logic bears on the logical correctness of a reflective inference only if the argument expresses a type of reflective inference. Accordingly, fixing the logic requires a prior account of reflective inferences that informs which arguments express reflective inferences. More generally, how a logic is normative if at all for reasoning turns on the nature of the reasoning.

Pragmatic norm, *Doxastic norm*, and *Dialectical norm* support thinking that a reason-giving use of an argument is good only if the associated inference claim is true. It isn't true unless the premises are reasons—in the intended sense for the conclusion—and they have any intended epistemic import as support for the conclusion. If an inference claim says that the premises of the corresponding argument are *conclusive or inconclusive* reasons for believing the conclusion, then it isn't true unless the argument is demonstrative or ampliative, respectively.

6

Reason-Giving Uses of Arguments, Invitations to Inference, and Rational Persuasion

6.1. Preamble

In an effort to persuade Shannon that the car needs service, Matthew communicates to her that the car's brakes squeak when wet and that the car is due for an oil change. Unbeknownst to Matthew, Shannon learned just recently that Beth got the oil changed. However, Shannon thinks that the brakes squeaking when wet is a sufficiently good reason to believe that the car needs service. So she infers that the car needs to be serviced and tells Matthew that she will schedule it.[1] Was Shannon persuaded by Matthew's reason-giving use of argument?

More generally, what is required in order for a reason-giving use of an argument to persuade an addressee to accept its conclusion? My response distinguishes between direct and indirect persuasion. In a nutshell, one is directly persuaded by a reason-giving use of an argument to accept its conclusion only if one accepts the associated inference claim. One is indirectly persuaded by a reason-giving use of an argument to accept its conclusion only if one believes that the argument provides at least one reason, perhaps among others, one has to believe the conclusion, but doesn't accept the associated inference claim. Hence, whether one accepts the associated inference claim matters to whether one is directly or indirectly persuaded by a reason-giving use of an argument to believe its conclusion.

Matthew's reason-giving use of argument has persuasive force for Shannon even though she doesn't believe Matthew's inference claim to the effect that the premises advanced are reasons for Shannon to believe the conclusion. I describe this by saying that Shannon is indirectly persuaded by Matthew's

---

[1] Matthew's argument is a conductive argument. See Govier 2010, pp. 353–67.

Arguments and Reason-Giving. Matthew W. McKeon, Oxford University Press. © Oxford University Press 2024.
DOI: 10.1093/oso/9780197751633.003.0006

reason-giving use of argument to believe its conclusion. Put succinctly, the two central claims of Chapter 6 are as follows.

(I)   An addressee R is directly persuaded by S's reason-giving use of an argument to believe its conclusion only if R believes S's inference claim.

(II) An addressee R is indirectly persuaded by S's reason-giving use of an argument to believe its conclusion only if R believes the argument provides at least one reason, perhaps among others, R has to believe the conclusion, but R doesn't accept the associated inference claim.

According to (I), a person S does not directly persuade an addressee R of the conclusion of S's argument unless R accepts S's inference claim, which S believes and conveys (recall from Chapter 3, *asserts*) in stating the argument. So direct persuasion by means of a reason-giving use of an argument turns on agreement between speaker and addressees regarding the truth of the associated inference claim. According to (II), a speaker S's reason-giving use of an argument can indirectly persuade an addressee R to accept S's conclusion even though R does not accept S's inference claim. So indirect persuasion by means of a reason-giving use of an argument does not turn on the speaker and addressees agreeing about the truth of the associated inference claim.

Direct and indirect persuasion are forms of *rational* persuasion because an invitation-to-inference's addressees are persuaded to accept the conclusion advanced in light of premises they believe are reasons they have to believe the conclusion. For example, if you are rationally persuaded by my reason-giving use of an argument to believe the conclusion, either directly or indirectly, then you believe the conclusion because you take the argument that I use to provide at least one reason you have to believe the conclusion. Accordingly, you believe the conclusion in light of reason(s). So, when you are persuaded, indirectly or otherwise, by an invitation to inference to accept its conclusion, you are rationally persuaded to accept it.

I start by developing Robert Pinto's (2001c) notion of an argument as an *invitation to inference* that aims to persuade addresses of the conclusion. I'll say that such an invitation to inference is a use of an argument to invite an addressee to believe the conclusion by inferring it from the given premises. Next, I distinguish between inferences that merely correspond to an argument used in a reason-giving way and those that are also expressed by it. One's inference is expressed by an argument so used only if one infers the conclusion from the premises because one accepts the associated inference claim. Using this idea, I generate a rationale for (I). After briefly reviewing the difference between being *directly* and *indirectly* persuaded by an invitation to inference, I argue for (II) and enhance its plausibility by exploring different forms of indirect persuasion. I argue that intuitively bad arguments can indirectly persuade addressees of their conclusions by inducing an addressee's performance of an intuitively good reflective inference.

Finally, I connect invitations to inference to reflective inferences by arguing that if you are persuaded, directly or indirectly, by an invitation to inference to accept its conclusion, then the inference you perform is a reflective inference. I then show that as a consequence when you are persuaded by an invitation to inference to accept its conclusion, you are *rationally* persuaded to accept it. This serves as a nice segue to Chapter 7.

In Chapter 7, I ask: When does your reason-giving use of an argument rationalize your believing the conclusion? I make the case that if you author an argument whose premises are not good reasons for you to believe the conclusion, then your believing the conclusion may nevertheless be rational. I show how this divorces argumentative rationality from good argumentation in the sense that whether your believing the conclusion of your argument is rational is prior to whether it is good by the lights of a theory of argument.

6.2. Invitations to Inference Are Reason-Giving Uses of Arguments

Pinto (2001c) advances a notion of an argument as an *invitation to inference*. I use this notion to enhance understanding of reason-giving uses of arguments that aim to persuade addresses of their conclusions. My discussion will relate reason-giving uses of arguments to inferences and to acts of persuasion. This prepares my consideration in the next section of why an addressee R is not directly persuaded by your reason-giving use of an argument unless R's inference is expressed by your argument as you use it. I now begin.

Pinto characterizes an argument as "a set of statements or propositions that one person offers to another in the attempt to induce that other person to accept some conclusion" (2001c, p. 32). Recall from Chapter 2 that I define arguments structurally and so independently of how they are used. So I concur with Pinto that an argument is a set of propositions (i.e., an ordered pair of a set of premises and a conclusion-proposition). However, I disagree with Pinto in that I think that this is all there is to arguments. Characterizing arguments independently of their potential uses serves as a heuristic for taking seriously the distinction between arguments and uses of them. Many informal logicians think that this distinction should be accommodated by any plausible full-blown theory of argument (e.g., Blair 2004; Hitchcock 2007a).

According to Pinto's understanding of arguments as essentially instruments of persuasion (2001c, p. 36), arguments are what he calls *invitations to inference*.

> [T]he premisses that are put forward by the arguer are intended to elicit assent to the argument's conclusion by forming the basis of an inference drawn by the person to whom the argument is addressed. (p. 37)

To get Pinto's conception of *invitations to inference* to fit with my conception of argument, I take an invitation to inference to be an argument used to invite its audience to perform an inference from its premises to conclusion. Arguments do not invite inferences, people do. An invitation to inference is a person's *use* of an argument to invite addressees to perform an inference from its premises to conclusion in order to elicit their assent to the conclusion.

Invitations to inference so construed are reason-giving uses of arguments. That is, an invitation to inference that is extended to addressees to persuade them of the conclusion is a reason-giving use of an argument. When you use an argument in a reason-giving way to persuade an interlocuter that the conclusion is true, you invite your interlocuter to accept the conclusion by inferring it from the premises you advance as reasons for believing it.

For example, suppose your invitation to inference advances the premises as reasons your interlocuter R has to believe the conclusion. Accordingly, you intend and so believe that the premises are such reasons. So (a) you believe that the premises you advance are true. Also, (b) you believe that R believes or should believe the premises (say, because they are obviously true, presupposed by what R explicitly believes, or are obvious consequences of what R explicitly believes). Furthermore, (c) you believe that the conclusion follows from the premises.

If any of (a)–(c) fail, then you are not using your argument to advance reasons your interlocuter has to believe the conclusion. However, suppose that you aim to persuade your interlocuter R to accept your conclusion by advancing the premises as reasons for R to believe the conclusion. In this case, you may argue from R's beliefs and commitments not all of which you accept. Accordingly, (d) you believe that R believes or should believe the premises (say, because they are presupposed by what R explicitly believes, or obvious consequences of what R explicitly believes). Also, (e) you believe that R is committed to the conclusion following from the premises. If either (d) or (e) fails, then you are not advancing your premises as reasons for R to believe the conclusion. Persuading R to accept the conclusion by advancing the premises as reasons for R to believe the conclusion does not necessarily bring either (a) or (c) into play.

Pinto's uses his notion of an invitation to inference to connect argument, inference, and persuasion.

> [I]magine a situation in which the presentation of an argument caused assent to its conclusion but in which the addressee did not make an inference from the argument's premisses to its conclusion. For example, the argument is actually too complicated for the addressee to follow, but worn down by its length and caught up by the arguer's charm, the addressee's resistance to the conclusion disappears. Would we count this as a case in which the addressee was persuaded by the argument to accept its conclusion? Caused, yes. But not, I maintain, persuaded. (2001c, p. 37)

An addressee isn't persuaded by your argument to accept the conclusion unless they infer the conclusion from the premises you advance.

> Arguments succeed when the persons to whom they are addressed accept their conclusions on the basis of their premisses. Arguments fail when the addressee either refuses to accept their premisses, or accepting their premisses does not draw the intended conclusion from those premisses. (Pinto 2001c, p. 37)

According to Pinto, the rhetorical success of an invitation to inference consists of the addressee's being persuaded by the argument as this is signaled by their performance of an inference from the argument's given premises to its conclusion. To illustrate, consider the following exchange.

MATTHEW: Miguel Cabrera is one of the greatest hitters in Major League Baseball history.

SHANNON: Really?

MATTHEW: Yes. He is one of seven players in MLB history to have at least five hundred home runs and three thousand hits.

SHANNON: OK. He is one of the greatest hitters in MLB history.

The argument that Matthew presents may be displayed as follows.

> He is one of seven players in MLB history to have at least five hundred home
> <u>runs and three thousand hits</u>
> Miguel Cabrera is one of the greatest hitters in MLB history

Matthew uses this argument in a reason-giving way, since he advances the premise as a reason to believe the conclusion. Shannon acknowledges that she agrees with Matthew's asserted conclusion. However, Shannon is not directly persuaded by Matthew's argument unless the premise Matthew gives is a reason for which she believes the conclusion. For example, if Shannon's acknowledges Matthew's conclusion just because she doesn't want to disagree with him and perhaps upset him, then she is not necessarily persuaded by his argument to accept the conclusion. Also, Shannon is not persuaded by Matthew's argument if she believes the conclusion but thinks that having the batting statistics Matthew highlights does not indicate that one is among the greatest hitters of all time. Clearly, for Shannon to be persuaded by Matthew's argument, she and Matthew must agree that the premise Matthew gives is a reason to believe the conclusion. That is, they have to agree that Matthew's inference claim is true.

In sum, an addressee R is persuaded by your invitation to inference to accept the conclusion of the argument you use just in case R performs an inference that your invitation to inference invites. Of course, this leaves open the question whether you should have performed the inference. I now make two observations important to what follows.

First, Pinto seems to think that your inference is invited by an invitation to inference if you infer the conclusion from the given premises. This makes Pinto's claim about direct, as opposed to indirect, persuasion. Second, it is plausible to think that an invitation to inference that aims to induce acceptance of the conclusion invites a *belief-inducing* inference. I now briefly elaborate, starting with the first observation.

Taking invitations to inference to be reason-giving uses of arguments motivates thinking that an addressee R's believing the operative inference claim matters to whether R is directly persuaded by an invitation to inference. Recall from Chapter 3 that an argument may be used in different reason-giving ways, which are distinguished by their different associated inference claims. The inference claim associated with a reason-giving use of an argument should matter in some way to what inference it invites. This is the import of (I), one of the two central claims of this chapter mentioned at the start.

> (I) An addressee R is directly persuaded by S's reason-giving use of an argument to believe its conclusion only if R believes S's inference claim.

Elaboration and defense of (I) is given below. I now turn to my second observation.

The persuasive force of invitations to inference that aim to elicit belief of the argument's conclusion is manifested in terms of the addressees' acceptance of the conclusion as an outcome of inferring it from the given premises. Such persuasion registers the addition of a belief or registers an increase in credence of a belief acquired by some other means. Accordingly, in what follows I take an invitation to inference intended to elicit addressees' belief of the conclusion to be invitations to *belief-inducing* inferences. Recall from Chapter 5's discussion of belief-inducing reflective inferences that if your inference from p to q is belief-inducing, then there is a transfer of credence from your acceptance that p to your acceptance that q. A necessary outcome of your performance of a belief-inducing inference from p to q is that p becomes a reason *for which* you believe q; i.e., p is the actual basis of your belief that q.

Certainly, as Pinto acknowledges (2001a, sec. 2), not all inferences are belief-inducing. The cognitive import of inferences is broadly construed by Pinto. As Hitchcock notes, on Pinto's view, "[In] inferring, a person adopts or reinforces an attitude towards the proposition embedded in the conclusion" (2007a, p. 106). For Pinto, these attitudes include a range of doxastic attitudes beyond merely accepting the truth of the conclusion (e.g., considering the conclusion possible), and also include a range of non-doxastic attitudes (e.g., worrying that the conclusion is true) (p. 41). Accordingly, the persuasive force of an invitation to inference may be registered not in terms of believing that the conclusion is true, but in terms of worrying that it may be true.

The following claim, which I label *Pinto's claim*, encapsulates the spirit of Pinto's conception of arguments used as *invitations to inference* that aim to persuade addressees to believe the conclusion.

> (Pinto's claim): You are directly persuaded by an invitation to inference to accept its conclusion if and only if you perform the belief-inducing inference that is invited.

Clearly, if you are persuaded by an argument to accept its conclusion by inferring it from the premises, then the argument has persuasive force for you. However, the persuasive force of an argument needn't be registered in terms one's coming to believe that the conclusion is true.

To further illustrate, suppose that S extends a belief-inducing invitation to a respondent R with the aim of persuading R that the conclusion is true. Suppose further that this induces R's performance of an inference from premises to conclusion that is not belief-inducing, because, unbeknownst to S, R already accepts the conclusion. R might nevertheless find S's argument persuasive because R recognizes that the premises provide further grounds for R's conclusion-belief which R accepts for independent reasons. R's recognition registers the persuasive force that S's argument has for R.

6.2.1. Summary

Suppose that you use an argument in a reason-giving way to rationally persuade an addressee R that the conclusion is true. Your reason-giving use of the argument you present is an invitation to inference. By Pinto's claim, your invitation to inference *directly* persuades R to accept your conclusion just in case R performs the belief-inducing inference that you invite. This raises the question of how invited inferences are determined by an invitation to inference. This is addressed in the next section.

6.3. Invitations to Inference Invite Only the Inferences Expressed by the Arguments Used

An addressee R's inference is invited by your invitation to inference only if it is expressed by the argument so used. R's inference is expressed by your argument as used only if R draws the conclusion from the premises because R accepts your inference claim. In such a case, your inference-claim belief is R's linking belief associated with R's inference. Generally, an inference is expressed by an argument used in a reason-giving way only if the inferer draws the conclusion from the premises because they accept the associated inference claim.

I now elaborate. I first discuss when arguments correspond to inferences (or, equivalently, when inferences correspond to arguments) in order to distinguish between inferences that merely correspond to an argument and those that, in addition, are expressed by the argument. Next, using the notion of an inference being expressed by an argument, I make the case for (I) repeated several pages back.

Recall from Chapter 5 (e.g., section 5.2), that an inference corresponds to an argument just in case the propositional contents of the initial premise-beliefs of the inference are the argument's given premises, and the propositional content of the conclusion-belief is the propositional content of the argument's conclusion. In Chapter 5, I illustrated that whether an argument is deductive or inductive is relative to how it is being used. These illustrations suggest that different inferences may correspond to one and the same argument. For example, consider the basic argument pattern of an appeal to popular opinion given in Chapter 5.

(A)

It is widely held among population P that p

p is true

Suppose that for a given instantiation of P and p, Beth and Matthew both infer the conclusion from the premise. Beth believes that premise conclusively supports the conclusion. Matthew believes that the premise provides inconclusive, abductive support for the conclusion. Matthew takes the truth of the conclusion to be the best explanation for the truth of the premise. Beth's and Matthew's inferences are different because they view differently the epistemic import of the premises as reasons for believing the conclusion (i.e., conclusive and inconclusive, respectively). Beth's deductive inference may well commit the *ad populum* fallacy, because she accepts that the premise is a conclusive reason that she has to believe the conclusion. However, where the members of P are in a position to know about p, or when the best explanation of the prevalence of the belief that p among P is that p is true, Matthew's inference (to the best explanation) may well be cogent. So Beth's and Matthew's inferences are importantly different. Nevertheless, they both correspond to argument (A).

For another illustration of different inferences corresponding to one and the same argument, suppose that you and I infer (1) *that Beth is not at work* from our belief (2) *that her car is in the driveway*. Suppose further that our inferences are reflective. I believe that (2) is a conclusive reason to believe (1), because I believe that whenever Beth's car is in the driveway, she is not at work. You believe (2) is an inconclusive reason to believe (1), because you think that it is usually but not always true that when Beth's car is in the driveway, she is not at work (say, because you believe that Beth infrequently carpools to work). We believe that Beth is not at work for the exact same reason: her car is in the driveway.

However, we differ with respect to the epistemic import of (2) as a reason to believe (1). You and I take (2) to be a conclusive and inconclusive reason, respectively, to believe (1). Accordingly, our reflective inferences are different because our associated linking beliefs are different. Nevertheless, our inferences correspond to argument (B), displayed as follows.

(B)
<u>Beth's car is in driveway</u>
Beth is not at work
For a final illustration, consider the following formally valid argument (C).

(C)
(1) If Beth is at home, then her car is in the driveway
<u>(2) Beth's car is not in the driveway</u>
(3) Beth is not at home

Suppose that Kelly, Paige, and Shannon perform deductive, reflective inferences from (C)'s premises to its conclusion. All believe that (1) and (2) are reasons to believe (3). Kelly, untutored in logic, performs her inference on the basis of her intuition that it seems right. She does not recite or conceptualize her reasoning process, nor does she intend that her premise-beliefs have any particular epistemic support for her conclusion-belief, conclusive or otherwise.

However, Paige and Shannon both take (1) and (2) to be conclusive reasons to believe (3). Both recently completed formal logic courses. Paige infers the conclusion directly from the premises appealing to the logical principle modus tollens. Shannon never learned modus tollens in her logic class. Shannon reasons as follows. By the logical principle contraposition, she infers from (1) that if Beth's car is not in the driveway, then Beth is not at home. From this and (2) Shannon infers (3) by the logical principle modus ponens. Paige's and Shannon's inferences differ. Paige's inference is immediate; she directly infers (3) directly from (1) and (2). However, Shannon's inference is not immediate. She infers the conclusion from the premises by means of an intermediate inferential step.

The three different inferences correspond to argument (C) because the premises and conclusion of (C) are the propositional contents of the (initial) premise-beliefs and conclusion-beliefs of the inferences. Note that whether an inference corresponds to an argument is independent of how that argument is being used. For example, we determine that (C) corresponds to the three inferences independently of determining how it is being used.

The three scenarios involving arguments (A), (B), and (C) highlight that among the distinguishing features of reflective inferences are the following:

(i)   The content of the associated linking belief
(ii)   The contents of the premise- and conclusion-beliefs
(iii) The inferential connection between premise-beliefs and conclusion being direct or indirect

For example, with respect to argument pattern (A), Beth's and Matthew's inferences that correspond to an instantiation of (A) differ in regard to (i). With respect to argument (C), Kelly's and Paige's corresponding reflective inferences differ from Shannon's in regard to (iii). Note that (ii), but not (i) and (iii), matters to whether an inference corresponds to an argument. Two reflective inferences correspond to an argument just in case they are indistinguishable in regard to (ii); i.e., the contents of their respective premise- and conclusion-beliefs are the same. In short, different inferences (immediate and otherwise) can be expressed by a reason-giving invitation to inference as long as the operative linking beliefs are the inference-claim belief associated with the invitation to inference.

Certainly, one may use a proof to invite the performance of a deductive inference whose inferential transition from premise-beliefs to conclusion-belief mirrors the steps of the given derivation from the initial premises of the proof to its conclusion. In such a case, one may think that whether one's inference is immediate or otherwise does matter to whether it is expressed by the proof. However, arguments are not proofs and here we construe, following Pinto, invitations to inferences as reason-giving uses of arguments and not reason-giving uses of proofs. Of course, one may consider proofs as invitations to inferences. Such an invitation to inference invites the inference from the initial premises to conclusion via the inferential route represented by the given deduction. The deduction guides the inferer's inferential transitions in drawing the conclusion from the set of initial premises.[2]

This concludes my discussion of when an inference corresponds to an argument. I now respond to the following question: When is an inference expressed by an argument used in a reason-giving way? My response: an argument used in a reason-giving way *expresses* your inference only if your inference corresponds to the argument, and, in addition, you believe the associated inference claim. Accordingly, whether your inference is expressed by an argument is relative to how it is being used, because it turns on your believing the inference claim associated with a particular reason-giving use of the argument.

To elaborate, I've said that invitations to inference are reason-giving uses of arguments. The inference that is invited by an invitation to inference is the inference expressed by the argument so used. As inference claims are essentially associated with arguments in use, i.e., with reason-giving uses of arguments, we can't determine what inference is expressed by an argument until we know how it is being used. This involves knowing what the associated inference claim is.

The features that matter to whether a reflective inference is expressed by an argument used as an invitation to inference are (i) and (ii), but not (iii) (all given above). Since (iii) doesn't matter to whether an inference corresponds to an argument used in a reason-giving way, it shouldn't matter to whether an inference is expressed by an argument. For example, suppose that you use argument (C) as an invitation to inference in an effort to induce Kelly, Paige, and Shannon to accept the conclusion. Further suppose that your inference claim is in effect that the premises are conclusive reasons to believe the conclusion. As described above, Paige's and Shannon's inferences are invited, even though their inferential transitions differ in regard to (iii). Kelly doesn't perform the inference that is invited because she doesn't believe your inference claim. However, intuitively, your invitation to inference has persuasive

---

[2] For example, it is hard to see why the exact order of the steps comprising an inferential transition should matter to whether the inference is invited. It is easier to see why the explicit use of theory-centric inference rules does matter (e.g., intuitionistic modus ponens is different from *classical-logic* modus ponens). I can't adequately address here the complications concerning what counts as the same inferential transition for purposes of persuasion. In substructural logics, order of premises does matter. For an substantive introduction to substructural logics, see Restall 2000.

force for Kelly. Below, I'll say that Kelly was *indirectly persuaded* by your invitation to inference. In contrast, Paige and Shannon were *directly persuaded* by your invitation to inference because they performed the inference you invited.

Appealing to this understanding of when an inference is expressed by an argument, I now give the argument for (I), one of the two central claims of Chapter 6.

(1) An addressee R is directly persuaded by S's reason-giving use of an argument to believe its conclusion only if R performs the inference that S's argument expresses.

(2) If R performs the inference that S's argument expresses, then R believes S's *inference claim*.

(I) An addressee R is directly persuaded by S's reason-giving use of an argument to believe its conclusion only if R believes S's inference claim.

The rationale for premise (1) is twofold. First, by Pinto's claim, (i) if an addressee R is directly persuaded by S's reason-giving use of an argument to believe its conclusion, then R performs the (belief-inducing) inference that S invites R to perform. Second, (ii) if R performs the inference invited by S, then R performs the inference expressed by S's argument.

As indicated, Pinto's claim secures (i). The primary rationale for (ii) is accounting for the fact that it is up to S what inference S invites in extending an invitation to inference. The inference that is expressed by S's invitation to inference is entirely a function of S's argumentative intention and S's choice of argument. S's argumentative intention fixes S's inference claim, which determines the linking belief of the expressed inference. S's given premises and conclusion determine the content of the invited inference's initial premise- and conclusion-beliefs. Hence, it is plausible to understand the inference that S invites in terms of the inference that S uses the argument to express.

In a short, the motivation for (ii) is as follows. You are in charge of what inference is expressed by the argument associated with your invitation to inference. The inference you invite is the inference expressed by the argument that you use to invite it. So you are in charge of what inference your invitation to inference invites. Hence, if R performs the belief-inducing inference invited by S, then R performs the inference expressed by S's argument. This is (ii).

To illustrate the force of the motivation for (ii), consider the following conversational exchange.

SHANNON: Paige and Kelly want to buy that guitar for $2,000, but they don't
   have the money to pay for it.
MATTHEW: That's wrong. *Beth gave $1,000 to Paige and Kelly.* So they have
   the money.
SHANNON: That doesn't follow. Where did they get the other $1,000?

Matthew's italicized statement is ambiguous; perhaps this is intentional. Did Beth give $1,000 to each of them or to both? Shannon declines Matthew's invitation to inference, because she uncharitably interprets Matthew to mean that Beth gave $1,000 to both of them, which if accurate problematizes Matthew's inference. However, what Matthew exactly meant by uttering what's italicized isn't up to Shannon, it is up to Matthew. The proper disambiguation of Matthew's premise turns entirely on what he intended to mean by uttering it. Given the context, it is plausible that he meant that Beth gave $1,000 to each of them. This is the interpretation of his premise that should figure in determining the inference that Matthew invites Shannon to perform.

Again, arguments don't invite inferences. Arguers do. What inference your invitation to inference invites is entirely a function of the inference you intend your argument to express. Consider argument (D).

(D)
Matthew will pitch in Friday's doubleheader
Matthew will pitch in the second game

Argument (D) can be used to invite a variety of inferences, not all of them belief-inducing. To illustrate, consider the following scenario.

Shannon and Beth are discussing when they need to leave to watch Matthew play baseball. Suppose toward an effort to convince Shannon that she can leave work later rather than earlier in order to see Matthew play, Beth makes one of the following three different statements of (D).

(i) Matthew will pitch in Friday's doubleheader; so he will certainly pitch
   in the second game.

(ii) Matthew will pitch in Friday's doubleheader; so he probably will pitch in the second game.

(iii) Supposing that Matthew will pitch in Friday's doubleheader; it follows that he'll probably pitch in the second game.

Each of (i)–(iii) states (D) in a such a way that if one is used by Beth to invite Shannon to perform the inference that is expressed, Beth would invite a unique inference as determined by the unique inference claim that Beth conveys. For each, we may take the premise to qualify as a reason of some sort for believing the conclusion only if (P) is true.

(P): When Matthew pitches in Friday doubleheaders, he pitches in the second game.

If Beth states (i), her inference claim is that (D)'s premise is a conclusive reason for Shannon to believe the conclusion. Accordingly, Shannon's corresponding inference is invited by this invitation to inference only if Shannon's associated linking belief is that (D)'s premise is a conclusive reason for her to believe the conclusion. Such a linking belief is true only if (P) is necessarily—in some sense—true.

If Beth states (ii), her inference claim is that (D)'s premise is an inconclusive reason for Shannon to believe the conclusion. So Shannon's inference from the premise to the conclusion is expressed by the argument so used only if Shannon's associated linking belief is that (D)'s premise is an inconclusive reason for her to believe the conclusion. Such a linking belief is true only if (P) is true more often than not.

If Beth states (iii), she advances (D)'s premise as an inconclusive, suppositional reason to believe the conclusion. Accordingly, unlike with (i) and (ii), she is not trying to persuade Shannon of the truth of the conclusion. The inference Beth invites is what we have called a suppositional inference. If Shannon believes that in fact Matthew will pitch in the doubleheader and comes to believe that Matthew will pitch in the second game on the basis of Beth's presentation of (D), then she didn't perform the inference that Beth invited.

I've said more than once now that arguments don't invite inferences, people do. Therefore, what inference is invited by an invitation to inference is complicated by what fixes the intentions of the arguer. Among other indicators of an arguer's intensions are an arguer's use of conclusion modifiers, e.g., "certainly," "possibly," in presenting their argument which serve to indicate how the premises are to be taken to support the conclusion. Also, argument patterns, e.g., enumerative induction, modus ponens, that the arguer's argument clearly instantiates may indicate the arguer's intentions regarding not only how but the way they take the premises to support the conclusion.

Again, premise (2) of my argument for (I) is this: if R performs the inference that S's argument expresses, then R believes S's inference claim. This claim reflects my response to the question posed above, when is an inference expressed by an argument used in a reason-giving way? An argument used in a reason-giving way *expresses* your inference only if your inference corresponds to the argument, and, in addition, you believe the associated inference claim. So, that a person S's inference is expressed by an argument used in a reason-giving requires that S believe the associated inference claim. Hence, premise (2).

This understanding of when an inference is expressed by an argument used in a reason-giving strengthens Chapter 4's two central claims.

(I) If you perform a reflective inference, then you use the corresponding argument in a reason-giving way.

(II) If you use an argument in a reason-giving way, then you have performed a reflective inference from its premise(s) to conclusion.

Regarding the strengthening of (I), I now say that the argument corresponding to your reflective inference expresses your reflective inference, since your inference-claim belief associated with your reason-giving use of argument is the linking belief of the corresponding reflective inference. Accordingly, when you perform a reflective inference, you are directly persuaded by the corresponding argument to accept its conclusion. Regarding the strengthening of (II), when you use an argument in a reason-giving way, the reflective inference you perform from its premise(s) to conclusion is the inference that is expressed by the argument.

6.3.1. Summary

In argumentative exchanges, whether an addressee R is directly persuaded by your invitation to inference to believe the conclusion turns on whether R performs the inference you invite. What is the inference invited by an invitation to inference? In this section, I have defended (I), which speaks to this. An addressee R is directly persuaded by S's reason-giving use of an argument to believe its conclusion only if R believes S's inference claim. By the lights of (I), R performs the inference you invite only if R's inference is expressed by the argument you use. Accordingly, the given premises and conclusion of your argument must be the propositional contents of the initial premise- and conclusion-beliefs of R's inference. Furthermore, R must believe your inference claim. The content of R's linking belief associated with R's inference is the same as the content of your inference-claim belief as this is fixed by your argumentative intention in extending your invitation to inference.

6.4. Indirect Persuasion

My primary task in this section is to elaborate and defend (II), the second central claim of Chapter 6. I repeat it here.

(II) An addressee R is indirectly persuaded by S's reason-giving use of an argument to believe its conclusion only if R believes the argument provides at least one reason, perhaps among others, R has to believe the conclusion, but R doesn't accept the associated inference claim.

Recall Pinto's claim:

You are directly persuaded by an invitation to inference to accept its conclusion if and only if you perform the belief-inducing inference that is invited.

However, Pinto's claim does not account for how an invitation to inference may persuade an interlocuter R to accept the conclusion even though R does not perform the invited inference, because R does not accept the associated inference claim. In such a case, R takes the argument to provide at least one reason for R to believe the conclusion. I label such persuasion *indirect persuasion* to distinguish it from *direct persuasion*. Claim (II) highlights a necessary condition in order for an addressee to be indirectly persuaded by an invitation to inference.

Put succinctly, my case for (II) runs as follows. Suppose that an addressee R accepts the conclusion of an invitation to inference because R believes that the argument provides a reason for R to believe the conclusion. This is compatible with R's believing that not all the premises are such reasons. Therefore, the invitation to inference has persuasive force for R sufficient enough to elicit R's acceptance of the conclusion. Accordingly, R is persuaded by the invitation to inference to accept its conclusion. Generally, an invitation to inference may provide a reason for one to believe the conclusion even though one does not accept the inference claim. In such a case, one is indirectly persuaded by the invitation to inference.

The plausibility of this case for (II) turns on (i) clarifying how an argument associated with an invitation to inference can provide a reason for one to believe the conclusion even though one does not believe the associated inference claim (say, because one rejects it). Also, (ii) motivation must be provided for why we should count "indirect persuasion" as form of persuasion. The remainder of this section is devoted to tasks (i) and (ii). I start with (i).

Consider Roy Sorenson's case for thinking that the syntactic circularity of an argument doesn't rule out it being rationally persuasive. Sorenson (1991, p. 248) maintains that the following argument is rationally persuasive and so not objectionably circular.

(E)
Some arguments are written in black ink
∴ Some arguments are written in black ink

He holds that since the argument itself is evidence for the truth of the conclusion, and is, therefore, what he calls an *ontic reason* for accepting the truth of the conclusion, (E) provides the basis for rationally accepting the conclusion (1991, pp. 253–54). According to Sorenson, this illustrates that (E) is not objectionally circular, since it provides a rational basis for accepting the conclusion. Sorenson's general point is that whether or not an argument is objectionally circular turns on its epistemic properties, not its syntactic properties.

Alvin Goldman (2003) is not persuaded by Sorenson's use of (E) to illustrate a syntactically circular argument that is rationally persuasive. He claims that presented with (E), an addressee is likely to deploy another argument such as (F) to reach the conclusion (2003, p. 56).

(F)
The displayed argument (E) is written in black ink
∴ Some arguments are written in black ink

Argument (F) is epistemically sound: the conclusion logically follows, and its premise is supported by the perceptual evidence that (E) is written in black ink. Goldman remarks,

> It is highly plausible that [(F)] is what a reader would think to himself in reasoning to the indicated conclusion, and this mode of reasoning or inference is unobjectionable. Of course, the premise of [(F)] refers to [(E)] so [(E)] does get appealed to in the reader's thought process. (2003, p. 56)

Goldman concludes,

> It is clear that a reader/inspector of [(E)] can become rationally persuaded of [(E)]'s conclusion, but not so clear that this is *via* an inference that uses [(E)]. So, this example does not clearly identify a non-defective argument with the syntactic form 'P; therefore, P'. (2003, p. 56)

Recall from Chapter 5, that the explicit circularity of (E) rules out its expression of the contents of a possible belief-inducing inference. It can't express such an inference since the premise and conclusion are one and the same. So, if the contents of the belief-inducing inference that must be performed in order to be rationally persuaded by (E) to accept its conclusion must be expressed by (E), then (E) can't be a rationally persuasive argument.

However, as Goldman admits in the first quotation above, the inference whose content is expressed by (F) does appeal to (E). Plausibly, (E) serves as a guide to the inference expressed by (F) since it provides the evidence for the starting point of the inference and by providing the endpoint, i.e., the intended conclusion. So, borrowing from Sorenson (1991, p. 255), even if Goldman is right that when presented with argument (E) in a context of persuasion an addressee's belief-inducing inference would be expressed by (F), (E) nevertheless guides the addressee's inference. Argument (E) indirectly persuades the addressee of (E)'s conclusion.

There are many forms of indirect persuasion that do not bring self-referential arguments into play. For example, suppose that a classical logician S advances the premises of the following disjunctive syllogism (G) as conclusive reasons for an addressee R to accept the conclusion.

(G)
The keys are in the kitchen or in the car
The keys aren't in the car
∴ They are in the kitchen

Further suppose that unbeknownst to S, R is a paraconsistent logician who thinks that although (G) is deductively invalid, it provides strong but non-conclusive reasons for R to believe the conclusion in part because R thinks that the situation is consistent and thus there is no truth-value glut.[3] R accepts the premises on the basis of S's testimony and infers—in a belief-inducing way—the conclusion. Argument (G) expresses the content of S's inference. However, this is not the inference invited, since R does not accept S's inference claim because R does not take the premises to be conclusive reasons for R to believe the conclusion. Nevertheless, R is indirectly persuaded by S's invitation to inference since (G)'s premises provide (non-conclusive) reasons for which S accepts the conclusion.

Here's another example of indirect persuasion. To save space, I'll use propositional variables. Suppose for some propositions p, q, and r, S advances argument (H) as an invitation to inference in order to elicit an addressee R's acceptance of r.

(H)
p or q
if p then r
if q then r
∴ r

Further suppose that R explicitly takes the premises to be reasons for R to believe the conclusion. However, R believes that p or q only because R believes p. R infers the conclusion from R's beliefs that p and *if p then r*, explicitly following a modus ponens inference rule. R's inference is not the one argument (H) is used to invite: although R takes (H)'s premises to conclusively support the conclusion, R doesn't perform the inference because of this fact.

---

[3] For example, Priest (2008, p. 155) accepts that situations in which a statement is both true and false can be used to generate counterexamples to disjunctive syllogism (DS). Paraconsistent logic blocks explosion, e.g., p & ~p, so q, by rejecting the validity of DS, which is needed to derive q from p & ~p. However, Priest thinks DS cannot lead us from truth to untruth with respect to consistent situations, which are the norm, and so he thinks DS may express inductively strong inferences.

The argument that expresses R's inference is derived from (H) *via* R's *premise pruning*. Intuitively, (H) guides R's reasoning since it provides its endpoint and a starting point that, in conjunction with R's *p*-belief, licenses R's use of modus ponens.

In agreement with Sorenson, the explicitly circular argument (E) can be used as an invitation to inference that is rhetorically successful by virtue of guiding the performance of an epistemically sound inference that it does not invite. In such a case, the addressee is indirectly persuaded by the invitation to inference. However, against Sorenson, this doesn't require that (E) be non-defective. This is because defective arguments may guide the performances of epistemically sound inferences whose contents they do not express. Therefore, in agreement with Goldman, that (E) can be successfully used to rationally persuade (in an indirect way) an addressee of its conclusion does not show that it isn't objectionably circular. To elaborate by way of another illustration, consider the following.

Suppose that a person S uses argument (I) as an invitation to inference in order to persuade an addressee R of its conclusion.

(I)

Kelly, Paige, Shannon, Beth, and Matthew need a ride to the beach
∴ We can't take the Smart car

Suppose that R just learned that Matthew now no longer needs a ride to the beach, but correctly believes that the others do on the basis of S's testimony. Suppose further that from this premise-belief, R infers—in a belief-inducing way—(I)'s conclusion because R correctly believes that the Smart car is too small to transport the others. R's inference is not invited since S does not take the premise to support the conclusion. R would take the premise to support the conclusion, except R thinks it's false (given the premise, R thinks the conclusion is more likely than it would be otherwise). Nevertheless, R is indirectly persuaded by (I); the argument guides R's inference. In conjunction with R's background beliefs, (I) generates the starting pointing via *premise weakening* and provides the endpoint, which is (I)'s conclusion. In this scenario, a defective invitation to inference (e.g., defective because a premise is false) guides the performance of an epistemically sound inference.

Enthymemes provide further material for examples of indirect persuasion. To illustrate, suppose that a person S presents the following enthymeme as an invitation to inference to person R in order to persuade R of the conclusion.

<u>Kelly is a member of the NRA</u>
∴. Kelly is a gun owner

Suppose that S's implicit premise is that *every NRA member is a gun owner*. Suppose further that S advances the premise in conjunction with this suppressed premise together as conclusive reasons for R to believe the conclusion. In advance of fact-checking, R thinks it plausible that there might be members of the NRA who do not own guns. Suppose R draws the conclusion from the premise by means of an inductive inference with the suppressed premise being that *most NRA members are gun owners*. R's inference is not the one invited. Nevertheless, R is indirectly persuaded by the enthymematic argument to accept the conclusion because it guides R's inferential performance by supplying a starting point and endpoint of R's belief-inducing inference.

If you perform an epistemically sound inference because you are *indirectly* persuaded by an invitation to inference, then the argument used needn't be non-defective. This reflects that bad arguments may guide addressees' performances of epistemically sound inferences.[4] However, if you perform an epistemically sound inference because you are *directly* persuaded by an invitation to inference, then the argument used must be non-defective since the premises must be reasons you have to believe the conclusion.

My second task in this section is to motivate why we should count "indirect persuasion" as form of persuasion. The above illustrations of indirect persuasion suggest that if an invitation to inference provides at least one starting point and the endpoint of an addressee's inference, then it guides the reasoning even though the inference performed may not be the one that is invited. An invitation to inference provides a starting point either by expressing the contents of some premise-beliefs (e.g., as with (G) and (H)) or by providing evidence for some premise-beliefs (e.g., as with (E) and (I)). Argument (E) itself is the evidence for the premise-belief of an inference whose content is expressed by (F). The premise of argument (I) provides evidence by virtue of entailing a truth that is the content of the premise-belief of an epistemically sound inference. An invitation to inference provides the

---

[4] Goldman (1994, p. 45) briefly acknowledges this in a note and takes this to show that the theory of folk-argumentative rules he presents is incomplete. Even if one follows Goldman and takes true-belief consequences to be the sole end of argumentation, this does not rule out that an invitation to inference might be good because it *indirectly persuades* the addressee to accept the truth of the conclusion on the basis of an epistemically sound inference guided by the argument.

endpoint of an addressee's inference by virtue of its conclusion being the propositional content of the addressee's conclusion-belief.

By guiding an addressee's inference in these ways without inviting it, an invitation to belief-inducing inference indirectly persuades the addressee to accept its conclusion. This makes the invitation to inference rhetorically successful. On my view, an invitation to belief-inducing inference doesn't guide the performance of an uninvited inference unless it provides a starting point as well as the endpoint of the inference in the ways just explained. It has to provide a starting point; otherwise, the invitation to inference merely plays a causal role in inducing the addressee's acceptance of the conclusion.[5] It has to provide the endpoint; otherwise, its persuasive force can't get cashed out in terms of its rhetorical success, i.e., persuading the addressee of the conclusion.

One may question whether an invitation to inference must involve an argument or whether it must provide the inference's conclusion in order to invite the inference. To briefly elaborate by way of an illustration, suppose Kelly and Paige have demonstrated a reluctance to eat their peas. Observing this, Dad says, "No dessert unless you eat your peas!" with the intention of inducing Kelly and Paige to generate a belief by way of an inference from their acceptance that eating their peas is a requirement for dessert. Dad wants to wrap up dinner. The sisters reason as follows.

KELLY: no dessert unless I eat my peas, I will not eat my peas; therefore, no dessert for me.

PAIGE: no dessert unless I eat my peas, I want dessert; therefore, I will eat my peas.

Their different conclusion-beliefs prompt different actions: Kelly pushes the plate away and leaves the table; Paige eats her peas. Dad uses his assertion to induce inferences that his assertion does not express. Nevertheless, one might think that Dad's invitation to inference is successful because Kelly and Paige reasoned to beliefs that prompted them to finish—in different ways—their dinners. It is unclear to me that the sister's inferences

---

[5] Borrowing from Pinto (see above, section 6.2), an invitation to inference persuades an addressee to accept its conclusion as opposed to merely causing the addressee to accept it by virtue of its premises providing starting points of an inference that induces acceptance of the conclusion. What I am pointing to here is that an invitation to inference can be (indirectly) persuasive even if it provides just some of an inference's starting points.

are invited by Dad's statement made in order to induce some inference or other.[6]

The question arises whether non-arguments can have indirect persuasive force measured in terms of belief-inducing inference. That is, can a non-argument provide—in some sense—the starting point and endpoint of a belief-inducing inference and thereby serve as a proper guide to belief-inducing inferences? An affirmative response, which seems initially plausible to me, complicates the story about how the starting point and endpoint are "provided" in a way that engenders indirect persuasion.

For example, Beth experiences a beautiful sunset that both invokes feelings of gratitude and calls to mind her dad saying in the past that experiencing nature can dignify human existence. She realizes for the first time that experiencing nature can invoke gratitude and infers in a belief-inducing way that what Dad used to say is true. It is at least initially plausible to think that Beth's experience of the sunset provided the starting point and endpoint of her inference by virtue of suggesting them or causing her to think of them. This is plausible grounds for thinking that Beth's experience of the sunset indirectly persuaded her of the truth of her dad's comment.

In general, a non-argument can properly guide a reasoner S to entertain and then perform a belief-inducing inference by providing—in some way—a starting point and endpoint of the inference. This accounts for the potential of a wide variety of things to have indirect persuasive force: e.g., non-argumentative speech acts such as a poem or a story; acts that aren't speech acts such as a dance or gesture; artifacts like a painting or a garden; and natural objects like a rock or a mountain. The phenomenon of indirect persuasion highlights that the persuasiveness of an invitation to inference, and therefore its rhetorical success, turns on the psychological makeup of the addressees (e.g., their belief-sets), and not merely on the intentions of arguers or the contents of their arguments. This is in sync with the argumentation motto: know your audience!

---

[6] A reviewer observes that there are cases where some version of the preferred inference can be pretty clear with some "pregnant premises." So: drive hammered, get nailed; park here and get towed; if slavery isn't wrong, then nothing is. Perhaps there are other felicity conditions given audience commitment, shared knowledge, and so on. In such cases, there does seem that there are inference expectations in these cases. What I am gesturing at here is that Dad's inference expectations may be satisfied by his daughter's inferences even though he doesn't specifically invite them. Accordingly, we may think that Dad's inference expectations are satisfied by his daughters' inferences which neither correspond to nor are expressed by an argument Dad gives. In such a case, it is wrong to think that Dad rationally persuaded Paige to finish her peas and Kelly not to finish her peas by means of expressing an argument their inferences somehow correspond to.

6.4.1. Summary

If an addressee R is directly persuaded by your invitation to inference to accept the conclusion, then R accepts your inference claim. If R is indirectly persuaded, then although R does not accept your inference claim, R thinks the argument you use provides at least one reason for R to believe the conclusion. Hence, the difference between one being directly or indirectly persuaded to accept the conclusion of an invitation to inference turns on whether one accepts the associated inference claim.

A takeaway is that a bad argument may *indirectly* persuade an addressee R, inducing R's performance of a corresponding inference that is epistemically good. Accordingly, a bad argument may function to rationally persuade an addressee of its conclusion (contra Lumer 2005; Biro and Siegel 2006a). In such a case, the evaluative dimensions of arguments do not ground the normative quality of the inference it guides.

6.5. Conclusion

One way of trying to persuade an interlocuter R to believe something is to advance premises for it that you think are reasons of some sort for R to believe it. Specifically, in service of your aim to persuade R, you think that the premises are reasons R has to believe your conclusion or reasons for R to believe it. In the former case, you take the premises you advance to be normative reasons to believe the conclusion and so believe that that they are true and are evidence of some kind for the conclusion. In the latter case you do not and are arguing from R's commitments and beliefs not all of which you accept. If you do not intend and so believe that the premises you advance are reasons—in some sense—for your interlocuter to accept the conclusion, then your act of persuasion, successful or otherwise, does not involve a reason-giving use of argument.

If you use an argument in a reason-giving way in order to persuade an interlocuter R of the conclusion, then your reason-giving use of the argument is rhetorically successful if R is persuaded to accept the conclusion. By Pinto's claim, if R is directly persuaded, then R performs the invited inference, which is the inference expressed by the argument as you use it. Direct persuasion requires that R accept your inference claim. If R is indirectly persuaded, then although R does not accept your inference claim, R believes that your argument provides a reason for R to accept the conclusion.

Suppose that your invitation to inference is rhetorically successful because your interlocuter R is either directly or indirectly persuaded by your argument to believe the conclusion. Accordingly, R's inference is the one you invite, or it is expressed by R's argument derived from yours that R uses in a reason-giving way. The conclusion of R's argument is the same as yours and R takes your argument to provide at least one reason for R to believe the conclusion, which is represented by a premise of R's argument.

When we argue with someone in order to rationally persuade them of something, we seek to elicit their belief of something in light of the reasons we advance for believing it. Advancing reasons for believing something as a means of persuading someone of its truth concords with acknowledging their autonomy as reasoners with the wherewithal to decide for themselves whether the premises we advance are, in fact, reasons for them to accept the conclusion.

Direct persuasion counts as rational only if two conditions obtain. First, the relevant reason-giving use of argument is a rationality generator in the sense that the premises advanced are reasons for the person convinced by the argument to believe the conclusion. Second, the person, in fact, believes the conclusion in light of the premises. Indirect persuasion associated with a reason-giving use of argument counts as rational only if the person induced to accept the conclusion believes it in light of what they take to be reasons for them to believe the conclusion that includes at least one of the premises. Additionally, the premises of the argument that expresses their inference must be reasons for them to believe the conclusion.

By the lights of this understanding of the rationality of argumentative persuasion, that a reason-giving use of argument rationally persuades an interlocuter of the conclusion, directly or indirectly, does not require that one's reasons for believing what one is persuaded of be good reasons for believing it. This suggests that a reason-giving use of an argument may rationalize your believing the conclusion even though the argument you use is not good as judged by a plausible theory of argument. The plausibility of this claim turns, in part, on the plausibility of understanding argumentative rationality as somehow prior to an account of the good-making features of arguments. This understanding is developed in the next chapter, which is devoted to addressing the following question: When does a reason-giving use of argument rationalize one's believing the conclusion?

7

Reason-Giving Uses of Arguments and Argumentative Rationality

7.1. Preamble

Willard remarks that "not all rationality theories include argument in their definitions, but virtually all argument theories include rationality in theirs" (1989, p. 152). This highlights the idea that rationality is in some way central to argumentation. As I noted in Chapter 1, this idea is widely held. Taking rationality as the basic evaluative ideal of argument makes it "a fundamental task of any theory of argument . . . to supply, by manufacture or import, some theory of rationality" (Godden 2015, p. 136). Following Godden (2015), I will call these theories of *argumentative rationality*. Argumentative rationality concerns the rationality of believing the conclusion of an argument in light of believing its premises. The central question of this chapter is, when does one's reason-giving use of an argument rationalize one's believing the conclusion? Presumably, a theory of argumentative rationality should deliver a response. Toward developing my response, I consider three general approaches to argumentative rationality: the well-known epistemic and pragma-dialectic approaches,[1] and what I call the pragma-epistemic approach.

The *epistemic approach* (e.g., Biro and Siegel 1992; Feldman 1994; Lumer 2005) reduces argumentative rationality to what is commonly referred to as the standard picture of epistemic rationality.[2] According to this picture (see

---

[1] As I will discuss below, the epistemic and pragma-dialectic approaches to argumentative rationality are associated with the epistemic and pragma-dialectic theories of argumentation. My rationale for focusing on these two approaches to argumentative rationality to contrast with the pragma-epistemic approach I favor is twofold. First, the epistemic and pragma-dialectic theories of argumentation that I consider advance substantive approaches to argumentative rationality. See Corner and Hahn 2013 for a useful discussion of the two approaches to what I am calling *argumentative rationality*. Second, these well-known versions of the epistemic and pragma-dialectic theories of argumentation are explicit in advocating competing accounts of what is necessary and sufficient for one's use of an argument to rationalize one's believing the conclusion in a way that highlights competing conceptions of the centrality of rationality to argumentation.

[2] Epistemic theories of argumentation can be classified as objective (e.g., Biro and Siegel 1992) or as subjective epistemic theories (e.g., Feldman 1994). For a substantive discussion of the distinction

Arguments and Reason-Giving. Matthew W. McKeon, Oxford University Press. © Oxford University Press 2024.
DOI: 10.1093/oso/9780197751633.003.0007

Rysiew 2008 for a good review), believing that something is the case is epistemically rational just in case it is justified to so believe it. On the epistemic approach, your reason-giving use of argument rationalizes your believing the conclusion only if your premises justify believing it. So, to get at argumentative rationality on this approach requires an account of epistemic justification.

The *pragma-dialectic approach* (e.g., van Eemeren and Grootendorst 2004; van Laar 2003) understands argumentative rationality in terms of procedural rationality (for a good discussion of procedural rationality, see Corner and Hahn 2013). A reason-giving use of an argument in a dialogical exchange devoted to resolving a difference of opinion rationalizes the participants' accepting the conclusion just in case the use of the argument accords with the procedural rules that should guide the interlocuters' dialogical exchanges toward resolving their difference of opinion. Hence, to understand argumentative rationality on this approach requires an account of the rules operative in an ideal dialogical exchange devoted to resolving a difference of opinion.

What I call the *pragma-epistemic approach* adopts a reasons-first notion of rationality to characterize argumentative rationality. Your reason-giving use of argument rationalizes your believing the conclusion just in case your premises are either reasons you have to believe the conclusion or reasons for you to believe the conclusion. On this approach, your use of an argument to advance reasons you have to believe the conclusion suffices to rationalize your believing it independently of whether the premises justify your believing the conclusion and independently of whether your use of the argument is in accordance with ideal procedural rules for dialogues conducted to resolve a difference of opinion. To develop this initial understanding of argumentative rationality, we need an account of these two types of *reasons for belief* (introduced in Chapter 3) according to which believing that something is true in light of them suffices to rationalize believing it. Also, we need clarification of the associated reasons-first rationality according to which one's premises being such *reasons for believing* the conclusion of one's argument rationalizes one's believing the conclusion.

I favor the pragma-epistemic approach so understood over the epistemic and pragma-dialectic approaches. In this chapter, I appeal to the pragma-epistemic approach to account for the centrality of rationality to

see Lumer 2005. Each type is associated with a distinct understanding of argumentative rationality. Below I focus on the objective version of Biro and Siegel for the reasons mentioned in note 1.

argumentation. Argumentative rationality serves to make the norms of argumentation bear on the evaluation of arguers' believing the conclusions of their arguments. Specifically, that a person S's reason-giving use of an argument is good or bad bears on the evaluation of S's believing the conclusion just in case S's use of the argument rationalizes S's believing the conclusion. In what sense does it *rationalize S's believing the conclusion*? In the sense that S's premises are reasons S possesses for believing the conclusion. If the premises are such reasons, then they are either reasons S has to believe the conclusion or reasons for S to believe it. By the lights of the pragma-epistemic approach, if the premises qualify as either type of reason, then S's use of the argument rationalizes S's believing the conclusion in light of the premises. Accordingly, S's reason-giving use of an argument bears on the evaluation of S's believing the conclusion in light of the premises just in case S's use of the argument rationalizes S's believing the conclusion as understood on the pragma-epistemic approach.

For example, that your reason-giving use of argument is good bears on the rational evaluation of your believing the conclusion in light of the premises only if your premises are reasons you possess for believing the conclusion. Put another way, if your use of an argument doesn't involve giving reasons that you possess for believing the conclusion, then that it is a good use of argument doesn't bear positively on your believing the conclusion. Also, criticism of your reason-giving use of argument is relevant as rational criticism of your believing the conclusion in light of your premises just in case the premises are reasons that you possess for believing the conclusion. So criticism of your reason-giving use of argument counts as rational criticism of your believing the conclusion just in case your reason-giving use of argument rationalizes your believing the conclusion as understood on the pragma-epistemic approach.

As I will explain below, the epistemic and pragma-dialectic stories about why rationality is central to argumentation require that it is only uses of good arguments that rationalize believing their conclusions. Accordingly, the epistemic and pragma-dialectic theories of good argumentation ground the epistemic and pragma-dialectic approaches to argumentative rationality, respectively. This contrasts with the pragma-epistemic approach.

To elaborate, the pragma-epistemic story why rationality is central to argumentation does not require that your premises be *good* reasons for believing the conclusion in order for your use of the associated argument to rationalize your believing the conclusion in light of the premises. Rather, what is required is that your premises be *reasons you possess for believing the conclusion*, good or otherwise. Accordingly, argumentative rationality as understood on the pragma-epistemic approach is prior to an account of what makes reason-giving uses of arguments good. One's reason-giving use of an argument may rationalize one's believing the conclusion even though it is not a *good* use of the argument as judged by one's favorite theory of argumentation.

Chapter 7 runs as follows. In section 7.2, I clarify the type of *reasons for belief* operative in pragma-epistemic argumentative rationality. Specifically, I sharpen the distinction introduced in Chapter 3 between reasons one has to believe that a proposition is true and reasons for one to believe that it is true. I then show how these two different types of reasons for belief ground a distinction between what I call objective and subjective rationality. Next, in section 7.3 I develop the pragma-epistemic approach, drawing on section 7.2's discussion of reasons for belief. On the pragma-epistemic approach, objective and subjective rationality are two dimensions of argumentative rationality.

In section 7.4, I discuss the epistemic and pragma-dialectic approaches to argumentative rationality in order to further distinguish the pragma-epistemic approach. Working from Siegel and Biro (e.g., 1992, 1997, 2008) and van Eemeren and Grootendorst (e.g., 1988, 1995, 2004) I argue that both approaches presuppose that one's use of an argument rationalizes one's believing the conclusion if and only if the argument used is good as understood by the epistemic and pragma-dialectic theories of good argument, respectively. Then in section 7.5 I argue against this claim in defense of the pragma-epistemic approach. Finally, in section 7.6 I conclude the chapter by summarizing the import of its central claims.

In Chapter 8, I discuss why believing your inference claim is necessary for your reason-giving use of argument to be intellectually honest. Recall that when you use an argument in a reason-giving way, you intend the premises to serve as reasons for believing the conclusion and you claim that your premises are such reasons. Assuming that your argumentative intention satisfies the inference-claim belief requirement for rationality, you believe what you claim. Intellectual honesty demands that you believe what you claim. Accordingly, the reason-giving uses of arguments of interest in this book are intellectually honest insofar as users believe their inference claims. A liar's dialectical argument is at best a pseudo-reason-giving use of it. I then use the book's account of reason-giving uses of arguments as a framework to distinguish between the intellectual honesty and intellectual integrity of reason-giving uses of arguments. For example, your intellectually honest reason-giving use of argument displays intellectual integrity only if the premises you advance are reasons for which you believe the conclusion.

7.2. Reason for Belief and the Rationality of Belief

In this section, I revisit *reasons one has to believe something* and *reasons for one to believe something*, both introduced in Chapter 3. Recall that the former are normative, subjective reasons for belief, and that the latter are non-normative, subjective reasons for belief.[3] On the pragma-epistemic approach to argumentative rationality these are the two types of reasons that figure in how our reason-giving uses of arguments rationalize our believing the conclusion. My discussion of these types of reasons for belief serves as a starting point for my development in the next section of the pragmatic-epistemic approach to argumentative rationality. First, some preliminaries.

As I mentioned in Chapter 3, I take reasons for belief to be propositions.[4] My chief rationale for understanding reasons for belief in terms of propositions is that when one uses an argument in a reason-giving way one advances the premises as reasons for believing the conclusion. If successful, the premises are such reasons. As discussed in Chapter 2, I take the premises and conclusion of an argument to be propositions. Hence, my view that reasons for belief, in the context of reason-giving uses of argument, are propositions. In this context, the ontology of reasons for belief turns on the ontology of arguments.

---

[3] The expression *my belief* can be used to mean either my believing something or what I believe. Consistent with the discussion of *reasons for belief* in Chapter 3, my focus is on the second meaning. For example, I understand *p is a reason for my belief that q* to mean *p is a reason for my believing that p*.

[4] There is no consensus in the literature on the ontology of reasons for belief. For useful discussion of various views and involved problematics in giving an account of reasons for belief see Ginsborg 2006 and Turri 2009. Some scholars think that nothing counts as a reason for belief except another belief (e.g., Davidson 1986, p. 10) or, more generally, another mental state (Turri 2009, p. 492). Some think that perceptual experiences can count (e.g., McDowell 1997, p. 14). Others think that only facts or true propositions count as reasons for belief (e.g., Alvarez 2009; Stampe 1987, pp. 337, 343; Skorupski 1997, p. 345) As I discuss below, since I take a reason for one to believe something to be a false proposition, I don't think that a proposition needs to be true in order to qualify as a reason for belief, i.e., a reason for one to believe something.

A proposition is only a reason to believe in relation to another proposition, i.e., the proposition it is a reason to believe.[5] Also, a proposition p may be a reason for believing another proposition q only in conjunction with other propositions that taken together along with p are reasons for believing q. That *Paige is Shannon's sibling* is a reason to believe *Shannon is Paige's sibling*. That *Paige is home only if Shannon is home* is a reason to believe that *Shannon is home* only in conjunction with other proposition(s), e.g., that *Paige is home*. Note that your reason-giving use of argument may rationalize your believing the conclusion even though you don't believe the conclusion, or you do but for other reasons. This is because that you possess reasons for believing the conclusion doesn't imply that you believe the conclusion or that they are reasons for which you believe it.

I now sharpen my story about reasons a person has to believe something and reasons for a person to believe something. To simplify, I will initially speak in terms of a single reason for believing a proposition rather than a collection of reasons for believing it. My characterizations of each type of reason for belief put succinctly are as follows.

If p is a reason a person S has to believe something, say, q, then (a)–(c) obtain.

(a) p is true.
(b) S believes p or should believe p given the information available to S.
(c) q follows in some way from p.

If p is a reason for S to believe q, then (b), (c) and (d) obtain.

(d) p isn't true.

So whether or not p is true is the crucial difference between p being a reason S has to believe q and being a reason S for to believe q. I now review the rationales for (a)–(d).

In regard to (a), a reason p a person S has to believe q is a normative reason for S to believe it by virtue of being a reason to believe q. A reason to believe q is a true proposition from which q follows. Borrowing from Alvarez (2009, pp. 182–83), I understand the normativity of a reason to believe to be,

---

[5] Some believe that the involved relation is three-place, involving a believer (for discussion see Kiesewetter 2017, pp. 8–9). Audi raises the interesting question whether for every true proposition p there is another such that it is a good reason to believe p (1993, p. 235).

at minimum, as follows. *That p* makes believing *q* in light of *p pro tanto* correct. Believing *q* in light of *p* is *pro tanto* correct by virtue of *p* being true and *q* following from *p*. The force of *pro tanto* correctness is that it may be otherwise wrong for you to believe *q* because, say, it is epistemically irresponsible, or unintelligent. Hence, the normativity of a reason *p* person has to believe *q*, understood in this minimal sense, requires the truth of *p*, and it requires that *q* follow from *p*. I take these requirements to make the truth of *p* a sufficient indicator of the truth of *q*.

My initial rationale for (b) is that a reason a person S has to believe something is *subjective* in the sense that it is a proposition that S believes, or would acknowledge as true if S explicitly considered it, say when questioned about whether it is true. This reflects the idea that a reason S has to believe something or a reason for S to believe it is a reason that S in some way *possesses*.[6] That the square root of 2 cannot be expressed as a fraction is a reason to believe that it is an irrational number, but it may not be a reason little Johnny has to believe this unless he has the necessary math background.

According to condition (c), if *q* doesn't follow from *p*, then it is neither type of reason for you to believe the conclusion. Even stronger, if *q* doesn't follow from *p*, then it isn't a reason of any type introduced in Chapter 3. Accordingly, the requirement that *q* must follow from *p* in order for *p* to be a reason person S has to believe *q* is not grounded on the normativity of reasons for one to believe something. Rather, it is grounded on what I take to be an essential feature of a reason for belief. I now elaborate.

An intuitive starting point for accounts of reasons accepted by many is that reasons count in favor of (or against) what they are reasons for (against) (e.g., among many others, see Broome 2013, p. 54; Kiesewetter 2017, p. 5; Scanlon 1998, p. 17; Thomson 2008, p. 237). Different accounts of reason emerge from different understandings of the ways reasons count in favor or against what they are reasons for (see Alverez 2009 and Kiesewetter 2017, pp. 5–13, for discussion). Intuitively, I don't see how *p* can count in favor of the truth of *q* if *q* doesn't follow from *p*. This motivates thinking that *p* isn't a reason someone possess for believing *q*, unless *q* follows from *p*.

---

[6] Some think that this is an essential feature of a reason to believe something and so are skeptics of the category for belief that I have labeled, following Audi (1993, pp. 237–38), reasons to believe, which are normative and objective (e.g., Broome 2013, p. 66; Kiesewetter 2017 p. 6; Schroeder 2007). Being objective, such reasons are not subjective and so not possessed by a believer. For discussion of the manner reasons may be possessed, see Sylvan 2016, pp. 367–70.

For example, if p is a reason a person S has to believe q, then it seems to me that the truth of p must be indicative of the truth of q. That is, p being true constitutes evidence, conclusive or otherwise, for the truth of q (this follows, among others, Kelly 2007; Kiesewetter 2017, p. 12; Worsnip 2021, p. 12). That p is true signifies that q is true and so the truth of q follows from the truth of p. In ordinary circumstances, my hearing the whistle of the teapot in the kitchen indicates that the water is boiling, because ordinarily that the teapot is whistling indicates this. Given that I believe that the teapot is whistling based on what I hear, that the teapot is whistling is a reason I have to believe that the water is boiling. If I mistakenly believe that the teapot is whistling, then nevertheless this is a reason for me to believe that the water is boiling. For, if it were true that the teapot is whistling then, ceteris paribus, this would be evidence that the water is boiling because that the teapot is whistling in ordinary contexts is a typical indicator that the water is boiling.

Consider hypothetical or supposition reasons. Again, from Chapter 3, p is a hypothetical reason to believe q just in case p is merely possibly true and if it were true, it would be a reason, conclusive or otherwise, to believe q. That Lee wins at Gettysburg in 1863 may be a hypothetical reason to believe that the South wins the US Civil War, but it is obviously implausible to think that it is a hypothetical reason to believe that the Mafia was involved in President Kennedy's assassination in 1963. A win for the Confederacy at Gettysburg isn't even a bad hypothetical reason for believing that the Mafia was involved in President Kennedy's assassination, because if true that the Mafia was involved doesn't follow from this.

Condition (c) motivates a response to the following question. What distinguishes a proposition p as a bad reason for believing q as opposed to p being no reason at all for believing q? Drawing on (c), it is that q must follow from p to be even a bad reason for believing q. To elaborate, I use Kornblith's discussion of two common-sense distinctions which he thinks any plausible epistemological theory needs to preserve.

> When Jack believes that it will rain tomorrow because he noticed that his tea leaves were wetter than usual, while Jill believes that it will rain tomorrow because she carefully examined the local weather patterns, the obvious thing to say is that Jill has good reasons to believe as she does, while Jack does not. We need to preserve the distinction between beliefs like Jack's and beliefs like Jill's lest we lapse into a view which sees all beliefs as epistemologically on a par, and the obvious way to draw this distinction is just the

way we do in everyday parlance: Jill holds her belief for good reasons, while Jack does not. (2015, p. 225)

Condition (c) accommodates the distinction Kornblith highlights as follows. That Jill has good reasons to believe that it will rain tomorrow is compatible with (c). However, by (c) Jack does not hold his belief that it will rain for good reasons because he does not believe it for reasons, good or otherwise. Presumably, that his tea leaves were wetter than usual has nothing to do with the following day's weather. For example, that his tea leaves were wetter than usual is no more a (bad) reason to believe that it will rain the following day than is the proposition that $2 + 2 = 4$. Suppose, instead, Jack misreads the barometer on his deck and mistakenly thinks that the air pressure is below 29.00 inHg. He infers that it will rain tomorrow. As such low pressure is associated with rainstorms, the proposition that *the air pressure is below 29.00 inHg* is a reason for Jack to believe that it will rain tomorrow. However, since Jack misread his barometer, Jack's mistaken belief does not provide him with a reason he has to believe that it will rain tomorrow.

> There is also another distinction which commonsense draws. When Jack falls down and hits his head on a rock, and then, on returning to consciousness, holds a belief which he never held before—that he is the present King of France, say—we need to contrast this case, and cases like it, with beliefs such as Jill's, that Jack has had a concussion, and that it would be wise for him to seek medical attention immediately. Jill's belief is based on reasons, and good ones at that, but Jack's belief is not based on reasons at all, not even bad ones. His belief was caused, to be sure; it was caused by his unfortunate encounter with the rock. But there is a distinction, it seems, between coming to believe for reasons, whether good or bad, and merely being caused to believe. We need to advert to reasons, of course, to make this important distinction. Any plausible epistemological theory, it seems, should thus incorporate such a distinction, and give us an account of it. (2015, p. 225)

Condition (c) is compatible with this common-sense distinction between coming to believe for reasons, whether good or bad, and merely being caused to believe. However, (c) motivates drawing the distinction differently from what Kornblith may have in mind. For example, Jack doesn't possess reasons either for his belief that he is the present king of France or for his belief that it will rain tomorrow. In the second scenario, Jack's belief that he is the present king of France is merely caused by his head hitting a rock. He doesn't possess reasons for believing this. Similarly, in the first scenario Jack's belief that it will rain tomorrow is merely caused. It is merely caused by his belief that his tea leaves are wetter than usual for he (erroneously) takes the state of his tea leaves to be indicative of the following day's weather. The difference is that in this scenario, unlike in the second in which Jack hits his head, Jack (wrongly) thinks that he has a reason for the truth of his belief.

In short, if you believe a proposition p because of your other beliefs, whether their propositional contents count as reasons you possess for your believing p turns on whether p follows from them.[7] On this view, that one's reasoning to a conclusion from a set of premises is *logically* fallacious nullifies the premises as reasons one possesses for one's believing the conclusion. For example, consider the following scenario.

(1) Every student in Mr. Avery's class is a sophomore.
(2) Jane is not a student in Mr. Avery's class.
(3) Jane is not a sophomore.

Suppose that Jack believes (3) because he believes (1) and (2) and takes (1) and (2) to be reasons to believe (3). Presumably, reasoning from (1) and (2) to (3) is logically fallacious because (3) does not follow from them. Accordingly, (1) and (2) are not reasons for which Jack believes (3) even if Jack thinks otherwise. Suppose that Jill believes (2) because she believes (1) and (3) and takes (1) and (3) to be reasons to believe (2). Since (2) follows from (1) and (3), they may count as reasons for which Jill believes (2) regardless of whether Jill explicitly acknowledges their status as such reasons. Whether (1) and (3) are reasons Jill has to believe (2) or reasons for her to believe (2) turns on whether (1) and (3) are true.

To summarize, I take an internalist approach to reasons for believing a proposition q to involve the claim that if a person S's believing q is caused in the right (i.e., non-deviant) way by S's belief that p and S takes p to be a reason S has to believe q, then p qualifies as a reason of some sort that S possesses to

---

[7] It also turns on the causal link being non-deviant between these other beliefs and your believing p. For a good discussion of the challenge deviant causal chains involving coming to believe something present to characterizing *believing for a reason*, see Wedgewood 2006. I find Wedgewood's proposed response to the challenge plausible.

believe q. Here to get at whether there are reasons for which S holds a belief we determine the origin of S's belief. Jack's belief that he is the present king of France is not caused in the right way from his other beliefs. For example, he doesn't believe this because he takes some propositions to be reasons he has for believing that he is the present king of France. Hence, Jack doesn't possess reasons for which he believes that he is the present king of France. On an internalist approach, since Jack holds his belief that it will rain tomorrow because he believes that his tea leaves are wetter than usual and takes this to be a reason to believe that this is indicative of tomorrow's weather, he possesses a (bad) reason for believing that it will rain tomorrow (assuming that the causal connection is legit).

I take an externalist approach to reasons for belief to involve the denial of the claim that if a person S's belief that q is caused in the right way by S's belief that p and S takes p to be a reason to believe q, then p qualifies as a reason that S possesses to believe q. An externalist approach endorses condition (c) and so motivates thinking that in order for p to be a reason for S believing q, q must follow from p. So on an externalist approach Jack's belief that his tea leaves are wetter than usual provides a reason for which he believes that it will rain tomorrow only if the latter follows from the former. Whether this is the case is independent of whether the operative causal connection between his two beliefs is legit.

A combined internalist + externalist approach may be construed as involving the claim that if a person S's belief that q is caused in the right way by S's belief that p, S takes p to be a reason to believe q, **and** q follows from p, then p is a reason that S possesses to believe q. On the combined approach, that Jack holds his belief that it will rain tomorrow because he believes that his tea leaves are wetter than usual and takes this to be indicative of rain tomorrow does not suffice for his possession of a (bad) reason for believing that it will rain tomorrow. In addition, that it will rain tomorrow must follow from the proposition that his tea leaves are wetter than usual.

I take the determination of the status of a proposition p as a reason to believe q on an externalist approach to be an a priori matter. Deductive logic or probability theory confirms that p is so related to q. Whether p is a reason that a particular person S possesses for believing q requires empirical inquiry into what else S believes. For example, to determine whether S's belief that p provides a reason for which S believes q calls for an empirical inquiry into the origin of S's q-belief, and S's capacity to ascertain the evidential connection between p and q.

To summarize, the account of reasons for belief adopted here has two central claims. First, if p is a reason for believing q, then q follows from p. So, if q doesn't follow from p, then p isn't a reason for anybody to believe q. This reflects an externalist approach to reasons for belief. Put loosely, p has to be relevant as sufficient support for believing q; i.e., q has to follow from p, in order for p to be a reason for believing q. So if p is a reason you have to believe q or a reason for you to believe q, then q follows from p. Second, p is a reason that a person S possesses for believing q if S believes or should believe p and S correctly takes p to be a reason to believe q. Taking p to be a reason to believe q is correct only if q follows from p in the way S thinks.

Of course, that p isn't a reason for anybody to believe q doesn't rule out reasoning in some sense from p to q. For example, taking a person S's inference from (1) *All my relatives that are Republican think the election was stolen* to (2) *it is most likely the case that all Republicans think the election was stolen* to commit the fallacy of hasty generalization does not problematize the status of S's inference as reasoning. After all, logically fallacious reasoning is nevertheless reasoning (but see Grice 2001, p. 6). Rather, taking S's inference to be logically fallacious rules out the status of (1) as a reason S has to believe (2) or as a reason for S to believe (3). My point here is that the starting points of a piece of reasoning collectively are not reasons for believing the endpoint unless the endpoint follows from the starting points.

To avoid misunderstanding it is worth emphasizing that I am discussing what counts as reasons for belief, not what counts as *good* reasons for belief. Obviously, more is involved in spelling out the latter than spelling out the former. For example, p may be a reason you have to believe q but it may not be a *good* reason you have to believe it because, say, your believing p is defeated by your other beliefs. In such a case if you were to believe p this would contradict or be undercut by another belief of yours that you are far more certain of than you are of the truth of p. Good decision-making regarding what to believe as true goes beyond monitoring what counts as a reason for belief; e.g., it requires careful surveillance of one's belief set to ensure one's acquired beliefs are undefeated. Also, p may be a bad reason you have to believe q, because while your believing p is undefeated by your other beliefs you are not justified in believing p.

The last element of my account of reasons for belief to discuss is the claim that if p is a reason for S to believe q, then (d) p isn't true. As previously mentioned, this claim distinguishes reasons a person has to believe something from reasons for a person to believe it. The former are true propositions; the latter are false ones. My rationale for thinking that a proposition that isn't true can be a reason for a person to believe something is twofold. First, it reflects our practices of using arguments in reason-giving ways. Second, it reflects our second- and third-person ascriptions of intelligibility to believing something in light of reasons. I now elaborate, starting with the first rationale.

As I said in Chapter 2, it is widely acknowledged in the informal logic literature that among the variety of uses of arguments is their use to advance premises as reasons for believing the conclusion. In developing this point, I highlighted in Chapter 2 that among the different reason-giving uses of argument are those according to which the premises are advanced as hypothetical reasons for believing the conclusion or as reasons for one's interlocuter to believe the conclusion. For example, we may advance premises as reasons that we grant are true for the sake of argument. Of course, this doesn't necessitate that we believe that the premises are true even though we accept them as reasons for believing the conclusion. This is because suppose-for-the-sake-of-argument reasons needn't be true propositions.

As discussed in Chapter 2, when we use an argument whose premises we correctly think are our interlocuter's reasons for believing the conclusion, we use the argument in a reason-giving way. This is so even though we may also think at least one premise is false. To illustrate, consider the following scenario. You argue in order to persuade your interlocuter with their known Kantian sympathies that they wrongly did X from premises they accept that include their favorite version of the categorical imperative. However, you reject the categorical imperative from your act-utilitarian standpoint according to which you think your interlocuter's X-ing was wrong in a way that does not bring the categorical imperative into play. So you use an argument in a reason-giving way even though you reject one of your premises, because, say, you believe that it is vital that your interlocuter accept that what they did was wrong, and you believe that you are more likely to persuade them of this conclusion arguing from their premises rather than yours.

In short, to successfully use premises as reasons for believing the conclusion of an argument it is not required that one's premises be true or that one believes this. This motivates thinking that a proposition that isn't true can be a reason a person possesses for believing something. I now turn to my second rationale for this claim, drawing primarily on Ginsborg (2006) and Foley (1993, pp. 8–15).

Consider our past-tense ascriptions of reasons. For example, when discussing our past beliefs that we now view as mistaken, "[W]e often try to project ourselves into our past egocentric perspective" (Foley 1993, p. 12). We try to remember how things looked to us then in a way that makes sense of our maintaining the belief that we have now given up. This may enable us to present ourselves in a favorable light by identifying reasons we possessed for maintaining the belief that we now regard as mistaken. This is connected to the fact that our second- and third-person ascriptions of rationality may bring into play a person's beliefs that we think false in order to rationalize what they do or believe. A person in the know may think that Paige's belief that Beth is home is erroneous, but nevertheless think that it makes sense for her to believe this because she mistakenly believes that Beth's car is in the driveway. In short, our practices of reason ascription motivate thinking that proposition that isn't true can be a reason a person possesses for believing something.

I now connect (i) *reasons S has to believe something* and (ii) *reasons for a person S to believe it* to the rationality of S's believing it. I adopt a reasons-first conception of rationality: the rationality of S's believing something is a matter of S's possessing reasons for believing it. Since (i) and (ii) are different types of reasons for belief, intuitively they are associated with different notions of rationality. I develop this appealing to the notions of objective and subjective rationality, respectively.

If one believes that a proposition q is true in light of a proposition p that one correctly thinks is a reason one has to believe q, then one's believing q is *objectively rational*. If one believes that p is true in light of reasons one (incorrectly) believes are reasons one has to believe p, but which, in fact, are reasons for one to believe it, then one's believing p is *subjectively rational*. Hence, whether one's believing something is objectively or subjectively rational turns on whether one's reasons for believing it are reasons one has to believe it or merely reasons for one to believe it, respectively. I now illustrate the distinction between objective and subjective rationality.

As Beth prepares lunch, she mistakenly thinks (a) that there are two apples in the refrigerator and in light of this belief thinks (b) that Paige and Kelly can each have an apple for lunch. Intuitively, her believing (b) in light of (a) is rational even though (a) is not a reason she has to believe (b). After all, there are not two apples in the refrigerator and so (a) is false. However, (a) is a reason for Beth to believe (b), assuming that (b) follows from (a). Therefore, Beth's believing (b) in light of (a) is subjectively rational.

Suppose that Beth is justified in believing (a): she just checked and saw two apples. However, unbeknownst to her, just afterward Matthew took an apple from the refrigerator when Beth wasn't looking on his way out the door to baseball practice. Plausibly, Beth's believing (a) is justified even though it is not, unbeknownst to her, a reason she has to believe (b). Rather, it is a reason for Beth to believe (b) since it is false that there are two apples in the fridge. Accordingly, Beth believing (b) is subjectively rational.

Now suppose that in light of her mistaken belief (a), Beth believes (c) that each lunch attendee can have an apple, absentmindedly forgetting that she will join Paige and Kelly for lunch. It is not even (subjectively) rational for her to believe (c) in light of (a), since (c) does not follow from (a). This reflects that in order for p to be a reason for some person X's believing q, q must follow in some sense from p.

Finally, suppose that as Beth prepares lunch, she thinks (a) that there are two apples in the fridge on the basis of quickly glancing, without her glasses, at an apple and an adjacent tomato, mistaking the tomato for an apple. Further suppose that unbeknownst to Beth there is another apple in the fridge's dairy drawer, which is out of sight. Plausibly, Beth's belief (a) is unjustified. Nevertheless, (a) as a reason Beth has to believe (b). Accordingly, Beth believing (b) in light of (a) is objectively rational.

7.2.1. Summary

Your believing something is argumentatively rational only if it is the conclusion of an argument that you use in a reason-giving way. Accordingly, if your believing something is argumentatively rational, then you use an argument to advance its premises as reasons for believing the conclusion. So, to get at argumentative rationality we must understand the operative notion of reasons for belief. On my view, the operative notion is reasons one possesses for believing the conclusion understood in terms of reasons one has to believe the conclusion or reasons for one to believe it.

Specifically, if your believing something is argumentatively rational, then you use an argument to advance its premises as reasons you have to believe the conclusion and claim that the premises are such reasons. (A) If what you claim is true, then your use of the argument makes your believing the conclusion objectively rational. (B) If what you claim is false because, unbeknownst to you, a premise is false and collectively the premises are merely reasons for you to believe the conclusion, then your use of the argument makes your believing the conclusion subjectively rational. (C) If what you claim is false because, unbeknownst to you, the conclusion doesn't follow from your premises, then your use of the argument doesn't rationalize your believing the conclusion, objectively or subjectively. The premises are not reasons for believing the conclusion, contrary to what you think.

Claim (B) involves the idea that propositions that aren't true may nevertheless be non-normative reasons for somebody to believe something. Such reasons are non-normative in the sense that your believing something isn't correct if you believe it in light of reasons for you to believe it and so aren't reasons you have to believe it. Compare: if you if you believe something in light of what are reasons you have to believe it, then your believing it is *pro tanto* correct. Of course, there may be operative norms by which your believing something in light of reasons you have to believe it is legitimately criticizable.

Claim (C) presupposes that in order for some proposition to be reasons for believing another the latter must follow from the former. This reflects the externalist dimension of a reason for belief. My first-step clarification of the *follows-from* relation is that a proposition q follows other propositions just in case the truth of the latter is indicative of the truth of q in that their being true makes it more likely than not that q is also true. Without further information, that Beth is at home follows from that she said she was at home. That Beth is at home does not follow from the earth is the third planet from the sun. The latter proposition is too low in truth conducivity, as Alston (2005) puts it, to make that Beth is at home today probable enough to qualify as a reason for believing it. Since reasons for believing something must be relevant to believing that it is true, the *follows-from* relation has a relevance criterion.[8]

---

[8] This disqualifies consequence relations such as classical consequence, according to which the mere impossibility of true premises and a false conclusion is sufficient to make the conclusion a logical consequence of the premises. Plausibly, some sort of relevance (or, equivalently, relevant) consequence relation is needed to register the follows-from relation. See Priest 2008 for a good sample of relevance (relevant) logics.

7.3. The Pragma-epistemic Approach
to Argumentative Rationality

This section is devoted to explicating and motivating the pragma-epistemic approach to argumentative rationality, highlighting its pragmatic and epistemic dimensions. In the next section, I clarify what makes this approach to argumentative rationality distinctive by comparing it with the well-known epistemic and pragma-dialectic approaches. I start here by reviewing the book's notion of a reason-giving use of an argument, which informs the pragma-epistemic approach to argumentative rationality.

Recall that if you use an argument in a reason-giving way, you intend the premises you advance to be reasons for believing the conclusion. Assuming that your argumentative intention is rational insofar as it satisfies the inference-claim belief requirement, you believe that your premises are reasons for believing the conclusion (in the sense that you intend). In order for your reason-giving use of an argument to rationalize your believing the conclusion, you must intend and thereby believe that your premises are reasons you have to believe the conclusion.

From Chapter 3, your reason-giving use of an argument is not successful unless the associated inference-claim belief is true. That is, your use of the argument is successful only if your premises are reasons for believing the conclusion in the sense that you intend. Given that the premises are reasons for believing the conclusion only if the conclusion follows from them, no logically fallacious argument can be successfully used in a reason-giving way. It follows that no use of a logically fallacious argument can be a *good* reason-giving use of it. Logic and probability theory are tools for identifying what follows from what. Hence, they are a means for ruling out the capacity of arguments to be used in reason-giving ways.

Suppose that for some propositions p, q, you use p, *so* q to advance p as a reason you have to believe q. You intend your premise to be a reason you have to believe q. Assuming that your intention, i.e., your argumentative intention, is rational, you believe your inference claim that p is a reason you have to believe q. Your inference-claim belief isn't true unless the following two conditions hold.

(i) p is true.
(ii) q follows from p; i.e., the truth of p is indicative of the truth of q.

I now connect the notions of objective and subjective rationality to reason-giving uses of arguments by means of three claims, which for ease of reference I label (A), (B), and (C).

(A) If your inference claim is true and so both (i) and (ii) are true, then the premises are reasons you have to believe the conclusion and so believing it in light of the premises is objectively rational.

(B) If your inference claim is false just because (i) is false, then the premises are, unbeknownst to you, reasons for you to believe the conclusion and so believing the conclusion in light of them is subjectively rational.

(C) If your inference claim is false just because (ii) is false, then, your believing the conclusion in light of the premises is neither objectively nor subjectively rational.

Starting with (A), I briefly elaborate. If both (i) and (ii) hold, then your premise is a reason you have to believe the conclusion. Accordingly, your believing the conclusion in light of your premise is believing the conclusion in light of a reason to believe the conclusion that you possess. So your believing the conclusion in light of the premise is *objectively rational*.

With regard to (B) and (C), if your inference claim is false, then your reason-giving use of the argument isn't successful and so it isn't a good use of the argument since your premise is not a reason for believing the conclusion in the sense that you intend. However, if your inference claim is false just because your premise is false, then even though your reason-giving use of the argument isn't successful, you still give a reason for believing the conclusion, i.e., a reason for you to believe it. If your inference claim is false just because q doesn't follow from p, then your use of the argument is also unsuccessful. However, in this case your premise is not a reason for believing the conclusion. In such a case, your use of the argument fails to rationalize, objectively or subjectively, your believing the conclusion in light of the premises.

To elaborate further on (B), recall that if p is a reason for S to believe q, then p isn't true, S believes that it is true or should believe so given the information available to S, and q follows in some way from p. Suppose that you use p, *so* q to advance p as a reason you have to believe q. You intend your premise to be such a reason. Assuming that your argumentative intention is rational, you believe your inference claim to the effect that p is a reason you have to believe q. In effect, you believe (i) that p is true, and you believe (ii) that q follows from p, i.e., that the truth of p is indicative of the truth of q.

Say that (i) fails, i.e., *p* is not true, but (ii) holds. Then you believe incorrectly that *p* is true, and you correctly believe *q* follows from *p*. In this case, your reason-giving use of the argument is not successful as your inference claim is false. Nevertheless, your use of the argument subjectively rationalizes your believing the conclusion as the premise is, unbeknownst to you, a reason for you to believe the conclusion.

To summarize, if you use an argument to give reasons you intend to be reasons you have to believe the conclusion, then you believe your inference claim to the effect that your premises are such reasons. Your inference claim is either true or it isn't. If true, then you successfully use the argument in a reason-giving way and so your believing the conclusion is objectively rational. If your inference-claim belief is not true just because, unbeknownst to you, at least one premise is false, then your use of the argument is unsuccessful. However, your believing the conclusion is subjectively rational. You believe the conclusion in light of what are, unbeknownst to you, reasons for you to believe it.

By virtue of what does a person S's reason-giving use of argument rationalize S's believing the conclusion? According to the pragma-epistemic approach to argumentative rationality, it is by virtue of the premises being reasons that S possesses for believing the conclusion. The premises are reasons that S possesses for believing the conclusion just in case they are either reasons S has to believe it or reasons for S to believe it. So one's reason-giving use of argument rationalizes a person S's believing the conclusion because it is objectively or subjectively rational for S to believe the conclusion in light of the premises. However, if S's premises needn't be good reasons for S to believe the conclusion, then what, exactly, is the import of argumentative rationality understood in terms of objective and subjective rationality?

To put this question in terms of two others, what does pragma-epistemic argumentative rationality achieve? Why is such an achievement significant in argumentative contexts? To address these questions, I first highlight the pragmatic and epistemic dimensions of pragma-epistemic argumentative rationality.

A distinguishing feature of argumentative rationality is that it concerns believing the conclusion of an argument used in a reason-giving way in light of the argument's premises. The question of whether it is rational in an argumentative sense for one to believe a proposition only makes sense given that the proposition is a conclusion of an argument used in a reason-giving way. Accordingly, it is a category mistake to think that one's believing something is or isn't argumentatively rational divorced from an associated reason-giving use of argument of which it is advanced as the conclusion. This highlights the pragmatic dimension of argumentative rationality. An argument itself doesn't rationalize believing its conclusion. Rather, it is only an argument in use that does so. Specifically, it is only the use of an argument whose premises are advanced or considered as reasons for a person S's believing its conclusion.

Such a reason-giving use of an argument rationalizes S's believing the conclusion just in case the premises are reasons S possesses to believe the conclusion. Again, if the premises are reasons S possesses to believe the conclusion, then they are reasons S has to believe the conclusion or reasons for S to believe it. This highlights the epistemic dimension of argumentative rationality.[9]

To elaborate, recall that if you believe that the premises of the argument you advance are reasons you have to believe that the conclusion is true, then you (i) believe that your premises are true, and (ii) you believe that your conclusion follows from them in the way that you intend (conclusively or otherwise). Regarding (i), recall that you may successfully use an argument in a reason-giving way without believing that your premises are true. Clearly, such uses of arguments do not rationalize your believing the conclusion in light of the premises, as you don't believe that every premise is true. Regarding (ii), if you don't believe that the conclusion follows from the premises in some way, because you disbelieve it or don't have a clue, then this signals the absence of a rational argumentative intention necessary for your use of an argument to rationalize your believing the conclusion.

What pragma-epistemic argumentative rationality achieves must be understood across its pragmatic and epistemic dimensions. If your reason-giving use of an argument makes your believing the conclusion objectively rational, then your use of the argument is successful as your premises are reasons you have to believe the conclusion. Subjective rationality is indicative of the lack of such pragmatic success. That is, if your reason-giving use of an argument makes your believing the conclusion subjectively rational, then

---

[9] The epistemic dimension of argumentative rationality, as I understand it, reflects the idea that "to be a rational person is to believe and act on the basis of reasons" (Siegel 1988, p. 32). I take this to entail that your believing a claim is rational by virtue of your believing it in light of reasons. Accordingly, the epistemic dimension of argumentative rationality thus understood is a reasons-first conception of rationality in that crystalizing the standard or standards of rationality in play with respect to a given use of an argument involves the operative type of reason for belief that the premises are for believing the conclusion. Of course, one may use a reason-first conception of rationality to understand argumentative rationality but advance an account of reasons for belief different from the one I advance in section 7.2.

your use of the argument is unsuccessful as your inference-claim belief is false. In short, objective rationality is indicative of the (pragmatic) success of a reason-giving use of argument; subjective rationality is not.

Let us turn to the epistemic dimension of argumentative rationality: if your reason-giving use of an argument makes your believing the conclusion rational, objectively or subjectively, then it suffices to make your believing the conclusion intelligible. The intelligibility of your believing the conclusion is achieved by means of your providing reasons that you possess for believing it. That your reason-giving use of an argument makes your believing the conclusion intelligible in light of reasons you advance for believing it is an epistemic achievement. Both objective and subjective rationality achieve epistemic success so understood. For example, if your reason-use of an argument makes your believing the conclusion subjectively rational, then by means of this unsuccessful use of an argument you have made your believing the conclusion in light of your premises intelligible.

Why are such pragmatic and epistemic achievements significant to argumentation? Put succinctly, it is because they enable criticism of your reason-giving use of argument to serve as rational criticism of your believing the conclusion. I now elaborate.

Rational criticism of your believing the conclusion in light of premises you advance for the conclusion presupposes that your premises are reasons you possess for believing the conclusion. That is, such criticism presupposes that your premises are either reasons you have to believe the conclusion or reasons for you to believe it. This highlights that criticism of your reason-giving use of argument is relevant as rational criticism of your believing the conclusion only if your reason-giving use of the argument objectively or subjectively rationalizes your believing the conclusion.

Suppose that in an argumentative exchange with me you use an argument to advance reasons you take to be reasons you have to believe the conclusion. If I think that your use of the argument is successful and so I think, in effect, that it objectively rationalizes your believing the conclusion, then I believe that your believing the conclusion in light of the premises is correct because I believe that your premises are reasons you have to believe the conclusion. This makes inappropriate any criticism of mine to the effect that your premises are not evidence for the truth of the conclusion. However, if I think that your use of the argument is unsuccessful because I think, in effect, that it subjectively rationalizes your believing the conclusion, then criticism to the effect that your premises don't count as evidence for the truth of the conclusion is appropriate. It is appropriate because I reject as untrue at least one of your premises.

Pragma-epistemic argumentative rationality undergirds the significance of argumentation as a means of creating dialectical space for rational criticism of beliefs. If your reason-giving use of argument doesn't rationalize your believing the conclusion, objectively or subjectively, then critical evaluation of your use of the argument is not relevant as rational criticism of your believing the conclusion. The relevance of critical evaluation of your use of the argument to a rational criticism of your believing the conclusion presupposes that your premises are reasons you possess for believing the conclusion. Such relevance obviously does not require that your reasons for your believing the conclusion be true, justified, or compliant with agreed-upon dialectical norms. If either the conclusion of your argument doesn't follow from the premises or you don't believe that the premises are reasons you have to believe the conclusion, then valid criticism of your argument does not serve as criticism of your believing the conclusion. Of course, there may be value in such criticism of your act of arguing, but it doesn't serve as rational criticism of your believing the conclusion.

7.3.1. Summary

The pragmatic strand of what I call the pragma-epistemic approach to argumentative rationality may be articulated in terms of the claim that it is reason-giving uses of arguments and not arguments themselves that rationalize believing their conclusions. Recall that, to use an argument in a reason-giving way, one states the argument with the intention of advancing its premises as reasons for believing the conclusion. By so using the argument one thereby claims that the premises are reasons for the conclusion in the sense that one intends. Given that one's argumentative intention is rational, one believes one's inference claim. That is, one believes that one's premises are reasons for one to believe the conclusion.

The epistemic strand of the pragma-epistemic approach to argumentative rationality involves its reliance on a reasons-first notion of rationality to characterize argumentative rationality. Whether a use of an argument rationalizes one's believing the conclusion turns entirely on the status of the given premises as reasons to believe the conclusion and not on their status as *good* reasons to believe the conclusion, as spelled out by the correct theory of argumentation. Hence, the capacity of arguments as instruments of rationality does not depend on their possession of the good-making features of arguments. Whether or not your reason-giving use of an argument rationalizes your believing the conclusion turns exclusively on whether the premises you advance are reasons you possess for believing the conclusion. That is, your reason-giving use of an argument doesn't rationalize your believing the conclusion unless they are reasons you have to believe the conclusion or reasons for you to believe it. Accordingly, to get at argumentative rationality on the pragma-epistemic approach requires a characterization of the operative *reasons for belief.*

If you believe a proposition p in light of what you correctly take to be reasons you have to believe it, then your believing p is *objectively rational.* If you believe a proposition p in light of what you take to be reasons you have to believe p, but they are, unbeknownst to you, reasons for you to believe it, then your believing p is *subjectively rational.* To illustrate how the pragmatic and epistemic strands of the pragma-epistemic approach to argumentative rationality are intertwined, consider the following.

Suppose that you use an argument in a reason-giving way intending the premises to be reasons you have to believe the conclusion. You thereby claim that the premises are such reasons. Your associated inference claim is that your premises are such reasons. Your reason-giving use of the argument is good only if your inference claim is true. To explain what makes your inference claim true brings into play an account of reasons for belief. Your inference claim is true only if it is the case that (i) you believe or are committed to believing that your premises are true, and (ii) your premises being true indicates that your conclusion is true. Given that your argumentative intention is rational, you believe that your inference claim is true, and so you believe (i) and (ii).

If your inference claim is true, then your believing the conclusion is argumentatively rational because your reason-giving use of the argument makes your believing the conclusion objectively rational. If your inference claim is false because, unbeknownst to you, your premises are merely reasons for you to believe the conclusion, then your believing the conclusion is nevertheless argumentatively rational because your reason-giving use of the argument makes your believing the conclusion subjectively rational. Objective and subjective rationality are two dimensions of argumentative rationality.

If you use an argument to advance reasons for believing the conclusion and your premises are not reasons you possess for believing the conclusion, then your use of the argument does not rationalize your believing the conclusion. If so, whether your use of the argument is good according to some theory of argument doesn't matter to whether your believing the conclusion passes muster. For example, in such a case criticism of your argument doesn't count as rational criticism of your believing the conclusion.

If I think that your use of the argument makes your believing the conclusion in light of the premises objectively rational, then I believe that the premises are reasons you have to believe the conclusion and so I accept that they are true and that the conclusion follows from them. If I think that your use of the argument makes your believing the conclusion subjectively rational, then I think that the conclusion follows from the premises but that at least one premise is false. The objective or subjective rationality of your believing the conclusion make incorrect any criticism to the effect that the conclusion doesn't follow from the premises or that the premises are not reasons possessed by the arguer for believing the conclusion.

There are dialectical and epistemic touchpoints for criticism of a reason-giving use of an argument that are too numerous for me to engage here. The import of argumentative rationality on this pragma-epistemic picture of it is that it enables norms of argumentation, understood epistemically or dialectically, to bear on evaluation of our beliefs. For example, criticism to the effect that your reason-giving use of an argument is epistemically flawed because your believing a premise is unjustified or defeated by another of your beliefs bears on your believing the conclusion only if your use of the argument rationalizes your believing the conclusion, subjectively or objectively. Likewise, any dialectical flaw of your reason-giving use of an argument that bears on evaluation of your believing the conclusion in light of the premises in a given dialectical context presupposes that your use of the argument rationalizes your believing the conclusion, objectively or subjectively.

In sum, argumentation norms guiding your reason-giving use of argument matter as an evaluation of your believing the conclusion just in case the premises are reasons you possess for believing the conclusion, as understood in section 7.2. So your reason-giving use of an argument rationalizes your believing the conclusion in the pragma-epistemic sense if and only if the premises are reasons you possess for believing it. Accordingly, the import of argumentative rationality on the pragma-epistemic approach is that it enables norms of argumentation, understood epistemically or dialectically, to bear on evaluation of our beliefs.

Note that on the pragma-epistemic approach, argumentative rationality is characterized independently of what makes an argument or a reason-giving use of it *good*. For example, your reason-giving use of an argument rationalizes your believing the conclusion on this approach independently of whether your premises are *good* reasons for your believing the conclusion. So it is far from obvious that argumentative rationality so conceived is tracked by good arguments, as understood by the correct theory of argument. This runs counter to well-known approaches to argumentative rationality. I now elaborate.

7.4. The Epistemic and Pragma-dialectic Approaches to Argumentative Rationality

In order to highlight the distinctiveness of the pragma-epistemic approach to argumentative rationality, I now contrast it with the epistemic and pragma-dialectic approaches as developed by Siegel and Biro and by Van Eemeren and Grootendorst, respectively. As I explain below, these theorists develop their well-known accounts of good argumentation in a way that makes your argument being good (as captured by the associated epistemic or pragma-dialectic theory of argument) necessary and sufficient for your use of it to rationalize your believing the conclusion. As the pragma-epistemic approach to argumentative rationality doesn't bring into play an account of what makes arguments good, discussion of these versions of the epistemic and pragma-dialectic approaches is useful as a means of further distinguishing and motivating the pragma-epistemic approach.

I begin by summarizing Biro and Siegel's epistemic approach and van Eemeren and Grootendorst's pragma-dialectic approach to argumentative rationality. Toward this end, I explicate each in three steps. First, I identify the function or aim of arguments that is the focus of the associated theory of argument. Second, from the identified function I derive the theory's characterization of *good argument*. I take one's story about how arguments function as a motivator of one's account of what makes arguments so used good. Third, I illustrate how the approach's notion of argumentative rationality is grounded on the associated characterization of *good* argument. This highlights how these two approaches to argumentative rationality bring their accounts of good arguments into play in their characterizations of argumentative rationality. I then distinguish the pragma-epistemic approach from these two approaches, and make a case for preferring it over them. Before proceeding, it is worth highlighting the functional approach adopted in Chapter 5 to the normativity of argument. My framework for summarizing these two approaches to argumentative rationality presupposes this functional approach.

The functional approach to the normativity of argument I adopt involves the idea that an argument in use is good to the extent that its aims are realized.[10] This suggests the following line of thought. The features that make an argument (in use) good are those that together enable it to realize the intended aim in so using it. So a characterization of *good argument* is relative to some identification of the purpose or primary purpose of using arguments.

For example, I made the case in Chapter 5 that an argument used in order to advance reasons for believing its conclusion is good only if the premises are reasons in the intended sense for believing the conclusion, i.e., only if the associated inference claim is true. My chief rationale for this, recall, is that if the premises are not such reasons, then one's use of the argument doesn't succeed in realizing one's intended aim to give reasons for believing the conclusion in the intended sense. If, as is commonly acknowledged (e.g., Blair 2004; Meiland 1989), uses of arguments serve a variety of legitimate, distinct purposes, then it is far from obvious that there is just one set of features that an argument must possess in order to qualify as good. Putting this issue aside, according to this line of thought the defense that an argument is good invites the question, good for what?

In short, a functional approach to good arguments involves the idea that the good-making features of an argument are those that make the argument capable of realizing an aim of a given use of it. This functional approach motivates getting at a rationale for a given characterization of *good argument* in terms of identifying the associated function of arguments. Surely it

---

[10] To avoid misunderstanding, it is worth clarifying here my functional approach to the normativity of argument previously discussed in Chapter 5. Even those who reject versions of functionalism that defend specific ways of modeling the general functionality of argument typically agree that argument is functional, in a broad sense. For example, Goodwin remarks, "People aren't insane when they make arguments. In general, they are trying to get something done, and they expect their arguments make a difference. All discourse is functional in this sense, and argumentative discourse is no exception. I strongly endorse the functionality (purposiveness, usefulness, value, effectiveness, dignity) of argument in this broad sense" (2007, p. 70). My functional approach to the normativity of argument is intended to encapsulate functionality in this broad sense. For example, the functional approach I advocate reflects that arguers impose argumentation norms on themselves by virtue of using arguments to realize their particular aims. I take my functional approach to be roughly in the same ballpark as Goodwin's design view of argumentative pragmatics advanced in her 2007. I don't have the space to elaborate and defend this claim.

is not coincidental that, as a I highlight below, the typical starting points of accounts of good argument such as those advanced by Biro and Siegel and by van Eemeren and Grootendorst start from an identification of an aim or the primary of using arguments. Presumably, articulating a typical aim of using arguments motivates the associated characterization of the good-making features of arguments. An argument's possession of such features makes it capable of being used in the appropriate contexts to realize the intended aim(s).

7.4.1. The Objective Epistemic Approach to Argumentative Rationality

Biro and Siegel (1992) begin their sketch of the epistemic account of good argumentation and fallacies by claiming that it "founds itself on the claim that it is a conceptual truth about arguments that their central (not, of course, *only*) purpose is to provide a bridge from known truths or justified beliefs to as yet unknown (or at least unrecognized truths or as yet unjustified beliefs" (p. 92). I take their claim to provide a rationale for their account of good argument.[11] Biro and Siegel articulate this "central purpose" of arguments in different ways throughout their later writings in motivating their story of what makes arguments succeed or fail. Here are three samples.

(1) "An argument is understood as an attempt to affect a rational belief transition, or to justify such a transition in oneself or others" (Siegel and Biro 1997, p. 278).

(2) "The *raison d'etre* of arguments is to provide good reasons for belief" (Biro and Siegel 2006a, p. 94).

---

[11] I take the functional approach to good arguments to be reflected in why Biro and Siegel take aiming at truth to be an essential property of arguments. "Since the intrinsic goal of arguments is to provide reasons for belief, their quality must be judged by their success in providing such reasons. But a good argument, i.e., one that provides reasons for belief, provides reasons for believing that its conclusion is *true*. This follows directly from the truism that to believe something is to believe it to be true: if I believe that *p*, I believe that *p* is true; conversely, if I don't believe that *p* is true, I don't believe that *p*. From this, in turn, it follows that aiming at the truth is an essential property of arguments" (2006a, p. 94). As should be clear from Chapter 3, I understand there to be a variety of reasons for belief some of which are not reasons for believing that the conclusion is true. Accordingly, my skepticism that aiming at the truth so understood is an essential property of arguments is grounded on my different understanding of the goals of reason-giving uses of arguments. My primary point here is that different understandings of the goal(s) of reason-giving uses of arguments engenders different understandings of the good-making features needed to make them successful in providing such reasons. This point reflects the functional approach to the normativity of argument.

(3) Arguments aim at the achievement of knowledge or justified belief (Siegel and Biro 1997, p. 278; Biro and Siegel 2006a, p. 94). The point of giving an argument is, generally speaking, to show that knowing or being justified in believing the premises warrants knowing or being justified in believing the conclusion (1997, p. 286).

Using (1) to motivate (2), we may say that an attempt to affect a rational belief transition, or to justify such a transition in oneself or others, is an attempt to provide good reasons for believing the conclusion. This plausibly supposes that one's argument affects a rational belief transition, or justifies such a transition in oneself or others only if one's argument provides good reasons for believing the conclusion. To connect (2) and (3), we may say that arguments aim at the achievement of knowledge or justified belief insofar as they aim to provide good reasons for believing the conclusion. This supposes the plausible claim that the premises of an argument are good reasons for believing the conclusion only if knowing or being justified in believing the premises, taken together, warrants knowing or being justified in believing the conclusion. To further clarify this supposition, I now elaborate.

Plausibly, belief of a known proposition must be true, but a justified belief that some proposition is true needn't be. Accordingly, the aims of an argument to achieve knowledge and to achieve justified belief are importantly different. For example, in order to realize the former aim, the argument's premises must be true, but this isn't required in order to realize the latter aim (as Biro and Siegel seem to recognize, 1992, p. 98; 2006a, p. 94). So whether the premises of an argument must be true in order to qualify as good reasons for believing the conclusion turns on the argument being used to achieve knowledge as opposed to justified belief.

This brings a pragmatic element into play in what makes premises good reasons for believing the conclusion. Specifically, the manner in which premises are good reasons for believing the conclusion turns on whether the aim of the associated reason-giving use of argument is the achievement of knowledge or justified belief. This is in accordance with Siegel and Biro's acknowledgment of a distinction between abstracts arguments and arguments in use. It is only arguments in use that aim to provide good reasons for belief. More specifically, it is only arguments used in reason-giving ways that aim to provide good reasons for believing the conclusion (Biro and Siegel 2006a, p. 94). If you are not using an argument in a reason-giving way, then it is hard to see how you aim to provide good reasons for believing the conclusion. After all, good reasons for believing the conclusion are reasons for believing the conclusion.

To the best of my knowledge, nowhere do Siegel and Biro discuss what makes a use of an argument reason-giving. Nor do they convey anywhere in print that I am aware of what qualifies premises of an argument as reasons for believing the conclusion, good or otherwise. It is hard to see how getting at *good* reasons for belief sheds any light on the nature of reasons for belief. For example, suppose that we accept that *p* is a good reason for believing *q* only if believing *p* is justifiable and the justifiability of *p* transfers to *q*. Obviously, spelling this out involves an account of the operative sense of justification and its transference from *p* to *q*. However, an account of reasons for belief is prior to and informs an account of what make such reasons good. Again, a proposition is a good reason for believing *q* only if it is reason for believing *q*. Also, it is obvious that *p*'s not being a good reason for believing *q* doesn't necessarily disqualify it as a reason for believing *q*.

Biro and Siegel's focus on arguments used in a reason-giving way for the purpose of bridging known truths or justified beliefs to as yet unknown (or at least unrecognized truths or as yet unjustified beliefs) motivates their conception of good arguments as what they call epistemically serious arguments. They take good arguments to be epistemically serious ones (Biro and Siegel 1992, p. 92; Siegel and Biro 1997, pp. 278, 280), and hold in effect that the epistemic seriousness of an argument is necessary for a reason-giving use of it to rationalize believing the conclusion. I now elaborate in order to clarify the connection between epistemic seriousness and argumentative rationality.

> An argument succeeds epistemically to the extent that it advances the knowledge of the arguer or her audience or provides good reasons for the belief or acceptance of a proposition. Epistemically successful arguments are, in the sense explained above, epistemically serious. Epistemic success is a matter of justification, which is in turn a matter of *rationality*: an argument succeeds to the extent that it *renders beliefs rational*. (Biro and Siegel 1992, p. 96)

Epistemically serious arguments succeed epistemically. Since epistemic success is a matter of justification, an epistemically serious argument is one whose premises justify believing the conclusion. The operative notion of justification brings into play the notion of rationality. That is, the premises of an argument justify believing the conclusion just in case taken together they make believing the conclusion in light of them rational.

> Rationality is thus central to argument evaluation and theory, and is of course normative—it tells us, ideally, what we should and should not believe. This conception of argumentation presupposes that reasons can be *epistemically forceful* in warranting conclusion. Such force is related to rationality in the obvious way: a belief is rational to the extent that the reasons which support it are epistemically forceful. So understood, argument evaluation and argumentation theory rest heavily upon the theory of epistemic rationality. (Biro and Siegel 1992, p. 96)

Your believing the conclusion of an argument in light of its premises makes believing the conclusion epistemically rational only if the premises are *good* reasons for believing the conclusion in the sense that they are *epistemically forceful* in warranting the conclusion. I take premises being *epistemically forceful* in warranting the conclusion to be premises that provide adequate support for believing that the conclusion is true.

> So, an argument is bad if its premises taken together fail to provide adequate support for its conclusion. An argument is an epistemically unsuccessful one if it fails to warrant belief in its conclusion. This reflects that "the condition both necessary and sufficient for success in argumentation is that of rendering the conclusion warranted. An argument is successful to the extent that it provides warrant for its conclusion, and unsuccessful to the extent that it does not. (Biro and Siegel 1992, pp. 96–97)

The connection between epistemic seriousness and argumentative rationality is made by understanding argumentative rationality in terms of epistemic rationality. That is, an argument that you use rationalizes believing the conclusion in light of the premises only if the premises taken together are *good* reasons for believing the conclusion in the sense that together they warrant or justify believing that the conclusion is true. The reason why "argument evaluation and argumentation theory rest heavily upon the theory of epistemic rationality" (1992, p. 96) is that a reason-giving use of an argument is good just in case the argument so used rationalizes believing the conclusion in light of the premises. Accordingly, to get at what makes an argument good we need to understand argumentative rationality. An account of argumentative rationality draws on a theory of epistemic rationality, which tells us when one's premises qualify as *good* reasons for believing the conclusion.

Understandably, Biro and Siegel in their (1992) demur from providing their full-blown account of epistemic rationality, which is a substantive and controversial topic. I take it that their primary point is that argumentation theorists and informal logicians need such an account since epistemic rationality undergirds the normative dimensions of argumentation. Appealing to Blair and Johnson (1987), they illustrate how a first-step characterization of epistemic rationality figures in argument assessment. According to Blair and Johnson, in evaluating an argument we must look to (a) the acceptability of premises; (b) the relevance of premises to conclusion; and (c) the strength of support afforded by premises to conclusion (1987, p. 148). Biro and Siegel claim that (b) is simply a special case of (c) since if a premise is irrelevant, it offers no support for the conclusion and if it is relevant the crucial issue of the strength of support it affords the conclusion must still be addressed (1992, p. 98). So these three criteria collapse into two: (a) and (c).[12]

Both (a) and (c) are epistemic notions. Spelling them out is a substantive task. I take it that Biro and Siegel would take justifiability to be necessary for acceptability, and regard principles of reasoning to be principles that sanction that transfer of the justifiability of premises of an argument to its conclusion. Accordingly, such principles are many and varied and include principles of the probability calculus, formal validity, and content-specific principles germane to special fields of inquiry that account for the strength of support afforded by premises to conclusion.

To summarize, on Biro and Siegel's epistemic approach to argumentative rationality, your reason-giving use of argument rationalizes your believing the conclusion only if the argument you use is epistemically serious, i.e., only if the premises you advance are good reasons for believing the conclusion. If your premises are good reasons for believing the conclusion, then they provide sufficient justification for your believing the conclusion. So your reason-giving use of argument rationalizes your believing the conclusion only if

---

[12] Re (a), "An argument aims at, and a good one succeeds in, leading an inquirer or an audience from some propositions whose truth or justifiedness they accept to others whose truth or justifiedness they will see themselves as having good reasons to accept on its basis" (Biro and Siegel 1992, p. 92). Epistemic seriousness is "a property good arguments possess and bad ones, such as those that beg the question, lack. Epistemic seriousness, in turn, is defined generally as a matter of the relative knowability of premises and conclusion and, more particularly for the case of begging the question, as the knowability of the premises *independently* of the conclusion" (1992, p. 92).

your premises provide sufficient justification for your believing the conclusion. Drawing on (a) and (c) above, your premises do not provide sufficient justification for your believing the conclusion unless they are acceptable in the sense that they are justifiable and taken together they provide justification for the conclusion sufficient to warrant believing it.

Is the operative notion of justification in this characterization of argumentative rationality *propositional* or *doxastic*? I take it to be propositional justification, which I understand as follows.

> *Propositional Justification* (PJ): S has propositional justification to believe that *p* iff S has sufficient epistemic reasons to believe that *p*. (Silva and Oliveira 2023, p. 395)

Drawing on (a) and (c) above, let's say that the premises of an argument provide sufficient *epistemic* reasons for believing the conclusion just in case (a) they are acceptable and so justifiable and (c) together they provide sufficient support to warrant believing the conclusion. The premises of your argument provide sufficient epistemic reasons that you *have or possess* for believing the conclusion only if you believe that they are true. Bringing propositional justification into play in understanding epistemic seriousness, your argument is epistemically serious just in case your premises provide you with propositional justification for believing the conclusion, i.e., (a) the premises are acceptable and so justifiable, and (c) together they provide sufficient support to warrant believing the conclusion.

So, on my reading of objective-epistemic argumentative rationality, your reason-giving use of argument rationalizes your believing the conclusion just in case your premises provide you with propositional justification for believing the conclusion. If your premises provide you with propositional justification for believing the conclusion, then the argument you use is epistemically serious. Also, if the argument you use in a reason-giving way is epistemically serious, then your premises provide you with propositional justification for believing the conclusion and so your use of the argument rationalizes your believing the conclusion.

To clarify my use of propositional justification instead of doxastic justification in accounting for objective-epistemic argumentative rationality, I now introduce the notion of doxastic justification, distinguish it from propositional justification, and then explain why I think the latter and not the former is operative in the objective epistemic approach to argumentative rationality.

According to Siegel, "[t]o be a critical [i.e., rational] thinker is to be appropriately moved by reasons" (1988, p. 32), which he explains as follows: "[T]o say that one is *appropriately* moved by reasons is to say that one believes, judges, and acts in accordance with the probative force with which one's reasons support one's beliefs, judgments and actions" (1997, p. 2). I take being appropriately moved by reasons to involve properly basing one's beliefs on one's reasons.[13] One's rational beliefs must be *properly* based on reasons. If your belief is properly based on reasons, then you have doxastic justification for your belief.

> *Doxastic Justification* (DJ): S has a doxastically justified belief in p iff (i) S has propositional justification to believe that p, (ii) S believes that p, and (iii) S's belief in p is appropriately connected to S's sufficient epistemic reasons to believe it. (Silva and Oliveira 2023, p. 395)

Conditions (ii) and (iii) indicate that having propositional justification for a belief is not sufficient for having doxastic justification. The distinction between (PJ) and (DJ) is worth illustrating in order to sharpen the objective epistemic approach to argumentative rationality, understood in terms of (PJ). To illustrate, I draw on a scenario from Turri (2010) which he uses to illustrate that (PJ) doesn't suffice for (DJ). Consider two jurors, Miss Proper and Miss Improper, sitting in judgment of Mr. Mansour. Each paid close attention throughout the trial. As a result, each knows the following things.

(P1)   Mansour had a motive to kill the victim.
(P2)   Mansour had previously threatened to kill the victim.
(P3)   Multiple eyewitnesses place Mansour at the crime scene.
(P4)   Mansour's fingerprints were all over the murder weapon.

Since (P1)–(P4) are epistemic reasons each possesses for believing that Mansour is guilty, both Miss Proper and Miss Improper are propositionally justified in believing that Mansour is guilty. Suppose that each bases their

---

[13] Following Godden (2015 p. 140), it also seems to involve a standard of *evidence proportionalism*, which Engel defines as follows: "In general, a belief is rational if it is proportioned to the degree of evidence that one has for its truth" (2000, p. 3). Pinto similarly explains rationality along the lines of a qualitative evidence proportionalism whereby "rationality is a matter of making our *attitudes* toward propositions or propositional contents *appropriate to the evidence* which shapes them" (2006, p. 287).

acceptance that Mansour is guilty on the basis of (P1)–(P4) as the result of an episode of reasoning described as follows.

Miss Proper reasons like so: (P1)–(P4) make it overwhelmingly likely that Mansour is guilty; (P1)–(P4) are true; therefore, Mansour is guilty. Miss Improper, by contrast, reasons like this: the tea leaves say that (P1)–(P4) make it overwhelmingly likely that Mansour is guilty; (P1)–(P4) are true; therefore, Mansour is guilty. Suppose that each uses the following argument in a reason-giving way in coming to believe that Mansour is guilty.

(P1) Mansour had a motive to kill the victim
(P2) Mansour had previously threatened to kill the victim
(P3) Multiple eyewitnesses place Mansour at the crime scene
(P4) <u>Mansour's fingerprints were all over the murder weapon</u>
        Mansour is guilty

The argument, as they both use it to arrive at their conclusion-belief, is epistemically serious. The premises provide sufficient epistemic reasons for both to believe the conclusion. Accordingly, their believing the conclusion in light of the premises is argumentatively rational on the objective epistemic approach as the premises provide them with propositional justification for believing the conclusion.

Both Miss Proper and Miss Improper satisfy (PJ) conditions (i) and (ii), yet only Miss Proper's belief that Mansour is guilty is doxastically justified. Only Miss Proper is doxastically justified in believing as she does that he is guilty. Miss Improper's belief that Mansour is guilty is based on the reasons that propositionally justify that Mansour is guilty for her, but only in light of the tea-leaf reading. This makes her believe the conclusion in light of the premises doxastically *un*justified. Her belief is improperly based on (P1)–(P4). However, as Miss Proper's conclusion-belief is properly based, her believing the conclusion is doxastically justified.

On the objective epistemic approach to argumentative rationality theory, Miss Improper's use of the argument rationalizes her believing the conclusion as the argument she uses is good; i.e., it is epistemically serious. The premises provide her with propositional justification for believing the conclusion. Of course, her believing the conclusion is nevertheless subject to legitimate criticism because it isn't doxastically justified. That Miss Improper's belief that Mansour is guilty is argumentatively rational does not suffice to rationalize her believing this in the more epistemic full-blooded sense of rationality which demands that she possess doxastic justification for her belief. Here's another scenario, which is a version of an example from Biro and Siegel (2006a, p. 95ff.) they use to launch their case against the subjective epistemic theory of good argument.

Mr. Proper and Mr. Improper desire to learn where Twardowski attended college. They both learn and come to know the following.

(P1)   All the members of the club attended the University of Texas.
(P2)   Twardowski is a member of the club.

Since (P1) and (P2) taken together are epistemic reasons each possesses for believing that Twardowski attended the University of Texas, they are propositionally justified in believing that Twardowski attended the University of Texas. As it happens, each comes to believe that Twardowski attended the University of Texas as the result of an episode of reasoning described as follows.

Mr. Proper reasons like so: I know that (P1) and (P2) are true because I know that the club bylaws require that members attend the University of Texas and I know that Twardowski is on the membership roll; (P1) and (P2) if true together guarantee that Twardowski attended University of Texas; therefore, Twardowski attended University of Texas. Mr. Improper, by contrast, reasons like this: I know that (P1) and (P2) are true because each member of the club told me that they attended the University of Texas; (P1) and (P2) if true guarantee that Twardowski attended University of Texas; therefore, Twardowski attended the University of Texas.

I take each to use the following argument in a reason-giving way in coming to believe that Twardowski attended the University of Texas.

(P1)   All the members of the club attended the University of Texas
(P2)   Twardowski is a member of the club
          Twardowski attended the University of Texas

In so using this argument to arrive at their conclusion-belief, both Mr. Proper and Mr. Improper satisfy (PJ) conditions (i) and (ii), yet only Mr. Proper's belief that Twardowski attended the University of Texas also satisfies (iii). Accordingly, only Mr. Proper is doxastically justified in believing as he does that Twardowski attended University of Texas. Mr. Improper's belief that Twardowski attended the University of Texas is based on the reasons that provide him with propositional justification for thinking that Twardowski attended the University of Texas, but his epistemic route to (P1) spoils things as far as doxastic justification goes. His justification that (P1) is true calls upon the truth that Twardowski attended University of Texas, which is the conclusion of his argument. Accordingly, Mr. Improper's use of the argument is question begging. In short, his belief that Twardowski attended the University of Texas is improperly based on (P1)–(P2), whereas Mr. Proper's belief is properly based.

Biro and Siegel are committed to thinking that although Mr. Improper's use of his argument is question begging, the argument that he uses is good as it is epistemically serious (2006a, pp. 96–97, 99), which conflicts with the subjective-epistemic theory's assessment.[14] So the premises are good reasons for believing the conclusion in the sense that they provide those who believe the premises with at least propositional justification for believing the conclusion and thereby rationalize believing the conclusion in light of them. Given that rationality comes in degrees, intuitively Mr. Proper's belief that Twardowski attended the University of Texas is more rational than Mr. Improper's since only his use of the argument provides him with doxastic justification for his belief.

In sum, your successful use of an epistemically serious argument to advance your reasons for believing the conclusion indicates that you possess *good* reasons for believing the conclusion. Your premise-reasons are good in the sense that they provide you with propositional justification for believing the conclusion. However, as illustrated with Miss and Mr. Improper's uses of their epistemically serious arguments, one's premises being good reasons one possesses for believing one's conclusion may be rationally deficient unless one's conclusion-belief is properly based on the good reasons one possesses. The reason why their uses of the argument nevertheless rationalize their believing the conclusion is that argumentative rationality is a function

[14] In contrast to the *objective* epistemic theory, the *subjective* epistemic theory of good argument maintains that what counts as a good argument is relativized to users of arguments. For example, Feldman claims that an argument is good *for a person* S if and only if (i) S is justified in believing the conjunction of all the premises of the argument, (ii) S is justified in believing that the premises are "properly connected" to the conclusion, and (iii) the argument is not defeated for S (1994, p. 179). I read the operative sense of justification in (i) and (ii) as doxastic justification. Accordingly, I take the distinction between propositional justification and doxastic justification to be useful in distinguishing between the objective and subjective theories of good argument. The arguments Miss and Mr. Improper use are bad (for both) by the lights of the subjective epistemic theory since they don't provide either with doxastic justification for believing their conclusions. The same arguments used by Miss and Mr. Improper are good by the objective epistemic theory as they provide both with propositional justification for believing their conclusions.

of epistemic seriousness, and the epistemic seriousness of their arguments depends just on the propositional justification provided by their arguments for their conclusion-beliefs.

7.4.2. Summary

I understand the objective epistemic approach to argumentative rationality to essentially involve the following three claims. First, (1) a reason-giving use of an argument rationalizes believing its conclusion just in case the argument so used is good. Second, (2) an argument that is used in a reason-giving way is a good argument just in case it is an epistemically serious argument.[15] Third, (3) an argument that is used in a reason-giving way is epistemically serious just in case the premises constitute propositional justification the user has for believing the conclusion. Starting with (1), I briefly elaborate as a means of summarizing key points made in my discussion of the objective epistemic approach.

That the argument you use to give your reasons for believing the conclusion is good suffices to make your premises good reasons you possess for believing the conclusion. This in turn suffices to rationalize your believing the conclusion. Of course, that your reason-giving use of an argument so rationalizes your believing the conclusion does not rule out that your believing the conclusion is rationally deficient in other ways.[16]

Claim (2) highlights a central claim of an epistemic theory of argument. Namely, argumentation is fundamentally an epistemic affair whose purpose is to bring reasons from recognized truths or justified beliefs to previously

---

[15] Again, I take Biro and Siegel's focus on arguments as instruments of justification, which they acknowledge, to provide the chief rationale for (2). For example, *"Insofar as arguments have the purpose of (at least conditionally) warranting their conclusions by providing (in their premises) good reasons for them* [italics mine], fallacies—and failed arguments more generally—must be seen as failures of rationality. Hence the centrality of the normative notion of *rationality* to argument theory: an argument succeeds to the extent that it *renders belief rational* (Siegel and Biro 1997, p. 278). Clearly, their focus on this purpose of an argument shapes their conception of the centrality of rationality to argument theory. Accordingly, the viability of other conceptions of rationality is left open given a different theoretical focus on uses of arguments such as the pragma-dialectic focus discussed below.

[16] For example, Siegel remarks, "The rationality of beliefs or judgments depends (in part) upon the adequacy of their supporting reasons. That adequacy, like the goodness of judgment more generally, is a matter of satisfying relevant criteria (here of epistemic goodness)" (2004, p. 608). Understanding the adequacy of supporting reasons in terms of their providing propositional justification for what is believed or judged leaves open that additional criteria must be satisfied for the rationality of what is believed, perhaps understood in terms of the supporting reasons providing doxastic justification for what is believed or judged.

unrecognized truths or not otherwise justified beliefs (Biro and Siegel 1992, p. 99). Thus, arguments and episodes of argumentation need to be evaluated for their ability to provide warrant or evidential/probative force for believing their conclusions. "Fallacies are understood—whatever the intention of the argue—as epistemic failures, i.e., failed attempts to lead from recognized true or justified beliefs to hitherto unrecognized true or unjustified beliefs" (Biro and Siegel 1992, p. 99). Accordingly, it is absurd to think both that the premises of an argument are good reasons for believing the conclusion and that they do not justify believing the conclusion (2006a, p. 94).

I take the operative sense of justification here to be that of propositional justification. Hence, (3). Claim (3) highlights what I take to be a central claim of the *objective* epistemic theory of argument that distinguishes it from the *subjective* epistemic theory: that one's conclusion-belief is improperly based on one's premise-beliefs doesn't make one's argument being bad, because the premises may nevertheless provide justification for believing the conclusion. For example, your reason-giving use of an epistemically serious argument may provide you with propositional justification but not doxastic justification for your conclusion-belief. That your premises do not provide doxastic justification for your believing the conclusion does not suffice to disqualify your argument as good, because it may nevertheless be epistemically serious.

From (1)–(3) we may derive the following characterization of epistemic argumentative rationality.

> *Epistemic argumentative rationality* (EPIST AR): your reason-giving use of
> an argument makes your believing the conclusion argumentatively rational
> just in case the premises constitute propositional justification you have for
> believing the conclusion.

By comparison, pragma-epistemic argumentative rationality may be put as follows.

> *Pragma-epistemic argumentative rationality* (PRAGMA-EPIST AR): your
> reason-giving use of an argument makes your believing the conclusion argumentatively rational just in case the premises are reasons you possess for
> believing the conclusion.

I now make three observations about the relationship between (EPIST AR) and (PRAGMA-EPIST AR).

First, if your reason-giving use of an argument rationalizes your believing the conclusion according to (EPIST AR), then it does so according to (PRAGMA-EPIST AR). Suppose that you use an epistemically serious argument in a reason-giving way to have advance reasons you have to believe the conclusion. Then (EPIST AR) is satisfied. Accordingly, you have propositional justification for believing the conclusion and so your premises are reasons you possess for believing the conclusion. If your premises are true, then your believing the conclusion in light of the premises is objectively rational. If at least one premise is, unbeknownst to you, false, then your believing the conclusion in light of the premises is subjectively rational. Either way, your believing the conclusion in light of the premises is argumentatively rational according to (PRAGMA-EPIST AR). This makes perfect sense. If your premises are epistemically forceful reasons that you possess for believing the conclusion, then they are reasons you possess for your believing the conclusion regardless of how epistemic force is plausibly understood.

Second, it is not the case that if your reason-giving use of an argument rationalizes your believing the conclusion according to (PRAGMA-EPIST AR), then it does so according to (EPIST AR). This is obvious. Clearly, your premises being reasons you possess for believing the conclusion doesn't suffice for their being good reasons for believing the conclusion.

My third observation draws on the first of the three claims given above in support of (EPIST AR). Specifically, a reason-giving use of an argument rationalizes believing its conclusion just in case the argument used is good. Accordingly, (EPIST AR), unlike (PRAGMA-EPIST AR), supposes that your reason-giving use of an argument rationalizes your believing the conclusion only if the argument you use is good. Observe that this makes an account of good argumentation prior to an account of argumentative rationality. To elaborate, consider the following argument scheme.

(1) An argument is good if and only if (iff) it is F
(2) Your reason-giving use of an argument rationalizes your believing the conclusion iff the argument so <u>used is good</u>
(3) Your reason-giving use of an argument rationalizes your believing the conclusion iff your argument is F

Regarding premise (1), F stands for the conjunction of good-making features of arguments (the possession of which is both necessary and sufficient to make an argument good). Different theories of argumentation will generate different instantiations of F. On the objective epistemic theory of argumentation, F is *epistemic seriousness.*

Premise (2) makes an argument's being good both necessary and sufficient for a reason-giving use of it to rationalize believing the conclusion. In the context of clarifying argumentative rationality, the chief import of (2) is twofold. First, it distinguishes the concept of argumentative rationality in terms of what makes arguments that are used in reason-giving ways good. Second, and relatedly, it makes different accounts of good argumentation (e.g., different instantiations of F) generate different stories about argumentative rationality.

The conclusion grounds two evaluative criteria for any theory T of argumentation. First, if T correctly judges that your argument that you use to advance reasons you have to believe the conclusion is good, then it must be the case that your use of the argument rationalizes your believing the conclusion in light of the premises. Second, if it is true that your reason-giving use of an argument rationalizes your believing the conclusion in light of the premises, then T should judge that your argument is good.

7.4.3. The Pragma-dialectic Approach
to Argumentative Rationality

I begin by summarizing the pragma-dialectic account of good argumentation, drawing heavily on van Eemeren and Grootendorst (e.g., 2004, 1995, 1988). Next, I articulate the pragma-dialectic approach to argumentative rationality associated with the pragma-dialectic account of good argumentation. The pragma-dialectic approach understands argumentative rationality in terms of *reasonableness* (van Eemeren and Grootendorst 2004, pp. 123–34; 1988, pp. 272ff.), which I take to be a type of rationality distinct from epistemic rationality as discussed above in section 7.4.1. Some advocates of the epistemic approach complain that the pragma-dialectic notion of argumentative rationality is problematic because it is a consensual notion of rationality and therefore lacks normative oomph (Siegel and Biro 2008; Lumer 2010; but see Garssen and van Laar 2010; van Eemeren et al. 2014, pp. 595–600).

Below I push back against this criticism by highlighting what I take to be a non-consensual dimension of the pragma-dialectic normative framework that does not, contra Biro and Siegel 2006b, make it a version of the epistemic view of good arguments. The pragma-dialectic theory of argumentation is rather substantive, and the associated literature is enormous (for a sub-stantive review of the theory see van Eemeren *et al.* 2014, chap. 10). My aim in this section is to say enough about the pragma-dialectic theory of argu-mentation beyond what I discussed in Chapter 2 to motivate the pragma-dialectic approach to argumentative rationality and clarify its relation to pragma-epistemic rationality. I now begin.

Van Eemeren and Grootendorst characterize argumentation as follows.

> Argumentation is a verbal, social, and rational activity aimed at convincing a reasonable critic of the acceptability of a standpoint by putting for-ward a constellation of propositions justifying or refuting the proposition expressed in the standpoint. (2004, p. 1)

They regard this as a stipulative characterization of argumentation that provides the focus of their theorizing about argumentation (2004, p. 1). An argumentation considered as a product of the process of argumentation consists of "one or more expressions in which a constellation of propositions is expressed" (2004, p. 2). In the case of a positive standpoint, an argumen-tation qua product is used to justify the standpoint. In the case of a negative standpoint, the argumentation is used to refute it. In either case, to justify or to refute, the aim is to convince a reasonable critic to accept or reject, re-spectively, the standpoint presented (2004, pp. 2–3). A series of utterances constitutes an argumentation only if the expressions uttered are jointly used in an attempt to justify or refute a proposition, meaning that they can be seen as a concerted effort to defend a standpoint in such a way that the other party is convinced of its acceptability (2004, p. 3).

To simplify, I'll primarily focus on a person S's argumentation de-voted to a positive standpoint, according to which S's general aim is to re-solve a presumed disagreement by making S's standpoint acceptable to S's interlocutors who disagree by justifying it to their satisfaction (van Eemeren 1987, p. 207). In service of S's aim of justifying S's standpoint to the satis-faction of S's critical interlocuters, S advances premises that S intends to be reasons S's interlocuters have for accepting and so believing the standpoint.[17]

---

[17] Van Eemeren and Grootendorst understand "acceptance" in terms of public acknowledgment of a positive commitment to a proposition that is under discussion rather than as "being in a certain state of mind" (2004, pp. 54–55). In this book I have treated "acceptance" as being in a certain state of mind. Acceptance simpliciter of a proposition (as opposed to conditional acceptance, e.g., accepting a proposition for the sake of argument) involves believing that it is true, which I understand as an

Accordingly, argumentation so conceived is an argument used in a reason-giving way in order to *rationally* persuade a critic to accept the standpoint encapsulated by the conclusion. "The primary function of argumentation is to be a rational instrument for convincing other people" (2004, p. 15), by means of "expressions jointly used in an attempt to justify or refute a proposition" (2004, p. 3).

We may say a critical interlocuter C is *rationally* persuaded to accept the standpoint S argues for only if it is reasonable for C to be persuaded by S's argument for it. When is it reasonable for C to be so persuaded? It is reasonable for C to be persuaded by S's argument only if (i) S's premises are acceptable to C and (ii) the conclusion of S's argument follows from the premises. Regarding (ii), it is only when the conclusion follows from S's premises that C's commitment to accepting the premises transfers to C's commitment to accepting the conclusion. In short, a critical interlocuter C is rationally persuaded by S's argument to accept S's standpoint as expressed by the conclusion only if C accepts the conclusion directly because C accepts the premises and is correct in accepting that the conclusion follows from them. C's acceptance of the premises commits C to their joint truth and justifiability. C's correctly accepting that the conclusion follows from the premises amounts to C's acknowledging that C's acceptance of the premises transfers to the conclusion. Such acknowledgment makes C aware of C's commitment to accepting the conclusion.

In the context of a disagreement, you use an argument in a reason-giving way to rationally persuade your interlocuter C to accept your conclusion. To realize this aim, it must be reasonable for C to accept the conclusion in light of your premises. Hence, it must be reasonable for C to accept your inference claim to the effect that the premises are reasons C has to believe the conclusion. Accordingly, your argument isn't good unless it is reasonable for C to accept this inference claim. It is so reasonable if your premises are acceptable to C and C is thereby committed to accepting the conclusion.

To illustrate with a simple example, suppose Pro and Con are interlocuters engaged in a dialectical exchange with the aim of settling a disagreement. Suppose further that Pro gives an argument to advance reasons Con has to believe the conclusion in an effort to rationally persuade Con of the truth of the conclusion. When is such an argument good? Plausibly, it is when the

---

internal psychological state. I take this to be compatible with there being a public dimension of acceptance as understood by Van Eemeren and Grootendorst.

premises are acceptable to Con and the conclusion, in fact, follows from them. If the argument possesses these features, then the aim of using it to rationally persuade Con is realizable.

There are at least three dimensions of the persuasive force of Pro's good argument for a standpoint. First, (1) the premises are acceptable to Con given what else Con believes. Second, (2) upon reflection, Con would accept that the conclusion follows from the premises. Third, (3) Con desires to settle the disagreement regarding Pro's standpoint, and Con recognizes a commitment to accepting the standpoint given what Con takes to be a good argument for it. If (1) and (2) are satisfied, then Con should think that Pro's argument for the standpoint is persuasive. Given (3), Con should accept the standpoint if Con thinks that Pro's argument for it is persuasive. It is unreasonable for Con not to accept the standpoint, given that (1)–(3) are satisfied. Accordingly, argumentative rationality understood in terms of reasonableness so conceived makes it so that Pro's argument rationalizes believing the conclusion when the premises are acceptable to their interlocuter Con and the conclusion follows from them.

To generalize: an argument used in order to rationally persuade an interlocuter C that its conclusion is true is good when (i) the premises are acceptable to C and (ii) the conclusion follows from them. Using pragma-dialectic terminology, an argument is good just in case (i) it is *conventionally* (i.e., *intersubjectively*) *valid* and (ii) *problem valid* (van Eemeren and Grootendorst 2004, p. 17). A resolution or settlement of a disagreement regarding a standpoint that turns on the use of an argument that fails (i) or (ii) is a pseudo-resolution. A genuine settlement of a disagreement regarding what is true is reached by means of arguments that are both intersubjectively valid and problem valid. I now clarify the pragma-dialectical normative framework that grounds the pragma-dialectic account of good argumentation.

Pragma-dialectical rules for critical discussion (van Eemeren and Grootendorst 2004, chap. 6) combine to form a discussion procedure that provides normative guidance for the speech acts performed by the parties in a dialectic exchange devoted to settling a difference of opinion. The speech acts occurring at any stage of the discussion should satisfy the operative pragma-dialectical rules in order to contribute to the resolution of the difference of opinion, a presumed desideratum of the discussants (van Eemeren and Grootendorst 2004, p. 187). The reasonableness of the procedure is derived from the possibility it creates to resolve differences of opinion (its *problem validity*) in combination with its acceptability to the discussants (its *conventional validity*) (van Eemeren and Grootendorst 2004, p. 132).

At the opening stage of the critical discussion (for their account of stages of critical discussion, see van Eemeren and Grootendorst 2004, chap. 3), the parties decide procedural issues. For example, what are the starting points taken for granted? What argument schemes are to be excluded as inappropriate? The overarching norm in engaging such questions is that what should be adopted for discussion is only what is instrumental to rationally resolving the conflict of opinion at hand and what hinders or obstructs such rational conflict resolution should be excluded (van Laar 2003, pp. 14–15).

An argument used in a critical discussion aimed at resolving a difference of opinion is problem valid and conventionally valid just in case its use accords with the pragma-dialectical rules for critical discussion. More specifically, an argument so used is problem valid just in case the adoption of the scheme it instantiates is admissible by the lights of the pragma-dialectical rules for critical discussion (Garssen and van Laar 2010, p. 128). Again, these are the discussion rules that should be accepted by the discussants who aim to rationally resolve their difference of opinion. An argument so used is conventionally valid just in case its use accords with the discussion rule that demands the premises of arguments be acceptable to all parties.

In sum, if an argument is problem valid and conventionally valid, then its use in a dialectical exchange accords with the pragma-dialectical rules for critical discussion in which that exchange occurs. If an argument used in a dialectical exchange accords with the pragma-dialectical rules for critical discussion, then it is reasonable for the participants to accept the conclusion in light of the premises. Plausibly, if this acceptance is so reasonable, then the premises are reasons the participants possess for believing the conclusion. Specifically, the premise are reasons they have to believe the conclusion or reasons for them to believe it (as I have clarified these reasons for belief in section 7.2). Accordingly, it is reasonable for the participants to accept the conclusion in light of the premises only if the conclusion follows from them. Hence, if an argument is problem valid and conventionally valid, then the conclusion follows from the premises all of which are acceptable to the participants.

The acceptance of an argumentation implies that the (declarative) propositions used are accepted and that the constellation formed by argumentative utterances is regarded as *legitimizing (pro-argumentation) or refuting (contra-argumentation) the proposition to which the standpoint obtains* (van Eemeren and Grootendorst 2004, p. 144). The argumentation achieves its status as legitimizing or refuting the proposition to which the standpoint obtains only if it has the *force of a justification or refutation* (van Eemeren and Grootendorst 2004, rules 6, 8, and 9, pp. 144–51). I take an argument to have such force to the degree to which there is a transfer of acceptability from the premises to the conclusion which expresses the standpoint at issue or its negation.

Such a transfer of acceptability with respect to an argument deployed in a critical discussion is enabled by the fact that the conclusion follows from the premises according to the logical theory that is accepted as a starting point (van Eemeren and Grootendorst 2004, note 19, p. 194). It is worth spelling this out in order to crystallize what I take to be a significant non-consensual dimension in the overarching pragma-dialectical norm. Again, I take this overarching norm to demand that what is adopted for discussion is only what is instrumental to rationally resolving the conflict of opinion and excluding what hinders or obstructs such rational conflict resolution. A rational resolution of a conflict of opinion is a resolution grounded on reason-giving uses of arguments. I take this to entail that if a resolution of a conflict of opinion turns on an argument whose premises are, in fact, not reasons the parties possess to believe the conclusion, then it isn't a rational resolution of the disagreement.

To articulate what I take to be a non-consensual dimension of the pragma-dialectic normative framework for argumentation, I highlight simplified versions of two of the ten rules for critical discussion given by van Eemeren and Grootendorst (1995, p. 136). I gloss over subtleties that should be developed in a complete account of pragma-dialectic argumentation norms.

7. A party may not regard a standpoint as conclusively defended if the defense does not take place by means of an appropriate argumentation scheme that is correctly applied.
8. In his argumentation, a party may only use arguments that are logically valid or capable of being validated by making explicit one or more unexpressed premises.

Rule 7 highlights two normative criteria for argument schemes. They are evaluable in terms of their (i) appropriateness and their (ii) correct application. Hence, a protagonist can violate rule 7—at the argumentation stage of a critical discussion—by relying on an inappropriate argumentation scheme or using an appropriate argumentation scheme incorrectly (van Eemeren and Grootendorst 1995, p. 140). Here, I'll focus on (ii).[18]

Toward illustrating a protagonist's use of an inappropriate argument scheme, Van Eemeren and Grootendorst say such a scheme is inappropriate

[i]f a standpoint is presented as right because everybody thinks it is right (populistic variant of *argumentum as populum*, and, as such, also a special variant of *argumentum as verecundiam*) or if a standpoint is a generalization based upon observations that are not representative or not sufficient (*hasty generalization* or *secundum quid*). . . . Similarity argumentation is being used incorrectly, if, for instance, in making an analogy, the conditions for a correct comparison are not fulfilled (*false analogy*). (1995, p. 140)

Van Eemeren and Grootendorst illustrate violations of rule 8 as follows.

Rule 8 can be violated—at the argumentation stage—by the protagonist in a variety of ways. Some logical invalidities occur with a certain regularity and are often not immediately recognized. Among them are violations that have to do with confusing a necessary condition with a sufficient condition (or vice versa) in arguments with an "If . . . then . . ." premise (*affirming the consequent, denying the antecedent*); other violations amount to erroneously attributing a (relative or structure-dependent) property of a whole to its constituent parts or vice versa (*fallacies of division* and *composition*). (1995, p. 141)

That the logical norm of validity gets its proper (and limited) place in the argumentation stage (van Eemeren and Grootendorst 1995, pp. 142–43) is captured in commandment 7, which is one of ten argumentation commandments advanced as practical normative guides for discussants that reflect the pragma-dialectic discussion rules.

---

[18] See van Eemeren and Grootendorst 1995, pp. 133–34. Van Laar illustrates with the example that argument from analogy is excluded in penalty lawsuits (2003, p. 14). Here's another quick illustration. Obviously, an argument scheme used by the classical logician that is classically valid but not intuitionistically valid to advance their case against the intuitionist is inappropriate in a critical discussion devoted to settling a disagreement about the correct account of validity.

Commandment 7 is the validity rule: Reasoning that in an argumentation is presented as formally conclusive may not be invalid in a logical sense. (van Eemeren and Grootendorst 2004, p. 193)

Commandment 7 is designed to ensure that protagonists who resort to formal reasoning in resolving a difference of opinion use only reasoning that is valid in a logical sense. Also, "This makes it possible to examine whether a contended proposition is defensible in relation to the premises (viewed as a concession) that constitute the argumentation" (2004, p. 198). Presumably, such defensibility requires that the contended proposition deductively follow from the concessions.

I now summarize by means of two observations. First, any resolution of a dispute that is an outcome of a proper critical discussion that turns on an incorrect use of an argument scheme (a violation of rule 7) or the use of an invalid argument resulting in a violation of rule 8 and commandment 7 is at best a pseudo-resolution of the dispute. "The problem-validity of a discussion procedure depends on its efficiency in achieving a resolution to the disagreement and its efficacy in furthering the resolution process while avoiding 'false' resolutions" (van Eemeren and Grootendorst 1995, pp. 133–34).[19]

Second, I take it that whether an argument scheme is correctly used and whether an argument is formally valid are not merely consensual matters, as is the case with the determination of discussion starting points (this accords with Garssen and van Laar 2010, p. 129). For example, whether a generalization is based upon observations that are representative is not a consensual matter. That is, whether an argument is a *hasty generalization* and so defective is not a matter decided by fiat by the discussants. They might be incorrect in thinking a generalization is/isn't hasty. Also, whether necessary and sufficient conditions are being confused in an argumentation resulting in, say, a fallacy of denying the antecedent is not decided by means of a consensus among the discussants. Whether an argumentation commits this fallacy is independent of discussants being aware of this.

I understand the "force of justification or refutation" of an argumentation (van Eemeren and Grootendorst 2004, p. 144) to be, at least in part, the

---

[19] This accords with Garssen and van Laar's understanding of the import of the pragma-dialectic notion of problem validity to the successful resolution of a dispute: "The notion of problem validity ... is used by van Eemeren and Grootendorst (2004, pp. 22, 134) to refer to discussion rules that are instrumental for resolving differences of opinion, including rules that concern the logical or argumentative relations between propositions. If arguers start from logical schemes or argument schemes that lack problem validity, the result of the discussion is at most a pseudo-resolution" (2010, p. 128).

degree to which the acceptability of the premises is transferable to the conclusion that expresses the standpoint at issue (2004, p. 4). Argument schemes are more or less conventionalized ways of achieving this transfer (2004, p. 4). Let's label this *acceptability transference*. An argumentation displays acceptability transference just in case the degree to which the acceptability of the premises is transferable to the conclusion suffices to make the argumentation have the "force of justification or refutation." If an argument scheme is not used correctly or an argumentation commits a logical fallacy, then it lacks acceptability transference and so lacks the "force of justification or refutation" required for a genuine resolution of the dispute. If there is no acceptability transference with respect to an argument, then its conclusion does not follow from the premises and so the premises are not reasons for the discussants to believe the conclusion.

The logical theory that guides a critical discussion determines the acceptability transference of the discussants' argumentation. The discussants choice of a logical theory at the start is *correct* insofar as the argument schemes it endorses enables the parties to offer arguments that promote criticisms in line with points of departure adopted by the parties (Garssen and van Laar 2010, p. 128), which thereby qualifies them as problem valid. To emphasize, the choice of a logical theory is correct by the general pragma-dialectic norm that what is adopted for discussion is only what is instrumental to rationally resolving the conflict of opinion and excluding what hinders or obstructs such rational conflict resolution.

Accordingly, the correct choice of a logical theory relative to a critical discussion is a function of its utility in critically assessing the standpoint at issue. For example, if the conclusion of an argumentation that encapsulates the standpoint at issue doesn't follow from the premises and so lacks the force of justification or refutation, then critical evaluation of the premises does not serve critical evaluation of the standpoint (this echoes Garssen and van Laar 2010, pp. 128–29). Accordingly, the argumentation is an obstacle, or at least useless, toward a rational resolution of the operative dispute.

What I have referred to as a consensual dimension of pragma-dialectic norms concerns matters relevant to the successful outcome of a critical discussion devoted to dispute resolution that are a matter of mere agreement among discussants. A non-consensual dimension of pragma-dialectic normativity guiding a given critical discussion is the *correct* choice of a logical theory, and the argument schemes it validates. This accords with Garssen and van Laar.

[T]he [correct] use of argumentation or logical schemes is, unlike the choice for material starting points, not a matter of mere agreement between participants, although for a resolution this agreement is a necessary condition, but a scheme has as an additional requirement that it furthers critical testing. The problem validity of the discussion rules in general, and of the appropriateness of the argumentation and reasoning schemes in particular, is the result of assessing them, not in view of their epistemic worth, but rather in view of the degree to which they promote criticism. (2010, p. 129)

The idea of a logical theory being correct to the degree that its adoption in a critical discussion promotes rational criticism of the standpoint at issue is compatible with both monist and pluralist views of logic (see Beall and Restall 2006 for discussion and defense of logical pluralism). My point here is that the correct logical theory that guides a critical discussion is not a matter of mere agreement among discussants that it is so. Additionally, to be correct the logical theory must further criticism by correctly endorsing as valid argument schemes that are in play (i.e., that are appropriate) in the critical discussion.

Obviously, in a critical discussion between a theist and an atheist the theist's use of the following argument is inadmissible.

If God doesn't exist, then it is false that if I pray, my prayers will be answered. I don't pray. So God exists!

Criticism of the premises doesn't bear on criticism of the conclusion as the conclusion doesn't follow from the premises. That classical logic judges the argument valid indicates that this logic is the wrong logic to guide the critical discussion even if incorrectly chosen initially by the discussants. (It is wrong to treat the conditionals used as material conditionals.)

In sum, I understand the pragma-dialectic approach to argumentative rationality to essentially involve the following three claims. First, (1) a reason-giving use of an argument makes believing the conclusion argumentatively rational just in case the argument used is good. Second, (2) an argument that is used in a reason-giving way for the purpose of rational persuasion is good when it is both conventionally valid and problem valid. Third, (3) an argument that is both conventionally valid and problem valid is an argument whose premises are acceptable to both the protagonist and the antagonist and this acceptability transfers to the conclusion. I now briefly elaborate on (1)–(3).

Regarding (1), argumentative rationality is understood in terms of reasonableness. Accordingly, what is argumentatively rational to believe is relative to a dialectical context in which interlocuters participate in order to resolve their disagreement about a standpoint. Your reason-giving use of an argument rationalizes your believing the conclusion in the intended sense just in case it makes your believing the conclusion in light of the premises reasonable. Claim (2) is the pragma-dialectic characterization of good argument. The norms guiding reason-giving uses of arguments are those procedural norms that guide dialectical exchanges between interlocuters who aim to resolve their disagreement about a given standpoint.

Claim (3) highlights consensual and non-consensual dimensions of the pragma-dialectic argumentation norms. Conventional (intersubjective) validity highlights a consensual dimension: an argument isn't good unless its premises are acceptable to the interlocuters. So the conventional validity of an argument depends on the common ground of acceptability relative to the dialectical exchange in which it is used. The problem validity of an argument is a non-consensual dimension of good argumentation. For example, if Pro and Con settle their difference of opinion by means of an argument that commits a logical fallacy, then at best the outcome is a pseudo-resolution of their disagreement. To further illustrate, consider the following.

Suppose that both Pro and Con disagree about whether candidate D should be elected US president. Further suppose that Pro presents argument (A) in order to persuade Con of the truth of its conclusion.

(A)
No Democrat should be US president
Candidate D is not a Democrat
Candidate D should be US president

Further suppose that Pro and Con accept the premises and so both are committed to their truth and justifiability. In this scenario, Con is persuaded by Pro's argument to accept the conclusion just on the basis of Con's acceptance of the premises, erroneously thinking that the conclusion follows from the premises. As (A) is not problem valid, its use to settle the disagreement results in a pseudo-resolution of it. Since (A) is not a good argument as used in this dialectic exchange, it does not make believing the conclusion in light of the premises pragma-dialectically rational.

Suppose that instead of being persuaded by (A), Con replies to Pro's presentation of (A) by reminding Pro that actually Candidate D is a Democrat and counters with argument (B).

(B)
No Democrat should be US president
<u>Candidate D is a Democrat</u>
Candidate D shouldn't be US president

Con's reminder in effect judges argument (A) to be conventionally invalid. Unlike (A), argument (B) seems problem valid as the conclusion follows from the premises. Given both interlocuters' acceptance of the major premise, (B) may well be a good argument in this dialectical context and so this reason-giving use of it may make the interlocuters' believing the conclusion reasonable and so argumentatively rational. That this use of argument (B) makes Pro's and Con's believing the conclusion argumentatively rational entails that both Pro and Con accept that the premises are justifiably true and are correct in accepting that the conclusion follows from them. Of course, this does not mean that the premises are, in fact, true or justifiable. This makes whether believing the conclusion of an argument used in a reason-giving way in a given dialectical exchange is, in fact, true or justifiable irrelevant to whether it rationalizes the interlocuters' acceptance of the conclusion.

The rationale for the pragma-dialectic norms' guiding resolution of a disagreement about what is true is that following them ensures that any settlement of the disagreement will be *rational*. Intuitively, there are more or less rational ways of resolving such a disagreement. From claims (1)–(3), we may derive a simplified characterization of pragma-dialectic argumentative rationality.

Pragma-dialectic argumentative rationality (PRAGMA-DIALECTIC AR): a reason-giving use of an argument makes your believing the conclusion argumentatively rational (i.e., reasonable) just in case the premises are acceptable to the interlocuters (e.g., protagonist and antagonist) and this acceptability transfers to the conclusion.

I now make three observations about how (PRAGMA-DIALECTIC AR) and (PRAGMA-EPIST AR) are related.

First, if your reason-giving use of an argument rationalizes your believing the conclusion according to (PRAGMA-DIALECTIC AR), then it does so according to (PRAGMA-EPIST AR). Suppose that you use a conventionally and problem valid argument in a dialogue with an interlocuter aimed to rationally resolve a disagreement about the truth of your standpoint. Then your premises are reasons you and your interlocuter possess for believing the conclusion. If your premises are true, then your both believing the conclusion in light of the premises is objectively rational. If at least one premise is false, then your both believing the conclusion in light of the premises is subjectively rational. Either way, believing the conclusion in light of the premises is argumentatively rational according to (PRAGMA-EPIST AR). This makes perfect sense. If your premises are good reasons for you to believe the conclusion because the argument is problem and intersubjectively valid, then they are reasons you possess for your believing the conclusion.[20]

Second, it is not the case that if your reason-giving use of an argument rationalizes your believing the conclusion according to (PRAGMA-EPIST AR), then it does so according to (PRAGMA-DIALECTIC AR). This is obvious, as (PRAGMA-EPIST AR) doesn't secure conventional validity. In a dialectical exchange, your use of an argument that advances reasons you possess for believing the conclusion isn't conventionally valid unless they are reasons also possessed by your interlocuters. Note that (PRAGMA-EPIST AR) does secure problem validity, which, as I claimed earlier, demands that the conclusion follows from the premises of problem valid arguments.

My third observation draws on the first of the three claims given above in support of (PRAGMA-DIALECTIC AR). Specifically, a reason-giving use of an argument rationalizes believing its conclusion just in case the argument used is good. Accordingly, (PRAGMA-DIALECTIC AR), unlike (PRAGMA-EPIST AR), supposes that your reason-giving use of an argument rationalizes your believing the conclusion only if the argument you use is good. Observe that, as with the epistemic approach to argumentative

---

[20] Biro and Siegel (2006b) note, in effect, that argumentation so understood makes it an instrument of epistemic justification. They think that this interpretation of argumentation makes the pragma-dialectic and objective epistemic theories of good argument compatible as epistemic norms are in play. However, that one's premises are reasons one possesses for believing the conclusion may not warrant believing the conclusion unless they are sufficient to justify believing it. Hence, argumentation that is conventionally and problem valid is not necessarily an instrument of epistemic justification.

rationality, this makes an account of good argumentation prior to an account of argumentative rationality.

7.5. Argumentative Rationality and Good Argumentation

To elaborate, consider again the following argument scheme.

(1) An argument is good if and only if (iff) it is F
(2) Your reason-giving use of an argument rationalizes your believing the <u>conclusion iff argument so used is good</u>
(3) Your reason-giving use of an argument rationalizes your believing the conclusion iff your argument is F

Recall that on the objective epistemic approach F is instantiated as *epistemic serious*. It's instantiated as *conventionally valid and problem valid* on the pragma-dialectic approach. Thus instantiated, the argument provides the rationales for (EPIST AR) and (PRAGMA-DIALECTIC AR), respectively, which, again, are as follows.

(EPIST AR): your reason-giving use of an argument makes your believing the conclusion argumentatively rational just in case the premises constitute propositional justification you have for believing the conclusion.

(PRAGMA-DIALECTIC AR): a reason-giving use of an argument makes your believing the conclusion argumentatively rational (i.e., reasonable) just in case the premises are acceptable to both the interlocuters (e.g., protagonist and antagonist) and this acceptability transfers to the conclusion.

For convenience, I repeat (PRAGMA-EPIST AR).

(PRAGMA-EPIST AR): a reason-giving use of an argument makes your believing the conclusion argumentatively rational just in case the premises are reasons you possess to believe the conclusion.

If one's argument rationalizes one's believing the conclusion according to (PRAGMA-DIALECTIC AR) or (EPIST AR), then it does so according to (PRAGMA-EPIST AR). This must be true since the premises of an argument are good reasons you possess for believing the conclusion only if they are reasons you possess for believing the conclusion.

However, the converse fails. That is, it is false that if one's argument rationalizes one's believing the conclusion according to (PRAGMA-EPIST AR), then it does so according to either (PRAGMA-DIALECTIC AR) or (EPIST AR). Obviously, merely possessing reasons for believing the conclusion does not suffice for possessing good reasons for believing it, however "good" gets spelled out. According to (PRAGMA-EPIST AR), if the premises of an argument you use in a reason-giving way are reasons (good or otherwise) you have to believe the conclusion or reasons for you to believe it, then it thereby rationalizes your believing the conclusion. Accordingly, the pragma-epistemic approach is incompatible with premise (2) of the above argument scheme. So defense of (PRAGMA-EPIST AR) must argue against (2).

I deny that your reason-giving use of an argument rationalizes your believing the conclusion only if your argument is good. My rationale turns on my conception of the centrality of rationality to argumentation. Specifically, I take the centrality of rationality to argumentation to involve a univocal standard of argumentative rationality across the variety of aims served by reason-giving uses of arguments. I now explain.

That theories of argument like the objective epistemic and pragma-dialectic theories generate different accounts of good-making features of arguments is partly explained by their different theoretical starting points concerning how arguments are used.[21] This way of theorizing about what counts as a good argument motivates thinking that the good-making features of arguments turn on how they are being used. This reflects what I am calling the functional approach to good argumentation. Given (2), it follows that there isn't a univocal standard of argumentative rationality, but different

---

[21] This partly accounts for why criticisms of a theory of argument from the perspective of another have an inherent risk of begging the question or involving a non sequitur. For example, Biro and Siegel argue against the pragma-dialectic theory by sampling an argument they claim doesn't rationalize believing the conclusion, but is nevertheless counted as good according to the pragma-dialectic theory (e.g., 1992, pp. 87, 90). The argument is similar to (A), given above. Given their assumption that what is argumentatively rational turns on an account of good argumentation, this line of argument is question begging as it presupposes their epistemic theory of argument. Also, given that a theoretical characterization of good argumentation works from certain uses of arguments, it is wrong to think that an argument that is pragma-dialectically good but doesn't make believing the conclusion epistemically rational is evidence that favors the epistemic theory over the pragma-dialectic theory (e.g., a line of thinking I see in Biro and Siegel 2008, pp. 193–94). This commits a non sequitur since, as I noted, the two theories focus on different uses of arguments. Furthermore, given that there are different degrees of rationality, that your believing something is argumentatively rational doesn't rule out that it is rationally deficient in other ways. Accordingly, that believing the conclusion of an argument is rationally deficient in some sense doesn't entail that it isn't argumentatively rational.

standards of argumentative rationality. Which one is in play with respect to one's reason-giving use of an argument depends on one's aims in so using the argument. Against this, I propose a standard of argumentative rationality that is invariant across various aims of reason-giving uses of argument.

Such a standard is triggered by your use of an argument to advance reasons you have to believe the conclusion. In this way, the standard of argumentative rationality is self-imposed. Given your argumentative intention that the premise you advance are reasons you have to believe the conclusion, your premises should be reasons that you possess for believing the conclusion. Accordingly, the standard of argumentative rationality in play with such reason-giving uses of arguments is twofold: there's a sincerity standard and an epistemic standard. The sincerity standard is, in effect, that you really believe what you claim in using the argument to advance reasons you have to believe the conclusion. The epistemic standard is that your conclusion should follow from your premises in the sense that your premises being true is indicative of your conclusion being true.

The sincerity and epistemic standards involved in argumentative rationality are brought into play when you intend the premises of your argument to be reasons you have to believe the conclusion. If the epistemic standard fails, then, contrary to what you intend, your premises are not *reasons for believing the conclusion*. If the sincerity standard fails, then, contrary to what you intend, your premises are not *your* reasons for believing the conclusion. They are not reasons you possess for believing the conclusion. In short, on the pragma-epistemic approach, if your reason-giving use of argument satisfies the honesty and epistemic standards so understood, then your use of the argument rationalizes your believing the conclusion. Of course, satisfying either standard doesn't require that the argument you use is good. This motivates thinking that it is false that your reason-giving use of an argument rationalizes your believing the conclusion only if your argument is good.

The chief positive consideration in favor of the pragma-epistemic approach to argumentative rationality is that it makes the centrality of rationality to argumentation turn on the role of reason-giving uses of arguments as a means of evaluating a person's believing the conclusion. For example, in order for norms that guide your reason-giving use of argument to matter to an evaluation of your believing the conclusion, the premises that you advance must be reasons you possess for believing the conclusion. By so rationalizing your believing the conclusion, evaluation of your reason-giving use of argument by the lights of a theory of argumentation serves as an evaluation of your believing the conclusion in light of the premises.

What counts as a reason-giving use of argument underpins this pragma-epistemic understanding of argumentative rationality. The centrality of rationality to argumentation highlights those uses of arguments that are genuinely reason-giving. Your use of an argument doesn't rationalize a person S's believing the conclusion unless the premises are reasons S possesses for believing the conclusion. If you don't succeed in advancing premises that are such reasons for S's believing the conclusion, then your use of the argument does not rationalize S's believing it. Whether you so succeed is independent of whether the argument you use is good. Accordingly, abandoning (2) enables a univocal standard of argumentative rationality uniform across various conceptions of good argumentation and so enables a notion of argumentative rationality that is ecumenical with respect to what makes a reason-giving use of argument good.

7.5.1. Summary

I understand the *epistemic* and *pragma-dialectic approaches* to argumentative rationality to make what is argumentatively rational to believe turn on the *epistemic* and *pragma-dialectic* accounts of good argumentation, respectively. Specifically, I take both approaches to make what is argumentatively rational to believe a function of the premises of an argument for it being *good* reasons for believing it. On the *epistemic* and *pragma-dialectic approaches*, *good* reasons for believing the conclusion are premises of arguments that are epistemically serious and both conventionally valid and problem valid, respectively.

However, arguments that are epistemically serious or conventionally and problem valid rationalize your believing the conclusion only if the premises are reasons you possess for believing the conclusion. If the premises are such reasons, then your believing the conclusion is argumentatively rational by the lights of the *pragma-epistemic* approach. On the pragma-epistemic approach, argumentative rationality makes an evaluation of the argument you use in a reason-giving way matter as an evaluation of your believing the conclusion. In other words, an evaluation of your reason-giving use of an argument has normative import for your believing the conclusion only if the premises are reasons you possess for believing the conclusion.

To illustrate, say that an argument you use is/isn't epistemically serious. This matters to your believing the conclusion just in case the premises are reasons you possess for believing it, i.e., just in case your use of the argument makes your believing the conclusion argumentatively rational in the pragma-epistemic sense. Suppose that you present an argument for believing its conclusion in the course of arguing that the conclusion is true. Your interlocuter criticizes your use of the argument by pointing out, in effect, that your argument is not epistemically serious. If correct, the premises of your argument do not warrant believing the conclusion. When does this epistemic criticism of your use of the argument count as a criticism of your believing the conclusion? Intuitively, just in case they are reasons you possess for believing the conclusion.

Suppose that in the heat of an argumentative exchange, an argument you give for believing the conclusion merely parrots one that you heard given on a television talk show. Actually, you are agnostic about the truth of the premises. That the argument you give isn't epistemically serious doesn't count as a rational criticism of your believing the conclusion in light of the premises, because the premises are not reasons you possess for believing the conclusion. In such a case, the judgment that your argument isn't epistemically serious doesn't count as a rational criticism of your believing the conclusion, because your use of the argument doesn't rationalize your believing it. Of course, your use of an epistemically non-serious argument to justify believing the conclusion does problematize it in other ways. For example, it seems intellectually dishonest.

The *epistemic* and *pragma-dialectic* approaches to argumentative rationality presuppose that uses of arguments that rationalize believing their conclusions are reason-giving uses of arguments. Accordingly, both presuppose that a use of an argument rationalizes believing the conclusion only if the premises are reasons for believing it. Clarifying what qualifies premises of an argument as such reasons sharpens the import of the norms determining good argumentation.

For example, on the *pragma-dialectic* approach if your argument that you give in a dialectical exchange devoted to (rationally) resolving a difference of opinion is not problem valid, then the premises are not good reasons for you or your interlocuters to believe the conclusion. On my understanding of reasons for belief as reflected on the *pragma-epistemic* approach, the premises are not good reasons for believing the conclusion because they are not reasons for believing the conclusion. The conclusion doesn't follow from them. Of course, the pragma-dialectic scholar may not adopt my understanding of reasons for belief. My point here is twofold. First, some notion of reasons for belief is presumed on the pragma-dialectic (and *objective epistemic*) approach to argumentative rationality. Second, spelling this notion out can clarify the normative import of the criteria of good argument as just illustrated.

7.6. Conclusion

When does your reason-giving use of an argument rationalize your believing the conclusion? In short, just in case you intend and thereby believe that your premises are reasons you have to believe the conclusion and your reason-giving use of the argument succeeds in advancing premises that are reasons you possess for believing the conclusion. Reasons you possess for believing the conclusion are either reasons you have to believe the conclusion or reasons for you to believe it. Argumentative rationality so understood has internalist and externalist dimensions. I now elaborate starting with the first.

The reason-giving uses of arguments of interest in this book provide a framework for understanding argumentative rationality that makes it essentially reflective in the sense that if one's use of an argument rationalizes one's believing the premises, then one believes, perhaps incorrectly, that one's premises are reasons one has to believe the conclusion. Hence, the internalist dimension of *pragma-epistemic* argumentative rationality. That argumentative rationality is essentially reflective by virtue of this internalist dimension explains why genuine reason-giving by means of using an argument satisfies a necessary requirement for a reason-giving use of argument to be intellectually honest. This is discussed in Chapter 8.

The externalist dimension of pragma-epistemic argumentative rationality is that your use of an argument rationalizes your believing the conclusion only if your conclusion follows from your premises. Obviously, whether the conclusion follows is independent of your thinking that it does. If you are wrong in thinking that it does follow from your premise, then your use of the argument fails to advance reasons for believing the conclusion. The externalist dimension of pragma-epistemic argumentative rationality is grounded on the account of reasons for belief according to which p is not a reason for anyone to believe q unless q follows from p.

Again, on the pragma-epistemic approach to argumentative rationality your reason-giving use of an argument rationalizes your believing the conclusion just in case it makes your believing the conclusion in light of the premises objectively or subjectively rational. The internalist and externalist dimensions of pragma-epistemic argumentative rationality are in play here. If you rationally intend the premises of the argument you use to be reasons you have to believe the conclusion, then you believe your inference claim to the effect that your premises are such reasons. If your inference claim is true, then your use of the argument objectively rationalizes your believing the conclusion. If your inference claim is false just because your premises are merely reasons for you to believe the conclusion, then your use of the argument subjectively rationalizes your believing the conclusion. Either way, you believe, perhaps incorrectly, that your premises are reasons you have to believe the conclusion, which reflects the internalist dimension of argumentative rationality. Also, either way, your conclusion, in fact, follows from your premises. This reflects the externalist dimension of argumentative rationality.

Of course, that your believing the conclusion of your argument is argumentatively rational does not suggest that you should believe it or that it is immune from cogent criticism.[22] Rather, the import of argumentative rationality is, drawing from Sellars (1956),[23] that it anchors your believing the conclusion in the logical space of reasons. Your believing that your conclusion is true is a world-directed thought that is made intelligible by your use of an argument whose premises you successfully advance as reasons you possess for believing that the conclusion is true. McDowell (2018), drawing on Davidson ("Mental Events" in his 1980), is useful as a means of highlighting the special character of this "space-of-reasons intelligibility" (2018, p. 5) engendered by reason-giving uses of arguments.

> Placing items in the space of reasons, to put it in Sellarsian terms, serves the purpose of displaying phenomena as having a quite special kind of

[22] Argumentative rationality thus understood reflects Foley's observation: "An impulse that is common in much of philosophy is the impulse to turn every human shortcoming into a failure of rationality. The way to thwart this impulse is to remind ourselves that the charge of irrationality is not the worst, much less the only, criticism we can hurl at one another. We can criticize others as being unimaginative, or hypocritical or self-pitying or cowardly or even unintelligent without implying that they are thereby irrational" (1993, p. 7).

[23] In *Empiricism and the Philosophy of Mind*, Sellars writes that "in characterizing an episode or a state as that of *knowing*, we are not giving an empirical description of that episode or state; we are placing it in the logical space of reasons, of justifying and being able to justify what one says" (1956, pp. 298–99). I follow McDowell (2018) in taking Sellars to believe that his remark generalizes. For example, McDowell remarks, "In characterizing an episode or a state in terms of actualization of conceptual capacities, as we do when we say that someone is thinking of a celestial city, or that something looks, for instance, red to someone, we are placing the episode or state in the logical space of reasons, no less than when we characterize an episode or a state as one of knowing" (2018, p. 3).

intelligibility, the kind of intelligibility a phenomenon is revealed as having when we enable ourselves to see it as manifesting responsiveness to reasons as such . . . we place beliefs and desires in the space of reasons by putting them in a context that includes other beliefs, other desires, and valuations, in the light of which the beliefs and desires we are aiming to understand are revealed as manifestations of rationality on the part of their possessors. (2018, p. 4)

Only if your reason-giving use of the argument rationalizes your believing the conclusion does it make your believing the conclusion in light of the premise-reasons intelligible, thereby indicating your responsiveness to reasons as such. This doesn't require that your use of the argument be good. It does require that you rationally intend that your premises be reasons you have for believing the conclusion. In short, that your argument makes your believing the conclusion argumentatively rational in the pragma-epistemic sense indicates your being responsive to reasons as such in the way that allows for reflectively stepping back and raising critical questions.

8

Reason-Giving Uses of Arguments, Intellectual Honesty, and Intellectual Integrity

8.1. Preamble

Distorting the truth when we argue is generally frowned upon. Ordinarily, we expect our interlocuters in an argumentative exchange to be committed to speaking the truth and avoiding distortion. Intuitively, you don't argue well even if the argument you advance is good unless your arguing is honest. Of course, arguing well thus understood may not be obligatory in all argumentative contexts. There may be occasions when being honest is not in play, or when there are good reasons for being deceptive.[1]

In this chapter, I consider two questions. When are your reason-giving uses of argument intellectually honest? When do they have intellectual integrity? My responses draw on essential facets of the reason-giving uses of arguments that I have discussed in earlier chapters. Accordingly, using the book's understanding of reason-giving uses of arguments as a framework for shedding some light on intellectual honesty and intellectual integrity is useful as a means of summarizing the book's central claims—hence, one of my rationales for a final chapter on intellectual honesty and intellectual integrity. Another rationale is that the book's concept of reason-giving uses of argument is a useful backdrop for distinguishing between intellectual honesty and intellectual integrity in a way that I think informs how both are realized in our practices of using arguments in reason-giving ways.[2] To

---

[1] See Blair 2011. What counts as a "good reason" for being deceptive when arguing will vary depending on your preferred ethical theory. For example, Kant famously insists that even if a murderer is at the door seeking out a victim, you ought not lie in order to protect the victim's life. A rule utilitarian, in contrast, might endorse lies that can generally be expected to maximize expected utility (including, presumably, lying to murderers about the whereabouts of their intended victims).

[2] As Miller and West note (2020, pp. xv–xvi), the literature focused on the virtues of integrity and honesty is thin. For brief literature reviews on honesty and integrity see Miller and West 2020, introduction, and Scherkoske 2013, chap. 1, respectively. As far as I am aware, discussion of intellectual

Arguments and Reason-Giving. Matthew W. McKeon, Oxford University Press. © Oxford University Press 2024.
DOI: 10.1093/oso/9780197751633.003.0008

help introduce the chapter, I now briefly summarize my responses to the two questions posed above. They identify some necessary conditions for reason-giving uses of arguments to be intellectually honest and have intellectual integrity.

My response to the first question runs as follows. Your reason-giving use of an argument is intellectually honest only if you are being truthful in stating your argument. Drawing on Williams (2002), if you are truthful in stating your argument, then you believe what you claim and you have taken care to ensure the accuracy of what you claim. So your reason-giving use of argument displays intellectual honesty only if you believe what you claim and you have taken care to ensure the accuracy of what you claim. This highlights that what qualifies your reason-giving use of an argument as intellectually honest partially turns on what claim(s) you make in stating your argument. In stating an argument that you use in reason-giving, you make the associated inference claim. So your reason-giving use of an argument is intellectually honest only if you believe your inference claim and have taken care to ensure its accuracy. Here I get at intellectual honesty by making essential use of the book's understanding of reason-giving uses of arguments.

Intellectual honesty subsumes intellectual integrity in the sense that if a reason-giving use of an argument has intellectual integrity, then it is intellectually honest. However, I do not take the converse to hold. In order for your intellectually honest reason-giving use of an argument to display intellectual integrity, the premises you advance must be reasons that sustain your believing the conclusion as a manifestation of your intellectual autonomy, i.e., as a manifestation of *your properly thinking for yourself*. If a reason-giving use of an argument has intellectual integrity, then your associated reflective inference is an instance of your *properly thinking for yourself*. So getting clear on intellectual integrity in the context of reason-giving uses of arguments involves getting clear on when one's reflective inference is an instance of *properly thinking for oneself*.

The chapter's major tasks are elaboration and defense of these two claims about intellectual honesty and intellectual integrity with respect to reason-giving uses of arguments. Each advances necessary conditions for a reason-giving use of an argument to be intellectually honest or have intellectual integrity. I do not have space to address questions about when case-making

---

honesty and intellectual integrity in the context of reason-giving uses of arguments is absent from the literature.

should display intellectual honesty[3] or when one's reason-giving use of an argument should display intellectual integrity. Plausible answers are parasitic on what makes reason-giving uses of argument intellectually honest in the first place and when they have intellectual integrity. Also, I take it that the topic of when reason-giving uses of an argument are intellectually honest or have intellectual integrity is different from the topic of when arguers are intellectual honesty or have intellectual integrity. Plausibly, one's reason-giving use of an argument may be intellectually honest or have intellectual integrity even though one isn't an intellectually honest person or isn't a person who has intellectual integrity. Compare: one's thinking can on occasion exhibit open-mindedness without one being an open-minded person. Here I will not address what is required to be intellectually honest or to be a person with intellectual integrity, although, as I indicate below, I will draw from the literature on these virtues to advance my discussion of reason-giving uses of arguments that are intellectually honest and that have intellectual integrity.

I begin in section 8.2 by making some general remarks about intellectual honesty and truthfulness germane to developing my response to the above intellectual honesty question. Again, when does your reason-giving use of argument display intellectual honesty? Next, in section 8.3 I explore the import of the idea that your reason-giving use of argument displays intellectual honesty only if you believe your inference claim and have taken care to ensure that what you claim is accurate. For example, what, exactly, intellectual honesty involves turns on the content of the inference claim you make. That is, what exactly believing your inference claim involves turns on the type of reasons that you claim the premises are for believing the conclusion. In section 8.4, I address the intellectual integrity question: When do your reason-giving uses of argument have intellectual integrity? In response, I distinguish between reason-giving uses of arguments that are intellectually honest and those that have intellectual integrity in the way sketched above.

My main point in section 8.4 is that an intellectually honest reason-giving use of an argument doesn't have intellectual integrity unless the premises you advance sustain your believing the conclusion in a way that reflects your intellectual autonomy. This point sharpens the import of intellectual honesty in reason-giving uses of arguments. For example, if you advance your

---

[3] My discussion in Chapter 1 on the importance of reason-giving uses of arguments in our current climate of arguing highlights the significance of our case-making's being constituted by reason-giving uses of argument as understood in this book.

premises as reasons for your interlocuter to believe the conclusion, then you don't believe that they are true. You may not even accept the conclusion. In such a case, the question of whether your use of the argument is intellectually honest is germane, but the question of whether it has intellectual integrity in the sense developed in this chapter is not in play. Finally, I conclude in section 8.5 by summarizing the chapter's central claims.

8.2. Intellectual Honesty and Truthfulness

Here I connect *intellectual honesty* with a notion of *truthfulness* that I derive from Williams (2002). This will prepare my response in the next section to the intellectual honesty question posed above. First, I do some general stage-setting. I then sketch the notion of intellectual honesty that I will use in the next section to discuss intellectually honest reason-giving uses of arguments.

Typically, intellectually honest acts are distinguished from morally honesty ones in terms of the operative motive for being honest (e.g., see Miller 2021, p. 111; King 2021, p. 135; Wilson 2018, p. 278). For example, being honest on a certain occasion solely out a love or reverence for truth may be distinguished from being honest solely out of respect for one's interlocuters. The former is associated with being intellectually honest and the latter with being morally honest.[4] Generally, the motivational component of an intellectual virtue such as intellectual honesty is understood as involving the desire to promote epistemic goods for oneself or others (e.g., see Zagzebski 1996; Roberts and Wood 2007; Baehr 2011; Battaly 2014; and King 2021). Of course, both types of motivations may be simultaneously operative. So if we distinguish the virtues of intellectual and moral honesty solely in terms of their motivational components, they are not mutually exclusive.

Miller (2021) offers the following taxonomy for the virtues of honesty: *truthfulness, forthrightness, being respectful of property, proper compliance, fidelity to promises* (2021, pp. 20–21).

---

[4] As King states, "The intellectually honest person is motivated by a desire to convey and not distort the truth because she cares about truth as such. The morally honest person need not care about truth in precisely the same way. She might instead be motivated to speak the truth and avoid distorting it because she wants to respect others, to avoid harming them, to be kind to them, or the like" (2021, p. 135).

Truthfulness: The virtue of being disposed to reliably tell the truth for good
moral reasons.

Forthrightness: The virtue of being disposed to reliably avoid misleading
by giving a sufficient presentation of the relevant facts for good moral
reasons.

Being respectful of property: The virtue of being disposed to reliably respect the property of others for good moral reasons.

Proper compliance: The virtue of being disposed to reliably follow the relevant rules in a situation of voluntary participation when they are fair
and appropriate and when there are good moral reasons to do so.

Fidelity to promises: The virtue of being disposed to reliably keep promises
for good moral reasons.

Following Miller, a desideratum of any account of moral honesty is meeting
what he calls the unification challenge: "What is it exactly that these various
virtues have in common such that they all pertain to the virtue of honesty?"
(2021, p. 24). Miller claims that acts of dishonesty essentially involve the intentional distortion of the truth (2021, pp. 19–20). This motivates thinking,
toward meeting the unification challenge, that at the core of honesty is "a
commitment to representing the truth (as we see it) accurately" (King 2021,
p. 141). King's characterization draws on Miller's identification of the core of
moral honesty as "the virtue of being disposed, centrally and reliably, to not
intentionally distort the facts as the agent sees them" (Miller 2021, p. 38).[5]

Such a commitment seems to rationally demand that when one makes a
claim one has taken care to ensure that what one claims is true.[6] As a starting
point for getting at intellectual honesty I propose thinking of intellectual
honesty in terms of truthfulness.[7] My understanding of truthfulness draws
from Williams (2002, e.g., p. 11).

Williams identifies what he calls two basic virtues of truth as *sincerity* and
accuracy. The virtue of sincerity includes "a disposition to make sure that

---

[5] See Byerly 2022 for useful discussion of the connection of King's conception of intellectual
honesty and Miller's conception of the core of moral honesty, and how both related to intellectual
transparency.

[6] Here I follow King's understanding of the notion of truth needed to make sense of honesty and
dishonesty (2021, p. 141). A proposition *p* is true just in case things are as *p* describes. "On this way
of thinking, truth is determined by the way things are, and not by our beliefs, desires, conceptual
schemes, or social mores" (King 2021, p. 141).

[7] Here I borrow from the characterization of the virtue of moral honesty given by Roberts and
West (2020, p. 101). They articulate two dimensions of moral honesty: *honesty as truthfulness* and
honesty as justice. As I state just below, I focus on honesty as truthfulness.

one's assertion expresses what one actually believes" (2002, p. 96). Accuracy is a virtue that concerns belief acquisition: reliably doing and being capable of ensuring that the information you report is reliable (2002, pp. 124–25). Miller claims that what Williams calls the virtue of sincerity seems to be a combination of Miller's virtues of truthfulness and forthrightness (2021, note 49, p. 21). On this interpretation of Williams's notion of sincerity, it is a moral virtue since truthfulness and forthrightness both are. Accuracy is an epistemic virtue as it is exclusively concerned with excellence regarding the process of acquiring true beliefs.

Two paragraphs back, I said that a commitment to representing the truth (as we see it) accurately seems to rationally demand that when one makes a claim, one has taken care to ensure that what one claims is true. This grounds a link between the virtues of sincerity and accuracy. Williams highlights that sincerity implies a seriousness about truth that is essential to accuracy as reflected in being careful in confirming that what one claims is true (2002, chap. 6, e.g., pp. 124–26). Intuitively, following Roberts and West (2020, p. 103),[8] if you are serious about what you claim being true, then you will be serious about how you come to believe what you claim. For example, it's incompatible with a serious commitment to the truth to engage in wishful thinking, make claims solely out of a need to be agreeable, or make claims without checking one's investigations, say out of laziness (Williams 2002, p. 125).[9]

As applied to reason-giving uses of arguments, I drill down on sincerity and accuracy as follows.

Sincerity: Your reason-giving use of an argument is sincere only if you believe that what you claim in stating the argument is true.

Accuracy: Your reason-giving use of an argument is accurate only if you have taken care to ensure that what you claim by virtue of so using the argument is accurate.

---

[8] Roberts and West remark that "the untruths characteristic of an untruthful person sometimes stem less from the intention to deceive than from careless inquiry. The truthful person thus cares about truth both in the context of communication with other persons, and in the context of investigations and knowing" (2020, p. 103).

[9] Intuitively, if you desire to comply with a commitment and knowingly act in ways contrary to your commitment, then such acts aren't fully rational. See Worsnip's discussion of structural (ir)rationality (2021, chap. 1).

I'll say that your reason-giving use of an argument satisfies *Sincerity* and *Accuracy* when you believe that what you claim in stating the argument is true and you have taken care to ensure that what you claim is accurate, respectively.

That the virtues of sincerity and accuracy are dimensions of the virtue of intellectual honesty makes plausible that your reason-giving use of an argument is intellectually honest only if your statement of the argument is truthful. If your statement of the argument so used is truthful, then your use of it satisfies *Sincerity* and *Accuracy*. Accordingly, your reason-giving use of an argument is intellectually honest only if it satisfies *Sincerity* and *Accuracy*. That is, only if you believe what you claim in stating the argument and you have made what Williams calls an *investigative investment* in ensuring that what you claim is accurate (2002, p. 87).

Honesty may be applied to people ("He is the most honest person that I have ever known"), their actions ("He did what was right and honest"), or to things ("He just wants to make an honest living"). When intellectual honesty is attributed to people, it may connote that the person possesses the associated virtue(s), or merely the associated reliable disposition(s) to behave honestly when honesty is called for. When applied to one's act, we may think that one's act is the manifestation of someone who possesses the virtue or disposition of honesty (e.g., it's how such a person would act in similar circumstances). Here I am concerned with what makes correct the attribution of intellectual honesty to reason-giving uses of arguments. Of course, that your reason-giving use of an argument satisfies *Sincerity* and *Accuracy* does not suffice for your possession of the virtue of intellectual honesty.

Clearly, that a person S's reason-giving use of an argument is intellectually honest does not suffice for S being an intellectually honest person, which is a matter of S's psychological makeup and character (e.g., see Miller 2021, p. 41; King 2021 pp. 131–51 Baehr 2016). For example, S may display honesty on an occasion but not be acting from honesty, because, say, it suits S's needs at the time to be sincere, or S is coerced in some way into ensuring the accuracy of what S claims. Furthermore, being an intellectually honest person requires that one is *reliably disposed* to being sincere and accurate. A person who just makes sincere and accurate claims to the best of their ability every now and then doesn't seem to qualify as intellectually honest.

In short, I claim that satisfying both *Sincerity* and *Accuracy* is necessary for a reason-giving use of argument to qualify as intellectually honest. Again, your use of an argument isn't intellectually honest unless your statement of the argument is truthful. If it is truthful, then your use of the argument is intellectually honest insofar as it satisfies *Sincerity* and *Accuracy*. I now elaborate on what *Sincerity* and *Accuracy* involve with respect to the claims one makes in stating an argument that one uses in a reason-giving way. In the next section, I review the types of claims one makes in stating arguments so used, which will highlight the import of *Sincerity* and *Accuracy* to determining the intellectual honesty of a reason-giving use of an argument.

Sincere communication demands that it reveals what you believe, either directly or indirectly. If directly, then what you communicate expresses your belief in the sense that the meaning of what is uttered is the content of your belief. Here I take such an act of communication to be the act of assertion. If an act of communication reveals what you believe indirectly, then what you believe is communicated either as an implication or implicature of what you utter. Accordingly, *Sincerity* requires (i) that one really believe what you claim. Additionally, *Sincerity* seems to require that (ii) one not intentionally implicate or imply by one's utterance what one doesn't believe. I now address (i) and (ii), starting with (i). Consider the following scenario from Lackey.

> *Creationist teacher.* Stella is a devoutly Christian fourth-grade teacher, and her religious beliefs are grounded in a personal relationship with God that she takes herself to have had since she was a very young child. This relationship grounds her belief in the truth of creationism and, accordingly, a belief in the falsity of evolutionary theory. Despite this, Stella fully recognizes that there is an overwhelming amount of scientific evidence against both of these beliefs. Indeed, she readily admits that she is not basing her own commitment to creationism on evidence at all but, rather, on the personal faith that she has in an all-powerful Creator. Because of this, Stella thinks that her religious beliefs are irrelevant to her duties as a teacher; accordingly, she regards her obligation as a teacher to include presenting material that is best supported by the available evidence, which clearly includes the truth of evolutionary theory. As a result, while presenting her biology lesson today, Stella asserts to her students, "Modern day *Homo sapiens* evolved from *Homo erectus*," though she herself does not believe this proposition. (2013, p. 243; 2007, p. 599)

Lackey uses this example to illustrate two key points. First, Stella *asserts* that modern-day *Homo sapiens* evolved from *Homo erectus*, though she does not believe this proposition (2007, p. 599). Second, even though she does not believe what she asserts, Stella's assertion that modern-day *Homo sapiens* evolved from *Homo erectus* doesn't count as lying because there is no intent to deceive her students regarding the claim that she makes (2013, pp. 243–45).[10] Rather, her intention in making the assertion is to comply with what she takes to be "her obligation as a teacher to include presenting material that is best supported by the available evidence, which clearly includes the truth of evolutionary theory."

However, perhaps Stella is not being completely honest with respect to her communicative act of claiming that modern-day *Homo sapiens* evolved from *Homo erectus* even though she does not lie in claiming so. One may think that she is less than fully honest here by not explicitly canceling implicatures that she doesn't believe. This seems especially so if her obligation as a teacher involves being sensitive to the implicatures of her utterances in the classroom that are reasonable for her fourth-grade students to draw (one being that she believes what she claims), and explicitly canceling those that she rejects. In any event, it is at least initially plausible to think that Stella's satisfies (i) and (ii) when stating that modern-day *Homo sapiens* evolved from *Homo erectus*.

Suppose that in presenting her biology lesson, Stella uses an argument that she puts on the chalkboard to display the support for evolutionary theory. The premises encapsulate the support for the conclusion that modern-day *Homo sapiens* evolved from *Homo erectus*. Lackey's scenario so buttressed doesn't automatically rule out that Stella uses the argument she states in a reason-giving way, despite her not believing the conclusion due to her believing in a personal creator as a matter of her religious faith. That is, Stella may rationally intend the evidence that she gives to be reasons to believe that the conclusion is true. She takes the conclusion to follow from premises that she regards as true. We may take it that she believes that the premises are reasons she and her students have to believe the conclusion. *Sincerity* is satisfied because she believes her inference claim. Furthermore, she doesn't intend to deceive by implication or implicature. Plausibly, Stella's use of the argument is intellectually honest insofar as it satisfies *Sincerity*. For a comparison, consider the following scenario.

---

[10] Lackey remarks that "when Stella states to her students a proposition that she believes is false, her aim is not to bring about a false belief in her students or conceal her own beliefs on the matter" (2013, p. 244). For discussion, see Miller (2021, pp. 40–42), who agrees with Lackey's assessment that Stella isn't lying when she states that modern-day *Homo sapiens* evolved from *Homo erectus*.

BETH: Can you take my leftovers from dinner last night out of the fridge. I'll
    have them for my lunch today.
PAIGE: Someone ate your leftovers from dinner last night. So you'll have to
    make your lunch.

Paige advances the premise as a reason to believe that the conclusion is
true. Paige believes her associated inference claim and reflectively thinks
that her inference-claim belief is well grounded. Given the obvious background assumptions, she and Beth discern that the conclusion follows from
the premise, which is understandably upsetting to Beth as she now has to
rush and cobble together her lunch before dashing out the door to make it
to work on time. Paige knows that the premise is true because she is the one
that ate Beth's leftovers. So Paige isn't being completely honest in light of the
fact that her utterance intentionally implicates what she believes to be false,
namely that someone other than her ate Beth's leftovers. Accordingly, one
may plausibly think that her reason-giving use of the argument is not completely honest even though it satisfies *Sincerity*. Recall from Chapter 3 that
implicatures are not assertions.

However, perhaps Paige's reason-giving use of her argument is intellectually
honest, even though it involves her deceptive communicative act of implicating
what she believes is false. Honesty comes in degrees (Miller 2021, p. 31). There
may be dimensions of your communicative act that are dishonest because intentionally misleading, while there are other dimensions according to which
your communicative act is honest. It is hard to fault Paige's act of reason-giving
by means of stating an argument as dishonest, but it is easy to fault her utterance of the premise as dishonest. I think that it's an honest use of the argument,
but Paige's statement of it involves an infelicitous, deceptive utterance.

At any rate, I acknowledge that one's intuitions may run counter to
mine. Since what Paige implicates she does not assert (again, as discussed
in Chapter 3), one may think that even though Paige's use of the argument
satisfies *Sincerity* it is nevertheless dishonest. This is not a strike against
Sincerity because it only states a necessary condition for the intellectual honesty of a reason-giving use of an argument. Specifically, *Sincerity* focuses on
what is asserted in stating an argument so used. In order to further clarify
Sincerity, I now discuss the operative notion of *assertion*.

In Chapter 3, I considered assertion as an expression of belief. According
to Williams, an assertion is one person's *telling* something to oneself or
to another (2002, p. 71). This seems to involve a notion of assertion as an

expression of belief, but Williams thinks such a notion incorrectly ignores insincere assertions.

> The basic idea of an assertion might seem to lie just in a speaker's expressing a belief by uttering an appropriate sentence. Rather more strictly, we might say that A asserts P in uttering a sentence which means that P, in doing which he expresses his belief that P. But this cannot be the only kind of assertion. A can express his belief that P only if he has that belief, that is to say, if he is sincere. An account of assertion must leave room for *insincere assertions*, and this suggestion does not yet do so. (2002, pp. 72–73)

The notion of an insincere assertion fits with Williams's taking "a lie to be an assertion, the content of which the speaker believes to be false, which is made with the intention to deceive the hearer with regard to that content" (2002, p. 96). But why take insincere assertions to be a type of assertion? Why not think of *insincere assertions* like we think of fool's gold. Fool's gold is a mineral (e.g., pyrite, chalcopyrite, or weathered mica) that appears gold-like but isn't gold.[11] Why not take insincere assertions to be utterances that merely mimic assertions well enough that they may be mistaken for assertions?

What does an insincere assertor do? Williams remarks, "In a certain sense he pretends to be expressing his belief, and this means, as with all pretence, that up to a point he does exactly what someone does who is doing the real thing: for instance, he utters the same sentence, in the same manner, as one who was expressing that belief" (2002, p. 73). But this applies to someone who speaks ironically or to an actor stating something in a role, neither of which involves assertions. Williams thinks that this motivates an additional condition on insincere assertions.

> I think it is clear that in giving an account of insincere assertion, we do have to put back the idea of a speaker's trying to affect the beliefs of the person he is addressing. I have made the point that sincere assertions do not necessarily have the aim of informing the hearer; but insincere assertions do have the aim of misinforming the hearer. In the primary case, they have the aim to misinform the hearer about the state of things, the truth of what the speaker asserts. Derivatively, they may aim to misinform the hearer about the speaker's beliefs: the speaker may know that the hearer will not believe

---

[11] https://www.usgs.gov/faqs/what-fools-gold, accessed on April 12, 2023.

what he falsely asserts. But he wants her to believe that he himself believes it. (2002, p. 73)

For Williams, the standard conditions of A asserting that P are that "A utters a sentence 'S' where 'S' means that P, in doing which either he expresses his belief that P, or he intends the person addressed to take it that he believes that P" (2002, p. 74). The first disjunct captures sincere assertions, the second captures insincere assertions.

Williams claims, rightly on my view, that the notion of an insincere notion is conceptually dependent on the notion of a sincere assertion. He takes the rationale for this dependence to be twofold. First, "Quite generally it is true that we have to understand what it is to do X before we can understand what it is to pretend to do X" (2002, p. 75). Compare: to understand what passes as counterfeit X, or an imitation of X, we need to understand what counts as X.

Second, in their most primitive form expressions of belief are spontaneous (2002, p. 75). In the most basic case, expressions of belief are involuntary as to what is expressed; in the first instance and in the simplest cases we are disposed spontaneously to come out with what we believe.

> Sincerity at the most basic level is simply openness, a lack of inhibition. Insincerity requires me to adjust the content of what I say. Of course, this does not mean that all adjustment or reflective thought about what I should say is insincerity . . . there are other demands on what I say, and, again, I may have reasons for not concealing the truth but for expressing it very carefully. (2002, p. 75–76)

What counts as an assertion is controversial. On Williams's account, Stella's claim that modern-day *Homo sapiens* evolved from *Homo erectus* doesn't seem to be an assertion, contrary to Lackey's view. Stella's claim is not an expression of her belief, and she doesn't intend that her students take it that she believes what she claims. She doesn't seem to be intentionally pretending to express her belief. This is controversial and intuitions may vary here. What I am pointing to here is that Williams's distinction between sincere and insincere assertions doesn't require treating insincere assertions as assertions any more than distinguishing between gold and fool's gold requires treating fool's gold as a type of gold. Liars mimic assertion in order to intentionally deceive listeners into thinking that they genuinely express their belief that what they claim is true.

I take the upshot here to be as follows. Sincerity, as Williams understands it, requires that what one claims to be a fact be a sincere assertion and so be an expression of one's belief that what one claims is true. Insincere assertions, of course, fail this requirement. By failing this requirement, I say, insincere assertions are not assertions. This claim is no more paradoxical than saying that counterfeit money, while it may look like real money, is not legal tender and so is not money. As with counterfeit assertions, counterfeit bills are typically produced with the intention of deceiving others into accepting them as the real McCoy. In short, working within Williams's conceptual framework for understanding the act of assertion, I take assertions to be essentially expressions of belief and so essentially sincere. Accordingly, on my view insincere assertions are not, strictly speaking, assertions. I turn now to Williams's notion of accuracy.

Williams's notion of accuracy seems akin to the notion of *epistemic diligence*. Plausibly, *truthfulness* is always accompanied by *epistemic diligence*. If your stating something is sincere, then what you claim you really believe. If your stating something satisfies accuracy to a degree, then you have exercised epistemic diligence to the corresponding degree in forming the belief(s) of what you state. Toward clarifying what I have in mind, let's sample some failures of epistemic diligence.

Self-deception: Suppose Igor had never considered before whether his son was using illegal drugs. But one day a neighbor tells Igor what she saw his son doing secretly in the backyard. Igor also begins to notice that money is missing from his bank account. He realizes that his son's behavior has changed significantly in recent months. A look at his son's texts shows dates, cash amounts, and locations for meetings with a stranger. Yet despite all of this evidence, Igor comes to form the belief that his son is not using illegal drugs. (Miller 2021, p. 58)

Igor seems self-deceived about his son's behavior. Certainly, "[H]e is not engaging in an honest manner with the overwhelming evidence of his son's drug use" (Miller 2021, p. 59). He is not exercising epistemic diligence. Igor forms his belief that his son is not using illegal drugs in an untruthful way, because the formation of his belief fails to reflect the overwhelming evidence he possesses to the contrary. Hence, his belief fails *Accuracy*, because he ignored his evidence which is sufficient to indicate that his son was using illegal drugs. Igor is not being epistemically diligent in forming his belief that his son isn't involved with illegal drugs.

> *Epistemic misrepresentation:* Dr. X's patient asks her about the health benefits of a particular exercise therapy for low mood that he's come across. Dr. X vaguely remembers seeing someone tweet about this therapy once, and thinks they were moderately positive about it. Dr. X has never looked at the clinical evidence base, NHS guidelines or had firsthand experience of it. Nevertheless Dr. X figures it can't hurt and replies, "Oh yes—I've heard of that. It's supposed to be good." (Brown 2022)[12]

As Brown (2022) comments, Dr. X doesn't distort the facts as she sees them, since she thinks that the therapy will probably help. Dr. X's statement doesn't count as a lie because she doesn't intend to mislead her patient about the truth of what she utters. She thinks it will probably help. The problem is that Dr. X has not taken care to check how good the therapy is and thereby misrepresents her state of knowledge in communicating with her patient. This is a failure of epistemic diligence. The patient reasonably expects Dr. X to know what she's talking about when making assertions about medical treatments. Presumably, in her role as a doctor she should possess good reasons to believe that her medical advice is true (Brown 2022).

> *Intellectual laziness:* Sam is a student in a logic class, which they find very difficult. This is worrisome to Sam as getting a good grade in the class is important to them. Sam is working on a homework assignment, and believes that they have figured out the solution to one of the logic problems. They know that they frequently make mistakes in doing such logic problems, and they are unsure of their solution to this problem. Sam is aware of how to check their solution and knows that this will increase the likelihood of its being correct. Nevertheless, Sam doesn't feel like devoting more effort to the homework assignment and turns in a solution without checking it, thinking that it is probably correct anyway.

> *Intellectual laziness:* Sonny saw on their social media account that someone posted that the pandemic outbreak was intentionally planned by the US government, which is what they suspected all along. Afterwards, Sonny

---

[12] I have converted Brown's first-person scenario to third person.

learns from an online post that there was a government virus lab at the source of the outbreak. Although Sonny thinks that many posts convey falsehoods, Sonny takes this post to confirm that the US government planned the outbreak without understanding the underlying reasons for why the US government would do this and without doing any fact-checking regarding whether the alleged leak from the lab was accidental. Sonny on occasion vigorously argues against the idea that the virus had animal-to-human origins in the locale of the nearby farmer's market in light of their belief that the US government planned the outbreak. Sonny implies on such occasions that they are better informed than they really are.

Sam and Sonny fail to devote the intellectual effort needed to ensure the accuracy of thinking that the homework solution is correct, and that the US government intentionally planned the pandemic outbreak, respectively. Sam had the time and wherewithal to confirm the correctness of their solution to the homework problem. Moreover, Sam is aware that such confirmation is worthwhile given past mistakes, but nevertheless does not confirm it. Clearly, Sam didn't take the care necessary in this case as described to ensure the accuracy of their solution. This is a failure of epistemic diligence. Although Sonny understands the need to fact-check online posts, Sonny nevertheless does not do so with respect to the post aligned with their hunch about the US government's intentional involvement in what triggered the pandemic. Since Sonny doesn't take any steps to ensure the accuracy of this claim, using their conjecture to argue against other origins of the virus exhibits a lack of epistemic diligence.

A lack of epistemic diligence is a lack of truthfulness. Since truthfulness is a criterion of intellectual honesty, a lack of epistemic diligence is a lack of intellectual honesty. Accordingly, intellectual honesty demands that you shouldn't imply that you are better informed than you really are (e.g., as with Dr. X and Sonny), that you don't believe what your evidence is sufficient to rule out (e.g., as with Igor), and that your reasoning isn't careless when such care is called for (e.g., Sam). In short, intellectual dishonesty involves either misrepresenting what you actually believe in making statements or misrepresenting the epistemic status of your beliefs that your statements express.

If my seven-year-old son asks me how clouds are formed, a correct response involves some reference to the process of condensation, which occurs when warm, moist air rises and cools, causing the water vapor in the air to condense into the liquid droplets or ice crystals that constitute clouds.[13] Without checking first, which may not be practical at the time, I would probably end up giving my son misleading information, because I just don't understand cloud formation all that well. However, this is not a barrier to my response displaying intellectual honesty as long as I do not respond with undue confidence. As long as I do not give my son the impression that I know anything about the process of cloud formation and so don't misrepresent the epistemic status of my beliefs expressed in my response, my response may be intellectually honest. In this instance, my taking care to ensure the accuracy of what I claim involves being fairly guarded and more uninformative than I would otherwise be if I were, say, a meteorologist.

Taking care to ensure that what you claim is true qualifies as being careful in making the claim. Being careful in claim-making manifests a degree of epistemic diligence that is effortful. One is mindful to take the care one thinks necessary to ensure the accuracy of what one claims. On my view, whether such epistemic diligence counts as sufficient to qualify as being epistemically responsible in claim-making depends on the context, i.e., what's at stake, one's epistemic role, etc. For example, what counts as *due* epistemic diligence when claim-making in the context of one's profession and vocation turns on what is required to be responsible by the standards set by one's professions and vocation such as academics, journalism, police, courts, and the foreign intelligence field.[14]

Drawing from Williams, I have said that your making a claim displays the virtue of *Accuracy* when you have taken care to ensure the accuracy of what you claim. On my view, taking care to ensure the accuracy of what you claim may fall short of exercising *due* epistemic diligence. In such a case, your claim-making may not be epistemically responsible even though you took care to ensure the accuracy of what you claim. When taking care to ensure the accuracy of what you claim suffices to make your claim-making epistemically responsible is a complicated matter. I take it as a start that what is involved is different for a philosopher talking about cloud formation with his son than for a doctor talking about medical treatments with her patient. This reflects an earlier point that a lack of knowledge needn't be a barrier to

---

[13] See https://www.nasa.gov/audience/forstudents/5-8/features/nasa-knows/what-are-clouds-58.html, accessed on April 20, 2023.

[14] For a detailed example, see Hayward 2019 for a discussion of what Hayward sees as three duties of epistemic diligence that "academics in general, and social philosophers more particularly, may have to check claims of knowledge emanating from fields beyond their professional expertise or individual competence" (p. 536).

honesty. The doctor's status as an expert in this domain means that the evidentiary basis for her belief is expected to be stronger (certainly stronger than a half-recalled tweet).

In sum, your reason-giving use of an argument satisfies *Accuracy* when you have taken care to ensure that what you claim by virtue of so using the argument is accurate.

> *Accuracy*: Your reason-giving use of an argument is accurate only if you have taken care to ensure that what you claim by virtue of so using the argument is accurate.

Satisfying *Accuracy* means that you are careful in what you claim when stating your argument in the sense that you have taken steps to ensure that accuracy of what you claim. However, your involved claim-making may nevertheless not fulfill your duties of epistemic diligence. My motivation for this claim appeals to my conceptual framework for understanding the virtue of intellectual honesty.

Recall that I understand the virtue of intellectual honesty in terms of Williams's virtues of accuracy and sincerity. If you possess the former virtue, you possess the latter two. Applying this to assertion, your assertion is intellectually honest only if it is sincere and you have taken care to ensure that what you claim is accurate. Doing the best that you can to be careful in making a claim may fall short of fulfilling all of your operative epistemic responsibilities. In such a case, I think it is wrong to make this count against your intellectual honesty in making your claim. Your intellectual honesty in claim-making doesn't guarantee that you are epistemically justified or meeting all of your epistemic obligations in making your claim. This is somewhat in sync with the idea that "honest actions don't require that the beliefs of the agent be true" (Miller 2021, p. 38). Rather, being honest involves not intentionally distorting the facts as the agent sees them (Miller 2021, pp. 38ff.). I now connect this course-grained picture of intellectual honesty with the more developed and well-known accounts by Guenin (2005) and King (2021).

According to Guenin (2005), the kernel of intellectual honesty consists in "a virtuous disposition to eschew deception when given an incentive for deception" (p. 179). He takes intellectual honesty to be but one component of honesty in general that is concerned with "truthfulness and veraciousness" (2005, p. 180). Guenin understands these, respectively, as "the attribute of being truthful" and "the disposition to be truthful" (p. 180). When acting truthfully, an agent does not assert anything that the agent believes false" (2005, p. 183). Plausibly, when an agent asserts something that they believe false, then they make an insincere assertion. Being truthful in what one claims requires that your assertions not be insincere, as understood above. *Veraciousness* is the disposition to be truthful. To possess that disposition is to be *veracious*. Guenin summarizes his understanding of intellectual honesty as follows.

> I suggest that the kernel of *intellectual honesty* consists in a disposition of an agent such that when presented with an incentive to deceive in any way, the agent will not deceive. This virtue fosters fulfillment of a duty (per deontological views) promotes good ends (per consequentialism), and constitutes a virtue possessed by a virtuous person (per virtue ethics). The whole of intellectual honesty includes a disposition or dispositions such that notwithstanding contrary incentives, the agent refuses, in respect of assertion or other means of communication, to gain an unfair advantage, to indulge laziness diminishing the quality of the impression left, or to indulge in exaggeration. Consistently with the etymology of "honest," acting in accordance with intellectual honesty is acting honorably. (2005, pp. 217–18)

I now make three observations. First, possessing the disposition of intellectual honesty is ethically motivated. The ethical value of intellectual honesty across different ethical theories generates motivational grounds for being intellectually honest. Earlier, I said that intellectual honesty and moral honesty are distinguished in terms of motivation. Guenin blurs this distinction: moral motivations (e.g., fulfillment of a duty, promoting good ends) may be operative in an instance of intellectual honesty. Intellectual honesty has a motivational component that is moral. Guenin understands this as a duty to be non-deceptive (2005, p. 178).

Second, Guenin's notion of *veraciousness* is in the ballpark of Williams's notion of the virtue of sincerity. One's claim that such and such is the case is an instance of what Guenin calls *truthfulness* only if it counts as a *genuine* assertion, i.e., counts as an expression of belief.[15] However, a genuine assertion

---

[15] Guenin clarifies as follows: "Although veraciousness may be inferred from instances of truthfulness, veraciousness the disposition is not the same as the set of those instances. A stronger disposition than veraciousness, a disposition to render what one says (including nonverbally) wholly in accord with what one thinks, is sincerity" (2005, p. 227). I say that Guenin's notion of *veraciousness* is *in the ballpark* of Williams's notion of the virtue of sincerity, because Guenin's account of assertion,

may nevertheless mislead and so count as an instance of dishonesty in virtue of an intentional, misleading implicature (Guenin 2005, p. 201). Among the conversational maxims that truthfulness, in Guenin's sense, demands is that the speaker not exceed what the speaker's evidence supports (2005, p. 200). This suggests that one's assertion fails to be intellectually honest unless one has taken care to ensure that what one claims is accurate. Honoring one's duty to be non-deceptive involves such epistemic diligence in forming beliefs that one expresses. This leads to my third observation.

If by means of one's assertion one mispresents the epistemic status of one's belief that is expressed, then such misrepresentation is intellectually dishonest (2005, p. 222). If one is justifiably taken to be in the know when one isn't, then an unfair epistemic advantage is accrued in relation to one's less-informed interlocuters (2005, p. 218). A pretense to be authoritative puts one in an unfair advantage as one's assertions merely appear to epistemically trump one's interlocuter's less authoritative assertions to the contrary. This brings Williams's notion of accuracy into play. If you express your belief formed without taking care to ensure the accuracy of what you believe, then you mispresent the epistemic status of your belief and thereby deceive. Accordingly, you are not being truthful and so you are being intellectually dishonest. I now turn to King.

King's characterization of the virtue of intellectual honesty explicitly expresses its motive-oriented feature in epistemic and not moral terms.

> Intellectual honesty is a disposition to express the truth (as we see it) through our thought, speech, and behavior, to avoid intentionally distorting the truth (as we see it), and to do so because we revere the truth and think it is valuable. (2021, p. 145)

"It's a motivation for truth that makes the difference between merely morally honest behavior and the virtue of intellectual honesty" (King 2021, p. 145; see also Wilson 2018). Transferring this idea to assertion, one's assertion is intellectually honest only if one communicates the truth as one sees it and does so because, in part, one reveres the truth (as one sees it) and thinks it is valuable. Plausibly, if one communicates the truth as one sees it and does so

---

which he spells out in terms of what he calls the *Signal condition* (2005, pp. 181–82), differs from Williams's account of assertion reviewed above. As the details of the difference between the two accounts of assertion do not matter to what follows, I do not rehearse them here.

partly because one reveres the truth and thinks it is valuable, then one's act of communication is sincere; i.e., one believes that what one communicates is true (as one sees it). Sincerity is a component of an intellectually honest act of communication if the motivational component for being sincere with respect to this act of communication includes a reverence for truth and acceptance of its value. The reverence for truth grounds one's intention to be truthful in communicating with others (King 2021, p. 145).

While King does not explicitly connect intellectual honesty with epistemic diligence, I think such a connection is implicit in his characterization of intellectual honesty. Roughly, the motivational component of the virtue of intellectual honesty suggests that the intellectually virtuous person reliably takes care to ensure the accuracy of their claims. If one expresses what one takes to be true partly because one reveres the truth and thinks it is important, then ordinarily one will have taken care to ensure that what one claims is accurate. One's intellectual laziness, for example, is symptomatic of not revering the truth or not appreciating its importance in the context that occasions this intellectual laziness. Of course, epistemic diligence is no guarantee that our beliefs are error free.

King briefly illustrates Frege's display of intellectual honesty upon learning of what is known as Russell's paradox in terms of Frege's "fervent desire to get at the truth, and to avoid distortion, even in the face of professional loss and embarrassment" (2021, p. 147). Such a desire motivates the intellectual rigor and carefulness exemplified in Frege's published work and illustrates, King claims, that Frege's virtue of intellectual honesty is among a network of other intellectual virtues Frege possessed alongside others such as intellectual perseverance and intellectual humility. I conjecture that the motivational component of intellectual honesty motivates the dispositions of intellectual rigor and carefulness indicative of the disposition to reliably take care to ensure that one's claims are accurate.

8.2.1. Summary

Drawing on Williams's notions of the virtues of sincerity and accuracy, I propose that one's act of claiming that something is the case is intellectually honest only if one is sincere; i.e., one believes what one communicates, and one has taken care to ensure that what one communicates is accurate. As illustrated with Guenin's and King's characterizations of intellectual honesty, it is fairly straightforward to think that an intellectually honest act of assertion requires sincerity. An insincere assertion does not ordinarily count as intellectually honest assertion. On my view, it doesn't count as a genuine assertion. I see three bases, pragmatic, psychological, and conceptual, for how an intellectual honesty act of assertion involves accuracy.

A pragmatic basis is as follows. If you make a serious claim about what is the case and thereby implicate that you are in the know and so have taken are to ensure the accuracy of what you claim, then if this implicature is not true, you misrepresent the truth regarding the epistemic status of your belief. That we have exercised epistemic diligence so construed is implicated by our assertions, and so if this implicature is false, our assertions are untruthful and so intellectually dishonest (Guenin 2005, pp. 200–201). For example, you may bluff your epistemic credibility by deceptively implicating by means of your assertion that you have taken care to ensure the accuracy of what you assert (King 2021, pp. 136–37). In such a case any confidence you convey in expressing your belief deceptively masks your failure to ensure the accuracy of what you claim.

A psychological basis for how an intellectually honest act of assertion involves accuracy is that if we revere the truth and appreciate its value (King 2021, p. 141) or are intentional about honoring the duty to be non-deceptive in our acts of communication (Guenin 2005, p. 202), then we will reliably take care to ensure the accuracy of what we claim. Reverence for the truth is compatible with failures of such epistemic diligence every now and then. But it is incompatible with gross cases of self-deception (e.g., as with Igor) or of laziness (e.g., as with Sam), or not reliably taking care to ensure the accuracy of what we claim when such care is called for (e.g., as with Dr. X).

I conceive of a conceptual basis for a connection between an intellectual honesty act of assertion and Williams's notion of accuracy that draws from Miller's brief remarks regarding *epistemic honesty*.

> I understand epistemic honesty as primarily concerned with how someone comes to form beliefs. Following Bernard Williams such a virtue leads you to "do the best you can to acquire true beliefs" [Williams 2002, p. 11], with "effective investigation" that involves "resistance to wishful thinking, self-deception, and fantasy" [2002, p. 127]. (Miller 2021, p. 111–12)

Conceptually, *epistemic honesty* essentially involves *honest belief formation*. Plausibly, this in turn essentially involves Williams's notion of accuracy (as noted by Miller 2021, note 39, p. 112). Miller proposes unpacking the motivational dimension of epistemic honesty, following Wilson's approach (2018), using notions such as *being concerned about finding the truth*, *loving the truth*, and *caring for the truth* (2021, p. 112). A conceptual connection between intellectual honesty and *accuracy* may be put as follows. An intellectually honest act of assertion is epistemically honest in that the belief that is expressed is honestly formed. If the belief that is expressed is honestly informed, then the believer exercised care in ensuring its accuracy in forming it. Hence, if your act of assertion is intellectually honest, then you have taken care to ensure that what you claim is accurate.

Williams's notions of the virtues of sincerity and accuracy motivate *Sincerity* and *Accuracy*, which focus on claims, i.e., assertions, made by virtue of stating an argument used in a reason-giving way.

> *Sincerity*: Your reason-giving use of an argument is sincere only if you believe that what you claim in stating the argument is true.

> *Accuracy*: Your reason-giving use of an argument is accurate only if you have taken care to ensure that what you claim by virtue of so using the argument is accurate.

The absence of any mention of a motivational dimension in my statements of *Sincerity* and *Accuracy* is intentional. This reflects my view that one's specific motivation for stating an argument one uses in a reason-giving way is irrelevant to whether one's use of it is intellectually honest. This accommodates a notion of an intellectually honest reason-giving use of argument that is compatible with different views of the motivational component of the virtue of intellectual honesty as well as being sensitive to the variety of motivations for using arguments in reason-giving ways that we might think are intellectually honest uses of arguments. One's motivation does matter to whether one is being intellectually honest in stating an argument, whether this be reverence for truth, honoring a duty to be non-deceptive, or something else. Obviously, one's intellectually honest use of an argument is not sufficient for one's possession of the intellectual virtue of intellectual honesty any more than an occasion of truth-telling suffices for being an honest person. If one thinks that a motivational component to *Sincerity* and *Accuracy* is essential for them to matter as necessary conditions to the intellectual honesty of a reason-giving use of argument, then one may incorporate the needed motivational component.[16]

8.3. Reason-Giving Uses of Arguments and Intellectual Honesty

In this section, I develop my response to the question posed at the start of Chapter 8: When are your reason-giving uses of argument intellectually honest? In section 8.2, I advanced two necessary conditions: satisfying *Sincerity* and *Accuracy*. What, specifically, must be true about a given reason-giving use of argument for it to satisfy *Sincerity* and *Accuracy*? This raises other questions. What, exactly, is being claimed when stating an argument used in a reason-giving way? How, exactly, is taking care to ensure that what one claims in stating the argument is accurate a dimension of reason-giving uses of arguments? My responses draw heavily from earlier chapters.

Recall that a reason-giving use of argument essentially involves an act of communication (even if to oneself). When you use an argument in a reason-giving way, you state the argument with the intention of advancing its premises as reasons for believing the conclusion in the sense that you intend. What does one claim when stating an argument so used? From Chapter 3, one makes the associated inference claim. When you use an argument in a reason-giving way, you claim that the premises are reasons for believing the conclusion in the sense that you intend. Assuming that your intention is rational insofar as it satisfies the inference-claim belief requirement, you believe what you claim. From Chapter 3, you assert your inference claim since what you claim expresses what you believe. Accordingly, when you genuinely use an argument in a reason-giving way, you satisfy *Sincerity* insofar as your inference claim expresses your belief that your premises are reasons for believing the conclusion in the sense that you intend. However, whether this involves your believing that your premises and conclusion are true

---

[16] For example, a reason-giving use of argument satisfies *Sincerity* and *Accuracy* only when you believe that what you claim in stating the argument is true, you have taken care to ensure that what you claim is accurate, *and* your motivation for believing what you claim and ensuring its accuracy includes a reverence for the truth. Of course, not including a motivational component in characterizing intellectually honest reason-giving uses of argument is compatible with the aforementioned psychological basis for a link between Williams's notions of sincerity and accuracy with respect to acts of assertion.

depends on the type of reasons that you claim the premises are for believing the conclusion.

For example, if you claim that your premises are reasons you have to believe the conclusion, then you claim (i) that your premises are true and (ii) that the conclusion follows from them. Here I bypass whether you also claim that the conclusion is true or whether this is merely implied. At any rate, (i) and (ii) involve your believing that the premises and conclusion are true. If your inference claim is, in effect, that your premises are hypothetical or suppositional reasons for believing the conclusion, then you claim (iii) that they are merely relevantly possible and (iv) that the conclusion follows from them. Taken together, (iii) and (iv) do not involve your believing that the premises or the conclusion are true. Finally, if you claim that your premises are reasons for your interlocuter to believe the conclusion, then you claim that (v) your interlocuter believes the premises or is at least committed to them, and that (vi) the conclusion follows from them.

In short, insofar as you are engaged in reason-giving by means of stating an argument, you believe that the conclusion follows from the premises. That is, you believe that taken together the premises being true is indicative of the truth of the conclusion. If this belief is false, then the premises aren't reasons of any kind for believing the conclusion. In such a case one's statement of the argument is a pragmatic failure since one fails to use the argument in a reason-giving way as one intends. As *Sincerity* does not suffice for *Accuracy*, that you believe your inference claim is insufficient to qualify your reason-giving use of an argument as intellectually honest. In addition, you must take care to ensure that your inference claim is true.

Plausibly, such epistemic diligence is a feature of the reflective inferences expressed by arguments used in reason-giving ways. Recall from Chapter 4, the argument you use in a reason-giving way expresses your reflective inference. The linking belief of the reflective inference is the belief of the associated inference claim. Also recall from Chapter 4 that a reflective inference is (i) active, (ii) persistent, (iii) purposeful, and (iv) criterial in the sense that the inferer is trying, perhaps unsuccessfully, to fulfill appropriate standards of adequacy.

As an instance of reflective thinking, reflective inference is careful in part by being self-regulating. As Lipman writes, reflective thinking is "*thinking about its procedures* at the same time it involves *thinking about its subject matter*" (2003, p. 26). Being self-regulating, performing a reflective inference involves one taking care to ensure that an inference-claim belief is accurate. This involves understanding what one must attend to in order to ensure the accuracy of one's inference claim. Of course, being self-regulating does not thereby make a reflective inference good. What I am pointing to here is that if you perform a reflective inference, then its being self-regulating involves your taking care to ensure that your associated inference claim is true.

In sum, if you use an argument in a reason-giving way, then you have performed a reflective inference from the premises to conclusion. Since such an inference is self-regulating, your use of the argument satisfies *Accuracy*. However, a reason-giving use of an argument satisfying *Accuracy* does not suffice to make the associated inference claim true, and so does not make the use of the argument good.

8.3.1. Summary

Your reason-giving use of an argument is intellectually honest only if it satisfies *Sincerity* and *Accuracy*. For convenience, I repeat both.

> *Sincerity*: Your reason-giving use of an argument is sincere only if you believe that what you claim in stating the argument is true.

> *Accuracy*: Your reason-giving use of an argument is accurate only if you have taken care to ensure that what you claim by virtue of so using the argument is accurate.

Your use of the argument satisfies *Sincerity* and *Accuracy* when you believe that what you claim in stating the argument is true and you have taken care to ensure that what you claim is accurate, respectively.

Plausibly, the intellectual honesty of your reason-giving use of argument may not turn exclusively on what you claim, i.e., on what you assert, in stating the argument. If one thinks that complete honesty is required in order for a reason-giving use of argument to be intellectually honest, then one will require in addition to *Sincerity* and *Accuracy* that in stating one's argument one must not intentionally implicate by means of one's utterances what one believes to be false. At any rate, I take *Sincerity* and *Accuracy* to be necessary conditions for the intellectual honesty of a reason-giving use of argument.

Since an inference-claim belief is an essential dimension of reason-giving use of arguments, such a use of argument is essentially intellectually honest insofar as what is claimed in stating the argument is believed. A liar who deceives by stating an argument intending that their audience take them to be using the argument in a reason-giving way even though they do not believe their own inference claim isn't genuinely using the argument in a reason-giving way. It's a pseudo-reason-giving use of the argument, as the liar doesn't believe their associated inference claim and so doesn't rationally intend their premises to be reasons for believing the conclusion.

In Chapter 4, I argued that if you use an argument in a reason-giving way, then you perform a reflective inference that is expressed by the argument as you use it. Your inference-claim belief is the linking belief of your reflective inference. By the lights of Chapter 4's account of reflective inference, one's reflective inference is self-regulating. A feature of such self-regulation is that the inferer takes care to ensure that their inference-claim belief is accurate. So if you use an argument in a reason-giving way, then your use of the argument satisfies *Accuracy*. Again, this doesn't qualify it as a good use of the argument.

In short, reason-giving uses of arguments as I understand them are intellectually honest uses of arguments insofar as they necessarily satisfy *Sincerity* and *Accuracy*. Ordinarily, one argues well only if one's arguing is honest. So if one's reason-giving use of an argument doesn't satisfy *Sincerity* or *Accuracy*, then one's arguing for the conclusion is not honest. This is prima facie grounds for thinking that one isn't arguing well.[17]

8.4. Reason-Giving Uses of Arguments and Intellectual Integrity

When does a reason-giving use of an argument have intellectual integrity? After noting that integrity is a property that can be applied to a wide variety of things other than to persons, Halfon draws on the *Oxford English Dictionary* definition of the expression *integrity* to generally characterize integrity as the "state or quality of wholeness, completeness, pureness" or "an unimpaired or unmarred state" (1989, pp. 6–7). Admittedly, it isn't easy to understand what exactly one attributes to a reason-giving use of argument when one thinks that it has integrity, intellectual or otherwise.[18]

---

[17] As commented in note 1, merely prima facie grounds, as there may on occasion be good reasons for being deceptive.

[18] Halfon distinguishes between different kinds of integrity as applied to persons such as personal integrity, intellectual integrity, artistic integrity, professional integrity, or moral integrity (1989, Chapter 5). But see Scherkoske 2013, pp. 139–40, who advances a unified account of integrity

Recall the argue$_1$-argument$_8$ link from Chapter 2. If you argue$_1$, then you give reasons in support of an idea, action, or theory. An argument$_8$ is a coherent series of reasons, statements, or facts intended to support or establish a point of view. When you argue$_1$, you use an argument in a reason-giving way. You state an argument$_8$. That is, you state an argument whose premises you intend to be reasons for the truth or desirability of some idea, action, or theory. I propose that the wholeness and completeness of your reason-giving use of argument in a context of your arguing$_1$ includes its integration with your epistemic stance regarding the truth of the conclusion. I understand such integration to demand at minimum that you believe the conclusion.

In sum, the attribution of *integrity* to a reason-giving use of argument makes sense when the attribution of a kind of *completeness* or *wholeness* to your use of argument makes sense. This makes sense when you use the argument to argue$_1$ for the conclusion and so state an argument$_8$. When you use an argument to argue$_1$ for its conclusion and so state an argument$_8$ your reason-giving use of the argument has intellectual integrity only if it is integrated with your epistemic stance regarding the truth of the conclusion. My response to the question posed at the start of this section clarifies the operative integration needed for a reason-giving use of argument to have intellectual integrity. Toward this end, the discussion that follows focuses on two dimensions of the virtue of intellectual integrity that have been highlighted in the literature: its *performance dimension* and its *reflective resoluteness dimension*.[19] I now discuss each, starting with the first.

The *performance dimension* of integrity "isolates what persons of integrity characteristically *do* with their convictions besides adhere to them" (Scherkoske 2013, p. 148). In her seminal work on integrity, Calhoun argues that a display of integrity requires standing for one's convictions in public settings, particularly in the face of resistance, out of a desire to make known to others what one takes to be one's reasons for maintaining their conviction (1995, pp. 256–60). "An act of standing for one's convictions or commitments is to stand for them before others, to propose them as worthy of others'

---

according to which it is a virtue of "epistemic agency—as an excellence of the myriad ways in which people form, revise and express their convictions" whether their convictions be aesthetic, moral, prudential, or empirical beliefs.

[19] I borrow the turn of phrase *performance dimension* from Scherkoske (2013, p. 148). For better or worse, I coined the expression *reflective resoluteness dimension*. My conception of this dimension of integrity draws on some of Scherkoske's discussion of what he calls the "data points" that talk of integrity picks out (2013, pp. 5–9; in particular, pp. 8, 15).

endorsement. It involves submitting one's judgment to others' critique" (Herdt 2020, pp. 65–66). This idea that the paradigmatic display of integrity is standing for one's convictions before others is widely acknowledged in the literature (e.g., in addition to the three above, see Walker 1998; McLeod 2005; and Mendus 2002).

According to Calhoun, standing for something essentially involves publicizing one's conviction and insisting on its *endorsability* before others (1995, p. 246). To stand for one's best judgment about what the truth is regarding some matter involves deliberately advancing one's reasons for one's conviction. Here I develop Calhoun's notion of "standing for something" in terms of reason-giving uses of arguments. When does a reason-giving use of an argument count as instance of standing for something? To simplify, let's consider the following question. When does arguing for the truth of a conclusion before others count as standing for something in a way that displays intellectual integrity?

Plausibly, arguing for the truth of a conclusion before others doesn't count as standing for something unless one believes that one's conclusion is true. So, (i) in order for one's reason-giving use of an argument to have intellectual integrity, one must believe that one's conclusion is true. Furthermore, (ii) one's premises must be *reasons for which* one believes the conclusion. That is, they must be reasons that sustain one's believing the conclusion. Third, (iii) one's reason-giving use of an argument has intellectual integrity only if one believes that the premises are reasons to believe the conclusion, and so they are reasons for anyone to believe the conclusion.

Condition (i) rules out as occasions for intellectual integrity your reason-giving uses of arguments that do not involve your believing the conclusion. The literature on integrity suggests that the conclusion-belief expressed on occasions for intellectual integrity must have the status of a conviction (e.g., Calhoun 1995, p. 259; Scherkoske 2013, p. 6). I take a conclusion-belief that has the status of a conviction to be one held with a high degree of certainty, transferred from the associated premise-reasons. Hence, they too are believed with a high degree of certainty.

Condition (ii) makes one's inference that is expressed by one's reason-giving use of argument what I have called in Chapter 6 a belief-inducing reflective inference. If you are making a stand before others for the truth of a claim by providing reasons for believing it, then in order for your use of the argument to have intellectual integrity the argument must express your belief-inducing reflective inference. Otherwise, your arguing$_1$, i.e., your act(s) of reason-giving, is incomplete as it lacks the needed harmony with your intellectual identity with respect to the matter at hand.

Condition (iii) highlights that you take the premises you advance to be normative reasons for believing the conclusion. This reflects your stance regarding the endorsability of your conclusion-belief. You regard the premises as reasons to believe the conclusion and thus worthy of consideration by your interlocuters as reasons they have to believe the conclusion.

There is a lot more to say about the *performance dimension* of integrity (for discussion, see Scherkoske 2013, e.g., chap. 5, who draws heavily on Calhoun 1995). I believe that I have said enough to make plausible the claim that a reason-giving use of an argument has intellectual integrity only if it satisfies *Sustenance*.

> *Sustenance*: Your reason-giving use of an argument displays how you sustain your conclusion-belief only if the premises are reasons for which you believe the conclusion.

A reason-giving use of an argument satisfies *Sustenance* when the premises are reasons for which the arguer believes the conclusion. The *performance dimension* of integrity speaks to the occasions for displaying intellectual integrity. A display of intellectual integrity (such a display could be a painting, a song, a scientific conjecture) that occasions a reason-giving use of an argument is taking a stand publicly by providing reasons for one's conviction. More specifically, they are occasions when one advances before others what one takes to be reasons one has to believe the conclusion. You rationally intend your premises to be reasons you have to believe the conclusion. Hence, you believe that your premises are such reasons. Furthermore, occasions for intellectual integrity are occasions for advancing premises that are reasons for which you believe the conclusion. Your premise beliefs *sustain* your believing the conclusion. This motivates thinking that a reason-giving use of an argument must satisfy *Sustenance* to have intellectual integrity.

Recall Stella's reason-giving use of the argument. It clearly fails *Sustenance*. Stella does not believe the conclusion she states to her students and so the reasons she advances are not reasons for which she believes the conclusion. Nevertheless, as previously stated, it is plausible to take her reason-giving use of the argument to be intellectually honest. Again, Stella accepts her inference claim that the premises she advances are reasons she and her students have to believe the conclusion. This highlights that satisfying *Sustenance* is not necessary for a reason-giving use of argument to count as intellectually honest.

Suppose that there is no proposition that you are more certain of than some proposition p (e.g., *that you exist, that there is an external world*). It seems possible that you may have reasons to believe p even though such reasons do not sustain your believing that p. For example, suppose that Paige is convinced of the truth of a proposition p that is an instance of the law of excluded middle. She is intuitively certain of p and can't imagine it false. After taking a logic class, she comes to believe both that the classical account of the truth-conditional properties of disjunction and negation is correct, and that the truth of p may be derived from it. I don't see why she can't use an argument for p that advances what she takes to be reasons she has to believe p that draws on the classical account. Even though she may be more certain of p than the classical account of the connectives and she doesn't believe p because of that account, Paige's belief that the classical account of the truth-conditional properties of disjunction and negation is correct counts as a reason she has to believe p. It is reasonable for her to call upon her belief that the classical account is correct in response to a request to justify her belief that p. It is far from obvious that her corresponding reason-giving use of argument satisfies *Sustenance* even though it may count as an intellectually honest reason-giving use of argument. Given that her reason-giving use of argument doesn't satisfy *Sustenance*, her justification of her belief that p is not an occasion for her act of reason-giving to display intellectual integrity.

There are situations in which being certain that a proposition p is true does not obviate one's need for finding reasons that one takes to be reasons one has to believe p. For example, Beth's husband is accused of embezzling a large sum of money. Beth loves her husband dearly and believes that she knows him as well as anyone can know anyone else. She cannot imagine that he could do this. Beth sets out to prove her husband's innocence by finding the real embezzler. She uncovers evidence sufficient to prove that her husband's brother took the money. The evidence Beth collects produces what she takes to be reasons she has to believe that her husband is innocent, which may give her knowledge where before she only had firm conviction. However, Beth's newly won reasons she has to believe in her husband's innocence need not add any force to her conviction in her belief that her husband is innocent, which may be so strong that nothing could shake it.[20] Her reason-giving

---

[20] This scenario is adapted from one given by Harman (1973, pp. 31–32), which he uses to illustrate reasoning that may explain an individual's knowledge but not the acquisition of their corresponding belief.

use of argument in defense of her husband's innocence may be intellectually honest, but it doesn't display intellectual integrity as it doesn't satisfy *Sustenance*.

The idea that an intellectually honest use of an argument needn't display intellectual integrity reflects that the demand for a reason-giving use of an argument is not always dictated by the need to show an audience that its conclusion is true. For example, Kelly is certain of the answer to the geometry problem because her professor has given it to her. However, she would like to figure out the answer on her own to better prepare for the final exam. Over the weekend, she ends up identifying certain propositions from which she deduces the answer. Since these propositions represent her evidence for a conclusion which is the answer to the geometry problem, she has constructed an argument. Indeed, she correctly sees that these propositions are reasons she has to believe the conclusion. She tests this argument by presenting it to a fellow student who is unsure of the answer to the geometry problem, and convinces them that she has the answer.

Since one can have reasons to believe a proposition p that are not the reasons for which one believes p, it is possible that one's certainty of a conclusion is not derived from the certainty of one's premises. One needn't be more certain of a proposition than another in order for the first to qualify as a reason one has to believe the second. I can construct an argument whose premises I acknowledge as reasons I have to believe the conclusion without there ever having been a transfer of certainty from my premises to my conclusion. This is in sync with the fact that there are contexts in which one's search for reasons for one to believe a proposition is not motivated by a need to determine the truth of that proposition or by a need to enhance one's certainty of it.

I now turn to what I label the *reflective resoluteness dimension* of intellectual integrity. Suppose that in your best judgment you believe that some proposition p is true in light of reasons that you possess to believe p. Drawing from Calhoun (1995), your believing p in light of such reasons has integrity only when you have a proper regard for your judgment that p is true. What is it to have a proper regard for your judgment about the truth of p? Calhoun spells out *proper regard for one's best judgment* in terms deciding what is worth doing.

> To have integrity is to understand that one's own judgment matters because it is only within individual persons' deliberative viewpoints, including one's

own, that what is worth our doing can be decided. Thus, one's own judgment serves a common interest of co-deliberators. Persons of integrity
treat their own endorsements as ones that matter, or ought to matter, to
fellow deliberators. Absent a special sort of story, lying about one's views,
concealing them, recanting them under pressure, selling them out for
rewards or to avoid penalties, and pandering to what one regards as the bad
views of others, all indicate a failure to regard one's own judgment as one
that should matter to others. (1995, p. 258)

Plausibly, trying to have integrity so understood brings into play the possession of a host of other virtues.

[I]ntegrity may be a master virtue, that is, less a virtue in its own right
than a pressing into service of a host of other virtues-self-knowledge,
strength of will, courage, honesty, loyalty, humility, civility, respect, and
self-respect.... What is a person who tries to have integrity trying to do? I
have not rejected (though I have revised) the ideas that she is trying to be
autonomous, or loyal to deep commitments, or uncontaminated by evils.
But I have tried to argue that this is not the whole story. She is also trying
to stand for what, in her best judgment, is worth persons' doing. (1995,
p. 260)

In spelling out a connection between trying to have integrity and trying to be
autonomous, Calhoun qualifies the operative notion of autonomy in order
highlight that treating one's endorsements as ones that matter, or ought to
matter to fellow deliberators, does not involve being close-minded or dog-
matic in engaging them with one's endorsements.

This is to say that when what is worth doing is under dispute, concern to
act with integrity must pull us both ways. Integrity calls us simultaneously
to stand behind our convictions and to take seriously others' doubts about
them. Thus, neither ambivalence nor compromise seem inevitably to be-
token lack of integrity. If we are not pulled as far as uncertainty or compromise, integrity would at least demand exercising due care in how we go
about dissenting. (1995, p. 260)

Generalizing, proper self-regard for one's best judgment involves regarding it
as "one that should matter to others" and involves thinking autonomously in

supporting it.[21] In order to clarify the connection between intellectual integrity and intellectual autonomy, I now briefly discuss intellectual autonomy. My aim is to use the notion of intellectual autonomy to highlight a necessary condition for a reason-giving use of argument to have intellectual integrity.

In general, autonomy is "correctness in the avoidance and acceptance of the testimony and guidance of others. Autonomy is a proper degree and reliance on the authority of others, what is proper being determined by the end of the activity in which one is engaging" (Benson 1983, pp. 9–10). This echoes King's characterization of intellectual autonomy, which "requires thinking *for* ourselves but not *by* ourselves" (2021, p. 88). How independently we should think in deciding what to believe or do depends on what we are thinking about, and on how well equipped we are to think about it (King 2021, p. 99). This echoes Kant's elaboration of his oft-cited remark, "*Sapere Aude!* [dare to know] Have courage to use your own understanding!—that is the motto of enlightenment" (1784, p. 17). That is, the degree to which one should think independently on a given topic turns in part on the expected level of one's understanding about the relevant subject matter. Accordingly, "[U]nderstanding is the seed of autonomy" (Roberts and Wood 2007, p. 263).

I can take it properly on authority that whales are viviparous, that my car needs a new alternator, and that my dental health is good, because it is not my business to understand such matters deeply enough to warrant intellectual self-sufficiency. Accordingly, it is appropriate to outsource my thinking about such matters to sources that exemplify the needed expertise. For example, that the reason for which I believe that whales are viviparous is that it is so stated in a reliable textbook is not a strike against my intellectual integrity as it is not expected that I have the requisite zoological understanding. However, if I am a marine biologist and take it on the authority of a reliable textbook that whales are viviparous, then my believing that this is so does not display intellectual autonomy (following Roberts and Wood 2007, p. 264). My introductory logic students reasonably expect me to possess reasons for why the argument in our textbook is valid beyond the say so in the book's answer key. Such a reliance on the answer key evinces an understanding of validity that lacks the depth normally expected of a logic instructor. So,

---

[21] Scherkoske highlights how Calhoun's view of integrity may be descriptively inadequate because of its focus on the public expression of convictions concerning "what would be just or what lives are acceptable forms of the good" (Calhoun 1995, p. 254). However, this view of integrity "seems, in fact, not to capture the sense in which a person's integrity can be expressed in regard for judgments other than those concerning good ways to live" (Scherkoske 2013, p. 24).

outsourcing my judgment that the argument is valid to the book's answer key would be a failure of intellectual autonomy.

Proper self-regard for one's judgment involves one sustaining one's judgment in light of reasons that display one's intellectual autonomy. Your reasons for belief display the intellectual autonomy of your act of believing only if they are indicative of the level of understanding that you should have of why what you believe is true. So you have proper self-regard for your judgment only if your reasons that sustain your judgment are indicative of the level of understanding that you should have of why your judgment is true. To illustrate, I borrow from Benson (1983).

The government warns that smoking can damage your health
The government would not have issued the warning without good reasons
<u>for its belief</u>
Smoking can damage your health

Suppose that Shannon uses this argument to advance reasons for which she believes the conclusion. Whether Shannon's use of the argument has intellectual integrity turns on the level of understanding that she should have with respect to why the conclusion is true. For example, suppose that Shannon lacks any scientific understanding of the health effects of smoking. She reminds herself that there have been investigations by competent people, whose reports are publicly available and have been assessed by other competent people who advise the government. Plausibly, reminding herself about these points indicates that Shannon is thinking for herself about the topic to the appropriate degree and so she displays a proper self-regard for her judgment insofar as the premise-reasons that sustain her judgment are indicative of the level of understanding of why her judgment is true that it is reasonable to expect of her. Obviously, the expectations are raised with respect to the health experts responsible for advising the government. Plausibly, if one were to use the above argument to advance reasons for which they believe the conclusion, such a use of the argument would not display a proper self-regard for their judgment that smoking can cause cancer. Indeed, it is hardly imaginable that a person with such scientific understanding would so use the argument.

Let's pause to summarize. Proper self-regard for one's best judgment that *p* involves thinking autonomously in supporting such a judgment. To think autonomously in supporting such a judgment is to maintain one's belief that

p in light of reasons that, taken together, are indicative of the level of understanding one should have of why p is true. So one has proper self-regard for one's best judgment that p only if the reasons one possesses that sustain one's belief that p reflect the understanding one should have of why p is true. Presumably, the less one understands why p is true the more reliant one is on expert opinion as reflected in one's reasons in support of believing that p is true. In short, one has proper self-regard for one's best judgment only if one's reasons that sustain one's judgment reflect the understanding one should have of why p is true. *Deference* connects this claim to reason-giving uses of argument.

> *Deference*: Your reason-giving use of an argument displays your proper self-regard for your conclusion-belief only if the premises you use for believing the conclusion taken together are indicative of the depth of understanding you should have of why the conclusion is true.

A reason-giving use of argument satisfies *Deference* when the premises the arguer uses for believing the conclusion taken together are indicative of the depth of understanding the arguer should have of why the conclusion is true. Intuitively, Shannon's use of the above argument satisfies *Deference*. A healthcare expert's use of it to advance reasons for them to believe the conclusion most likely does not.

How does one determine the required level of understanding needed for a reason-giving use of argument to satisfy *Deference*? Drawing from Benson (1983, pp. 11–13), King (2021, pp. 98–99), and Roberts and Wood (2007, pp. 263–65) a first-step response runs as follows. The depth of understanding you should have of why the conclusion is true turns on the relevant subject-specific domain and the level of expertise it is reasonable to expect of someone relative to their various roles in their personal and professional life such as autonomous moral agent, citizen, parent, auto mechanic, professional philosopher, etc. The depth of understanding you should have of why the conclusion is true depends on the understanding of the relevant subject matter expected of you under some description of a specified role you have in your personal or professional life.

To borrow an example from King (2021, p. 98): if I need to replace an engine starter in my car, I'll most likely end up forming all sorts of false beliefs and break something if I do it by myself. The risk of intellectual disaster of proceeding alone is high enough for me that I should rely on the expertise of a certified mechanic. However, it would be inappropriate for such an expert to need expert advice to replace the same part in order to avoid intellectual disaster. In their role as a certified mechanic, it is to be expected that they have the necessary understanding to think on their own in replacing the engine starter. As a professional philosopher of logic, it is reasonable to expect that I have a deeper understanding of the concept of logical consequence than the garage mechanic. Of course, intellectual outsourcing in one's area of intellectual expertise is not always inappropriate. It may well be appropriate for a mechanic to defer to another in deciding what to think with respect to complex engine repair tasks that demand a high degree of sophistication.

What I am pointing to here is that the premises you use for the conclusion taken together are not indicative of the depth of understanding you should have of why the conclusion is true if you inappropriately outsource your thinking in support of your conclusion-belief. What's inappropriate in this regard is a function of the level of understanding expected of you relative to the specific subject matter at hand. I have suggested that such an expectation is a matter of whether and to what extent it is your business to understand such subject matter. This idea is illustrated by Benson's remark concerning how the expected degree of epistemic self-sufficiency may vary from one subject matter to another.

> It may be consistent with the role of critical enquirer to ask a competent authority whether smoking will damage my health, but it is not consistent with the role of critical moral agent to ask anyone whether I ought to be a conscientious objector, practice contraceptive intercourse, or approve of abortion . . . to be autonomous in morality involves a greater degree of self-sufficiency than to be intellectually autonomous. (1983, p. 211)

Again, Shannon taking it on someone else's authority that smoking is unhealthy is not a strike against her intellectual autonomy because it is not her business to have the scientific understanding that obviates the need to outsource what she should believe about such matters. However, as Roberts and Wood put it (2007, p. 264), because it is everyone's business to understand why, say, torture is wicked, it is inappropriate for Shannon qua autonomous moral agent to merely take it on authority that torture is wicked.

A reason-giving use of argument has intellectual integrity only if it satisfies *Deference*. This is because only then does your believing the conclusion in light of the premises display proper self-regard for your best judgment that the conclusion is true. One has proper self-regard for one's best judgment that p only if the reasons one possesses that sustain one's belief that p reflect the understanding one should have of why p is true. The level of understanding one should have of why p is true turns in part on whether it is one's business to understand why p is true. Admittedly, this is vague. However, if I am right, whether it is one's business to understand why one's conclusion is true matters to whether one's reason-giving use of argument has intellectual integrity.

8.4.1. Summary

The attribution of *integrity* to a reason-giving use of argument makes sense when the attribution of a kind of *completeness* or *wholeness* to your use of argument makes sense. Appealing to the argue$_1$-argument$_8$ link introduced in Chapter 2, we can say that your act of arguing$_1$ for a conclusion by means of stating an argument$_8$ for it is incomplete unless your use of the argument is integrated with your epistemic stance regarding the truth of the conclusion. Such integration is necessary for your use of the argument to have intellectual integrity. My clarification of this integration of one's reason-giving use of argument with one's epistemic stance appeals to the performance and reflective resoluteness dimensions of intellectual integrity.

Specifically, the performance and reflective resoluteness dimensions of intellectual integrity motivate *Sustenance* and *Deference*, respectively. Your reason-giving use of an argument satisfies *Sustenance* when the premises you advance are reasons for which you believe the conclusion. It satisfies *Deference* when your believing the conclusion in light of them is indicative of the depth of the expected understanding of why the conclusion is true. Your reasons for believing the conclusion are indicative of the degree of understanding of why the conclusion is true that you should have given your roles in your civic (e.g., citizen), personal (e.g., parent), and professional (e.g., auto mechanic) life.

Your reason-giving use of an argument is integrated with your epistemic stance regarding the conclusion only if it satisfies *Sustenance* and *Deference*. Accordingly, if your reason-giving use of an argument has intellectual integrity, then it satisfies *Sustenance* and *Deference*. My elaboration and defense of this claim has drawn on the literature on the virtue of intellectual integrity. Obviously, the attributions of intellectual integrity to arguers and reason-giving uses of arguments are related. If an arguer possesses the virtue of intellectual integrity, then when arguing₁, their reason-giving uses of arguments will reliably satisfy *Sustenance* and *Deference*. However, that your reason-giving use of an argument occasionally satisfies *Sustenance* and *Deference* does not suffice for your possession of the virtue of intellectual integrity.

8.5. Conclusion

I have supposed that it makes sense to attribute intellectual honesty and integrity to reason-giving uses of arguments. I have posed two central questions. When are your reason-giving uses of argument intellectually honest? When do they have intellectual integrity? Each of my responses identifies two necessary conditions.

In order for your reason-giving use of an argument to be intellectually honest it must satisfy both *Sincerity* and *Accuracy*.

> *Sincerity*: Your reason-giving use of an argument is sincere only if you believe that what you claim in stating the argument is true.

> *Accuracy*: Your reason-giving use of an argument is accurate only if you have taken care to ensure that what you claim by virtue of so using the argument is accurate.

That is, your reason-giving use of an argument is intellectually honest only if you believe that what you claim in stating the argument is true and you have taken care to ensure that what you claim by virtue of so using the argument is accurate.

Your reason-giving use of an argument lacks intellectual integrity unless it satisfies *Sustenance* and *Deference*.

> *Sustenance*. Your reason-giving use of an argument displays how you sustain your conclusion-belief only if the premises are reasons for which you believe the conclusion.

> *Deference*. Your reason-giving use of an argument displays your proper self-regard for your conclusion-belief only if the premises you use for believing

the conclusion taken together are indicative of the depth of understanding you should have of why the conclusion is true.

So your reason-giving use of an argument has intellectual integrity only if the premises are reasons for which you believe the conclusion and they are indicative of the depth of understanding you should have of why the conclusion is true. As previously illustrated, the intellectual honesty of your reason-giving use of argument does not suffice for it having intellectual integrity. For example, that it satisfies *Sincerity* and *Accuracy* does not suffice for its satisfaction of *Sustenance* and *Deference*. Accordingly, that a reason-giving use of argument lacks integrity does not necessitate that it is intellectually dishonest (recall Stella's reason-giving use of argument).

However, as I said in the preamble, it is plausible to think that intellectual honesty subsumes intellectual integrity. Plausibly, if a reason-giving use of an argument has intellectual integrity, then it is intellectually honest. Toward a partial defense of this claim, I end by sketching why if your reason-giving use of an argument has intellectual integrity, then it is intellectually honest insofar as it satisfies *Sincerity* and *Accuracy*.

If your reason-giving use of an argument has intellectual integrity, then, by *Sustenance*, the premises you advance are reasons for which you believe the conclusion because you accept the associated inference claim, which says in effect that the premises are reasons you have to believe the conclusion. Hence, you believe that your premises and conclusion are true, and that the former constitutes evidence that warrants believing the conclusion. Hence, your reason-giving use of the argument satisfies *Sincerity*. In short, if *Sustenance* is satisfied, so too is *Sincerity*.

However, it is less clear that if a reason-giving use of argument satisfies *Deference* then it satisfies *Accuracy*. Can't the premises you use for believing the conclusion be indicative of the depth of understanding you should have of why the conclusion is true even though you have not taken care to ensure that what you claim by virtue of so using the argument is accurate? It seems so. It might be appropriate for you to cite an authority instead of giving your reasons for what you believe regarding a subject matter that is outside of your range of competence. Your appeal to authority indicates that the authority you cite could give good reasons for what you believe. But perhaps you haven't done your homework and your appeal to authority is faulty in any one of a number of ways. Say, you could have easily checked to see that the authority you cite is not in fact an authority in the appropriate area or that the matter of whether your conclusion is true is not a settled by expert consensus (see Sinnott-Armstrong and Fogelin 2010, pp. 360–64). When appeals to authority are legitimate is a complicated matter. My point here is just to show that it is far from obvious that a reason-giving use of argument satisfying *Deference* ipso facto satisfies *Accuracy*.

Nevertheless, my intuitive sense of *intellectual integrity* suggests that if your reason-giving use of an argument has intellectual integrity, then it does satisfy *Accuracy*. To elaborate, I draw on the link acknowledged in the literature between integrity and having reasons for one's convictions (e.g., Calhoun 1995; McLeod 2005; and Scherkoske 2013) that exemplifies the self-trust dimension of autonomous thinking.

To draw from my earlier discussion of Calhoun: a person with intellectual integrity has a proper self-regard for their best judgment, which involves regarding their judgment as one that should matter to others and involves thinking autonomously in supporting their best judgments. If one thinks autonomously in supporting one's best judgment, then one's confidence or certainty in the truth of that judgment is derived in part from one's taking care to ensure that what one believes is true.

To elaborate, recall the *reflective resoluteness dimension* of intellectual integrity that motivates *Deference*. Suppose that in your best judgment you believe that some proposition p is true in light of reasons that you possess for believing p. Drawing from Calhoun (1995), we can say that your believing p in light of such reasons has integrity only when you have a proper regard for your judgment that p is true. If your judgment that p is true has the status of a conviction, then to so regard it properly requires that you have taken care to ensure that it is true. Calhoun remarks that, according to our intuitive sense of integrity, "people with integrity decide what they stand for and have their own settled reasons for taking the stands they do. They are not wantons or crowd followers or shallowly sincere" (Calhoun 1995, p. 237). Taking a stand regarding one's conviction about the truth of some claim in light of one's own settled reasons for believing it is an expression of the self-trust in deciding what to believe that is indicative of persons with integrity. The certainty that matters to sustaining one's convictions with integrity is derived, in part, from the care one has taken to ensure that one's conviction is accurate and not a function of dogmatism, fanaticism, and ideological blindness (Scherkoske 2013, p. 139).

In short, your reason-giving use of an argument has intellectual integrity only if your certainty that the conclusion is true is an expression of your self-trust in ensuring the accuracy of what you claim. Obviously, how one ensures the accuracy of what one claims is a partly a function of one's level of competence in the relevant subject matter. Our earlier arguer Shannon, not having any competence in the health field, will have to convince herself that the government would not have issued the warning about the harm of smoking without good reasons for its belief. The health expert's self-trust is exemplified in a more direct confrontation with the evidence, e.g., studying the reports of the various investigations, looking at the statistics, sampling methods, etc.

So, if your reason-giving use of an argument has intellectual integrity, then it satisfies *Accuracy* because you have assumed responsibility as an autonomous thinker for ensuring that what you claim is accurate in a way that accounts for your certainty of your conclusion-belief. Accordingly, your believing the associated inference claim with a high degree of confidence is grounded on the care that you have taken to ensure that your inference claim is true. Following Calhoun (1995, p. 248) and McLeod (2005, pp. 116–17), we can say that the reasons one possesses that sustain one's convictions needn't be good reasons (against this, see Scherkoske 2013, pp. 61, 89, and 130). This accords with my understanding that your reason-giving use of argument satisfying *Accuracy* doesn't guarantee the premises are, in fact, good reasons for you to believe the conclusion. However, one might think that an argument that one uses must rationalize one's believing the conclusion in order for it to have intellectual integrity. Perhaps, even stronger, the premises must be reasons for one to believe the conclusion. On this line of thought, at the very least in order for a reason-giving use of an argument to have intellectual integrity the premises must be either reasons one has to believe the conclusion or reasons for one to believe it.

In sum, it is intuitive plausibility that intellectual honesty subsumes intellectual integrity. It is a strike against any story about the intellectual honesty and integrity of reason-giving uses of argument that is incompatible with this. I hope I have said enough to at least convince the reader that my responses to the two central questions of this chapter are compatible with the claim that if your reason-giving use of an argument has intellectual integrity, then it is intellectually honest.

Bibliography

Abbott, B. 2006. "Where Have Some of the Presuppositions gone?" Pp. 1–20 in *Drawing the Boundaries of Meaning: Neo-Gricean Studies in Pragmatics and Semantics in Honor of Laurence R. Horn*. B. Birner and G. Ward, eds. Philadelphia: John Benjamins.

Aikin, S. F. and R. B. Talisse. 2019. *Why We Argue (and How We Should)*. 2nd ed. New York: Routledge.

Alston, W. 2005. *Beyond Justification: Dimensions of Epistemic Evaluation*. Ithaca, NY: Cornell University Press.

Alvarez, M. 2008. "Reasons and the Ambiguity of 'Belief.'" *Philosophical Explorations* 11, 53–65.

Alvarez, M. 2009. "How Many Kinds of Reasons?" *Philosophical Explorations* 12, 181–93.

Aristotle. 1985. *The Complete Works of Aristotle*. J. Barnes, ed. Princeton: Princeton University Press.

Audi, R. 1993. "Belief, Reason, and Inference." Pp. 233–73 in Audi, *The Structure of Justification*. Cambridge: Cambridge University Press.

Audi, R. 1998. "Reasons for Belief." In *Routledge Encyclopedia of Philosophy*. Taylor and Francis. https://doi.org/10.4324/9780415249126-P043-1.

Bach, K. 1994. "Conversational Implicature." *Mind and Language* 9, 124–62.

Bach, K. 1999. "The Myth of Conventional Implicature." *Linguistics and Philosophy* 22, 262–83.

Bach, K. and R. Harnish. 1979. *Linguistic Communication and Speech Acts*. Cambridge, MA: MIT Press.

Baehr, J. 2011. *The Inquiring Mind: On Intellectual Virtues and Virtue Epistemology*. New York: Oxford University Press.

Baehr, J. 2016. "The Four Dimensions of an Intellectual Virtue." Pp. 86–98 in *Moral and Intellectual Virtues in Western and Chinese Philosophy*. M. Chienkuo, M. Slote, and E. Sosa, eds. New York: Routledge.

Bailin, S., R. Case, J. R. Coombs, and L. B. Daniels. 1999. "Conceptualizing Critical Thinking." *Journal of Curriculum Studies* 31(3), 285–302.

Barker, S. 2003. *The Elements of Logic*. Boston: McGraw-Hill.

Battaly, H. 2014. "Intellectual Virtues." Pp. 177–87 in *The Handbook of Virtue Ethics*. S. van Hooft, ed. New York: Routledge.

Beall, J. C. and G. Restall. 2006. *Logical Pluralism*. Oxford: Oxford University Press.

Benson, J. 1983. "Who Is the Autonomous Man?" *Philosophy* 58, 5–17.

Bermejo-Luque, L. 2011a. "Exchanging Reasons: Responses to Critics." *Theoria* 72, 329–34.

Bermejo-Luque, L. 2011b. *Giving Reasons: A Linguistic-Pragmatic Approach to Argumentation Theory*. Dordrecht: Springer.

Bessie, J. and S. Glennan. 2000. *Elements of Deductive Inference*. Belmont, CA: Wadsworth.

Biro, J. and H. Siegel. 1992. "Normativity, Argumentation, and an Epistemic Theory of Fallacies." Pp. 85–103 in *Argumentation Illuminated*. F. H. van Eemeren, R. Grootendorst, J. A. Blair, and C. A. Willard, eds. Amsterdam: SICSAT.

Biro, J. and H. Siegel. 2006a. "In Defense of the Objective Epistemic Approach to Argumentation." *Informal Logic* 26, 91–101.

Biro, J. and H. Siegel. 2006b. "Pragma-dialectic versus Epistemic Theories of Arguing and Arguments: Rivals or Partners?" Pp. 1–10 in *Considering Pragma-Dialectics*. P. Houtlosser and A. van Rees, eds. Mahwah, NJ: Lawrence Erlbaum Associates.

Blair, J. A. 2004. "Argument and Its Uses." *Informal Logic* 24, 137–51.

Blair, J. A. 2011. "The Moral Normativity of Argumentation." *Cogency* 3, 13–32.

Blair, J. A. 2012. "Argumentation as Rational Persuasion." *Argumentation* 26, 71–81.

Blair, J. A. and R. H. Johnson. 1987. "The Current State of Informal Logic." *Informal Logic* 9, 147–51.

Blanchette, P. 2001. "Logical Consequence." Pp. 115–35 in *The Blackwell Guide to Philosophical Logic*. L. Goble, ed. Oxford: Blackwell.

Boghossian, P. 2014. "What Is Inference?" *Philosophical Studies* 169, 1–18.

Bondy, P. 2017. "Epistemic Basing Relation." In *Routledge Encyclopedia of Philosophy*. Taylor and Francis. https://doi.org/:10.4324/0123456789-P070-1.

Bonevac, D. 1999. *Simple Logic*. Fort Worth: Harcourt Brace College Pub. Co.

Broome, J. 2013. *Rationality through Reasoning*. Oxford: Wiley Blackwell.

Broome, J. 2014. "Comments on Boghossian." *Philosophical Studies* 169, 19–25.

Brown, A. L. 1978. "Knowing When, Where, and How to Remember: A Problem of Metacognition." Pp. 77–165 in *Advances in Instructional Psychology*, vol. 1. R. Glaser, ed. Hillsdale, NJ: Erlbaum.

Brown, J. and H. Cappelen. 2011a. *Assertion: New Philosophical Essays*. New York: Oxford University Press.

Brown, J. and H. Cappelen. 2011b. "Assertion: An Introduction and Overview." Pp. 1–17 in *Assertion: New Philosophical Essays*. J. Brown and H. Cappelen, eds. New York: Oxford University Press.

Brown, R. 2022. "Epistemic Diligence and Epistemic Honesty." *Practical Ethics Blog*. Oxford University Press. https://blog.practicalethics.ox.ac.uk/2022/07/epistemic-diligence-and-honesty/. Accessed April 7, 2022.

Byerly, R. 2022. "Intellectual Honesty and Intellectual Transparency." *Episteme* 20, 1–19.

Calhoun, C. 1995. "Standing for Something." *Journal of Philosophy* 92, 235–60.

Carney, J. and J. Scheer. 1980. *Fundamentals of Logic*. 3rd ed. New York: Macmillan.

Chan, T. 2013. "Introduction: Aiming at Truth." Pp. 1–16 in *The Aim of Belief*. T. Chan, ed. Oxford: Oxford University Press.

Cherniak, C. 1986. *Minimal Rationality*. Cambridge, MA: MIT Press.

Copi, I. and C. Cohen. 2005. *Introduction to Logic*. 12th ed. Upper Saddle River, NJ: Pearson/Prentice Hall.

Copi, I., C. Cohen, and K. McMahon. 2014. *Introduction to Logic*. 14th ed. Essex, UK: Pearson Education.

Corcoran, J. 1993. "Editor's Introduction." Pp. xvii–xlvi in M. Cohen and E. Nagel, *An Introduction to Logic*, 2nd ed. J. Corcoran, ed. Indianapolis: Hackett.

Corner, A. and U. Hahn 2013. "Normative Theories of Argumentation: Are Some Norms Better Than Others?" *Synthese* 190, 3579–610.

Davidson, D. 1980. *Essays on Actions and Events*. Oxford: Clarendon Press.

Davidson, D. 1986. "A Coherence Theory of Truth and Knowledge." Pp. 307–19 in *Truth and Interpretation: Perspectives on the Philosophy of Donald Davidson*. E. Lepore, ed. Oxford: Blackwell.

Davies, M. 2015. "A Model of Critical Thinking in Higher Education." Pp. 41–91 in *Higher Education: Handbook of Theory and Research*. M. B. Paulsen, ed. Cham, Switzerland: Springer International Publishing.

Davies, M. and R. Barnett. 2015. "Introduction." Pp. 1–25 in *The Palgrave Handbook of Critical Thinking in Higher Education*. Davies M. and R. Barnett, eds. New York: Palgrave Macmillan.

Detlefsen, M., D. C. McCarty, and J. B. Bacon. 1999. *Logic from A to Z*. London: Routledge.

Dewey, J. 1933. *How We Think*. Boston: D.C. Heath.

Dutilh Novaes, C. 2015. "A Dialogical, Multi-agent Account of the Normativity of Logic." *Dialectica* 69, 587–609.

Dutilh Novaes, C. 2021. "Argument and Argumentation." In *The Stanford Encyclopedia of Philosophy* (Fall 2021 ed.). Edward N. Zalta, ed. https://plato.stanford.edu/archives/fall2021/entries/argument/.

Eemeren, F. H. van. 1987. "For Reason's Sake: Maximal Argumentative Analysis of Discourse." Pp. 201–16 in *Proceedings of Argumentation: Across the Lines of Discipline*. F. H. van Eemeren, ed. Dordrecht: Foris.

Eemeren, F. H. van, G. Garssen, E. C. W. Krabbe, A. F. Snoeck Henkemans, B. Verheij, J. Wagemans, and H. M. Wagemans. 2014. *Handbook of Argumentation Theory*. Dordrecht: Springer.

Eemeren, F. H. van and R. Grootendorst. 1984. *Speech Acts in Argumentative Discussions: A Theoretical Model for the Analysis of Discussions Directed towards Solving Conflicts of Opinion*. Berlin/Dordrecht: De Gruyter/Foris Publications.

Eemeren, F. H. van and R. Grootendorst. 1988. "Rationale for a Pragma-dialectic Perspective." *Argumentation* 2, 271–91.

Eemeren, F. H. van and R. Grootendorst. 1995. "The Pragma-dialectic Approach to Fallacies." Pp. 130–44 in *Fallacies: Classical and Contemporary Readings*. Hans V. Hansen and Robert C. Pinto, eds. University Park: Pennsylvania State University Press.

Eemeren, F. H. van and R. Grootendorst. 2004. *A Systematic Theory of Argumentation: The Pragma-dialectical Approach*. New York: Cambridge University Press.

Eemeren, F. H. van and P. Houtlosser. 2003. "The Development of the Pragma-dialectical Approach to Argumentation." *Argumentation* 17, 387–403.

Engel, P. 2000. "Introduction: The Varieties of Belief and Acceptance." Pp. 1–30 in *Believing and Accepting*. P. Engel, ed. Dordrecht: Kluwer.

Ennis, R. H. 1985. "A Logical Basis for Measuring Critical Thinking Skills." *Educational Leadership* 43, 44–48.

Ennis, R. H. 1991. "Critical Thinking: A Streamlined Conception." *Teaching Philosophy* 14, 5–24.

Epstein, R. L. 2001. *Propositional Logics*. 2nd ed. Belmont, CA: Wadsworth/Thomson Learning.

Epstein, R. L. 2002. *Five Ways of Saying "Therefore"*. Belmont, CA: Wadsworth/Thompson Learning.

Etchemendy, J. 2008. "Reflections on Consequence." Pp. 263–99 in *New Essays on Tarski and Philosophy*. D. Patterson, ed. Oxford: Oxford University Press.

Etchemendy, J. 2015. "Logical Consequence." P. 603 in *The Cambridge Dictionary of Philosophy*, 3rd ed. R. Audi, ed. Cambridge: Cambridge University Press.

Evans, J. St. B. T. 2017. *Thinking and Reasoning: A Very Short Introduction*. Oxford: Oxford University Press.

Evans, J. St. B. T. 2020. *Hypothetical Thinking: Dual Processes in Reasoning and Judgement*. New York: Routledge.

Facione, P. 1990. *The Delphi Report: Critical Thinking: A Statement of Expert Consensus for Purposes of Educational Assessment and Instruction*. Millbrae, CA: California Academic Press.

Feldman, R. 1994. "Good Arguments." Pp. 159–88 in *Socializing Epistemology: The Social Dimensions of Knowledge*. Frederick F. Schmitt, ed. Lanham, MD: Rowman & Littlefield.

Field, H. 2009. "What Is the Normative Role of Logic?" *Proceedings of the Aristotelian Society* supp. vol. 83, 251–68.

Fisher, A. 2019. "What Critical Thinking Is." Pp. 7–32 in *Studies in Critical Thinking*. J. A. Blair, ed. Windsor, ON: Centre for Research in Reasoning, Argumentation and Rhetoric, University of Windsor.

Fisher, A. and M. Scriven. 1997. *Critical Thinking: Its Definition and Assessment*. Norwich, UK: Center for Research in Critical Thinking, University of East Anglia.

Foley, R. 1986. "Is It Possible to Have Contradictory Beliefs?" *Midwest Studies in Philosophy* 10, 327–55.

Foley, R. 1987. *The Theory of Epistemic Rationality*. Cambridge, MA: Harvard University Press.

Foley, R. 1993. *Working without a Net: A Study of Egocentric Epistemology*. New York: Oxford University Press.

Franklin, B. [1793] 2022 . *The Autobiography of Benjamin Franklin*. N.p.: Independently published.

Freeman, J. 1988. *Thinking Logically: Basic Concepts for Reasoning*. Englewood Cliffs, NJ: Prentice Hall.

Gabbay, D. M. and J. Woods. 2005. "The Practical Turn in Logic." Pp. 15–122 in *Handbook of Philosophical Logic*, 2nd ed. D. Gabbay and F. Guenthner, eds. Dordrecht: Springer.

Garssen, B. and J. Albert van Laar. 2010. "A Pragma-dialectical Response to Objectivist Epistemic Challenges." *Informal Logic* 30, 122–41.

Ginsborg, H. 2006. "Reasons for Belief." *Philosophy and Phenomenological Research* 72, 286–318.

Glaser, E. M. 1941. *An Experiment in the Development of Critical Thinking*. New York: Bureau of Publications, Teachers College, Columbia University.

Godden, D. 2015. "Argumentation, Rationality, and Psychology of Reasoning." *Informal Logic* 35, 135–66.

Goldman, A. 1994. "Argumentation and Social Epistemology." *Journal of Philosophy* 91, 27–49.

Goldman, A. 2003. "An Epistemological Approach to Argumentation." *Informal Logic* 23, 51–63

Goldstein, L. 1988. "Logic and Reasoning." *Erkenntnis* 28, 297–320.

Goodwin, J. 2007. "Argument Has No Function." *Informal Logic* 27, 69–90.

Govier, T. 2010. *A Practical Study of Argument*. 7th ed. Belmont, CA: Wadsworth Cengage Learning.

Govier, T. 2018a. "Is a Theory of Argument Possible?" Pp. 20–55 in Govier, *Problems in Argument Analysis and Argumentation*, updated ed. Windsor, ON: University of Windsor.

Govier, T. 2018b. *Problems in Argument Analysis and Argumentation*. Updated ed. Windsor, ON: University of Windsor.

Govier, T. 2018c. "Reasons Why Arguments and Explanations Are Different." Pp. 242–70 in Govier, *Problems in Argument Analysis and Argumentation*, updated ed. Windsor, ON: University of Windsor.

Grennan, W. 1994. "Are 'Gap-Fillers' Missing Premises?" *Informal Logic* 16, 185–96.

Grennan, W. 1997. *Informal Logic: Issues and Techniques*. Montreal: McGill-Queen's University Press.

Grice, H. P. 1989. *Studies in the Way of Words*. Cambridge, MA: Harvard University Press.

Grice, H. P. 2001. *Aspects of Reason*. Richard Warner, ed. Oxford: Clarendon Press.

Groarke, L. 2021. "Informal Logic." In *The Stanford Encyclopedia of Philosophy* (Fall 2021 ed.). Edward N. Zalta, ed. https://plato.stanford.edu/archives/fall2021/entries/logic-informal/.

Groarke, L., and L. Groarke. 2002. "Hilary Putnam on the End(s) of Argument." *Philosophica* 69, 41–60.

Guenin, L. M. 2005. "Intellectual Honesty." *Synthese* 145, 177–232.

Gustason, W. and D. Ulrich. 1989. *Elementary Symbolic Logic*. 2nd ed. Long Grove, IL: Waveland Press.

Habermas, J. 1981. *The Theory of Communicative Action*. Vol. 1: *Reason and the Rationalization of Society*. T. McCarthy, trans. Boston: Beacon Press.

Halfon, M. S. 1989. *Integrity: A Philosophical Inquiry*. Philadelphia: Temple University Press.

Halonen, J. 1995. "Demystifying Critical Thinking." *Teaching of Psychology* 22(1), 75–81.

Halpern, D. 1998. "Teaching Critical Thinking for Transfer across Domains: Dispositions, Skills, Structure Training, and Metacognitive Monitoring." *American Psychologist* 53, 449–55.

Hamblin, C. L. 1970. *Fallacies*. London: Methuen.

Hanson, W. H. 1997. "The Concept of Logical Consequence." *Philosophical Review* 106, 365–409.

Harman, G. 1973. *Thought*. Princeton: Princeton University Press.

Harman, G. 1984. "Logic and Reasoning." *Synthese* 60, 107–27.

Harman, G. 1986. *A Change in View*. Cambridge, MA: MIT Press.

Harman, G. 2002. "Internal Critique: A Logic Is Not a Theory of Reasoning and a Theory of Reasoning Is Not a Logic." Pp. 171–86 in *Handbook of the Logic of Argument and Inference: The Turn towards the Practical*. D. M. Gabbay, R. H. Johnson, H. J. Ohlbach, and J. Woods, eds. Amsterdam: North Holland.

Hayward, T. 2019. "Three Duties of Epistemic Diligence." *Journal of Social Philosophy* 50, 536–51.

Herdt, J. A. 2020. "Enacting Integrity." Pp. 63–94 in *Integrity, Honesty, and Truth Seeking*. C. Miller and R. West, eds. New York: Oxford University Press.

Hitchcock, D. 1983. *Critical Thinking: A Guide to Evaluating Information*. Toronto: Methuen.

Hitchcock, D. 2007a. "Informal Logic and the Concept of Argument." Pp. 101–29 in *Philosophy of Logic*. D. Jacquette. Amsterdam: Elsevier.

Hitchcock, D. 2007b. "So." Pp. 1–8 in *Dissensus and the Search for Common Ground*. H. V. Hansen et al., eds. Windsor, ON: OSSA.

Hitchcock, D. 2011. "Inference Claims." *Informal Logic* 31, 191–228.

Hitchcock, D. 2017a. "Critical Thinking as an Educational Ideal." Pp. 477–94 in Hitchcock, *On Reasoning and Argument: Essays in Informal Logic and Critical Thinking*. Cham, Switzerland: Springer International Publishing.

Hitchcock, D. 2017b. *On Reasoning and Argument: Essays in Informal Logic and Critical Thinking*. Cham, Switzerland: Springer International Publishing.

Hitchcock, D. 2020. "Critical Thinking." In *The Stanford Encyclopedia of Philosophy* (Fall 2020 ed.). Edward N. Zalta, ed. https://plato.stanford.edu/archives/fall2020/entries/critical-thinking/.

Hoffman, M. H. G. 2016. "Reflective Argumentation: A Cognitive Function of Arguing." *Argumentation* 30, 365–97.

Hook, S. 1954. "The Ethics of Controversy." *New Leader*, February 1, 12–14.

Horn, L. 2004. "Implicature." Pp. 3–28 in *The Handbook of Pragmatics*. L. R. Horn and G. Ward, eds. Malden, MA: Blackwell.

Hume, D. [1739] 1978. *A Treatise on Human Nature*. 2nd ed. P. H. Nidditch, ed. Oxford: Oxford University Press.

Hurley, P. and L. Watson. 2018. *A Concise Introduction to Logic*. 13th ed. Boston: Cengage Learning.

Jackson, S. 2019. "Reason-Giving and the Natural Normativity of Argumentation." *Topoi* 38, 631–43.

Jeffrey, R. 1991. *Formal Logic: Its Scope and Limits*. 3rd ed. New York: McGraw-Hill.

Jennings, R. and N. Friedrich. 2006. *Proof and Consequences*. Peterborough, ON: Broadview Press.

Johnson, R. H. 2000. *Manifest Rationality: A Pragmatic Theory of Argument*. Mahwah, NJ: Lawrence Erlbaum Associates.

Johnson, R. H. 2014. *The Rise of Informal Logic: Essays on Argumentation, Critical Thinking, Reasoning and Politics*. Digital ed. Windsor, ON: University of Windsor Press.

Kahane, H. 1984. *Logic and Philosophy: A Modern Introduction*. 4th ed. Belmont, CA: Wadsworth.

Kahneman, D. 2011. *Thinking, Fast and Slow*. New York: Farrar, Straus and Giroux.

Kant, I. 1784. "An Answer to the Question, What Is Enlightenment?" Pp. 11–22 in Kant, *Practical Philosophy*. Mary J. Gregor, trans. Cambridge: Cambridge University Press.

Kelly, T. 2007. "Evidence and Normativity: Reply to Leite." *Philosophy & Phenomenological Research* 75, 465–74.

Kiesewetter, B. 2017. *The Normativity of Rationality*. Oxford: Oxford University Press.

Kim, M., and W. M. Roth. 2014. "Argumentation as/in/for Dialogical Relation: A Case Study from Elementary School Science." *Pedagogies* 9, 300–321.

King, N. L. 2021. *The Excellent Mind: Intellectual Virtues for Everyday Life*. New York: Oxford University Press.

Kornblith, H. 2015. "The Role of Reasons in Epistemology." *Episteme* 12, 225–39.

Korta, K. and J. Perry. 2020. "Pragmatics." In *The Stanford Encyclopedia of Philosophy* (Spring 2020 ed.). Edward N. Zalta, ed. https://plato.stanford.edu/archives/spr2020/entries/pragmatics/.

Kuhn, D. 1991. *The Skills of Argument*. New York: Cambridge University Press.

Kuhn, D. 1999. "A Developmental Model of Critical Thinking." *Educational Researcher* 28, 16–25, 46.

Kuhn, D. and D. Dean Jr. 2004. "Metacognition: A Bridge between Cognitive Psychology and Educational Practice." *Theory Into Practice* 43, 268–73.

Laar, J. A. van. 2003. "The Dialectic of Ambiguity: A Contribution to the Study of Argumentation." PhD dissertation, University of Groningen. http://irs.ub.rug.nl/ppn/249337959.

Lackey, J. 2007. "Norms of Assertion." *Noûs* 41, 594–626.

Lackey, J. 2013. "Lies and Deception: An Unhappy Divorce." *Analysis* 73, 236–48.

Lambert, K. and B. C. van Fraassen. 1972. *Derivation and Counterexample: An Introduction to Philosophical Logic*. Encino, CA: Dickenson.

Levinson, S. 1983. *Pragmatics*. Cambridge: Cambridge University Press.

Lipman, M. L. 1988. "Critical Thinking: What Can It Be?" *Educational Leadership* 46, 38–43.

Lipman, M. L. 2003. *Thinking in Education*. New York: Cambridge University Press.

Lumer, C. 2010. "Pragma-dialectics and the Function of Argumentation." *Argumentation* 24, 41–69.

Lumer, C. 2005. "The Epistemological Theory of Argument—How and Why?" *Informal Logic* 35, 213–43.

MacFarlane, J. 2004. "In What Sense (If Any) Is Logic Normative for Thought?" Unpublished.

MacFarlane, J. 2011. What Is Assertion? Pp. 79–96 in *Assertion: New Philosophical Essays*. J. Brown and H. Cappelen, eds. New York: Oxford University Press.

Marcus, R. B. 1981. "A Proposed Solution to a Puzzle about Belief." *Midwest Studies in Philosophy* 6, 501–10.

Mares, E. 2002. "Relevance Logic." Pp. 609–27 in *A Companion to Philosophical Logic*. D. Jacquette, ed. Malden, MA: Blackwell.

Mates, B. 1972. *Elementary Logic*. 2nd ed. New York: Oxford University Press.

McDowell, J. 1997. *Mind and World*. Cambridge, MA: Harvard University Press.

McDowell, J. 2018. "Sellars and the Space of Reasons." *Analysis* 21, 1–22.

Martinez, M. E. 2006. "What Is Metacognition?" *Phi Delta Kappan* 87, 696–99.

McLeod, C. 2005. "How to Distinguish Autonomy from Integrity." *Canadian Journal of Philosophy* 35, 107–34.

Meiland, J. 1989. "Argument as Inquiry and Argument as Persuasion." *Argumentation* 3, 185–96.

Mendus, S. 2002. *Impartiality in Moral and Political Philosophy*. Oxford: Oxford University Press.

Mercier, H. and D. Sperber. 2009. "Intuitive and Reflective Inferences." Pp. 149–70 in *In Two Minds: Dual Processes and Beyond*. J. Evans and K. Frankish, eds. New York: Oxford University Press.

Mercier, H. and D. Sperber. 2017. *The Enigma of Reason*. Cambridge, MA: Harvard University Press.

Mill, J. S. 1875. *A System of Logic, Ratiocinative and Inductive: Being a Connective View of the Principles of Evidence and the Methods of Scientific Investigation*. 9th ed. London: Longmans, Green, Reader, and Dyer.

Miller, C. B. 2017. "Honesty." Pp. 237–73 in *Moral Psychology*, vol. 5: *Virtue and Character*. W. Sinnott-Armstrong and C. B. Miller, eds. Cambridge, MA: MIT Press.

Miller, C. B. 2021. *Honesty: The Philosophy and Psychology of a Neglected Virtue*. New York: Oxford University Press.

Miller, C. B. and R. West, eds. 2020. *Integrity, Honesty, and Truth Seeking*. New York: Oxford University Press.

Mulnix, J. W. 2012. "Thinking Critically about Critical Thinking." *Educational Philosophy and Theory* 44, 464–79.

Neale, S. 1992. "Paul Grice and the Philosophy of Language." *Linguistics and Philosophy* 15, 509–99.

Owens, D. 2006. "Testimony and Assertion." *Philosophical Studies* 130: 105–29.

Packard, D. and J. Faulconer. 1980. *Introduction to Logic*. New York: D. Van Nostrand.

Pagin, P. 2016. "Assertion." In *The Stanford Encyclopedia of Philosophy* (Winter 2016 ed.). Edward N. Zalta, ed. https://plato.stanford.edu/archives/win2016/entries/assertion/.

Passmore, J. 1972. "On Teaching to Be Critical." Pp. 415–33 in *Education and the Development of Reason*. R. F. Dearden, P. H. Hirst, and R. S. Peters, eds. London: Routledge & Kegan Paul.

Paul, R. 1992. "Critical Thinking: What? Why, and How?" *New Directions for Community Colleges* 77, 3–24.

Paul, R., A. Fischer, and G. Nosich. 1993. *Workshop on Critical Thinking Strategies*. Rohnert Park, CA: Foundation for Critical Thinking, Sonoma State University.

Peirce, C. S. 1877. "The Fixation of Belief." Pp. 5–22 in *Philosophical Writings of Peirce*. J. Buchler, ed. New York: Dover Publications.

Peirce, C. S. 1955. "The Criterion of Validity in Reasoning." Pp.120–28 in *Philosophical Writings of Peirce*. J. Buchler, ed. New York: Dover Publications.

Perkins, D. 2002. "Standard Logic as a Model of Reasoning: The Empirical Critique." *Studies in Logic and Practical Reasoning* 1, 187–223.

Pinto, R. C. 2001a. *Argument, Inference and Dialectic*. Dordrecht: Kluwer Academic Publishers.

Pinto, R. C. 2001b. "Generalizing the Notion of an Argument." Pp. 10–20 in Pinto, *Argument, Inference and Dialectic*. Dordrecht: Kluwer Academic Publishers.

Pinto, R. C. 2001c. "The Relation of Argument of Inference." Pp. 32–45 in Pinto, *Argument, Inference and Dialectic*. Dordrecht: Kluwer Academic Publishers.

Pinto, R. C. 2006. "Evaluating Inferences: The Nature and Role of Warrants." *Informal Logic* 26, 287–317.

Pinto, R. C. 2010. "The Uses of Argument in Communicative Contexts." *Argumentation* 24, 227–52.

Pinto, R. C. 2011. "The Account of Warrants in Bermejo-Luque's *Giving Reasons*." *Theoria* 72, 311–20.

Pinto, R. C. 2019. "Argumentation and the Force of Reasons." Pp. 251–86 in *Informal Logic: A "Canadian" Approach to Reasons*. F. Puppo, ed. Windsor, ON: University of Windsor.

Potts, C. 2007. "Into the Conventional-Implicature Dimension." *Philosophy Compass* 2, 665–79.

Price, H. 1990. "Why 'Not'?" *Mind* 99, 221–38.

Priest, G. 1979. "Two Dogmas of Quineanism." *Philosophical Quarterly* 29, 289–301.

Priest, G. 1993. "Can Contradictions Be True?" *Supplementary Proceedings of the Aristotelian Society* 86, 35–54.

Priest, G. 1999. "Validity." Pp. 183–203 in *The Nature of Logic*, vol. 4. A. C. Varzi, ed. Stanford, CA: CSLI Publications.

Priest, G. 2008. *An Introduction to Non-classical Logic*. Cambridge: Cambridge University Press.

Quine, W. V. O. 1986. *Philosophy of Logic*. 2nd ed. Cambridge, MA: Harvard University Press.

Railton, P. 1999. "Normative Force and Normative Freedom: Hume and Kant, but Not Hume *versus* Kant." *Ratio* 12, 320–53.

Read, S. 1995. *Thinking about Logic: An Introduction to the Philosophy of Logic*. Oxford: Oxford University Press.

Restall, G. 2000. *An Introduction to Sub-structural Logics*. New York: Routledge.

Restall, G. 2005. "Multiple Conclusions." Pp. 189–205 in *Logic, Methodology and Philosophy of Science: Proceedings of the Twelfth International Congress*. P. Hajek, L. Valdes-Villanueva, and D. Westerstahl, eds. London: Kings' College Publications.

Restall, G. 2006. *Logic: An Introduction*. New York: Routledge.

Roberts, R. and R. West. 2020. "The Virtue of Honesty: A Conceptual Exploration." Pp. 97–126 in *Integrity, Honesty, and Truth Seeking*. C. Miller and R. West, eds. New York: Oxford University Press.

Roberts, R. and J. Wood. 2007. *Intellectual Virtues: An Essay in Regulative Epistemology*. New York: Oxford University Press.

Rysiew, P. 2008. "Rationality Disputes: Psychology and Epistemology." *Philosophy Compass* 3, 1153–76.

Sainsbury, R. M. 2001. *Logical Forms: An Introduction to Philosophical Logic*. Malden, MA: Blackwell.

Sainsbury, R. M. 2002. "What Logic Should We Think With?" Pp. 1–17 in *Logic, Thought and Language*. Anthony O'Hear, ed. Cambridge: Cambridge University Press.

Sainsbury, R. M. 2009. *Paradoxes*. 3rd ed. Cambridge: Cambridge University Press.

Scanlon, T. M. 1998. *What We Owe to Each Other*. Cambridge, MA: Belknap Press.

Scherkoske, G. 2013. *Integrity and the Virtues of Reasons*. Cambridge: Cambridge University Press.

Schroeder, M. 2007. "Reasons and Agent-Neutrality." *Philosophical Studies* 135, 279–306.

Scriven, M. 1976. *Reasoning*. New York: McGraw-Hill.

Scriven, M. and R. Paul. 1987. *Defining Critical Thinking*. http://www.criticalthinking.org/pages/defining-critical-thinking/766.

Searle, J. R. 1969. *Speech Acts: An Essay in the Philosophy of Language*. Cambridge: Cambridge University Press.

Searle, J. R. 1979. *Expression and Meaning: Studies in the Theory of Speech Acts*. Cambridge: Cambridge University Press.

Sellars, W. 1956. "Empiricism and the Philosophy of Mind." Pp. 253–329 in *Minnesota Studies in the Philosophy of Science*, vol. 1. H. Feigl and M. Scriven, eds. Minneapolis: University of Minnesota Press.

Shapiro, S. 2002. "Necessity, Meaning, and Rationality: The Notion of Logical Consequence." Pp. 227–40 in *A Companion to Philosophical Logic*. D. Jacquette, ed. Malden, MA: Blackwell.

Shapiro, S. 2005. "Logical Consequence, Proof Theory, and Model Theory." Pp. 651–70 in *The Oxford Handbook of Philosophy of Mathematics and Logic*. S. Shapiro, ed. Oxford: Oxford University Press.

Siegel, H. 1988. *Educating Reason: Rationality, Critical Thinking, and Education*. New York: Routledge.

Siegel, H. 1992. "The Generalizability of Critical Thinking Skills, Dispositions, and Epistemology." Pp. 97–108 in *The Generalizability of Critical Thinking*. S. P. Norris, ed. New York: Teachers College Press, Columbia University.

Siegel, H. 2004. "Rationality and Judgement." *Metaphilosophy* 35, 597–613.

Siegel, H. 2017. "Critical Thinking and the Intellectual Virtues." Pp. 89–107 in Siegel, *Education's Epistemology*. New York: Oxford University Press.

Siegel, H. and J. Biro. 1997. "Epistemic Normativity, Argumentation and Fallacies." *Argumentation* 11, 277–92.

Siegel, H. and J. Biro. 2008. "Rationality, Reasonableness, and Critical Rationalism: Problems with the Pragma-dialectical View." *Argumentation* 22, 191–203.

Siegel, H. and J. Biro. 2010. "The Pragma-dialectician's Dilemma: Reply to Garssen and van Laar." *Informal Logic* 30, 457–80.

Silva, P. and L. R. G. Oliveira. 2023. "Propositional Justification and Doxastic Justification." Pp. 395–408 in *The Routledge Handbook of the Philosophy of Evidence*. M. Lasonen-Aarnio and C. M. Littlejohn, eds. New York: Routledge.

Sinnott-Armstrong, W. and R. Fogelin. 2010. *Understanding Arguments: An Introduction to Informal Logic*. 8th ed. Belmont, CA: Wadsworth, Cengage Learning.

Skorupski, John. 1997. "Reasons and Reason." Pp. 345–67 in *Ethics and Practical Reason*. G. Cullity and B. Gaut, eds. Oxford: Oxford University Press.

Skyrms, B. 2000. *Choice and Chance: An Introduction to Inductive Logic*. 4th ed. Belmont, CA: Wadsworth/Thomson Learning.

Smiley, T. 1993. "Can Contradictions Be True?" *Supplementary Proceedings of the Aristotelian Society* 86, 17–33.

Smith, N. J. J. 2012. *Logic: The Laws of Truth*. Princeton: Princeton University Press.

Soccio, D. and V. Barry. 1998. *Practical Logic: An Antidote for Uncritical Thinking*. 5th ed. Belmont, CA: Wadsworth Cengage Learning.

Sorenson, R. 1991. " 'P Therefore P' without Circularity." *Journal of Philosophy* 88, 245–66.

Stampe, D. 1987. "The Authority of Desire." *Philosophical Review* 96, 335–81.

Stanovich, K. E. 2009. *What Intelligence Tests Miss: The Psychology of Rational Thought*. New Haven, CT: Yale University Press.

Stanovich, K. E. 2011. *Rationality and the Reflective Mind*. New York: Oxford University Press.

Steinberger, F. 2016. "Explosion and the Normativity of Logic." *Mind* 125, 385–419.

Streumer, B. 2007. "Reasons and Entailment." *Erkenntnis* 66, 353–74.

Swartz, R. J. and D. N. Perkins. 2017. *Teaching Thinking: Issues and Approaches*. New York: Routledge.

Sylvan, K. 2016. "Epistemic Reasons I: Normativity." *Philosophy Compass* 11, 364–76.

Tannen, D. 1999. *The Argument Culture: Stopping America's War of Words*. New York: Ballantine Books.

Tarski, A. [1936] 1983. "On the Concept of Logical Consequence." Pp. 409–20 in Tarski, *Logic, Semantics, Metamathematics*, 2nd ed. J. Corcoran, ed. Indianapolis: Hackett.

Tarski, A. [1941] 1995. *Introduction to Logic and to the Methodology of Deductive Sciences*. New York: Dover Publications.

Thompson, V. A. 2009. "Dual-Process Theories: A Metacognitive Perspective." Pp. 171–95 in *In Two Minds: Dual Processes and Beyond*. J. Evans and K. Frankish, eds. New York: Oxford University Press.

Thomson, J. J. 1967. "Reasons and Reasoning." Pp. 282–303 in *Philosophy in America*. M. Black, ed. Ithaca, NY: Cornell University Press.

Thomson, J. J. 2008. *Normativity*. Chicago: Open Court.

Tindal, G. and V. Nolet. 1995. "Curriculum-Based Measurement in Middle and High Schools: Critical Thinking Skills in Content Areas." *Focus on Exceptional Children* 27, 1–22.

Toulmin, S. E. 2003. *The Uses of Argument*. Updated ed. Cambridge: Cambridge University Press.

Toulmin, S. E., R. Rieke, and A. Janik. 1979. *An Introduction to Reasoning*. New York: Macmillan.

Turri, J. 2009. "The Ontology of Epistemic Reason." *Noûs* 43, 490–512.

Turri, J. 2010. "On the Relationship between Propositional and Doxastic Justification." *Philosophy and Phenomenological Research* 80, 312–26.

Van Benthem, J., 2008. "Logic and Reasoning: Do the Facts Matter?" *Studia Logica* 88, 67–84.

Vorobej, M. 2006. *A Theory of Argument*. Cambridge: Cambridge University Press.

Walker, M. U. 1998. "Picking Up Pieces: Lives, Stories, and Integrity." Pp. 103–30 in Walker, *Moral Understandings*. Oxford: Oxford University Press.

Walton, D. N. 1990. "What Is Reasoning? What Is an Argument?" *Journal of Philosophy* 87, 399–419.

Walton, D. N. 1996. *Argument Structure: A Pragmatic Theory*. Toronto: University of Toronto Press.

Wedgewood, R. 2006. "The Normative Force of Reasoning." *Noûs* 40, 660–86.

Willard, C. A. 1989. *A Theory of Argumentation*. Tuscaloosa: University of Alabama Press.

Williams, B. 2002. *Truth and Truthfulness*. Princeton: Princeton University Press.

Willingham, D. T. 2008. "Critical Thinking: Why Is It So Hard to Teach?" *Arts Education Policy Review* 109, 21–32.

Wilson, A. 2018. "Honesty as a Virtue." *Metaphilosophy* 49, 262–80.

Woods, J. 2002. "Standard Logics as Theories of Argument and Inference: Deduction." Pp. 41–103 in *Handbook of the Logic of Argument and Inference: The Turn towards the Practical*. D. M. Gabbay, R. H. Johnson, H. J. Ohlbach, and J. Woods, eds. Amsterdam: North Holland.

Worsnip, A. 2021. *Fitting Things Together*. Oxford: Oxford University Press.

Wright, L. 2001. "Justification, Discovery, Reason & Argument." *Argumentation* 15, 97–104.

Zagzebski, L. 1996. *Virtues of the Mind: An Inquiry into the Nature of Virtue and the Ethical Foundations of Knowledge*. New York: Cambridge University Press.

Index

For the benefit of digital users, indexed terms that span two pages (e.g., 52–53) may, on occasion, appear on only one of those pages.

Tables are indicated by *t* following the page number

demonstrative arguments and, 117,
164, 170–75
demonstrative inferences and, 172
good reasoning and, 163
reason-giving uses of arguments
and, 174–90
reflective inferences and, 163–64, 174–
75, 178–80, 184, 187–88
syllogisms, syllogistic reasoning
and, 185–87
forward reflective reasoning, 119–20
Franklin, Benjamin, 30
Freeman, J., 85
Frege, Gottlob, 308

Gabbay, D. M., 184–85
Garssen, B., 275n.19, 276–77
Godden, D., 25, 229, 261n.13
Goldman, A., 55, 220, 221, 223, 224n.4
good arguments and good argumentation,
81, 82, 83, 253–55, 258–59,
271, 281–86
Goodwin, J., 254n.10
Govier, T., 19n.4
Grice, H. P., 105n.9, 106nn.10–11, 107,
108, 108–9n.14, 109, 110, 110n.15,
111–12, 113
Groarke, L., 45, 84–85
Grootendorst, R., 19, 54, 54n.1, 56, 56n.3,
57, 232, 253–54, 268, 269, 269–
70n.17, 274–75
Guenin, L. M., 305–7, 306–7n.15, 308–9

Halfon, M. S., 314, 314–15n.18
Harman, G., 114, 190n.4
Harnish, R., 106, 107–8
Hitchcock, D., 1–2, 14n.3, 77, 94, 94nn.2–
3, 95, 95n.4, 103, 128–29, 209
Hoffman, M. H. G., 12–13
Hook, S., 11n.2
Horn, L., 109
Hume, David, 148
Hurley, P., 85
hypothetical inferences, 145, 146–47

illatives, 63–64, 104–5
indirect persuasion, 25, 203, 204–5, 219–
27, 224n.4, 228

inductive arguments, 23, 79, 80, 164
ampliative arguments and, 165–66, 168
deductive arguments and, 164–
65, 166–68
inductive inferences, 23, 168
inference-claim belief, 1–2
in active inferences, 146, 147
argumentative intention and, 71, 72, 73,
76, 93, 245
justification of, 152–53
objectively and subjectively rational
conclusions and, 6
reason-giving uses of argument and,
14–15, 70–71, 72, 163, 168, 192, 195–
96, 218, 245, 313–14
reasons for belief and, 72, 93–94, 202
requirement, 2, 3, 19, 71, 72, 73, 74–75,
76, 100, 232–33, 245, 311–12
inference claims, 3
argumentative intention and, 77, 251
assertions and, 111–14
belief in expression of, 99, 100, 102,
103–4, 108, 110, 112, 113
conventional implicature and, 108–11
conversational implicature and, 105–8
dialectical arguments and, 115
direct and indirect persuasion
and, 203–4
as mere implications, 103–5, 114
objective and subjective rationality and,
246–47, 251
as primary point in statement of
argument, 100, 101, 102, 104, 108,
111, 112–13
proto-inference claim, 89, 90,
95, 98, 99
reason-giving uses of argument and,
1–2, 4–5, 10, 13–15, 16–17, 20–21,
24–25, 70–71, 76, 77, 83–115, 199,
203–4, 214, 227–28, 232–33, 251,
290, 311–12
reasons for belief and, 14, 52, 84–95,
105, 202, 203–4
statement of an argument in
conveying, 99–115
value in expression of, 100–1, 102, 104,
108, 110, 112–13
inferences, critical thinking and, 145–55